Understanding Research Methods and Statistics in Psychology

Understanding Research Methods and Statistics in Psychology

Helen Gavin

Los Angeles • London • New Delhi • Singapore

SAGE Publications Ltd
1 Oliver's Yard
55 City Road
London EC1Y 1SP

SAGE Publications Inc.
2455 Teller Road
Thousand Oaks, California 91320

SAGE Publications India Pvt Ltd
B 1/I 1 Mohan Cooperative Industrial Area
Mathura Road
New Delhi 110 044

SAGE Publications Asia-Pacific Pte Ltd
33 Pekin Street #02-01
Far East Square
Singapore 048763

Library of Congress Control Number: 2008920885

British Library Cataloguing in Publication data

A catalogue record for this book is available from the British Library

ISBN 978-1-4129-3441-1
ISBN 978-1-4129-3442-8 (pbk)

Typeset by C&M Digitals (P) Ltd, Chennai, India
Printed in Great Britain by TJ International Ltd, Padstow, Cornwall
Printed on paper from sustainable resources

This book is dedicated to Garry for the grammatical conjunctions, definite articles and applications of *Theobroma cacao*.

CONTENTS

Preface   xvii

PART I   FIRST EXPLORATIONS   1

Chapter 1   The Range of Research   3

Studying the Invisible   5
Introspection   6
The Experimental Approach   8
   Falsifiability   9
   Demand Characteristics   11
   Control in Experimentation   12
Research Without Experimentation   15
   Psychometrics   15
   Direct Observation   16
   Self-reports   17
   Surveys   17
   Evaluation   17
Analysis of Psychological Data   18
Summary   19
Wilhelm Wundt (1832–1920)   19
Sir Karl Popper (1902–1994)   20

Chapter 2   Ethics in Research: Some Shocking Cases   **21**

Shocking Events in New Haven   23
Public Health Shame   25
Ethical Issues   26
How to Design Ethical Research   32
 General   32
 Consent   33
 Deception   34
 Debriefing   35
 Withdrawal   35
 Confidentiality   35
 Protection   36
 Observational Research   36
 Giving Advice   36
 Colleagues   37
Summary   37
Stanley Milgram (1933–1984)   38

Chapter 3   Some Basic Concepts in Psychological Research   **39**

Who Takes Part in Research?   42
 Populations   42
 Samples   43
Variables   43
 Independent   43
 Fixed   43
 Random   44
 Dependent   44
 Confounding   44
Level of Measurement   44
Quantitative Research Design   46
 Temporal Precedence   46
 Covariation   47
 Alternative Explanation   47
 Internal Validity   47

Replicability and Reliability	48
External Validity	48
Hypotheses	49
Handling Statistical Data	50
Qualitative and Quantitative Data	51
Why Use Qualitative Methods?	53
Reflexivity	54
Validity in Qualitative Research	55
Types of Qualitative Research	56
Ethnography	56
Phenomenology	57
Hermeneutics	57
Grounded Theory	58
Qualitative Data Collection	58
In-Depth Interviews	58
Direct Observation	59
Participant Observation	59
Case Studies	60
Diaries	60
Handling Qualitative Data	61
Summary	62
PART II BEGINNING QUANTITATIVE RESEARCH	**63**
Chapter 4 Using Numbers to Describe Behaviour	**65**
The Distribution	67
Building a Distribution	68
The Normal Distribution	70
Central Tendency	70
The Mean	71
The Median	71
The Mode	73
Which Central Tendency Measure?	73
Dispersion	74

The Sample Variance and the Standard Deviation 74
Standard Error of the Mean 77
The z-score 79
Disruptions to Normality – Skew and Kurtosis 80
Tabular Presentation 82
Summary 83

Chapter 5 Inferential Statistics – Why and What? **84**

Probability 88
Hypothesis Testing 93
Step 1: State the Hypotheses 93
Step 2: Set the Criterion for Rejecting H_0 94
Step 3: Compute the Test Statistic 96
Step 4: Decide About H_0 (Reject or Not Reject) 96
One-Tailed and Two-Tailed Significance Tests 97
Power 97
Parametric Tests and Assumptions 99
Normal Distribution 99
Homogeneity of Variances 100
Level of Measurement 100
Degrees of Freedom 101
Summary 101
Sir Ronald Aylmer Fisher (1890–1962) 102

Chapter 6 Simple Experimental Designs: Being Watched **103**

Who Is Watching You? 105
The Analysis of Data from Experiments with Two Conditions 107
The t test 108
Experiments with Within-Subjects Designs 109
Analysis of Data in Within-Subjects Designs 110
Experiments Using Between-Subjects Designs 113
Analysis of Data in Between-Subjects Designs 115
One- and Two-Tailed *t* Tests 118
Summary 120
Robert Zajonc 120

Chapter 7   Single Factorial Designs: The Levels of
Processing Experiments   **121**

Models of Memory   123
Designs with More Than Two Groups   125
Single Factor Designs   127
Analysis of Variance   127
    Total Sum of Squares (SST)   129
    Sum of Squares Between Groups (SS_B)   129
    Sum of Squares Within Groups (SS_W)   130
    Post-Hoc Tests in Single Factor Between-Subjects Designs 133
Non-parametric Tests in Single Factor Designs   135
    Single Factor Designs with Repeated Measures 139
    Non-parametric Tests in Single Factor Repeated
    Measures Designs   143
Tests of Trend   144
Summary   146
Fergus Craik   147
Robert Lockhart   147

Chapter 8   Survey Research: Who Is Afraid of Crime?   **149**

Measuring Attitudes Using Surveys   152
    Attitudes   152
    Attitude Measurement   153
    Writing Questionnaires   154
    Question Format   155
    Scaling   156
    Dimensionality   156
    The Major Unidimensional Scale Types   157
    Likert Scales   157
    Scoring and Analysis   159
    Level of Measurement   159
Sampling   160
    Answers to Our Crime Survey   162
Ethical Considerations of Performing Surveys   163
Summary   167

Chapter 9   Correlational Designs: The Poor Relation?   **168**

Correlational Designs and Analysis   171
Correlational Analysis with Interval-Level Data   173
Simple Linear Regression   176
Correlation with Non-continuous Data   178
Ordinal Data   180
Assumptions Made in Correlational Analysis   182
Partial Correlation   182
Summary   185
Hans Jurgen Eysenck (1916–1997)   186

PART III   COMPLEX QUANTITATIVE DESIGNS   **187**

Chapter 10   Factorial Designs with More Than One Factor:
**   A Closer Look at Memory**   **189**

Alternatives to the Levels of Processing Framework   191
The Principles of Encoding Specificity   192
Analysis of Factorial Designs with More Than One Factor   194
Reporting Factorial Results   194
Mixed Designs   202
Post-hoc Analysis   202
Simple Effects   203
Simple Main Effects for Between- and Within-Subjects Contrasts   205
Non-parametric Tests   205
Transformations   205
Friedman's Test   206
Summary   206
Endel Tulving   207

Chapter 11   Multivariate Statistics   **208**

Analysis of Covariance   210
Multivariate Analysis of Variance   214
Summary   218

Chapter 12   Complex Correlational Designs and Analysis:
                    Stats Can Be Murder   **219**

Murdering Stats   223
Multiple Linear Regression   225
  Multicollinearity   226
  Selection Methods   227
Getting Away with Murder   227
  Logistic Regression   228
Summary   229
Sir Edward Coke (1552–1634)   230

PART IV   BEGINNING QUALITATIVE RESEARCH   **231**

Chapter 13   Theory in Qualitative Research   **233**

The Alternative Paradigm?   234
  Qualitative Versus Quantitative Research Paradigms   235
Theoretical Viewpoints in Psychological Qualitative Enquiry   238
  Phenomenology   238
  Ethnomethodology   239
  Symbolic Interactionism   239
  Semiotics   240
  Hermeneutics   240
  Modernism, Post-modernism   241
Psychological Approaches to Qualitative Research   242
Summary   243

Chapter 14   Designing Qualitative Research   **244**

Features of Qualitative Research   246
The Role of the Researcher   246
Research Design   247
  Sampling Strategies   248
  Data Collection Techniques   248

Analysis of Data   248
Credibility of Qualitative Research   249
Summary   250

PART V   COMPLEX QUALITATIVE RESEARCH   **251**

Chapter 15   Interviews and Focus Groups   **253**

Market Research   254
Qualitative Interviews   257
   Conducting Interviews   258
Focus Groups in Qualitative Research   259
   Use of Focus Groups   260
   Questions for Focus Groups   261
Analysis of Interview and Focus Group Data   262
Summary   262

Chapter 16   Participant Observation: Girls, Gangs
**   and Aggression**   **263**

Observing Violence   265
Violent Women   266
Observation as Method   268
  Access   269
  Time   269
  Recording Data   270
  Analysing Data   270
  How to Be a Participant Observer   271
  Summary   271
  Anne Campbell   272

Chapter 17   Thematic Analysis   **273**

Research Diaries   274
The Effect of Recording Experience   275

The Analysis   277
The Outcomes   280
Summary   281

Chapter 18   Discourse Analysis: Power and Control   282

Language Structure   284
Syntax – Relation of Signs to Each Other   284
Semantics – Relation of Signs to Objects   285
Definitions of Discourse Analysis   287
Assumptions of Discourse Analysis   287
Issues of Reliability and Validity   288
How Do We Perform Discourse Analysis?   289
Gathering Data for Discourse Analysis   295
Natural Discourse   295
The Method of Discourse Analysis   295
Summary   296
Jonathan Potter   296
Margaret Wetherell   297

Chapter 19   Evaluation Research   298

Evaluation of Treatment Programmes   302
Sexual Offending, the Research, the Theory   302
Biological and Evolutionary Explanation of Sexual Aggression   303
Social and Psychological Explanations for Sexual Aggression   304
Treatment of Sexual Aggression and Sexual Offending   305
Evaluation Study Design   309
Effectiveness of Therapy   309
Summary   311

PART VI   COMMUNICATION OF RESEARCH   313

Chapter 20   Communicating Research   315

Journal Articles   317
Conference Proceedings   317

Books   317
Government/Corporate Reports   318
Newspapers   318
Theses and Dissertations   318
Internet   318
Research Paper Sections   319
    Abstract   319
    Introduction   320
    Method and Research Design   323
    Results   323
    Statistical Results   324
    Qualitative Results   324
    Discussion   325
Summary   327

Appendix A   Choosing a Statistical Test   328
Appendix B   SPSS Output for Data and Analysis
    Discussed in Chapter 6   330
    SPSS Output for Data and Analysis
    Discussed in Chapter 7   340
    SPSS Output for Data and Analysis
    Discussed in Chapter 9   352
    SPSS Output for Data and Analysis
    Discussed in Chapter 10   359
    SPSS Output for Data and Analysis
    Discussed in Chapter 11   365

Glossary   369
References   386
Index   393

PREFACE

This book takes us on a journey through research in psychology, with the aim of understanding why research is done and illuminating the methods by which it is carried out. Each chapter will explore an influential concept in psychology, and how each was developed through scientific and rigorous techniques of data collection and analysis. We are going to encounter a wide range of techniques used in psychological research and the analysis of data derived from the research. However, the emphasis will be on the method, so we will examine various pieces of research in psychology to discover why each was carried out in the way it was, and what was derived from it.

This book will explain the use and function of a range of methods of data collection and analysis in psychology, in easy-to-understand ways, relating each topic under discussion to well-established pieces of research. Each of the separate methods and techniques and pieces of analysis will be related to a research topic in psychology using those approaches. The scope of the book is deliberately broad and is intended to be used by students undertaking degrees in psychology. It will concentrate on the psychological aspects of the techniques, and will anchor them firmly to psychological research, laying a foundation of necessary skills, and developing them alongside relevant investigations.

Explanations of terms that will be new to the reader are embedded in the text. This prevents unfamiliar vocabulary getting in the way of learning about topics, as that can be daunting to those approaching them for the first time. We often feel overwhelmed by the topics contained here, and the language books use can be off-putting. Here everything is explained and complexity addressed appropriately. For example, in areas of quantitative analyses the statistical/mathematical content is kept to a minimum and in the qualitative areas the philosophy is explained and contextualised.

This book concentrates on the knowledge required to understand how to do research in psychology and how to analyse data collected, and not the technicalities of applying statistical formula. The SPSS method is used in the quantitative sections, but each step is explained and shown plainly, and the output spelt out clearly. Each chapter lists learning objectives and key terms at the beginning. The chapters (beyond the basic introductory ones) have, embedded in them, a description of a particular piece of research and an outline of its contribution to psychological knowledge. The development of the chapter then concentrates on how and why the research was (or might have been) carried out in the way described. Chapters end with a clear summary of what has been discussed. The chapters detailing quantitative analysis will also have an examination of how to carry out the analysis of data derived via computational methods, and in one of the appendices of the book there is a layout of the output from SPSS and how to interpret it.

HOW TO USE THIS BOOK

The chapters cover topics that undergraduate students in psychology will encounter in the first two years of their degree studies, in some cases beyond. Both quantitative (statistical) and qualitative methods are covered. In the first part of the book, the chapters cover some fundamental topics to take into account before embarking on any research, namely reasons why research is carried out, the ethical implications of doing research that should be considered, and the basic vocabulary of research in psychology. These chapters can be referred to while the rest of the book is being used. So Part I covers our first explorations in research. The chapters here explain why it is important to understand and be able to carry out research in psychology, and why there are considerations for those taking part to think about, both for the participants and for the researchers. We will then equip ourselves with some basic vocabulary in order to understand design, collection and analysis of research.

Part II looks at beginning quantitative research in psychology. Firstly, we will examine how to use numbers to describe behaviour, such as reducing, summarising and presenting data. We will then look at how to use numbers to predict behaviour, thinking about testing some theoretical questions about people. Once we know how to do this, we can move on to some simple experiments, where we will examine a simple social experiment: what happens when we are watched? From there it is a simple step to examining more complex pieces of human behaviour, such as what conditions will affect memory? However, experiments are not the only quantitative design in psychological research so in this part we will also look at survey approaches using an extract from the British Crime Survey as an example, and correlational designs, utilising Eysenck's theory of intelligence, to look at simple relationships between data. These chapters therefore cover the topics that are included in most first-year research methods modules in terms of quantitative methods and statistical analysis.

Part III examines more complex quantitative designs, such as those included in the studies for the second year of a psychology degree. Simple experiments can only go so far, and there are quantitative methods for examining several factors simultaneously. We will use some well-established theories of cognitive psychology to look at the interaction between events encountered every day, and how they affect the ways we think and behave. Cognitive psychology has some interesting applications, and in this part we will see how it can be applied to the perennial question of eyewitness testimony. Again, experiments are only one part of the story, so we will look at complex correlational designs and how they can allow us to navigate the complex data from areas of crime.

Part IV begins to address qualitative research in Psychology, but not merely as an alternative to quantitative. Qualitative research is a viable and developing area in psychology, and any new researcher needs an introduction to it that neither overwhelms with heavy philosophical arguments, nor denigrates a particular type of methodology. An overview of the paradigms and design issues in qualitative research is included in this part, which would be introduced in either the first or second year of a psychology degree.

Part V moves on to more complex qualitative issues, examining some popular data collection techniques. Here, we will examine market research that uses psychological theory, and then some of the issues surrounding observation of gang violence. The richness and sheer size of banks of qualitative data sometimes makes new researchers feel as if their data is out of control, so we will examine some essential techniques for organising and probing qualitative findings. Here we will use such diverse research topics as investigations into shop music, investigative interviews and treatment of sex offenders. These topics reflect the wealth of information that can be gleaned from qualitative approaches, together with ways of understanding how the data is produced and analysed in real-life settings, but without clouding the issues with intense philosophical discussion. In other words, these chapters concentrate on discussion of questions related to 'how to' rather than 'why'.

Part VI looks at the ways of communicating research, examining both the ways we gather information about research carried out and reporting on our own research.

At the end of a large number of chapters there is a small biography of a person or people who were influential in the area of psychology discussed in the chapter. These are there simply to acknowledge the contribution that these people made to the history of psychology, psychological research or, in one case, human rights. However, they may also be viewed as a starting point to the historical context of psychology and the research by which the discipline moves forward.

The appendices of the book are to be used as reference sections. Here also, there is a glossary of all the key terms in the book, including those that have been highlighted as key to a topic, and others that will be encountered in research and research methods studies.

The first appendix is a flowchart for deciding which test to use in quantitative analysis.

The second appendix shows figures of computer output for each of the quantitative methods chapters where analysis has been carried out. The chapters in the main parts of the book have the calculations in them as if we had carried them out by hand, but in most circumstances we would use computers to aid the analysis. The usual software package used in universities is SPSS, and this appendix includes 'screenshots' and explanations of each stage of SPSS navigation and output.

There is also a companion website available at www.sagepub.co.uk/gavin

ACKNOWLEDGEMENTS

I would like to thank Mike and Emily at Sage, without whose encouragement I would never have finished.

PART I

FIRST EXPLORATIONS

This first part of the book will introduce us to the reasons why research is carried out in psychology and the ways in which it is done. We will start to understand the range and scope of psychological research, together with the considerations we must take into account, both as ethical researchers and as participants in research. We will also learn some basic vocabulary used in the technical language of research.

CHAPTER 1

THE RANGE OF RESEARCH

Contents

Studying the invisible

Introspection

The experimental approach
Falsifiability
Demand characteristics
Control in experimentation

Research without experimentation

Psychometrics
Direct observation
Self-reports
Surveys
Evaluation

Analysis of psychological data

Summary

The Range of Research

The improvement of understanding is for two ends: first, our own increase of knowledge; secondly, to enable us to deliver that knowledge to others. (John Locke)

Learning Objectives

- To examine the range of research methods available to researchers in psychology.
- To understand some of the methods and the ways in which they might be utilised in psychology.

KEY TERMS

- Causality
- Conditions
- Demand characteristics
- Evaluation
- Experimentation
- Falsifiability
- Introspection
- Qualitative research
- Quantitative research
- Self-report
- Surveys

You have chosen to study psychology, which means that you are entering an area of exciting knowledge and research concerning the way we interact with the world. The term 'psychology' was probably first used by Goclenius, a German philosopher, who wrote about various philosophical positions in 1590 in a book called *Problematum logicorum*. But, consider the fact that, in the same year, he wrote about the best way to put witches to the test, and it might be thought that he was not writing about anything particularly scientific! The word itself comes from the Greek for 'soul' or 'spirit' (*psyche*), so psychology was originally termed to describe the study of the soul. However, in modern use, psychology is, for many people, a science, albeit a special kind of science, one of the most interesting sciences there is. This book will allow us to step into the world of research in psychology and understand the concepts by which we attempt to discover the hidden world of the mind.

Psychology deals with people (and other creatures), examining the behaviour, mind and internal world of each of us. It is the study of thoughts, feelings and actions, and is concerned with some of the most complex questions we know how to ask. It concerns many different variables, difficult to predict and measure, and for this reason it is divided into many different areas. However, overarching these divisions, and relating them together, is the concept of psychological research and the methods by which the research is carried out.

Science progresses slowly, and in a rigorous and methodical manner. It therefore requires some rigorous and methodical techniques by which progress can be made and measured. Much of science, including psychology, uses experimentation as its basic technique. However, psychology is also viewed as a social science and, as such, psychologists have at their disposal other techniques not usually available to natural scientists such as biologists and chemists. This book aims to explain the various techniques open to us. Let us begin by examining what these methods are.

STUDYING THE INVISIBLE

Much of science is concerned with processes and events that we cannot directly observe. For example, no one has seen subatomic particles moving in random paths, but predictions about the behaviour of atoms, based on the model, do work, providing support for the theory. This is the problem that psychology has: how to study what is going on in the mind when this activity is invisible to us. For example, we cannot see memory working; we can only observe the effect of its success or failure. So, psychology can be thought of as having a theoretical basis. However, this issue is made more challenging by the fact that, when we try to explore the workings of our minds, we are using the very processes under investigation. This makes the observation problematic in scientific terms, as a certain amount of detachment or objectivity might be lost, and the act of thinking about the contents of one's mind might change those contents. What is needed is a way of systematically examining behaviour without biasing the outcome. Hence,

KT

psychology also needs to be **empirical**.

Therefore, psychology is a blending of two approaches, theory and observation, and needs a rigorous way of combining them. Several methods have been developed to attempt this, each relying on applying meticulous techniques of observation and interpretation. These methods include introspection and experimentation, surveys and attitude scaling, observation and interviewing, and several more that we will examine. The sections below describe some of the research techniques and approaches used in psychology.

INTROSPECTION

KT

The first attempts to explore the contents of the mind were made by a technique called **introspection**. This means reflecting on one's own sensations and thoughts. Wundt established what came to be recognised as the first experimental psychology laboratory in Leipzig, Germany, in 1879. He trained students and colleagues to pay careful attention to what was going on in their minds and bodies, and to report on their observations objectively. These observers recorded their response to stimuli rather than the characteristics of the stimuli themselves, and attempted to avoid ascribing meaning to them. This research was the first to attempt to make some scientific sense from human experience in this way, and the project went on for about 50 years. Wundt concluded that, although some very interesting and useful observations were recorded, higher psychological processes were not really available to such techniques. A modern version of introspective methods is used alongside other data collection techniques, particularly in areas such as cognitive science, studying problem solving and knowledge representation. Examples of such methods are

KT

verbal protocols, self-ratings and focused diary keeping, and are called **self-reports**. When we wish to find out how an individual is accessing his or her own thoughts, asking the individual to verbalise is often a good technique to use alongside, for example, observation, and measurement of performance. This can give an individual insight that might be unavailable to other types of analysis. However, we cannot report on things of which we are unaware or not conscious and, indeed, reporting on one's own consciousness might become confusing. In addition, the very act of contemplating what you are doing might change the way in which you do it. To demonstrate this problem, try this test. Think about, and say out loud, the steps you take to open a can of beans. Now recall what you had for breakfast. Next, actually open a can of beans, saying out loud what you are doing. What differences are there between the reporting and the doing? This demonstrates the techniques, and one of its difficulties: the difference between imagination and reality. Alternatively, imagine being in a restaurant with several friends and working out how much of the bill each friend must pay. How much more difficult would it be if you had to tell someone else what you were doing as you were doing it? It requires a lot of practice to carry on this internal conversation with yourself, and it is likely that it will still affect the processes being considered.

Another problem is trying to do something that is outside of one's own experience. J.B. Watson, for example, completely rejected introspection after being asked to imagine himself as a rat in a maze and report on the *rat's subjective* experience. This is a difficult task unless you are very imaginative or have a lot of training in this introspective projection. Many researchers have challenged the validity of material derived from introspective techniques such as verbal protocols. According to Nisbett and Wilson (1977), the idea that we can access higher mental processes is ill-informed at best, and possibly bogus. The best we are achieving is a guess to explain our behaviour, not reporting on internal processes, and this could be done just as well by an external observer. This is supported by examples in which the verbal protocol has failed, because of either inability to report, or inaccuracies in the resulting data. However, these tend to be studies of processes that are more concerned with reactions and unreflective responses, and not problem solving, and there is more evidence that they are appropriate forms of data collection with tasks that require contemplation, rather than reactive responses or flashes of insight. Ahlum-Heath and Di Vesta (1986) showed that verbalising the cognitive strategies used when problem solving can aid the transfer of the strategy to similar problems. This suggests that the problem solver is becoming more aware of the strategy used and the internal state reached, which may be having an effect on the performance, but it is a positive one.

The self-report method has proved effective and supportable in such developments as work on the General Problem Solver or GPS (Newell & Simon, 1972). The GPS project was carried out in the theoretical framework of information processing and attempted to specify human behaviour as a collection of operations and rules that could be incorporated into a description of how humans solve problems, in order to produce a computer program that performed in the same way. Using verbal protocols, Newell and Simon and associates developed computer simulations and compared the action of the simulation with human behaviour in a given task. Ericsson and Simon (1984) describe such work as the GPS project as a defence of introspective methods used in this way, as the resulting model performs in such a way as to correspond to human behaviour, and they also showed that performance need not be affected by the need to verbalise. However, even they agree that GPS did not totally meet its original objective. GPS was intended to be a general problem solver, but it could only be applied to problems that could be specified in great detail, such as proving theorems in logic or geometry, word puzzles and chess. The conclusion is that the verbal report must be used in fitting circumstances, such as reporting on short-term memory contents, rather than material that may be affected by stored memories. In modern psychology, introspective methods have been developed in order to examine areas that lend themselves to revealing processes that involve the most accessible contents of the mind, such as problem solving. The data derived from introspective techniques tends to be rich and qualitative in nature, and the analysis of this is described in a later chapter.

Therefore, despite the fact that it is a useful method, and possibly a good starting point for self-observation and problem-solving strategy improvement, there are still major problems with the technique and with material derived from introspection. However, Wundt, and all the advocates of introspective methods, would stress that the techniques of applying objectivity and replication were important for studying such processes. This has been an important issue in psychology; principles such as these led to rigorous scientific elements being regarded as indispensable to psychological science and to be applied no matter what the method used to gather data about psychological behaviour. Using such ideological principles (but not introspection), Ebbinghaus tested himself and his memory by learning lists of nonsense words, and quantified his performance in terms of the amount he could remember, how much he forgot and how much this might vary when he altered the amount of material and the time between learning and recall. These are, perhaps, the first true experiments in the area of memory.

Experimentation, with its elements of control and inference, is one of the most useful approaches in psychology. A great deal of research in psychology involves the construction of theoretical models tested by experiments.

THE EXPERIMENTAL APPROACH

Experimentation has, as its basis, the elements of observation, inference, control and comparison. It attempts to build a relationship between what we see

KT

KT

happening, what we think is happening, and how we might test the resulting **theory**. One way in which we test the theoretical position we have is to generate questions, or **hypotheses**, which examine aspects of the way in which the theory would predict the way the world will work. Therefore, for example, we might observe that it is possible to remember a telephone number in the period between hearing it and reaching a telephone, so long as nobody asks the time on the way. This leads us to ask 'does distraction affect the retention of long numbers?' Note that this hypothesis does not specify in which direction the effect will be, whether recall will be worse or better. This is known as a non-directional hypothesis, a directional hypothesis would be 'does distraction make recall for long numbers worse?' The difference between these two types of hypothesis is discussed in more detail in Chapter 5. We can test this by comparing two situations that are as identical as we can make them. In one, the participants hear numbers, experience a waiting period, and then are asked to recall. In the other, they are distracted by another task instead of experiencing an undisturbed wait. Any difference between

KT

KT

performance in the two situations (or **conditions**) leads us to infer that doing the distracting task has had an effect on the subsequent recall. This simple **design** is the basis of experimentation, and it is a useful tool in studying some areas of psychology, in that it allows us to examine human performance. Our basic experiment here would test volunteers' ability to recall simple sequences of numbers or words, after they had been subjected to a distraction task, or not. A significant difference in the ability to recall in the two conditions would lead us to conclude, tentatively, that we have supported the hypothesis 'a distracting task between learning and recall has an effect on recall rate'. If we found no significant difference, then we would reject our hypothesis. In this way, we can test hypotheses, and relate them back to theoretical models. Such an approach also allows us to open our

KT

theory up to the possibility of **falsifiability**.

Falsifiability

Popper (1959) stated that if a theory was to be a good theory, then it must be testable, and that we have to be able to test the generated hypotheses to falsehood, and hence falsify the theory. Not that we actually have to prove it false, just that it should be possible to do so. This is an argument of logic that applies to the question of how to distinguish between science and 'non-science', and suggests how we should deal with theories and the attempts to test them.

It is not practical to know whether a scientific theory is correct in all cases. The theory may agree with all the evidence available today, but we cannot guarantee what will be discovered tomorrow. The next best stage we can reach is a logical principle stating that we can show a theory is wrong. If evidence can be found that contradicts a theory it is then falsified and stays that way, and allows us to eliminate that explanation, and move on. Thus, a scientific theory is one that can, *in principle*, be falsified. The theory has to make strong statements about evidence. If the statements are not strong, then the theory fits any evidence, and is unfalsifiable. This is problematic for several reasons. Firstly, a theory which cannot make predictions is a dead end, and impractical to use for scientific objectives. Secondly, if we have two rival theories, we want to use evidence to choose between them. If they are unfalsifiable, then evidence does not do that for us. For example, Einstein's theory of general relativity was not written with the expectation of blind belief. In 1916, Einstein predicted that the Sun's gravity would bend light, making the stars near the Sun appear in the wrong place, refuting the hitherto accepted Newtonian theoretical position of gravitational force. Einstein said that the evidence would be seen during a solar eclipse. The next solar eclipse was in 1919 and photographs showed that exact amount of bending. The evidence falsified Newton's theories and supported Einstein's. However, general relativity is not now proved right because it may still mis-predict something, so it remains forever tentative. On the other hand, consider the belief that Elvis Presley is alive and well. Can this ever be proved true? Presumably by the reappearance of the man himself, although he may be an impostor. Can it be proved false? Reports of his death may have been fabricated, the body lying in Gracelands Cemetery may not be his, and so on. However, some unfalsifiable theories do hold sway, and stay useful. Popper pointed out that nothing could, even *in principle*, falsify psychoanalytic theories, and that they have more in common with primitive myths than with genuine science! Psychoanalysis has as its chief source of strength, and the principal basis on which its claim to scientific status is grounded, a capability to accommodate and explain every form of human behaviour. This, in scientific terms, is its critical weakness, for it cannot be genuinely predictive. Nevertheless, psychoanalysis works when applied in various settings, so it has utility even if it is unscientific.

Popper drew a distinction between the logic of falsifiability and its applied methodology. The logic is simple: just because all the swans you have seen are white, it cannot be the case that all swans are white, as a black swan would falsify the assertion. Logically speaking, a scientific law is conclusively falsifiable, although it is not conclusively verifiable. Methodologically, however, the situation is much more complex: no observation is free from the possibility of error. Consequently we may question whether our experimental result was what it appeared to be.

So, in order to examine and verify a theory, we need to use a method by which we can see a way out of the vicious circle of collecting evidence and then refuting it, and one in which we have a certain amount of confidence. Classical experimentation allows this, as it sets up a direct comparison between the conditions, and has high internal validity. This means that the amount of control the experimenter has over the situation allows him or her to make direct inferences about what has happened, and allows it to be repeated in exactly the same format. This is called **replicability**. The replicability of experiments means that the same phenomena can be tested as many times as is wished with the capability of being able to observe exactly what has happened. However, this method has been criticised for being unable to provide **ecological validity**. This is the ability of theories to describe what happens in everyday situations, and critics point out that a laboratory study examining isolated pieces of behaviour is not an everyday situation. While this does not mean that we necessarily reject the use of laboratory-based data collection, we do have to be able to relate what we find to the outside world, and the theoretical position that is tested by experimentation must describe how we behave in natural circumstances. The benefit here is that psychologists now strive to explain theories and the testing of them in understandable ways, relating the findings to commonly experienced situations. A point to note here too is that a 'natural' setting does not necessarily mean that a study leads to being able to **generalise** everyday settings. In addition, consistent laboratory-based findings must be explained. Natural is not necessarily good, and laboratory is not necessarily bad, but meaning is everything.

Demand Characteristics

One other area in which experimentation is criticised is the tendency for participants to give in to **demand characteristics**. These are features of an experiment that leads a participant to behave in a way that he or she thinks is expected in that situation. This may mean that participants behave in an artificial and unnatural way. Participants know that they are taking part in experiments and look for cues in the experimental environment. No one is immune from this – we all attempt to interpret the situations in which we find ourselves. Demand characteristics can distort research findings. Aspects of a research procedure or the experimenter's behaviour or personal characteristics (known as experimenter effects) may cause the participants to guess the rationale of the study and attempt to confirm (or not) the experimenter's hypothesis. Due to this, many experiments are conducted in which the participants are kept 'naive' to the true nature of the experiment until they are told (or 'debriefed') at the end. See the chapter on research ethics for more details.

Control in Experimentation

Experiments in many areas of psychology include control, manipulation and replicability, but are still concerned with unobservable processes and events. We need therefore to be very careful about recording what we are observing, and controlling the variables when carrying out experiments. For example, what if we wanted to see how long it took someone to forget a new telephone number? We could tell them the number, and ask them to repeat it, and then ask them the next day, and then the next, and so on. What do you think might happen? They would probably never forget it as the very act of repeating it would make it more memorable. The person would also realise that you were continually asking them and think there was something special about the number! The construction of experiments is therefore not without difficulty, and the earlier chapters in this book are intended to lead you through the concepts of good experimental design.

One other item in good experimental design is the ability to compare two groups of data. To do this we need to setup the two conditions in the best way possible. What we would like to do is to be able to say that the two conditions are exactly the same except for the *manipulation* that we have carried out, in our telephone number case, the element of distraction. The major difference in two conditions is that they might be carried out on different people. One way of counteracting this is to carry out both sets of data collection on the same people, but this is not always possible. The other way of minimising the individual differences is to randomly allocate people to each of the conditions.

We need to make a distinction here between random selection and random allocation (or assignment). Random selection means that we have selected people to take part in the experiment from a population available to us and we have chosen those people using a randomisation method. Random allocation means that we have taken our group of people and split them into the required number of groups using some randomisation process. It is possible to have both of these elements, or one without the other. We could do our telephone number and distraction tasks and have at our disposal the group of psychology students in year one at a particular University. However, we do not want to use everyone in the group so we select 50 students out of the 150 in the class, and we do this by only including every third person sitting in the lecture theatre. This would be random selection. We now have 50 people and need to allocate them to one of two groups.

Random selection is part of a sampling technique and this is discussed in more detail in Chapter 8. It is one of the things we can do to improve how representative the sample is of the population. Random allocation, on the other hand, is part of the design, and is one of the things that distinguish a true experiment from other types of experiment (see Chapter 9 for more detail). Random allocation means that everyone in the sample has an equal chance of being in one or other of the groups. The simplest way would be to toss a coin, with heads meaning that the person is allocated to the group that will receive the distraction, and tails that they are in the other group, up to the point where we have 25 in one of the groups. The remaining people are then allocated to the other group. Random allocation only reduces the effect of individual differences though, and therefore statistical analysis is designed to take this into account. Again more detail about this can be found in later chapters.

The data derived from experiments tends to be highly structured and numerical in nature (although not always) and the analysis is described in later chapters. There are also several categories of experimental research, but all experimental studies are used to try to establish **causality** i.e. that there are casual relationships between variables. The underlying assumption is that the world works in a linear, cause-and-effect way and that science should identify causal laws.

KT

Therefore, we can see that experimentation is an extremely useful technique in psychology, and has added significantly to the body of knowledge. Historically, the use of experiments can be traced throughout the field and the development of theoretical positions. The contribution of experimental psychology is still so important today that learning how to carry out experiments will form a large part of your studies, which in turn will allow you to appreciate how experiments carried out have contributed and are contributing to the development of your discipline. There are various reasons why experimentation has been used so extensively:

- Experiments are the major, possibly only, way that we can attempt to establish cause and effect.
- Experiments allow for precise control of variables. In a lab setting, we have control over the environment, or can exert as much as possible, so that we can have confidence that it is our manipulation of the condition that has caused any observed effect.

- Experiments can be replicated. This means performing a complete repeat of the experiment under exactly the same conditions, because we cannot generalise from the results of a single experiment. The more replications that find the same result, the more confidence we have that the result shows us a true effect. Only experiments will really give us the opportunity for full replication due to the control we are trying to exert over the conditions.
- Most of the data can be subjected to statistical analysis, allowing us scientific confidence in the results and the level of predictability they give us.

Despite such utility, laboratory experiments have severe limitations:

- The experimental setup is not typical of real-life situations, and is highly artificial. Critics suggest that this means experiments are not ecologically valid and therefore we cannot generalise from the findings to real life.
- Behaviour in the laboratory can be narrow in its range. By controlling the conditions, behaviour may be very limited.
- Experimentation is open to distortion through demand characteristics. Some of the many confounding variables in a psychology experiment stem from the fact that a psychology experiment is a social situation in which no one involved is passive.
- Demand characteristics are all the cues that convey to the participant the purpose of the experiment.
- Historically, the participants of experiments have not been an unbiased or representative sample. A great many experiments use psychology students! It should be clear that we cannot generalise to the general population from a bunch of people studying the very subject under scrutiny. University students are not typical of any other group.
- One major element required of experiments is control, but it must be impossible to control for everything, in particular the internal, mental environment of participants.

In Chapter 2 we look at a major area of concern, which has been levied at experimentation, and that is ethics. Many experiments will involve deception, and other areas of unethical practice, and if the researchers are not careful, they will break guidelines. However, there is no evidence that experiments are any more likely to cause ethical dilemmas than surveys that ask sensitive questions or fieldwork that may entail intrusion into people's lives.

So experiments are criticised for a lack of ecological validity, and inherent difficulties with trying to get people to behave naturally in a lab setting. There are also simply some pieces of behaviour that cannot be accessed using experiments. So-called non-experimental methods describe behaviour, but do not let us identify the causes or reasons for the behaviour. However, they should *not* be regarded as non-scientific, which often happens due to common misuse of the term 'experiment' to mean any scientific study. Properly executed and analysed, non-experimental methods provide solid, scientific data. We do tend to place emphasis on causal explanations in psychology (and other fields) and **experimental methods** are attractive because we want to know why things happen and how to change things. However, non-experimental methods also tell us important things – what people do and think. They are useful when you cannot do an experiment because you

cannot practically or ethically manipulate the **predictor variable** (such as age or health status). For these reasons, many researchers will utilise a different

paradigm for thinking about their own research.

When we need to ask people about experiences, they have to reconstruct them. For this reason, some researchers call the methods used for this **reconstructive**

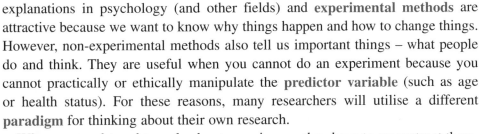

techniques, and they do not employ the same investigative techniques as experiments or introspection.

RESEARCH WITHOUT EXPERIMENTATION

Methods that do not involve experimentation can range from highly structured questionnaires and attitudes scales in correlational designs, to much less structured sets of questions used in unstructured interviews and focus groups. Correlational designs can use numerical data, but do not seek causal relationships as they are used to investigate the relationship between variables rather than the effect of one on another. The types of data derived from such techniques can range from the highly structured numerical data gathered from scales and validated questionnaires, to the very unstructured but rich information we get from allowing participants to talk freely about a topic. Data collection can be by questionnaire completion in psychometric testing, direct observation, diaries, interviews, postal or telephone questionnaires.

Psychometrics

Psychometrics is the science of measuring psychological aspects of a person such as knowledge, skills, abilities or personality. Measurement of these unobservable phenomena is difficult and much of the research in this discipline is designed to reliably define and then quantify these dimensions. Critics argue that such definition and quantification is impossibly difficult and that measurements are very often misused. Psychometricians respond to this by saying that the critics often misuse data by not assessing them with psychometric criteria!

Much of the early work in psychometrics was developed in order to measure intelligence, but recent developments include the measurement of attitudes and beliefs, academic achievement, quality of life and personality (particularly in clinical and occupational fields).

There are two branches to psychometric theory: classical test theory and item response theory. Classical test theory attempts to predict outcomes of psychological testing such as the difficulty of items or the ability of test takers. Generally speaking, the aim of classical test theory is to understand and improve the reliability of psychological tests. Key concepts of classical test theory are reliability and validity. In psychometrics, reliability is the accuracy of the scores of a measure. Reliability does not imply validity. That is, a reliable measure is measuring something accurately, but not, necessarily, what it is supposed to be measuring. For example, while there are many reliable tests, not all of them would validly predict job performance. A valid measure is one that is measuring what it is supposed to measure. Validity implies reliability. A valid measure must be reliable, but a reliable measure need not be valid. A reliable measure is measuring something consistently, while a valid measure is measuring what it is supposed to measure. A reliable measure may be consistent without necessarily being valid; for example, a measurement instrument like a broken ruler may always under-measure a quantity by the same amount each time (consistently), but the resulting quantity is still wrong, that is invalid. Both reliability and validity may be assessed mathematically and we will look at this later in the book.

Validity may be assessed by correlating measures with a **criterion validity** measure, a measurement known to be valid. When the criterion measure is collected at the same time as the measure being validated, the goal is to establish **concurrent validity**; when the criterion is collected later, the goal is to establish **predictive validity**. In psychometrics, predictive validity refers to empirical evidence that a scale has predictive power over the unobservable construct that it is intended to measure. In social science and psychometrics, **construct validity** refers to whether a scale measures the unobservable construct (such as 'ability to use a computer') that it purposes to measure.

Direct Observation

Experiments can be seen as direct observation, but we can also record behaviour outside the constraints of an experimental design. In direct observation, we record events during an experiment or record behaviour. However, we cannot observe people without informing them that we are doing so, and this complicates matters as behaviour might be changed because it is being observed. A classical form of observation is that used in **ethnography**, when a researcher joins a group of people to observe the life of the group and its constituents. The approach is phenomenological in that it attempts to represent the worldview of the people observed.

Observation can be achieved simply by observing behaviour without participating in it, or by a participation in the activity oneself. Both have difficulties but also advantages.

Self-reports

There are alternative forms of self-reports to those described above. The self-reports used in cognitive psychology involve scrutiny of the contents of the mind, whereas other forms involve reconstruction of experience. The data collection techniques include diaries, a wide range of interview types, focus groups and questionnaires.

Surveys

Many people confuse surveys and questionnaires. A questionnaire is a set of questions on a particular topic that requires answers from a participant. A survey is a research method for gathering data in a non-experimental way, and can include the use of questionnaires, interviews or unobtrusive observations. It is true that many surveys do employ the questionnaire technique, but can also be conducted using other tools, such as interviews. Properly constructed **surveys** can allow us to gather a great deal of information about a large number of people. However, there are difficulties with surveys, such as poor response rate (a poorly constructed method will not get a representative response) and there is a possibility that people may answer questions in a socially desirable way – the way that portrays themselves in a positive manner irrespective of accuracy.

Evaluation

A final type of research method to be considered in psychology is **evaluation**. The goal of evaluation research is data-based decision making. The types of evaluation research reflect different decisions to be made. Need assessment provides data to help make decisions about the need for a programme, its targets and its design. Process evaluation provides data on how the programme was delivered. Outcome evaluation provides data on the extent to which the programme met its intended objectives. It is useful in deciding whether to revise the programme, re-fund it, or to export it to other settings. Context evaluation provides information about the factors behind the programme, and what the constraints are on it. Context evaluation is necessary for fully understanding other aspects of the programme evaluation.

Evaluation is a useful technique in areas such as clinical and health psychology to evaluate parts of a programme that does not lend itself to experimental or correlational designs. For example, the evaluation of certain new therapeutic regimes can be evaluated by the use of clinical trials – a form of experimentation – but it might not be appropriate or ethical to deprive one set of patients of the new technique, or conversely subject them to a technique that is not yet established. Evaluation of current techniques and the possibility of the introduction of a new one could be much more effective.

ANALYSIS OF PSYCHOLOGICAL DATA

The above provides an idea of the range of research tools we use in psychology, but does not tell us very much about the analysis of any data. However, psychological research is broadly categorised into that requiring qualitative or quantitative analysis. The aim of qualitative analysis is a complete, detailed description. No attempt is made to assign numbers to the elements identified in the data, and the frequency with which the phenomena appear has no relevance. Qualitative analysis should allow for fine distinctions to be drawn because there is no attempt to reduce the data into a finite number of categories. Ambiguities, which are inherent in human language and behaviour, can be examined in the analysis. The main disadvantage of qualitative approaches is that the findings cannot be generalised to wider populations with the same degree of certainty that quantitative analyses can. This is because the findings of the research are not tested to discover whether they are statistically significant or due to chance. Quantitative research is used to classify features, count them, and construct statistical models. We can generalise our findings to a larger population, and direct comparisons can be made between two or more sets of data, allowing us to decide which phenomena are likely to be genuine observations of the behaviour we have observed. However, the view of the data that can be derived from quantitative analysis is not as rich as a qualitative analytical view. Quantitative analysis can be seen as an idealisation of the data, with the removal of rare occurrences. The most recent position on the analysis of psychological data is that both qualitative and quantitative analyses have something to contribute and there has been a move towards using mixed methodologies, multiple methods being employed, gaining the potential of a breadth of information which the use of more than one method may provide. The modern psychologist chooses the correct set of methods by which to carry out the research, and must therefore be aware of a wide range of techniques in order to choose appropriately.

Summary

We have been introduced to the concept of research and research methods in psychology, and have examined the form of some of the methods in detail. We have explored in some detail the experimental method but also examined the tensions between the possibility of control and causal inference and ecological validity and flexibility. We have considered the alternatives to experimentation and reasons they might be used.

Wilhelm Wundt (1832–1920)

Wilhelm Wundt was a German physiologist and psychologist. From 1875, he taught at Leipzig, where he established the first laboratory for experimental psychology. Wundt stressed the use of scientific methods in psychology, particularly through the use of introspection. He believed that the mind is active and creative. The process in which the mind functions to produce learning is not merely an accumulation of facts and instances, but a striving for understanding. Ironically, his findings from the process of introspection were not considered great work, but because of the work, psychology became a valid experimental science.

Sir Karl Popper (1902–1994)

Karl Popper was born in Vienna on 28 July 1902, and is viewed as one of the most influential philosophical theorists. He challenged mainstream philosophical viewpoints by asserting that scientific theories cannot be verified but only refuted. Popper promoted a critical culture in which we can debate in the knowledge that it is only by challenging the accepted perception and co-operation in science that we may get nearer to the truth. His contribution to psychology as a science is the establishing of scientific methods of examining questions about any phenomena. He was honoured many times, including receiving the Sonning Prize for merit in work that had furthered European civilization.

CHAPTER 2

ETHICS IN RESEARCH: SOME SHOCKING CASES

Contents

Shocking events in New Haven

Public health shame

Ethical issues

How to design ethical research
General
Consent
Deception
Debriefing
Withdrawal
Confidentiality
Protection
Observational research
Giving advice
Colleagues

Summary

Ethics in Research: Some Shocking Cases

The disappearance of a sense of responsibility is the most far-reaching consequence of submission to authority. (Stanley Milgram)

Learning Objectives

- To be aware of the concepts of ethics in research in the light of some infamous cases and the relevant professional body guidelines.

KEY TERMS

- American Psychological Association
- British Psychological Society
- Coercion
- Confederate
- Debriefing
- Deception
- Ethics
- Giving advice
- Informed consent
- Moral principles
- Privacy, confidentiality and anonymity
- Protection
- Responsibility of colleagues
- Right to service
- Risk of harm
- Voluntary participation
- Withdrawal

During the Second World War, as in many major conflicts, records show that ordinary people committed some inconceivable atrocities, genocidal acts that most of us would call inhuman. At the end of the war, some of the men who carried out these acts were tried at the Nuremberg War Criminal trials. Many offered in their defence a very bizarre reason for why they did such things, despite personal conscience that dictated they should not do them. They were 'only following orders'.

No one would do such things only to obey those they perceive to be in authority, would they?

SHOCKING EVENTS IN NEW HAVEN

In the 1960s the results of several experiments demonstrated that such behaviour was not confined to one nation (Germany) or to one situation (war), but that many people can be persuaded to behave in ways that conflict with their conscience.

In the experiments, 'teachers' (unsuspecting subjects) were recruited by Yale University psychologist Stanley Milgram. They were asked to administer an electric shock of increasing intensity to a 'learner' (an experimental **confederate**) for each mistake made during the experiment. The 'teachers' were told that the experiment was exploring effects of punishment on learning behaviour. The 'teacher' was not aware that the 'learner' in the study was actually an actor, or that the shocks were not real.

KT

When the 'teacher' asked whether increased shocks should be given he or she was verbally encouraged to continue. In most experiments 60% of the 'teachers' obeyed orders to punish the learner to the very end of the 450 volt scale and no subject stopped before reaching 300 volts. There are tapes and films of the experiments that show the setup and the obvious discomfort of the 'teachers'.

Milgram, S. (1963). Behavioral Study of Obedience. *Journal of Abnormal and Social Psychology*, 67(4), 371–378.

This article describes a procedure for the study of destructive obedience in the laboratory. It consists of ordering a naive S to administer increasingly more severe punishment to a victim in the context of a learning experiment. Punishment is administered by means of a shock generator with 30 graded switches ranging from Slight Shock to Danger: Severe Shock. The victim is a confederate of the E. The primary dependent variable is the maximum shock the S is willing to administer before he refuses to continue further: 26 Ss obeyed the experimental commands fully, and administered the highest shock on the generator; 14 Ss broke off the

(Cont'd)

experiment at some point after the victim protested and refused to provide further answers. The procedure created extreme levels of nervous tension in some Ss. Profuse sweating, trembling and stuttering were typical expressions of this emotional disturbance. One unexpected sign of tension – yet to be explained – was the regular occurrence of nervous laughter, which in some Ss developed into uncontrollable seizures. The variety of interesting behavioural dynamics observed in the experiment, the reality of the situation for the S, and the possibility of parametric variation within the framework of the procedure, point to the fruitfulness of further study.

Sometimes the 'teachers' questioned the experimenter, asking who was responsible for any harmful effects resulting from shocking the 'learner' at such a high level? They were told that the experimenter assumed full responsibility; they usually seemed to accept the response and continue shocking, despite their discomfort. The study raised many questions about how the subjects could bring themselves to administer such treatment. Also important to our interests as researchers are the ethical issues raised by such an experiment itself. Do we have the right to expose research participants to such stress and possible loss of self-esteem? Does the search for knowledge justify such costs to those who take part? Would we be less (or more) concerned if the experimental results had been different?

KT

We are going through a time of profound change in our understanding of the **ethics** of research. There has been a developing consensus about the major ethical principles that should underlie research. The Nuremberg trials brought to public view the ways that the Nazis had behaved, including how German scientists had used captive people in some horrific experiments. Milgram's experiments investigating the reasons why people might behave in this way have themselves been condemned as unethical. In 1962, a year before the appearance of his first journal article on the obedience research, the American Psychological Association put Milgram's membership application 'on hold' firstly because his undergraduate training was not in psychology, but also, and more importantly, because of questions raised about the ethics of that research. After an investigation produced a favourable result, the APA admitted him. In fact, as we will see, the results of the research may be appalling, but Milgram behaved in a perfectly ethical way in terms of the conduct of his own research.

Consider another situation that arises in research. Clinical trials are often carried out to determine the efficacy of a new treatment. This means withholding the treatment from one group of people and also trying out the new treatment, which may have its own attendant risks, on people who are ill.

PUBLIC HEALTH SHAME

Syphilis is a sexually transmitted disease caused by the bacterium *Treponema pallidum.* Early-stage syphilis produces hard red sores on the genitals, followed by flu-like symptoms. If untreated, the disease can progress, causing skin growths, disfigurement, bone decay, heart damage, blindness, insanity, paralysis and death. However, early-stage syphilis can be effectively treated with antibiotics. Aside from any moral stance an individual may have about STDs and their contraction, how would you feel if you knew that effective treatment might be withheld from people suffering from syphilis? Concerned, perhaps, even appalled?

In 1932, the US Public Health Service (PHS) recruited 600 African American men in Tuskegee, Alabama, to participate in a medical study; 399 of the men were diagnosed with syphilis, 201 uninfected men were included as a control group. Most of them were poor farm workers with limited education and access to medical care. The men and their families were not told that they had syphilis or that they were participants in an experiment. The researchers withheld effective treatment from the men. The study lasted for 40 years and was only stopped due to public protest, initiated by one of the health workers involved 'blowing the whistle'. By this time 28 men had died of syphilis, 100 others were dead of related complications, at least 40 wives had been infected, and 19 children had contracted the disease at birth.

The Tuskegee Syphilis study was not secret. Findings were regularly published and discussed in medical journals and public reports, yet the medical community did not object. In 1972, a series of Associated Press articles brought the study to general public attention. PHS officials immediately stopped the experiment, but still denied they had done anything wrong. A 1973 report commissioned by the US Department of Health, Education, and Welfare found that the study was 'ethically unjustified' because participants did not give their informed consent and that they should have been given penicillin when it became available as an effective treatment for syphilis in the 1940s. In 1997, US President Bill Clinton formally apologised for the study on behalf of the US government.

The Tuskegee Syphilis Study remains one of the most famous examples of violation of standards for ethical research. It also highlights the ethical conduct and, perhaps, some implicit racism, prevalent at the time. In a 1976 interview, John Heller, Director of the Venereal Diseases Unit of the PHS from 1943 to 1948, remarked: 'The men's status did not warrant ethical debate. They were subjects, not patients; clinical material, not sick people' (Jones, 1981: 179).

In the past few decades since the ending of the Tuskegee study and the publication of Milgram's findings, researchers have sought to examine the ways in which research is carried out. A consensus is evolving that involves the stakeholder groups most affected by a problem participating more actively in the formulation of guidelines for research. In the twenty-first century, the National Health Service is implementing its Research Governance Policy, which 'is intended to sustain a research culture that promotes excellence, with visible research leadership and expert management to help researchers, clinicians, and managers apply standards correctly' (Department of Health, 2005). These standards include the ethical conduct of research.

ETHICAL ISSUES

There are several key issues that are paramount in ethical research and the monitoring and governance of researchers and their ethical practice:

1   The principle of voluntary participation requires that people are not coerced into participating in research. This is especially relevant where researchers had relied on 'captive audiences' for their participants: prisons, schools and similar institutions.
2   Closely related to the notion of voluntary participation is the requirement of informed consent. This means that research participants must be fully informed about the procedures and risks involved in research and must give their consent to participate (**briefing**). Ethical standards also require that researchers do not put participants in a situation where they might be at risk of harm as a result of their participation. Harm can be defined as both physical and psychological.
3   There are two standards that are applied in order to help protect the privacy of research participants. Almost all research guarantees the participants' confidentiality: they are assured that identifying information will not be made available to anyone who is not directly involved in the study. The stricter standard is the principle of anonymity, which means that the participant will remain anonymous throughout the study including (in most cases) to the researchers. The anonymity principle is sometimes difficult to accomplish, especially in situations where participants have to be measured at multiple time points or in face-to-face interviews.
4   Increasingly, researchers have to deal with the ethical issue of a person's right to service. Good research practice often requires the use of a no-treatment control group, a group of participants who do not get the treatment or programme that is being studied, such as a drug or a new form of psychotherapy. But when that treatment or programme may have beneficial effects, people assigned to the no-treatment control may feel their rights to equal access to services are being curtailed.

Even when clear ethical standards and principles exist, there will be times when the need to do accurate research conflicts with the rights of potential participants. No set of standards can possibly anticipate every ethical circumstance. Furthermore, there needs to be a procedure that assures that researchers will consider all relevant ethical issues in formulating research plans. To address such needs, most institutions that are concerned with research, such as hospitals and universities, have internal review panels that review applications with the view to helping protect the organisation and the researcher against potential legal implications of neglecting to address important ethical issues of participants.

Many professional bodies have developed their own code of conduct and ethical principles.

The British Psychological Society (BPsS) is no exception; its code of conduct includes sections on ethical principles for those researching with humans and animals. The following points are condensed from the code of conduct, which can be obtained from the BPsS website (www.bps.org.uk). Each point is then placed in context for our two studies:

1   **General**   The first principle suggests that researchers must consider the ethical implications and psychological consequences for the participants in their research. A good point is made that researchers should consider the research from the perspective of all potential participants including 'foreseeable threats to their psychological well-being, health, values, or dignity' and that these should be eliminated. The BPsS recognises that we live in a multicultural and multi-ethnic society and researchers may not have sufficient knowledge of the implications of any investigation for different ages, sex, sexual orientation and social background, so the best judge of whether an investigation will cause offence will be members of the population from which the sample will be drawn.

   - There is very clear evidence that Milgram considered the consequences of his research, as he placed the research in front of the APA for investigation.
   - The Tuskegee researchers were also open about their study and the findings, but it is unclear (and unlikely) that any investigation took place before the study started.

2   **Consent**

   (a)   All participants should be informed about the objectives of the investigation, including all aspects of the research or intervention that might reasonably be expected to influence willingness to participate. Informed consent might be difficult for some categories of participants, such as children or those with learning impairments. Researchers must take responsibility for ensuring that the participants can give fully informed consent, or that carers or guardians can do so in their place. A researcher should also consider what might happen if, for example, a child's parent/guardian gives consent and the child does not, or vice versa.
   (b)   If the research is of such a nature (see point 3) that the researcher cannot reasonably explain all aspects, then additional safeguards to protect the welfare and dignity of the participants should be made.

      - Milgram's study was of such a nature, fully informing participants would have completely changed the nature of the experiments. However, he took care to ensure that subjects were fully debriefed and did follow up interviews to ensure that they were in a satisfactory frame of mind.

- The Tuskegee researchers did not inform participants, at any stage, that they were involved in the study, and there is no evidence that any debriefing took part. Men who died during the study would never have known what happened to them; the survivors and their families received an apology, but little further knowledge of their status.

(c) Researchers should ensure that participants have not been coerced (e.g. people detained in prison), or induced to take part and expose themselves to excessive harm by payment.

- Milgram neither coerced his subjects, nor withheld payment if they withdrew.
- The Tuskegee participants could not have been coerced as they did not know they were part of an experiment anyway.

(d) Researchers should remember that they represent authority, or may in fact be in authority over students, employees or clients, and should not pressure people to take part.

- Milgram's study demonstrates this effect very clearly. As he was studying this very phenomenon, Milgram was aware of its effect and took pains to ensure this was minimised after the experiment ended, and in follow-up.
- The Tuskegee researchers represented authority very clearly – they were medical personnel and, in the terms of the period in which the research was carried out, socially superior to the subjects. The men accepted what they were told and did as expected, never questioning the treatment they were being given, or the fact that they were not recovering.

(e) If harm, unusual discomfort or other negative consequences for the individual's future life might occur, the researcher must inform the participants, and obtain informed, real consent from each of them.

- Again, this was a difficulty for Milgram. It was clear that participants were distressed and may even have lost some self-esteem when they realised what they had done and that they had been 'duped' into doing it. Informed consent was not possible, though, and Milgram took steps to ensure the participants left the laboratory fully informed, but not feeling any worse than possible, then followed them up later to see if there were any ill-effects requiring any form of treatment.
- The Tuskegee subjects, particularly the infected group, were in very real danger from the outcomes of the study, but were never informed of the risks they were taking.

(f) In longitudinal research, consent may need to be obtained on more than one occasion.

- In Milgram's study the subject did only participate in one event, but Milgram obtained consent for follow-up interviews, allowing him to ensure that subjects were fully debriefed and no negative consequences accrued.
- The Tuskegee researchers never obtained consent even though the men took part in the study for some years.

3 Deception

(a) The withholding of information or the misleading of participants is unacceptable if the participants are typically likely to object or show unease once debriefed. Where this is in any doubt, appropriate consultation must precede the investigation. Consultation is best carried out with individuals who share the social and cultural background of the participants in the research, but the advice of ethics committees or experienced and disinterested colleagues may be sufficient.

- Milgram took the advice of the APA members who investigated his research. The APA committee considered the consequences of the study, agreed that the deception was necessary, and could be carried out with the condition of monitoring and follow-up that Milgram undertook.
- The Tuskegee study was never subjected to such scrutiny.

(b) Intentional deception of the participants over the purpose and general nature of the investigation should be avoided whenever possible. Participants should never be deliberately misled without justification. Even then, there should be strict controls and the disinterested approval of independent advisors.

(c) It may be impossible to study some psychological processes without withholding information about the true object of the study or deliberately misleading the participants. However, researchers should consider if alternative procedures are available, or that the participants are provided with sufficient information at the earliest stage and consider what effect the withholding of information might have on participants.

- This one could have been written for Milgram's study. Alternatives were considered and rejected, and the effects of the actual procedures were considered.

4 **Debriefing** Once the data has been collected, researchers should provide participants with enough information to complete their understanding of the research. This allows an opportunity to monitor any adverse effects that might occur, and does not provide a justification for unethical aspects of any investigation.

- Again, Milgram assiduously provided the information post-experiment and monitored his participants carefully for some time after the study was completed. (An even more effective and protective debriefing strategy is one which provides the participant with a justification for his or her behaviour (Ring, Wallston and Corey, 1970)).
- For the Tuskegee study, the adverse effects were the objectives of the study, so the researchers monitored this, but not with the intention to provide care and debriefing to the subjects.

5 **Withdrawal** Participants have the right to withdraw from the research at any time, irrespective of payment, inducement, or whether withdrawal will adversely affect the progress of the research. They should be informed of these rights before the data collection from any participant starts. This may be difficult in some settings but researchers should make all possible efforts to ensure that participants are aware of this right, including those for whom informed consent might have been difficult. Once the data collection is collected or after debriefing, the participant may wish to withdraw any consent given retrospectively, and to require that their own data, including recordings, be destroyed. The researchers must ensure the participant is aware of this right and put procedures in place to facilitate this withdrawal.

- Milgram's participants were told they could withdraw, but were encouraged by the experimenter to carry on. However, once debriefed they were allowed to withdraw permission to use the data if they wished.
- The men in Tuskegee were not informed they were in a study, so were unaware of any right to withdraw.

6 **Confidentiality** Subject to the requirements of legislation, including the Data Protection Act, information obtained about a participant during an investigation is confidential. Researchers should not be under pressure to disclose confidential information. Participants in psychological

research have a right to expect that information they provide will be treated confidentially and, if published, will not be identifiable as theirs.

- This directive does hold a problem for Milgram, as the films of the experiment do show the subjects quite clearly. However, their consent to use the film footage was obtained.
- Strangely enough, this was one directive with which the Tuskegee researchers complied.

7 **Protection** Researchers have a responsibility to protect participants from physical and mental harm during the investigation.

(a) Normally, the risk of harm must be no greater than in ordinary life, i.e. participants should not be exposed to risks greater than or additional to those encountered in their normal lifestyles. Where the risk of harm is greater than in ordinary life, then the participants must be in a position to give full informed consent and must be asked about any factors in the procedure that might create a risk, such as pre-existing medical conditions, and must be advised of any special action they should take to avoid risk.

  - Milgram's subjects were in distress, and when the objective of the study was revealed, may have lost self-esteem (Stollak, 1967). However, many safeguards were put into place. This is the major area of controversy with Milgram's research, and the one that makes most psychologists uncomfortable about the ethicality when considering the procedures.
  - The objective of the Tuskegee study placed the men in very real danger that could have been avoided.

(b) Participants should be informed about how to contact the researcher within a reasonable time following participation should stress, potential harm or related questions or concern arise despite the precautions made. Where research procedures might result in undesirable consequences for participants, the researcher has the responsibility to detect and remove or correct these consequences.

  - Milgram maintained contact with the participants himself.

(c) Where research may involve behaviour or experiences that participants may regard as personal and private, the participants must be protected from stress by all appropriate measures, including the assurance that answers to personal questions need not be given. There should be no concealment or deception when seeking information that might encroach on privacy.

  - Milgram's participants gave no information about private experiences, but the behaviour during the experiment can be construed as something the participants may not have wanted revealed about themselves. This is a contentious point about the research, but safeguards, such as withdrawal of data, were put in place.
  - The Tuskegee subjects, while anonymous, did reveal some information about themselves that they perhaps would not have wanted to – that they had a sexually transmitted infection.

(d) In research involving children, great caution should be exercised when discussing the results with parents, teachers or others acting in *loco parentis*, since evaluative statements may carry unintended weight.

8 **Observational research** Studies based upon observation must respect the privacy and psychological well-being of the individuals studied. Unless those observed give their consent to being observed, observational research is only acceptable in situations where those observed would

expect to be observed by strangers. Additionally, particular account should be taken of local cultural values and of the possibility of intruding upon the privacy of individuals who, even while in a normally public space, may believe they are unobserved.

9 **Giving advice**

(a) It is always possible that researchers may obtain evidence of problems of which a participant is unaware. In such a case, the researcher has a responsibility to inform the participant if the researcher believes that by not doing so the participant's future well-being may be endangered.

- It is clear that the Tuskegee researchers were aware of the life-threatening condition of the men who took part in the study, but carried on withholding treatment *and* information.

(b) If, in the normal course of psychological research, or as a result of problems detected as in 9(a), a participant solicits advice concerning educational, personality, behavioural or health issues, caution should be exercised. If the researcher is not qualified to offer assistance, the appropriate source of professional advice should be recommended.

10 **Colleagues** Researchers share responsibility for the ethical treatment of research participants with their collaborators, assistants, students and employees. A psychologist who believes that another psychologist or researcher may be conducting research that is not in accordance with the principles above should encourage that researcher to re-evaluate the research.

Let us examine these principles in the light of Milgram's research. Milgram was governed by the same principles as outlined above, as the APA has a very similar set. Remember, his research was examined by the APA before it proceeded too, as the APA had a responsibility to make sure that colleagues, in this case Milgram and his team, were acting ethically. In order to investigate the question of obedience and conflict, Milgram had to deceive his participants to some aspects. If they had known, beforehand, that the 'learner' was really a confederate, they would not have acted as they would in a 'real-life' situation. However, all participants were debriefed and those whose data was later included in the published articles gave full consent to its being included. Several months after debriefing, participants received follow-up interviews to ensure that there were no long-lasting effects of participation. Milgram's findings could not have been obtained any other way. So, Milgram did conform to all the requirements of his professional body's ethical principles and acted ethically. The major difficulties we have when viewing Milgram's work are the issue of deception and loss of self-esteem, and perhaps the inner worry of what we would do in the same situation. In one variation of the main procedure, the naive participants did not administer the shock; this was done by another participant, who was actually another confederate. Therefore, the real participants were one step removed from direct action; 37 out of 40 participants continued to the end, the highest obedience rate Milgram found in his whole series. Overall, he found that 65% of his participants were willing to give apparently harmful electric shocks to a protesting victim, because a scientific authority commanded them.

Perhaps we only perceive Milgram's experiments as unethical because of what they reveal, not because of the way they were conducted.

On the other hand, the Tuskegee Syphilis Study project leaders did not obtain consent and withheld potentially life-saving treatment. Furthermore, it transpires that the study was carried out in this way because some members of the US PHS openly held the belief that African Americans were biologically different to Caucasians and that this justified the way they were studied.

When designing our own research we have the responsibility to ensure that we comply with the guidelines outlined above, or their equivalent. As researchers in psychology we are all subject to the scrutiny of groups set up to review and monitor the procedures by which research is carried out, and it is the researcher's responsibility to seek out that scrutiny.

The design of a research project should be a good one and intended to add to the pool of knowledge about psychological processes and phenomena. Bad research is unethical research, as knowledge is sought for no good reason if it puts participants at any kind of risk for little or no scientific gain.

HOW TO DESIGN ETHICAL RESEARCH

When still learning about research and design, researchers should ensure that they have supervisors who are competent to aid the design of studies of this nature. The choice of methodology and design for the study should be appropriate to investigate the research question.

General

While designing research, we should attempt to consider how participation in the study will be perceived from the participants' point of view. One way to do this might be for the researcher to carry out the procedure on him- or herself, but this might not be possible in reconstructive techniques, those designed to elicit responses from people who have experienced something specific, or who possess attributes that the researchers do not, such as a specific illness. Therefore we must seek advice from people who may be able to give an opinion about those specific issues.

Consent

Research participants should give consent for their participation and/or for the data derived from their participation to be used for analysis. Some research will make it impossible for consent to be given *prior* to participation – protocols in which deception is necessary, or covert observation, for example – but then attempts should be made to achieve consent *after* participation. When writing a proposal for carrying out research it is always best to include the form on which the participant will be asked to indicate consent and the information the participant will be given in order to achieve fully informed consent. In that way the authority from which permission is requested (such as a university ethics committee or a local health authority research ethics committee) can satisfy itself that the researcher is aware of issues involved in consent.

Fully Informed Consent

Information given in order to gain consent must be couched in terms the participants will understand. The inclusion of scientific terms is not recommended unless they are fully explained.

Sometimes it is not possible to gain fully informed consent from the participants themselves. In the case of children, or adults with learning difficulties for example, it may be difficult for them to understand exactly what may be involved. Complete attempts must be made to explain what they are being asked to do, but in some cases it will be necessary to gain the consent of another person, usually the carer, parent or guardian. In these cases it must be considered what will happen if the carer gives consent and the potential participant does not, or vice versa. Consider for example the case where a researcher wishes to do something with a whole class of children, but one child's parents have declined permission to include their child. The exclusion from something that might be seen as fun by other children might be upsetting. What would you do in this case?

Coercion

In some categories of participant there might be the potential for **coercion** to take place. For example, those held in prisons and similar institutions can be coerced by the prison authorities either to agree or decline depending on how those authorities view the research. School children could be made to take part by teachers. As researchers we have responsibility to ensure that no coercion has been carried out by agencies (or gatekeepers in control of access to the participants). We also have responsibility to ensure that we do not use coercion either deliberately or inadvertently. We must also take care that there is no deliberate exclusion of potential participants; in a study on effective teaching methods, for example, it would be tempting for a teacher to select only the brightest pupils for inclusion.

Authority

Even as students, researchers represent authority – the university at which they study or the health authority which has granted permission for the research to be carried out, for example. Milgram's results show that participants in studies that are perceived to be high prestige will 'follow orders' even if they are counter to their own principles. Care must be taken therefore to ensure that the behaviour being observed is the way the participants would behave without complying with instructions from someone they perceive to be in authority. This is a special kind of demand characteristic, see Chapter 1.

Unusual Discomfort

Some procedures will require discomfort to the participants, such as studies of pain or stress. However, this discomfort should not be excessive, and steps should be taken to minimise it. Pain, psychological stress, noise, mood alteration are all things which could affect levels of discomfort. There are guidelines about use of such stressors, but a rule of thumb would be to ensure that participants leave the study in the same state or better than when they entered it.

Longitudinal Studies

Longitudinal studies are rare at undergraduate level, but many postgraduates may wish to do research that could be classified as such. The retention of identification is fraught with difficulty (see 'Confidentiality' below) but must be done in some reasonable manner if people are going to take part in several stages of a study. Consent must be gained and the evidence that it has been gained kept, at several stages, and participants need to be assured of the confidential manner in which the researchers are keeping this information.

Deception

KT

As Milgram's work shows us, **deception** is a useful device in psychological research. Deception can happen in many ways, much less obvious than the way it was performed in Milgram's case. If we tell participants that they are about to watch a film and then their attitudes to it will be measured, but in fact the researcher gives them a memory test, that is deception. Covert observation is a special kind of deception (see below). When proposing research we should always examine whether the procedure is deceptive, and consider what steps we are going to take to minimise the effect.

Debriefing

KT

One way of minimising the effect of deception is by **debriefing** the participants. In cases where the deception has led to participants behaving in a manner counter to their principles, then the debriefing should include a justification for the behaviour (Ring et al., 1970). However, debriefing should not only be considered in cases of deception. People are fascinated by psychology and psychological research and its findings. Many will ask 'what have you found out?' or more personally 'how did I do?'. If the research is such that people will find the result personally interesting, then the researcher could consider making a summary of the report available to those who took part, but never consider giving feedback on individual results (see 'Giving advice' below).

Withdrawal

KT

Participants are giving their time willingly to our research, and sometimes they give information about themselves that they may feel uncomfortable about revealing. This feeling of discomfort at revelations may not occur to them until after they have participated, so an ethical researcher should give participants the right of **withdrawal**, that is, the opportunity to withdraw permission to use their data at any time. This means failing to turn up to participate, walking away from the study during participation, and the withdrawal of data at any point up to final analysis.

Confidentiality

There is a tension between the need to allow participants to withdraw themselves or their data, and the need to keep all the information confidential, and, even more strictly, to allow participants to remain anonymous. Anonymity is achieved by the assignment of identification codes (id) to the data derived from a participant's behaviour, and the researcher should maintain a separate link between the id and participant's name (perhaps the consent forms) to facilitate the removal of the information relating to a participant should he or she wish to withdraw.

Confidentiality is a little different to that, in that all the information should be kept safe and away from anyone not involved with the project, so only the researcher and possibly the supervisor will have access to it. Locked filing cabinets and password-protected computer files are absolutely necessary. It might be reasonable for researchers and supervisors of research to familiarise themselves with at least the principles of the Data Protection Act (1998) (see http://www.legislation.hmso.gov.uk/).

Protection

All reasonable measures to protect participants from harm, either physical or psychological, should be taken. The potential for physical harm is sometimes easier to assess, and often there are other measures in institutions to ensure that physical risk is minimised. Risk assessment procedures are carried out alongside the assessment of ethical procedures, and if substances are being used researchers may be required to carry out a COSHH (Control Of Substances Hazardous to Health) assessment (see http://www.coshh-essentials.org.uk/assets/live/indg136.pdf) and even consult the institution's insurers. These last measures are unusual in psychology, but some research involving alcohol or other drugs may require this type of scrutiny.

Psychological harm is more difficult to assess. Such harm would include stressful procedures or mood alteration. Again, the rule of thumb here is that participants should leave in a reasonable state of mind. Interviews that are designed to elicit information and opinions about sensitive subjects should not place the participant in discomfort and the state of the interviewee should be monitored throughout the interview. Again procedures designed to maintain confidentiality and anonymity should reassure the participant.

Observational Research

Observation brings its own difficulties, as it may often need to be covert. Overt observation may make the participants change their behaviour, so a covert design may be needed. The behaviour being observed should always be something that could realistically be observed naturally, and not something that the participants would find problematic if revealed. So observing how the members of a choir interact with the conductor at rehearsal is acceptable, but observing how a singing teacher criticises a singer for intonation control is not.

Giving Advice

During the course of a procedure things may be revealed about the participant that require advice being given. For example, if we are measuring the changes in blood pressure due to a stressful task, and the participant's blood pressure appears quite high, it would be the act of a responsible and ethical researcher to suggest that the participant see his or her GP. However, many researchers would not be competent to give advice about the results of many tests and the researchers should therefore recognise their limitations and not attempt to. In this way, individual results of psychological tests should not be provided.

Similarly, interviews on sensitive topics may lead participants to start to disclose elements of their lives that require support. For example, in interviews about attitudes towards sex offenders, a participant may disclose that he or she had been sexually assaulted, or the victim of child sexual abuse. Even if the researcher is a trained counsellor, he or she should not attempt to start a counselling session, but refer the participant to a counselling service. The roles of researcher and practitioner should not be confused or conflict, and the researcher cannot ethically take on another role in the middle of an interview. Information sheets given to participants should include the appropriate agency referral information, and, if necessary, the researcher should make an individual referral.

Colleagues

As ethical researchers, we have a responsibility to conduct ethical research, and to ensure that our co-researchers and other colleagues are doing so too.

Summary

In this chapter we have explored two studies that appear to be unethical. One study was, in fact, carried out under ethical conditions, but it produced such disturbing findings, and the participants were clearly in such discomfort, that we must draw our own conclusion about its performance. The other study was clearly unethical and brings into sharp focus the responsibility that we all have to understand and monitor research.

If you are asked to take part in, carry out or observe research that you think is unethical but feel powerless to object, remember these words:

With numbing regularity, good people were seen to knuckle under the demands of authority and perform actions that were callous and severe. Men who are in everyday life responsible and decent were seduced by the trappings of authority, by the control of their perceptions, and by the uncritical acceptance of the experimenter's definition of the situation, into

(Cont'd)

performing harsh acts. … A substantial proportion of people do what they are told to do, irrespective of the content of the act and without limitations of conscience, so long as they perceive that the command comes from a legitimate authority. (Stanley Milgram, 1965)

The whole conspiracy idea is cockeyed. We had orders to obey the head of state. We weren't a band of criminals meeting in the woods in the dead of night to plan mass murders. (Hermann Goering, Reichsmarschall and Luftwaffe Chief; Nuremberg trials, 1946)

Stanley Milgram (1933–1984)

Stanley Milgram was born in New York in 1933. He graduated from James Monroe High School in 1950, where he was a classmate of Zimbardo. He went on to earn his bachelor's degree from Queens College in 1954. His PhD was from Harvard, in 1960, supervised by Gordon Allport. Milgram was interested in social issues and the emerging field of urban psychology. His thesis investigated cross-cultural differences in conformity that he conducted in Norway and Paris. Upon his return from Paris, Milgram spent 1959–1960 at the Institute for Advanced Study in Princeton with Solomon Asch. Asch was concerned with conformity and had completed his famous studies of conformity that required subjects to select lines judged to be the same size. The correct choices that would have been made were offset by false alternatives that were selected by the experimenter's confederates. These conflicting opinions induced the selection of lines that were not even close to the same length as the other. Milgram changed the design from lines to shocks and conducted his famous series of studies on obedience to authority.

Milgram much preferred to tackle subjects that affected the average person on the street. For example, once his mother-in-law asked him why people no longer gave up their seats on the subway. Milgram reasoned that New Yorkers were not hard and cold city dwellers, but instead were inhibited against engaging each other. He sent out his students to investigate this and concluded that his theory was accurate. In 1972, he returned to Paris to study Parisians' mental maps of their city with New Yorkers' mental maps of New York.

Milgram published *Obedience to Authority* in 1974 and received the Annual Social Psychology Award by the American Association for the Advancement of Science, for his life's work, but mostly for his work with obedience. He was also nominated for a National Book Award, in 1975, his book, by that time, had been translated into seven languages for international distribution.

One of the most important things that Milgram discovered was that the experimental subjects were allowing the authority figures to define the nature of the situation; in doing so, the subjects bypassed their own moral principles and accepted that their actions were already justified.

Stanley Milgram died of a heart attack in New York in 1984. He was 51 years old.

CHAPTER 3

SOME BASIC CONCEPTS IN PSYCHOLOGICAL RESEARCH

Contents

Who takes part in research?
Populations
Samples

Variables
Independent
Fixed
Random
Dependent
Confounding

Level of measurement

Quantitative research design
Temporal Precedence
Covariation
Alternative explanation
Internal validity
Replicability and reliability
External validity

Hypotheses

Handling statistical data

Qualitative and quantitative data

Why use qualitative methods?
Reflexivity

Validity in qualitative research

Types of qualitative research
Ethnography
Phenomenology
Hermeneutics
Grounded theory

Qualitative data collection
In-Depth interviews
Direct observation
Participant observation
Case studies
Diaries

Handling qualitative data

Summary

Some Basic Concepts in Psychological Research

Like other occult techniques of divination, the statistical method has a private jargon deliberately contrived to obscure its methods from non-practitioners. (G.O. Ashley)

Learning Objectives

- To examine the basic vocabulary of research.
- To examine some of the range of quantitative and qualitative methods.
- To understand the way that terms are used in research.
- To examine the debate over the nature of quantitative and qualitative research and the tension between them.
- To understand the various forms of variables.
- To introduce the concept of measurement and type of measurement.
- To introduce the concept of design and types of design.
- To introduce the concept of hypothesis generation and testing.
- To examine some of the ways that psychological data can be transformed into meaningful summaries.
- To discuss what each type of summary can be used to describe.

KEY TERMS

- Case studies
- Central tendency – mean, median and mode
- Design – temporal precedence, covariation alternative explanations
- Dispersion – maxima, minima, range, variance, standard deviation
- Display – graphs, tables
- Distribution – normal, skew, kurtosis
- Ethnography
- Grounded theory
- Hermeneutics
- Hypotheses – alternative, null
- Interviews

- Levels of measurement – nominal, ordinal interval/ratio
- Observation
- Phenomenology
- Populations and samples
- Variables – independent, fixed, random, dependent, confounding

Learning about research methods is like learning a new language, and learning a new language cannot start without understanding some basic rules and equipping ourselves with some basic vocabulary. This chapter will outline some of that vocabulary. Firstly, we will discover the language of quantitative research and examine some fundamental concepts that comprise the vocabulary on which we can build fluency in any area of statistical data analysis. We will then look at the ways in which qualitative methods allow us to approach research questions differently, not simply as a non-numerical alternative to quantitative methods, but as valuable ways of addressing the investigation of topics.

WHO TAKES PART IN RESEARCH?

Populations

In psychology, quantitative research is almost exclusively carried out on **samples** drawn from **populations**. Here the term population has a slightly different meaning from the one we use in everyday speech. It need not refer only to people or creatures, for example the population of London, or the population of hedgehogs in Huddersfield. In research, we can also refer to a population of objects, events, procedures or observations. A population is thus an aggregate of things.

We must always clearly define the population we are interested in, but we may not be able to describe and enumerate it exactly. For example, we might want to know the average IQ of psychology students, but who are these people? At any one time, the population of psychology students may contain people of different sexes, ages, socioeconomic and ethnic background, etc. Also, at one time, every psychology lecturer has been a psychology student. The researcher needs to provide a precise definition of a population and the constraints on that definition (such as time and location) in order to draw valid inferences from the sample that was studied, to the population being considered. Statistics that we will consider when taken from populations are referred to as population parameters. They are often denoted by Greek letters: the population mean is denoted by μ (mu) and the standard deviation denoted by σ (lower case sigma).

Samples

Even if a population can be defined, it will usually contain too many individuals to study, so research investigation is commonly confined to one or more samples drawn from it. A good sample will contain the information that the population does, so there must be an effective relation between the sample and the population. One way of providing this is to ensure that everyone in the population has a known chance of being included in the sample, and also it seems reasonable to make these chances equal. We also want to be certain that the inclusion of one population member does not affect the chance of others being included. So the choice is made by some element of chance, such as spinning a coin, or in large populations and samples by use of tables of random numbers. These are widely published alongside other tables used in statistical analysis.

VARIABLES

Variables are things that we can measure, control or manipulate in research because they can have more than one value. There are different types of variables, and we can consider numerical variables such as IQ, where the values would be the score measured, or non-numerical variables such as sex (values are male or female). Types include independent, fixed, random, dependent and confounding.

Independent

Independent variables are those that could have an effect on other variables. For example, it is possible that, as people get older, their short-term memory becomes less effective, and we could test that by comparing the performance on a memory test of several people who are deemed to be young adults and older adults. The variable that may be having an effect here is the age of the people being tested.

Fixed

A fixed variable is one where we have specific set values for the independent variable included in the study. For example, in our aging and memory study, although age changes every year, at the moment in which the participants take part they each have a particular measured age. Therefore, we can fix our variable 'age' in terms of specific groups, such as 18–25 and 65–75.

Random

In the study on aging and memory, we could fix our values at the age ranges in the fixed variable example. This might be representative of the aging process, but there are many more values available with the variable 'age'. With a variable that has many values, we would not necessarily wish to use every value, and could randomly select values from it. With age, this might not be appropriate as we wish to see the effect that aging has; a random selection of age groups does not necessarily give us the structure we need for our independent variable and we would prefer to use a fixed set for our variable.

Dependent

KT

A **dependent variable** is one that might be affected by the variations in the independent variable. In our memory study, the independent variable, age, might have an effect on short-term memory; our dependent variable is the scores achieved on a memory test. So a dependent variable is one whose values may *depend* on the different values in the independent variable.

Confounding

In some cases, there are variables that can affect the outcome, but which are not strictly part of the study. For example, in our memory study it might be thought that the effect of aging could be altered by certain types of drugs, so we might want to exclude people who are on certain types of medication. Or it may be that even though there is an established sex difference in memory, this difference varies with age (see Bleecker, Bolla-Wilson, Agnew and Meyers, 1988), so we might want to ensure that we have equal numbers of men and women in our samples of each age group to ensure we can compare them to see if this is the case. In

KT

this way, we **control** for **confounding variables**.

LEVEL OF MEASUREMENT

Variables differ in the way they can be measured, firstly in the amount of error that is inherent in the measurement (we will examine this later with respect to specific types of measurement) and secondly the amount of information that can be provided by a variable. This last is referred to as the type of measurement scale.

KT

Variables are classified as nominal, ordinal, interval or ratio, and this distinction is referred to as the **levels of measurement**. Each variable that we might investigate in psychology has a set of characteristics that indicate their nature, as a separate characteristic, irrespective of what we might do with them.

Nominal variables allow for only categorisation into named sets, and all we know is that individual items belong to some distinctively different categories, but there is no quantifying or ranking of items. So we can know whether individuals are male or female, but there is no indication that being in one category is better than the other (irrespective of your personal feelings!). We can know whether one category has

KT

more in it than another, so we can know the **frequency** of each category.

Ordinal variables are those in which we place items in rank order in terms of which has less and which has more of the quality represented by the variable, but not how much more. A typical example of an ordinal variable is socioeconomic status. We know that middle class is higher than working class but we cannot say that it is, for example, 30% higher.

Interval variables not only give rank order but also quantify and compare the sizes of differences (or interval) between them. Temperature is an interval scale. A temperature of 50 degrees is higher than a temperature of 40 degrees, and the increase from 40 to 50 degrees is half as much as an increase from 20 to 30 degrees.

In addition to all the properties of interval variables, *ratio* variables have an identifiable absolute zero point, thus they allow for statements such as 100 kg is two times more than 50 kg. Typical examples of ratio scales are measures of time or space. For example, as the Kelvin temperature scale is a ratio scale, not only can we say that a temperature of 200 degrees is higher than one of 100 degrees, but we can correctly state that it is twice as high, though this does not apply to the Fahrenheit scale. The zero point must be meaningful, and 0 degrees Fahrenheit is arbitrary. Most statistical data analysis procedures we use in psychology do not differentiate between the interval and ratio properties of the measurement scales and the distinction is unimportant.

One way to remember the distinction between different levels of measurement is to compile them all into one example. The one I liked to use when learning the differences is the idea of a foot race. There is a certain number of people who will take part, some professionals and some amateur, the numbers of whom are measured on a nominal scale, the number of different types of people, or the frequency with which each type is counted is the nominal category of measurement. When the race is ended, all the people will have finished in a particular order, first, second, third, etc.; these are ordinal numbers and in the ordinal category of measurement. Each person will have finished in a certain time and we can place them in order due to this, but also we can say that one person's time is less than another's so they have intervals between them that can be measured in seconds, or even minutes for a long race.

In psychology, although there may be more scope for flexibility than other sciences, we still need a systematic approach to research. If we are to make statements about human behaviour, we must do so in the light of good methods or we are simply speculating.

QUANTITATIVE RESEARCH DESIGN

Most empirical quantitative research belongs clearly to one of two general categories. In correlational research we do not (or at least try not to) influence any variables, but only measure them and look for relations (**correlations**) between some set of variables, such as weight and cholesterol level. If we see a relationship, we might conclude that being overweight causes high cholesterol levels, but it could be just as valid to say that high cholesterol means it is difficult to lose weight or prevent it going up. So correlation research does not seek to establish causal relationships between variables, just the strength and direction of the relationship.

In experimental research, we manipulate some variables and then measure the effects of this manipulation on other variables; for example, a researcher might have participants deliberately increase their weight and then record cholesterol level (not the most ethical of studies!). Only experimental data can conclusively demonstrate causal relations between variables. For example, if we found that whenever we change variable *A* then variable *B* changes, then we could conclude that *A* influences *B*. Data from correlational research can only be interpreted in terms based on some theories that we have; correlational data cannot conclusively prove causality.

In order to claim causality we need three elements:

- Temporal precedence
- Covariation of cause and effect
- No alternative explanation

Temporal Precedence

In order to be able to say that one thing caused another, the first thing has to happen before the second. This might not be quite as easy as you think and it could be a classic case of chicken and egg. For example, our study of weight and blood must establish which state happened first, the obesity or the high cholesterol.

Covariation

As well as establishing that our cause happens before the effect, we need to show that there is actually a relationship between them. In logic, we would express this as

if *A* then *B*
if not *A* then not *B*

So we can observe that whenever *A* is present, *B* is too and whenever *A* is absent, *B* is too, thus we have demonstrated that a relationship exists between them. However, this might not be reasonable. For example, in the days before family planning and probably electric lighting and widely available heating, more babies were born in the months of July to September (in the northern hemisphere). They are also the months when, in Europe, storks migrate. A plausible explanation might be that storks deliver babies... hmm. So, it can be dangerous simply to accept the causality of a relationship without examining the veracity of its nature. Simply because one thing happens before another, or seemingly at the same time, does not mean there is a relationship between them.

Alternative Explanation

So, with a relationship between two variables, we can show one happened before the other, but we still do not know that the relationship is a causal one. There is always the possibility that there is another variable/factor that is causing the outcome. This is the 'missing variable' problem, allied to the idea of extraneous or confounding variables, and is the core of internal validity.

Internal Validity

For research that measures the effects of treatments or interventions (independent variables), internal validity is a primary consideration. It is the ability to be able to say that our manipulation of the variables has led to an observed difference, such as it changes memory performance (a mnemonic strategy) or lower cholesterol (a new drug), for example. But there may be many reasons, other than our intervention, why memory scores may improve or symptoms may reduce. So we need to ask whether our observed changes can be attributed to our manipulations of differences in the levels of our independent variable and not to other possible causes.

Plausible alternative explanations or threats to internal validity can include flaws in design, such as testing only one group of people (there may be something special about this group that makes the results peculiar to them) or several groups of people who may not be comparable. There are also social threats, threats that arise because social research is conducted in real-world contexts where people will react not only to what affects them, but also to what is happening to others around them (see the section on demand characteristics in Chapter 1).

In order for us to argue that we have demonstrated internal validity, we have to eliminate the plausible alternative explanations. This can be done by making our research design as good as we can get it, minimising flaws. It can be demonstrated by ensuring that it is possible to find the same results again when the study is replicated, ensuring that our findings are reliable.

Replicability and Reliability

In order for quantitative research and its findings to be accepted, there must not only be no meaningful alternative explanation, but it must also be possible to find the same effect if the research is repeated in the same circumstances. This repetition is called replicability. A study is only replicable if the researcher clearly exposes his or her procedure to people reading about it. This means explaining how the design of the study was arrived at, how the sample was drawn, how the data was collected, etc. Everything pertinent to someone repeating the study must be explained. If this can be done, and the study can be repeated with (statistically) similar results, then the findings are said to be reliable. In order to make causal statements about the research findings, any procedures and instruments must have **reliability**, that is, must be stable and/or repeatable, and unbiased.

We will encounter reliability and validity in more detail when we look at psychometric measurements.

The final point about the utility and application of causal relationships is that of external validity.

KT

External Validity

Remember in Chapter 1 when we discovered that experiments have been criticised for lack of ecological validity? Well, many researchers using quantitative methods, in particular experimentation, attempt to ensure that the setting for the experiment has ecological validity: that is, they attempt to ensure that the experimental procedures resemble real-world conditions. This is linked to the concept of external validity, but should not be confused with it. External validity means whether or not experimental results can be generalised to a real-world situation. A study may possess external validity but not ecological validity, and vice versa.

If we have drawn a representative sample from our population, we should be able to generalise any findings from the sample to the population. However, it is not always possible to ensure that the sample is truly representative. One way of improving external validity is to improve the sampling procedure used. We will look at sampling more thoroughly in the chapter on surveys, as it is crucial to that method.

Demonstrating external validity can be done by carrying out the study in a variety of places, with different people and at different times. So, external validity will be more credible, the more replications of the study are performed

So, now we have determined what a causal relationship is, what elements do we also need in our quantitative research? Well, there are more things we need to consider before setting off to examine our psychological data.

HYPOTHESES

KT

In order to find an answer we have to know what the question is. A hypothesis is a formal way of expressing a question as a prediction that can be tested. It is a highly **operationalised** statement, or rather two statements, expressing the questions we have about our variables and their relationships. One statement describes what the relationship might be, the other describes all other possible outcomes with respect to the variables. For example, a structured statement about our aging and memory study could be 'there will be a difference in performance on short-term memory tests between 25 year olds and 65 year olds'. Note that there is no prediction that the difference is positive or negative. This would be called the alternative or research hypothesis, the one that you would carry out the study to investigate, denoted H_1. We could, however, due to previous research and clinical findings, suppose that there will be a difference in our age groups, and make our alternative hypothesis read '25 year olds will be better at a short-term memory test than 65 year olds'. So our hypothesis has a direction; when we look at how to test hypotheses statistically (see Chapter 5) we will see why that makes a difference, but for now remember that we call research hypotheses directional or non-directional depending on what the prediction is. The other type of hypothesis is

KT

called the **null hypothesis**. This is a hypothesis that states there will be no effect of the independent variable on the dependent variable. For example, '25 year olds and 65 year olds will not show any difference in memory test performance'.

Statistically, we test the null hypothesis and, if we can reject it, we seek evidence that we can support the alternative. So there is a logic in testing that has grown out of the form of science known as the hypothetico-deductive model, the traditional model of how science operates. Scientists begin with a theory or an observation, deduce a hypothesis, and then gather evidence to test the hypothesis. If the hypothesis is confirmed, the theory is assumed to be correct or useful. We observe and generate ideas, develop testable hypotheses, systematically observe and measure, and analyse data, thereby testing the hypotheses. This describes the whole process of quantitative research, but, as you might guess, there is a lot left out in between each bit! In the next chapters, we will discover how to do each of these pieces of the model. Firstly, a word about how to handle the data collected in quantitative research.

HANDLING STATISTICAL DATA

It is clear that many things about the way we live our lives have been altered by the advent of computers. No matter what we might think about this, it is certain that the analysis of large banks of numerical data has been aided by the use of computer programs (note the use of the American spelling to distinguish computer *program* from television or research *programme*!). The program most used in psychology is SPSS (Statistical Package for the Social Sciences) as it is relatively easy to use and contains some very powerful analytical tools. However, a package is only as good as the people using it and teaching others how to use it, and your university department will provide instruction in its use. The best way to learn how to use SPSS is being shown by someone who knows how to use it. This book will not therefore include detailed instructions in how to use SPSS, but will use 'screenshots' from running an SPSS analysis to illustrate the ways in which the package will show the analysis and how to navigate through it. There are other popular packages that you may encounter; the major competitors to SPSS are Minitab and SAS. However, once familiar with one package it is usually easy to transfer those skills to using another.

So, now we have discovered some of the basic vocabulary of quantitative research, examining how we use terms in different ways to everyday language, we need to look at how these concepts are used to describe and summarise data in the other major approach to psychological research, qualitative methods.

There are ways of collecting information that is not intended to be subject to statistical manipulation. The two approaches differ mainly in their fundamental purpose, as the aim of the qualitative researcher is an overall understanding of phenomena by stressing intriguing features and only possibly generating hypotheses. This can be contrasted to quantitative research, which tests predictions about events and assumes a certain level of isolation from other phenomena. Due to this, and various debates around this difference, we may be forgiven for thinking that there are two sorts of method – qualitative or quantitative – and that the two are mutually exclusive, that using one means that a researcher cannot or will not use the other. It may even be amusing to think that there is a fight going on about which is better. In fact, there is only one sort of method – the best one to investigate the question that is posed by some experience or incident. This correct method may even be a mixture of quantitative and qualitative techniques, and this should not be thought of as some sort of methodological sacrilege. The only problem that should be facing researchers is how to choose the most appropriate method. This will never be a simple yes–no decision, but a consideration of the benefits that every technique can bring. We should not choose qualitative methods simply because quantitative analysis is difficult, or discard qualitative because it lacks control and precision. Both of these reasons can be challenged, as statistical analysis has become so much easier to perform with the arrival of computers, and qualitative methods have rigour and precision if carried out systematically. There is even a position in which many researchers employ a mixed methodology because both approaches have value. In the next section, we will look at some of the range of qualitative methods, and examine this so-called tension between the methodological approaches a bit more closely.

It might be useful, when trying to decide on a methodological approach, to distinguish between the general assumptions involved in undertaking a research project (qualitative, quantitative or mixed) and the data that is collected. At the level of the data, there is really little difference between the qualitative and the quantitative. But, at the level of the assumptions that are made, the differences can be profound.

QUALITATIVE AND QUANTITATIVE DATA

In consideration of the data derived from qualitative and quantitative methods, there would seem to be a fundamental difference: qualitative data consists of words and quantitative data consists of numbers. In fact, those differences are not as deep-seated as first thought and there are several reasons for this:

1 All qualitative data can be coded quantitatively. We can assign numbers to anything that appears to be qualitative. For example, in surveys, questions are often included that take the format 'Please add comments'. The responses to these can be categorised and then coded numerically. This retains a qualitative distinction between categories but allows at least descriptive quantitative analysis.

2 All quantitative data is based on qualitative judgement. Numbers cannot be assigned or interpreted without understanding the assumptions that underlie them. In questionnaires, using Likert scales (see the chapter on survey methods), we can have a response from 'strongly agree' to 'strongly disagree'. If a respondent ticks one level what does that mean? We have to assume that the respondent read the statement properly, understood the terms in the statement, understood the level of response he or she was making, and a host of other underlying issues. The numerical data has many assumptions underlying it as any qualitative response.

So, in some ways quantitative and qualitative data are indistinguishable. To ask which type is better may be meaningless. However, it also begs the question 'what are researchers arguing about?' Well, there is still plenty of debate left here.

If we agree that qualitative and quantitative data are similar, we have still only started an examination of the debate. In reality, the contention is about epistemological and ontological assumptions underlying the approach to research, rather than data. In other words, the differences lie in *why* we use a particular method rather than what the data and its analysis entail.

So let us examine another 'belief' about the difference in the approaches: quantitative research is confirmatory and deductive in nature, whereas qualitative research is exploratory and inductive in nature. Is this correct? Well, not necessarily. There is a lot of quantitative research that can be classified as exploratory as well, and qualitative research can also be used to confirm specific deductive hypotheses. Belief in this difference is not acknowledging that both approaches can be rich and systematic. The difference is not then methodological but philosophical: qualitative research makes assumptions under a different **epistemology** from quantitative research. Qualitative researchers set out to understand phenomena by viewing them in context. Quantification appears limited from this viewpoint, as it only looks at a portion of reality that should not be removed from the whole. This 'in-context' examination may mean becoming immersed in the situation by moving into the culture under investigation.

KT

There is also an **ontology** about the world where assumptions appear to be different. Qualitative research does not assume that there is a single unitary reality

KT

that lies apart from our perceptions. Each of us experiences our own reality and therefore we must take into account the fact that the researcher's perception may be different from those researched, and each person involved has their own perception too. Therefore combining and summarising experience *across* individuals, in the way that quantitative research does, will not take into account a fundamental view of the individual, and the contribution of the researcher's own viewpoint.

Many qualitative researchers would not agree with some of the above, particularly about the connections between the data types. Of course, it is not possible to separate research assumptions from the data, and there is an argument that coding is simply the attempt of a quantitative researcher to impose those perspectives on qualitative data. However, a large majority of researchers who use qualitative methods have progressed to them from quantitative and believe that both can be used in harmony without imposing the values of one on the other.

No matter how we come to our conclusion about the use of qualitative or quantitative methods, it must be from the viewpoint of choice and information. Perhaps the major consideration here would be not whether we buy into one form or another, but which can approach the question in the best way. There is no resolution to this debate, but an informed choice is better than one driven by the need to fit with an uninformed standpoint. In that case, we had better inform ourselves about when and why we would choose qualitative methods.

WHY USE QUALITATIVE METHODS?

There are various reasons why we might choose to use qualitative methods. They allow us to approach research questions with flexibility and possibly allow access to participants who would not usually be comfortable taking part in more structured forms of research. Not only that, but the information derived from participants will be from their natural setting, placing them in natural context. Hence, qualitative research is interpretive and naturalistic, attempting to study psychological events in their natural settings, and interpreting meaning in context. It also acknowledges that there are several different ways by which we make sense of our environment. This last is often referred to as multiple realities, as we all have a different view of reality, and qualitative methods equip us more readily to access such subjective perceptions. However, there is also the danger that the researcher's own subjective perceptions will affect the process or outcomes of the research.

There are many ways that this can happen: a researcher's bias or personal involvement in the subject matter, or simply holding different views from the research participants, can alter the way in which the data is analysed and interpreted, or even how it is collected. To attempt to minimise this lack of neutrality there are theoretical tools that allow researchers to address any methodological and philosophical issues that may arise.

Reflexivity

No data collection can be truly neutral or free from the subjective perceptions of the data collector. This is a major criticism that qualitative researchers level at the experimental paradigm, that objectivity is impossible, so why attempt to achieve it? Conversely, qualitative research is criticised for the same thing, that it is too open to subjectivity and non-neutrality. The response is that qualitative research allows a researcher **reflexivity**. This means that the researcher acknowledges that he or she will affect the behaviour and interpretation of the behaviour of any system being observed or theory being formulated. Any observations cannot, therefore, be independent of the participation of the observer. Popper (see Chapter 1) said that reflexivity presents a problem for science, because, if a prediction can lead to changes in the observed behaviour, it becomes difficult to assess scientific hypotheses. In psychology, this causes a dilemma, as we are observing ourselves when we examine human behaviour. Qualitative researchers view this, not as a threat to the validity of the data and analysis, but as an opportunity to explore and reflect on their own views. In other words, researchers can afford to make critical reflections on the research process and their own input to it.

Being a reflexive researcher means having awareness of:

- theoretical assumptions and how they affect the research;
- how the research methods are chosen and used;
- what impact the research has on participants;
- self-involvement and how this may shape the research.

We can see that qualitative research has, as a fundamental perspective, a self-awareness of how each of us affects the world, and, specifically, how our own interpretation can affect our judgements in research settings and interpretation. According to Willig (2001), personal reflexivity means that we have to reflect on how our personal values, experiences and beliefs shape the research and how the research has affected us. She then suggests there is an alternative

KT

epistemological reflexivity in which we should think about whether the research question we have generated has limited the design and outcome and whether it could have been conducted differently. Would this then have stimulated a different view of the phenomenon?

This all suggests that a qualitative researcher spends a lot of time on the reflection rather than the performance of research. This is not really the case, but each is given sufficient value in the process to ensure the research is of good quality. When, in quantitative research, value is given to the design, the representativeness of the sampling and the generalisability of the results, this is establishing, or attempting to establish, the reliability and validity of any subsequent interpretation. There is a similar set of processes in qualitative research that attempts to ensure its integrity.

VALIDITY IN QUALITATIVE RESEARCH

KT

Some qualitative researchers reject the concept of, and adherence to, validity that is fundamental to quantitative research. Qualitative research is unconcerned with the idea of an external unitary reality to which we can **extrapolate** our findings. If we are to reject the assumption that there is a reality external to our perception of it, then it does not make sense to be concerned with the falsehood of an observation with respect to an external reality. Therefore, we need different standards for judging the quality of research.

Guba and Lincoln (1981) proposed four criteria for judging the veracity of qualitative research and said that these reflected the underlying assumptions better than the concepts of reliability and validity that quantitative research applies:

- Credibility (analogous to internal validity). This involves establishing that the results of qualitative research are credible or believable from the perspective of the participant. The participant then is the only one who can judge this.
- Transferability (analogous to external validity). This is the degree to which the results of qualitative research can be transferred to other contexts or settings. In a quantitative research perspective, this would mean generalising to a population's parameters from a sample's statistics. The researcher may not be the person doing the transferring; therefore, it is the responsibility of whoever wishes to do this to ensure that it is done properly. The person who wishes to place the results in a different context to the original is responsible for making the judgement of how sensible the transfer is.
- Dependability (analogous to reliability). The quantitative view of reliability is based on replicability. To what extent are we sure we will find the same result on repetition of the research? This is based on a possibly erroneous assumption that we can create the same

situation and control the environment to such an extent that the same conditions prevail. In order to estimate reliability, quantitative researchers construct various hypothetical concepts (such as **measurement error**) to try to get around this fact. Dependability, though, emphasises that the researcher must account for the changing context within which research occurs. The research is responsible for describing the changes that occur in the setting and how these changes affected the way the researcher approached the study.

- Confirmability (analogous to objectivity). Qualitative research assumes that each researcher brings a unique perspective to the study. Confirmability refers to the degree to which the results could be confirmed or corroborated by others. There are a number of strategies for enhancing confirmability, such as documenting the procedures for checking and rechecking the data throughout the study, and using several 'judges' of elements along the way. When the study is complete, a **data audit** could be conducted – an examination of the data collection and analysis procedures.

TYPES OF QUALITATIVE RESEARCH

As with quantitative methods, there are a range of possible methods within the qualitative approach. This variety arises firstly from the focus of the research, which can range from an examination of one's own experience to others' experiences examined through their speaking or writing, behaviours or products. Secondly, there is variety in how data is collected, which can focus on the past (such as an examination of historical documents or archaeological findings) or on the present, as in observation or introspection. Finally, there are different ways of analysing data from the highly structured repertory grid to forms that are viewed as more empathic such as phenomenology or hermeneutics. The processes of design, data collection and analysis are discussed in more detail in later chapters but let us just look at a few examples of these variations

Ethnography

The ethnographic approach to qualitative research comes primarily from the field of anthropology. Anthropology is the study of people and their lives and cultures *in situ*, with a central concept being that of culture. This is interpreted as the evolved capacity to perceive the world symbolically, and to transform the world based on the perception of those symbols. Symbols are any material artefact of a culture, such as art, clothing or even technology. The ethnographer strives to understand the cultural associations of symbols. Ethnographic research is holistic, believing that symbols cannot be understood in isolation, but, instead, are elements of a whole. The emphasis in ethnography is on studying an entire culture, but using the symbols as the process of accessing the culture. This 'culture' concept may be tied to notions of ethnicity and geography, but is actually broader and includes any group or organisation. Macro-ethnography is the study of broadly defined cultural groupings, and micro-ethnography is the study of narrowly defined cultural groupings. The most common ethnographic approach is participant observation in which the ethnographic researcher becomes immersed in the culture as an active participant and records extensive field notes.

An ethnographer can adopt an emic or an etic perspective when studying the culture. An **emic** perspective is the study of the way the members of the given culture perceive their world, and is usually the main focus of ethnography, whereas an **etic** perspective is the study of the way non-members perceive and interpret behaviours and phenomena associated with a given culture.

Phenomenology

Phenomenology is a philosophical perspective as well as an approach to qualitative methodology. It emphasises subjective experiences and interpretations of the world, so a phenomenologist sets out to understand how the world appears to others. However, there is an assumption that the researcher's own values and beliefs can be set aside, which is sometimes difficult to accept. Giorgi (1970) suggested that psychology approached from a phenomenological perspective provides an alternative paradigm to those found in an approach to psychology that follows methods of natural science.

Hermeneutics

The theory and practice of interpretation, **hermeneutics** originally, referred to the interpretation and criticism of biblical texts. However, it now has come to mean the removal of obstacles which may prevent readers from gaining the proper understanding of a text and analysing the necessary conditions for understanding. In hermeneutics, unlike phenomenology, there is an assumption that the researcher brings his or her own values and beliefs to the research and the examination of language. Hermeneutics does not rely on a deterministic or causal view of cultural influence; it suggests that the individual is not passive and powerless in relation to the culture in which he or she is found.

Grounded Theory

The purpose of **grounded theory** is to develop a theory about phenomena of interest. However, this is not in an intangible, abstract form, but rooted, or *grounded*, in systematic observation.

Grounded theory is referred to as a complex iterative process, which means we need to repeat processes, bearing in mind the findings or deliberations of the previous round of process. The research begins with the raising of *generative questions* that help to guide the research, but are not intended to confine the scope of the research to them. Data can be gathered and as this process happens, *core theoretical concepts* are identified together with tentative *linkages* between concepts and data. After this early, very open phase, the researcher engages in verification and summary, possibly leading to the evolution of one *core category*.

Analysis can take place in several ways:

- *Coding* is a process that allows categorisation of qualitative data and the description of the implications and details of these categories. Initially we can carry out *open coding*, considering the data in minute detail while developing some initial categories. Later, more *selective coding* allows systematic coding with respect to a core concept.
- *Memoing* is a process for recording the thoughts and ideas of the researcher as they evolve throughout the study.
- *Integrative diagrams* are used to group the detail together, to help make sense of the data with respect to the emerging theory. The diagrams can be any form of graphic that is useful at that point in theory development.
- By applying these analyses, a *conceptually rich* (or dense) theory emerges. New observation leads to new linkages that lead to revisions in the theory and more data collection, by which the core concept is identified and enriched. Grounded theory does not have a clearly demarcated point for ending a study but should lead to a well-considered explanation for the phenomenon of interest; this is our grounded theory.

The term 'qualitative data' covers a huge range of types of material, so perhaps the best way of examining it is to look at the ways in which it might be gathered.

QUALITATIVE DATA COLLECTION

In-Depth Interviews

In-depth interviews include both individual interviews as well as group interviews such as focus groups. In-depth interviews differ from direct observation primarily in the nature of the interaction. In **interviews**, it is assumed that there is a questioner and one or more interviewees and the interviewer will be probing to gain understanding of the ideas of the interviewees about the phenomenon of interest.

Unstructured interviewing involves direct interaction between the researcher and a respondent or group, but with no formal structured protocol or interview schedule. In addition, the interviewer is free to move the conversation in any direction of interest that may come up. Unstructured interviewing is useful for exploring a topic broadly, but there is a penalty for lack of structure. Each interview tends to be unique, with no predetermined set of questions asked of all respondents, it is usually more difficult to analyse unstructured interview data, effectively preventing comparison across respondents, making any construction of themes almost impossible.

Direct Observation

Direct observation does not involve the researcher actively questioning the respondent. This includes everything from field research, with the researcher living in culture, to examination of photographs.

Participant Observation

One of the most common methods for qualitative data collection, participant observation is also very demanding. It requires that the researcher become a participant in the culture or context being observed. If setting out to do this a researcher must consider how to enter and leave the context, what role to take, how to record the observations made, and how to analyse while still in the context.

At first glance, participant observation is a straightforward technique – we immerse ourselves in the subject being studied, and thereby gain understanding, perhaps more deeply than could be obtained by other means. Arguments in favour of this method include reliance on first-hand information, high face validity of data, and reliance on relatively simple and inexpensive methods. The hazards of participant observation as a data-gathering technique are an increased threat to the objectivity of the researcher, unsystematic gathering of data, reliance on subjective measurement, and possible observer effects (in that observation may distort the observed behaviour). However, these can actually be valued as important components of the approach.

Participant observation is particularly appropriate to studies of interpersonal group processes as long as, we as researchers, are clear about initial expectations and guard against the imposition of expectations on observations.

Case Studies

A **case study** is an intensive study of a specific individual. For instance, Freud developed case studies of several individuals as the basis for the theory of psychoanalysis and Piaget produced case studies of his children to study developmental phases. There is no single way to conduct a case study, and combinations of methods are often used.

Diaries

When the respondents themselves record data about what they are doing, or experience, they are writing a **diary**, a useful method. It is relatively cheap and relatively easy to administer. Diary methods have an established history in psychology, an example being an investigation of leisure behaviour by Harvey in 1990, in which time diaries were collected and analysed. Time diaries allow participants to record the total flow of activities and attendant perceptions. Such data can be studied at the macro and micro level. At the micro level, time points, individuals and events can be studied. At the macro level, it is meaningful to study subpopulations, bundles of time and aggregated events. Another example is the review of consumer time use by Robinson and Nicosia (1991). Their review highlighted studies in which diary use was prevalent and that identify certain aspects of consumer behaviour. However, the information is usually restricted to behavioural data, and difficult to verify, but there have been attempts to use diaries to expose perceptual responses to the environment. Here, however, the effect of diary keeping may itself be problematic. For example, Gavin (2006) describes a diary study carried out into the effects of hearing music that the participant had not chosen. Participants were directed to record accounts of episodes in which music was played in instances when they were not in control of the decision to play the music, and to record various items about the music, together with any effects on themselves. The data was analysed using a process of revealing themes inherent in the experience of the diarists. In addition to any other finding, the results also indicate some increased awareness of intrusive music, suggesting that some form of priming has occurred. As a direct result of keeping the diary, participants' perception of music had been heightened and thinking had been shaped by the diary-keeping task.

HANDLING QUALITATIVE DATA

Whatever form of qualitative data collection is used, a very large bank of information can be gathered. This data must be handled and summarised in some way. In the same way that quantitative data analysis has been moved forward by the use of computer packages, qualitative researches also have at their disposal several programs to aid in their analyses. This is a much more recent development than in quantitative research as it has evolved from complex text retrieval packages, rather than being a natural progression from calculators! This does not mean that using a program has answered every qualitative research problem, and some researchers are concerned that the forms in which computer-aided analysis is carried out present more restrictions than not using them. However, some packages in current use tend to be 'light touch' in nature, providing simple, but rapid, text retrieval with any transformation being under the control of the researcher. So, in the same way as statistical packages have to be used by someone who knows what test they wish to perform, the qualitative packages have to be used in such a way as to aid and not guide (or constrain) the form of analysis.

When choosing a package we would need to know what sort of organisation of the data is required. A word processing package is fine for a descriptive level of coding, as it would allow the writing of notes in a margin, which is often the first step to analysing a transcribed interview. Sentences could then be coded into various categories and so on. This does not allow a great dept of analysis, though, and a few dedicated packages allow much more than simple coding of words or sentences. The Ethnograph package can aid in identifying and retrieving text from documents as it allows the researcher to segment the text and identify it with several codewords. It can even allow us to interrelate segments and identify ways in which they generate a further set of segments (see the chapter on thematic analysis). HyperQual, on the other hand, allows us to integrate text and illustrations, which can be helpful when analysing data from several diverse sources. However, the most popular package used in qualitative research is NUD*ist. This stands for 'Non-numerical Unstructured Data Indexing, Searching, and Theorizing', and I have often wondered how long it took the producers of the program to come up with words that fit the memorable acronym!

NUD*ist allows the user to 'flag' and search text in order to construct a structured hierarchical database index. The index itself can then be searched for linkages and hierarchical categorisations that indicate meaningful themes or syntheses. These can themselves then be added into the indexing to produce further categories, which in turn allow emergent theoretical positions to be identified.

Summary

In this chapter we have looked at some of the basic vocabulary of quantitative and qualitative research, examining how we use terms in different ways to everyday language. This has equipped us with some of the basic terminology encountered when starting out in research. We have also examined the debate about the use of qualitative and quantitative research and the so-called tension between them. We could conclude that this tension is nonsensical and that we are now equipped with the fundamental tools to allow us to choose the most appropriate method for research rather than being swayed by extreme advocates of one or the other.

The next part of the book will examine some simple forms of quantitative research and how to carry out and interpret experiments and other forms of research that yield numerical data.

PART II

BEGINNING QUANTITATIVE RESEARCH

In this part, we will look at how psychologists can use numbers to describe and predict behaviour. Here we will encounter such concepts as summarising data and displaying it meaningfully. We will also look at how we can test hypothesis about behaviour scientifically. In order to demonstrate these topics we will look at studies that have examined why we perform differently when observed, and why we remember some things better than others do.

This part will also examine a type of study that everyone has taken part in, the survey, but looking at a particular type of survey, on crime.

CHAPTER 4

USING NUMBERS TO DESCRIBE BEHAVIOUR

Contents

The distribution
Building a distribution

The normal distribution

Central tendency
The mean
The median
The mode
Which central tendency measure?

Dispersion
The sample variance and the standard deviation
Standard error of the mean
The *z*-score
Disruptions to normality – skew and kurtosis
Tabular presentation

Summary

Using Numbers to Describe Behaviour

I abhor averages. I like the individual case. A man may have six meals one day and none the next, making an average of three meals per day, but that is not a good way to live. (Louis D. Brandeis)

Learning Objectives

- To examine some of the ways that psychological data can be transformed into meaningful summaries.
- To discuss what each type of summary can be used to describe.

KEY TERMS

- Central tendency – mean, median and mode
- Dispersion – maxima, minima, range, variance, standard deviation
- Display – graphs, tables
- Distribution – normal, skew, kurtosis

A major objective in quantitative research is to organise, summarise and simplify information about data collected from observing people. If we have gathered pieces of information from psychological observations and recorded these as numbers, then we have a set of data. This could be, for example, the scores on a psychological test or the time it takes to press a button after seeing a particular stimulus. So now we have a set of raw scores – interesting, but not very useful. However, we can represent this data in more manageable forms such as tables and graphs, and, even more usefully, as statistical summaries. **Descriptive statistics** are used to present our numerical descriptions in a

KT

manageable form, as we may have many measures or measurements from a large number of people on one variable. Descriptive statistics reduce what could be potentially a great deal of data into a simpler summary. For example, we can measure a large number of people on a memory test and find out what the average score is or we could record, over many cricket matches, the distance a batsman hits the ball and find his average distance. Very useful, but a warning! Every time we try to describe a large set of observations with a single indicator, we run the risk of distorting the original data or losing important detail. The average batting distance does not tell you whether the batsman is hitting a small number of sixes and many shorter hits, or just overall medium-distance hits. Therefore, we have some limitations, but even given these, descriptive statistics provide a powerful summary that may enable comparisons across our groups and variables of interest.

When we examine descriptive statistics, we are only concerned with that one set of measures, rather than a comparison of more sets. This is called a univariate analysis. There are three properties of our variable that we are interested in: the distribution, the central tendency and the dispersion.

THE DISTRIBUTION

The **distribution** is a summary of the frequency of individual values or ranges of values for a variable. The simplest distribution would list every value of a variable and the number of persons who had each value. For example, we could record how many people in your university year had birthdays in each month, listing the number of each student who celebrates in January, February, etc. Alternatively, we could describe the distribution of the sexes in your group by listing the number or percentage of men and women. In these examples, the variable has few enough values that we can list each one and summarise how many sample cases had the value.

Nevertheless, what do we do for a variable in which we have many values, with relatively few instances in each value? With variables such as this, there can be a large number of possible values, with relatively few people having each one. In this case, we can group the raw scores into categories according to ranges of values. For instance, there is a major concern about student debt. We might want to measure the amount of debt in your student group, but as this

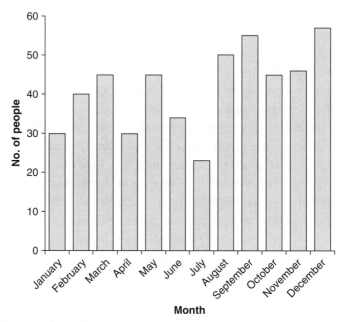

Figure 4.1 Number of people with birthdays in a specific month

could range from zero to thousands of pounds, we might group debt into four or five ranges of values.

Building a Distribution

One of the most common ways to describe a single variable is with a frequency distribution. In this we can do either of the above, represent all of the data values or group the values into categories. Frequency distributions can also be displayed in two ways, as a table or graph. Figure 4.1 shows a graph, in the form of a bar chart, of our distribution of birthdays, and Figure 4.2, the debt frequencies. Distributions may also be displayed in percentages instead of just frequencies. Table 4.1 shows the numbers of students in debt and the percentages of our student group in each debt category.

We can also use frequency summaries to describe more than one variable and to make a superficial examination of the relationship between them. For example, say we know how many male and female students are in each debt category and we want to show this. A useful display would be a contingency table, as in Table 4.1. Or a bar chart, as in Figure 4.3.

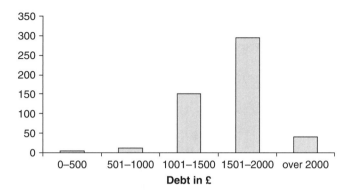

Figure 4.2   Number of students in debt

Table 4.1

Debt in £	Male	Female	Total
0–500	0	4	4
501–1000	4	7	11
1001–1500	20	130	150
1501–2000	200	95	295
over 2000	10	30	40
Total	234	266	500

Now consider what the bar chart might look like if we had many more measurements. In our debt example, we only have a few hundred students, but what if we could ask the whole population of students in the country about their debt? We would have many thousands of measurements, possibly stretching over a wider range of debt. We could carry on drawing bar charts like above, but what we would end up with is a set of small bars clustering closer and closer together the more measurements we made. In fact, it would look more like a curve, and representations of distributions of many measurements are usually drawn using a curve on a line graph. To illustrate this, let us look at a very special kind of curved distribution.

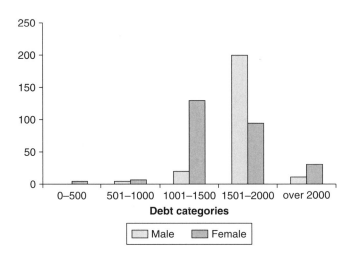

Figure 4.3 Number of male and female students in debt

THE NORMAL DISTRIBUTION

 A **normal distribution**, sometimes called a **Gaussian distribution**, is a frequency distribution in the shape of a bell curve, see Figure 4.4. It represents most variations in the frequency of appearance in such attributes as height, weight and IQ. Any variable with a normal distribution has a mean and also a standard deviation that indicates how much the data as a whole deviates from the mean. The distribution of many statistics test results is normal or can be derived from the normal distribution. The exact shape of the normal distribution is defined by a function which has only two parameters, mean and standard deviation, two friends we will return to several times!

So our variable can be summarised visually in frequency tables and graphs, but there are other ways we can summarise the data.

CENTRAL TENDENCY

 Measures of **central tendency** are those that describe where the middle of a distribution lies, and can be thought of as the balance point, with some exceptions.

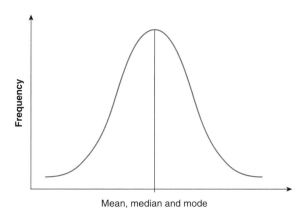

Figure 4.4   The normal distribution

The Mean

Probably the most often used measure of central tendency is the mean, sometimes called the arithmetic average. Many times in everyday life, we talk about the 'average', without really explaining what that represents. In order to calculate the mean we need to add all the scores in our sample and then divide by the number of scores:

$$\text{mean} = \frac{\text{sum of all observations}}{\text{number of observations}}$$

There are two types of mean we need to consider in psychological statistics: the population mean, represented by the Greek letter μ (mu), and the mean for a sample, represented by $\bar{X}$ (x-bar).

Another way of thinking of what the mean means is to regard it as a balance point for a distribution. If we add together all the scores above the mean, it equals the sum of the scores below it. Therefore, the sum of all observations expressed as positive and negative deviations from the mean is always zero.

The Median

On the other hand, other measures of central tendency can also be thought of as representing a balance point. The **median** is the score that also divides a distribution in half, with one-half of the scores less than or equal to the median and one-half of the scores equal to or greater than the median. There is no fancy Greek symbol for median. There are three basic ways of calculating the median; the one used depends on the number and type of scores.

Calculation 1 – Odd Number of Scores

This is the simplest calculation. The scores are listed in order of lowest to highest and the median is simply the middle score. For example, in this set of five scores, listed in order,

4	7	8	11	15

the middle score is 8. The median is therefore 8.0.

Calculation 2 – Even Number of Scores

Again, the scores are listed in order and the median is the point halfway between the middle two scores. For example, in the set of six scores,

4	4	5	6	8	14

the middle two scores are 5 and 6. The halfway point between 5 and 6 is 5.5.

Calculation 3 – Several Scores with the Same Value in the Middle of the Distribution

Consider the set of scores

1	3	3	4	5	5	5	5	7	8

There are 10 scores, so normally the process would be to average the middle two scores. The fifth and sixth scores are 5 and 5, so it looks like the median is 5.0. But we have other scores of 5 in the distribution, so the median is not 5. To clarify this, the score 5 does not mean exactly 5.0, but, more precisely, represents the interval 4.5 to 5.5. The median is held within this interval and, using the concept of a balancing point, it is clear that there are four scores below 5 and only two scores above 5 in the set of scores. The balance point will therefore be somewhere towards the lower end of the 4.5–5.5 interval. So how is the median calculated? As there are four scores of 5 to consider, the interval 4.5–5.5 must be divided into four. The interval has a length of 1.0, so each one-quarter is 0.25. The median would normally lie between the fifth and sixth scores, so we count the number of tied scores below (fifth score) and above (sixth, seventh and eighth scores) this mid-point. One-quarter of the tied numbers is below and three-quarters above, so the median lies one-quarter of the way along the interval 4.5–5.5. The median is therefore 4.5 + 0.25 = 4.75.

The Mode

KT

The **mode**, on the other hand, is the value of the most frequently occurring observation. To find the mode, the data may be plotted as a frequency distribution or table. The score or category that occurs with the highest frequency is the mode.

In some situations, there may be more than one mode. If there are two modes, we refer to the distribution as bimodal. If there are three modes, the distribution is trimodal etc. Consider the set of 20 scores

In ascending order these are

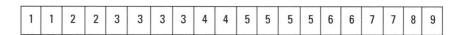

This is a bimodal case with the two modes, 3 and 5, both occurring four times.

Which Central Tendency Measure?

A recurring question is which measure of central tendency best describes the data? In a distribution that is completely symmetrical, like the classic normal distribution, the values of the mode, median and mean are the same. Any one of them could be used to describe the central tendency of the distribution. If the distribution is not symmetrical, if it shows any **skew**, it is better to use the median rather than the mean to represent the average for the distribution. Reporting both the mean and median can give an indication of how skewed the distribution is.

KT

However, the mean is the most preferred average for quantitative data. There are some reasons for this:

- It is a good indication of the balance point for most normally distributed data.
- It has numerical properties that allow it to be manipulated in useful ways, which we will examine when we look at further types of analysis.

The mode is usually the most appropriate measure of central tendency average for qualitative data. It represents what is the most common or fashionable response. The median can be used whenever it is possible to order qualitative data, or when the mean is not appropriate for seriously skewed quantitative data.

DISPERSION

Dispersion refers to the spread of the values within a distribution. The distribution has a maximum and a minimum value and one common measure of dispersion is the **range** (the maximum minus the minimum) but this is not a very useful description of the data. One with much more utility is a measurement that describes the relationship between the spread of scores and the mean of those scores. Such measures can be calculated as either variance or standard deviation.

The Sample Variance and the Standard Deviation

Each score in our sample differs from the mean (some of the difference might be zero, but most will be greater or smaller than zero), the difference for each score being known as a **deviation**. If we calculated each deviation, we would have a new set of scores, some of which will be negative. In order to deal with this we square each deviation, which gets rid of the minus sign, and then add all the squared deviations together. This is the sum of the squared deviations, usually called the **sum of squares**. Remember this term, it will be important! In order to derive the **standard deviation** we divide the sum of squares by $n-1$ (n is the number of scores in our sample). The standard deviation is a more accurate and detailed estimate of dispersion because a value that is exceptionally high or low in comparison with the rest of the distribution (called an **outlier**) can affect the range. The sample standard deviation shows the relation that a set of scores has to the mean of the sample. Consider a set of scores

15 20 21 20 36 15 25 15

To compute the standard deviation, we first find the distance (or deviation) between each value and the mean. The mean is 20.875:

$(15 + 20 + 21 + 20 + 36 + 15 + 25 + 15) \div 8 = 20.875$

So, the differences from the mean are

$$15 - 20.875 = -5.875$$
$$20 - 20.875 = -0.875$$
$$21 - 20.875 = +0.125$$
$$20 - 20.875 = -0.875$$
$$36 - 20.875 = -15.125$$
$$15 - 20.875 = -5.875$$
$$25 - 20.875 = +4.125$$
$$15 - 20.875 = -5.875$$

Notice that values that are below the mean have negative differences (or deviations) and values above it have positive ones. Next, we square each deviation (removing the laboriously calculated minus signs!):

$$-5.875 \times -5.875 = 34.515625$$
$$-0.875 \times -0.875 = 0.765625$$
$$+0.125 \times +0.125 = 0.015625$$
$$-0.875 \times -0.875 = 0.765625$$
$$15.125 \times 15.125 = 228.765625$$
$$-5.875 \times -5.875 = 34.515625$$
$$+4.125 \times +4.125 = 17.015625$$
$$-5.875 \times -5.875 = 34.515625$$

Now, we take these square deviations and sum them to get the sum of squares (SS) value. Here, the sum are 350.875. Next, we divide this sum by the number of scores minus one. Here, the result is 350.875/7 = 50.125. This value is known as the **variance**. To get the standard deviation, we take the square root of the variance (remember that we have squared the deviations earlier, so we are returning to a more accurate description):

$$\sqrt{50.125} = 7.079901129253$$

KT

So:

1 Find the mean.
2 Find the distance between each score and the mean.
3 Square each distance.
4 Add all the squared distances.
5 Divide the sum by the number of scores minus one.
6 Find the square root of the result.

Why do we use *n*–1 and not *n*?

We derive the population variance from the sample mean and the deviation of each score from the sample mean, but we need to be able to calculate it if any of this information was missing. So, of *n* scores, only *n*–1 of them are free to vary when we know the mean; *n*–1 is therefore the number of **degrees of freedom** of our data (see Chapter 6 for a more detailed explanation of degrees of freedom).

KT

Although this computation may seem rather complicated, it is actually quite simple. To see this, consider the formula for the standard deviation:

$$SD = \sqrt{\frac{\sum (X - \text{mean})^2}{n - 1}}$$

In the top part of the formula, we see that each score has the mean subtracted from it, the difference is squared, and the squares are summed. In the bottom part, we take the number of scores minus one. This ratio is the variance and the square root is the standard deviation. So we can describe the standard deviation as the square root of the sum of the squared deviations from the mean divided by the number of scores minus one.

The standard deviation is smaller for data clustered closely around the mean value and larger for more dispersed data sets.

The value of these two relatively simple to calculate descriptions of the distribution of a set of scores is very high in quantitative research. Basically, any other more complex calculation of sets of scores will use some variation of the mean and standard deviation. However, there is still one thing to establish, and that is how good a description of the set of scores is contained in the mean and standard

KT

deviation? We can find this out by the *standard error of the mean*, which is, simply put, a standard deviation measure of a mean. Well, it seems simple until you say it quickly.

Standard Error of the Mean

If we were to measure a variable with not just one sample taken from a population, but many samples, each set of scores would be slightly different, and yield a slightly different mean. This must be true, or we would already know what the population mean was and have no need to draw samples anyway. However, a frequency distribution histogram of these means would show a normal distribution. So, calculating the mean of the means and the standard deviation of all of the means in the distribution from it we have something called the standard error of the mean (SEM, denoted σ_n). There is a simple formula for the SEM:

$$\sigma_n = \frac{\sigma}{\sqrt{n}}$$

The standard error will be smaller than the standard deviation in most cases. If we take an example of a set of five scores used above

4   7   8   11   15

The mean is 9.2 and the standard deviation is 4.1473, so the standard error will be 9.2 divided by the square root of 5, or 1.8547.

The distinction between the two values or measurements has important implications for how we present our findings, and later we are going to look at a rather important usage of this term, one which initially prevented the execution of a convicted murderer in the USA (and sparked some ground-breaking legislation) and then put him right back on death row. But, firstly, we need to look at some important applications of our descriptive measures.

The standard deviation becomes very important in psychology when we relate it and the mean to the normal distribution. Psychometric tests (see Chapter 1) often yield a normally distributed set of scores in the population. For example, IQ, measured on various tests, is normally distributed, with a mean of 100. There are several difficulties with the validity of such a measure, as discussed in a later chapter, but for now we can use this well-known set of scores to illustrate the value of a normal distribution and items associated with it.

So, we know that if a person takes the test and scores 100, then they are of average intelligence as measured by that test, or that half the population scores lower than 100 (and half higher). What if someone scores something other than 100? How do we determine where on the scale of intelligence their score lies? We need to know what percentage of people is above or below the score, and how to compare scores across the distribution. Well, a large number of IQ tests yield a distribution with a mean of 100 and a standard deviation of 15. A score of 115 or 85 means that the people with those scores fall within one standard deviation either side of the mean. Relating this to the normal distribution curve, we can see that one standard deviation either side of the mean covers a large area under the curve. Remember: the curve of a distribution is not really a curve, but a very large number of very small bars representing the number of people at a particular score. The total area under the curve represents 100% of the scores we have plotted, so the area between the points 15 below and above the mean is also the percentage of scores falling between them.

Now, remember our example of how a convicted murderer had been released from a potential death sentence? In 1996, Daryl Atkins, then 18, and an accomplice called William Jones, abducted Eric Nesbitt, a 21-year-old US airman from Langley Air Force Base. They forced him to withdraw money from a cash machine, and then took him to an isolated field where he was killed by being shot eight times. The two men blamed each other for the actual murder, but Jones' argument was the more convincing, so, when, in 1998, the two men were tried, Jones got a life sentence but Atkins was sentenced to death. Perhaps the reason that Jones was more compelling was that Atkins was, in American legal terms, 'retarded'. His IQ in 1998 was measured at 59. Following the Atkins' case, the Virginia Supreme Court decided in 2002 that the State of Virginia would not execute people whose IQ was below 70. (For the legal case, see *Atkins v Virginia*, 2002.)

This cut-off point of 70 is two standard deviations below the average (100): 95% of the population will score within two standard deviations on either side of the average, with the remaining 5% being above or below this point (see Figure 4.5). This means that the legal definition of retardation, at least in Virginia, is having an IQ score in the bottom 2.5% of the population.

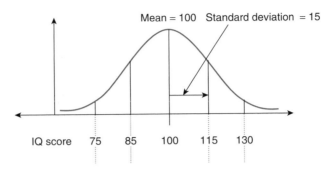

Figure 4.5   IQ scores

All well and good – Atkins was saved from the lethal injection by having a very low IQ. However, in 2004 his IQ was tested again and appeared to have risen to 74. There are several questions as to why this might be: he may have been able to fake his original score, or, as his defence lawyers say, his interaction with lawyers has raised his IQ. Rather strangely, the prosecution stated his IQ as 76, 2 points higher than the defence claimed. It seems rather arbitrary to argue over 2 points, when simply having a score over 70 would make the case. Well, this is due to the statistical nature of the IQ distribution, the standard deviation, and the standard error of the mean. The SEM of the IQ distribution is 5. If the SEM is taken as indication of a true score then 76 would inarguably lie above the level of retardation, but 74 would be ambiguous. At the time of writing, Atkins is still scheduled for execution.

The z-score

The z-score answers our question about the relative position of an individual's score in the distribution. It uses the mean and standard deviation to relate the score to the distribution in the following way:

$$z = \frac{x - \overline{x}}{sd}$$

that is, the difference between the score and the mean divided by the standard deviation. Scores below the mean will have negative values. A score of 115 in the

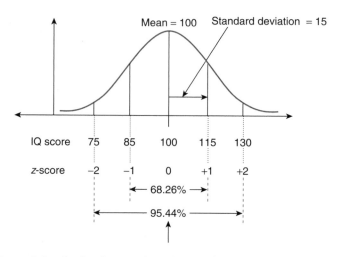

Figure 4.6 Area of distribution (proportion of scores) between $+z$ and $-z$

IQ distribution shown in Figure 4.6 (with a mean of 100 and a standard deviation of 15) would be 115 minus 100 divided by 15, which equals +1, and 85 would be −1.

We now have our *standard score* and we can say exactly what area of the distribution (and hence the proportion of all the values) lies between the two scores relating to IQ scores of 85 and 115. Using the z-scores we can look up the area in a table, and we find that the proportion of the area under the curve between −1 and +1 standard deviation from the mean is 68.26% (see Figure 4.6). So just over 68% of the population have IQs between 85 and 115. Just over 95% have IQs between −2 and +2 standard deviations from the mean, or between 75 and 130.

Many observed variables actually are normally distributed, which is another reason why the normal distribution represents a general feature of empirical testing. In the next chapter, we will look at how important this quality is. There are problems, however, if we want to use tests based on the normal distribution on variables that are not normally distributed themselves. Two qualities that might disrupt the normality of a distribution are skew and kurtosis.

Disruptions to Normality – Skew and Kurtosis

Skew means that the distribution around the mean is not symmetrical (Figure 4.7). Positive skew means that there are a few unusually high scores in the distribution,

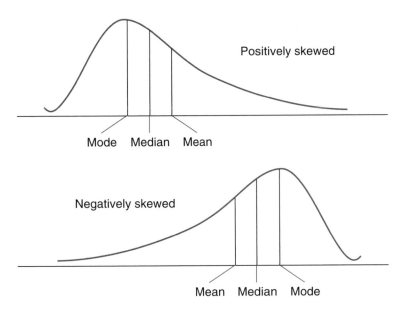

Figure 4.7   Skewed (non-normal) distributions

which makes the tail on that side longer. Negative skew is the opposite position, with fewer low scores. If the skew is large then the distribution is sufficiently non-normal enough to affect our use of it. The value of the skew can be calculated as

$$\text{skew} = \frac{\sum (y - \bar{y})}{(n - 1)\, s^3}$$

KT

Kurtosis describes how broad or wide (or perhaps flattened or pointed) a distribution is (Figure 4.8). If it is flattened and broad it is called platykurtic (think 'plateau') and if thin and pointed, leptokurtic.

Again, the amount of kurtosis can be calculated:

$$\text{kurtosis} = \frac{\sum (y - \bar{y})^4}{(n - 1)\, s^4} - 3$$

KT

So, we have looked at various ways of reducing data to manageable forms, but this all assumes that the data is ordinal- or **interval level data**. In the sections

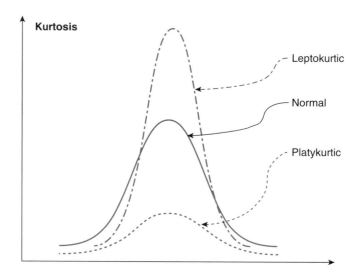

Figure 4.8

above, we looked at how to present data in tables, and this is often the best way to present purely nominal or **frequency data**.

KT

Tabular Presentation

The representation of data in a table is called a tabular presentation, which allows data to be organised for further analysis, allows large amounts of raw data to be sorted and reorganised, and allows the inclusion of only the most relevant data. When using a table as a final representation of data, we need to list specific data values or draw comparisons between variables by listing subtotals, totals, averages, percentages, frequencies, statistical results, etc. Data in a table should be relevant to the hypotheses. Using a table allows us to summarise frequency data clearly and concisely. A particular form of table that is very useful is called the contingency table. A contingency table is a table showing the responses of subjects to one variable as a function of another variable. For example, Table 4.1 (as above) shows the number of male and female students experiencing several levels of debt. We could further summarise this (Table 4.2) as male and female students who are in serious debt (owing over £1500) and not in serious debt (owing less than £1500).

Table 4.2

Serious debt	Male	Female	Total
No	24	141	165
Yes	210	125	335
Total	234	266	500

Out of 500 students, we have 335 in serious debt, but we would also like to know if this is dependent on the sex of the student. The chi-square test of independence is used to test the relationship between rows (debt status) and columns (sex) for significance, and we will examine this in the next chapter.

Summary

We now have some basic tools to examine data, so what can we find out with them? What we have learnt is some of the ways in which we can describe the data in one variable, particularly the use of descriptive statistics and how to construct and display distributions. We have also introduced measures of central tendency and dispersion and explored their relationship. In the next chapter, we will look at how we may use these elements to go beyond simple description.

CHAPTER 5

INFERENTIAL STATISTICS – WHY AND WHAT?

Contents

Probability

Hypothesis testing
Step 1: State the hypotheses
Step 2: Set the criterion for rejecting H_0
Step 3: Compute the test statistic
Step 4: Decide about H_0 (reject or not reject)
One-tailed and two-tailed significance tests

Power

Parametric tests and assumptions
Normal distribution
Homogeneity of variances
Level of measurement

Degrees of freedom

Summary

Inferential Statistics – Why and What?

Acceptance without proof is the fundamental characteristic of Western religion. Rejection without proof is the fundamental characteristic of Western science. (Gary Zukav)

Learning Objectives

- To examine hypotheses and their format.
- To examine how hypotheses can be tested.
- To introduce concepts of probability.
- To examine how probability is used in hypothesis testing.

KEY TERMS

- Degrees of freedom
- Hypothesis testing
- Level of significance
- Null hypothesis; alternative (research/experimental) hypothesis
- Power
- Probability
- Region of rejection
- Type I and Type II errors

In the previous chapter, we looked at how to reduce sets of numerical data to meaningful pieces of information. However, finding the mean and spread of a set of data, or displaying a distribution graphically, can only tell us things about that particular set of data. It is interesting to know that the means of two sets of data are different or that one has a higher spread than another. What we need to know next is whether this change is **significant** in any way, and whether we can predict that this would happen again. We also need to know whether we can generalise

KT

from a sample to the population (see Chapter 3). This is where we use **inferential statistics**, allowing us to test hypotheses to see if we can predict, within certain limits, that something is more likely to happen again than not. This means that we generalise from and beyond our data observations. Statistical tools in this area allow the use of a relatively small number of observations to make a generalised claim about an entire population from which the sample was taken. **Hypothesis testing** is a formal way of testing what our data tells us.

Remember when we looked at Popper's ideas of falsifiability (see Chapter 1)? We need to be able to test something to falsehood; in other words, we can disprove something in science, but not prove it. This is our basic tenet that we apply to hypothesis testing, and can also be seen in may other areas of life. We can draw a very direct analogy with how the criminal justice system works in most of the Western world (there are some notable exceptions). We have as the basis of our legal system the assumption that someone is innocent until shown, beyond reasonable doubt, to be guilty. Evidence is gathered and presented and this evidence has to show that someone is guilty, or their innocence is naturally assumed to have been demonstrated. So a jury has only two possible decisions, guilty or not guilty (note not 'innocent', just 'not guilty'). What happens if a mistake is made? If a person is really innocent but the jury decides they are guilty, then it has convicted an innocent person. If a person is really guilty, but the jury finds them not guilty, a criminal is walking free on the streets. In science, the first situation is known as a **Type I error**, deciding something has happened when, in fact, it is has not. Conversely, the second is a **Type II error**. In English law the first is considered more important, so erroneous guilty decisions are protected against. These possibilities are shown in Table 5.1.

Table 5.1

Jury verdict	Guilty	Not guilty
Real verdict		
Guilty	True	False negative (Type II error)
Not guilty	False positive (Type I error)	True

It is the same in science: we try to minimise the chance of making Type I errors, and use the rules of **probability** to do so. What we are trying to do is disprove unsatisfactory hypotheses and propose new ones, so the one we disprove is called the null hypothesis, often written H_0, the one which assumes no effect or difference or whatever. Our goal is to reject H_0 in favour of the alternative hypothesis, H_1, also termed the research hypothesis or sometimes the experimental hypothesis.

Research hypotheses are informed speculations about the likely results of an investigation. In a typical research design, researchers might want to know whether people in two groups differ in their behaviour. Returning to our running theme of memory and age, remember that we are asking if memory performance declines with age, and investigating this by comparing 25 year olds with 65 year olds. The hypothesis here might be that the mean score on a memory task is lower in the older age group. The problem is that even if we show a difference, we do not know if our hypothesis is confirmed. There may be other issues that are contributing to the difference, such as ability to learn or illness. When we set up studies we are trying to find out which of two conclusions is more likely, the research hypothesis (whether age affects memory) or its counterpart (whether age does not affect memory, the null hypothesis). The word 'null' means nothing or none, and here represents the idea that the independent variable 'age' has no effect on the dependent variable 'memory score'. What we are attempting to do in our experiments is to rule out the null hypothesis and to support the research hypothesis, because psychological research typically attempts to measure changes from one situation to the next, not failure to change. In hypothesis testing, it is always possible to make flawed conclusions. For example, we could reject the null hypothesis and conclude that memory of people in two groups is different; that is, that one group remembers more than the other because of the people's age. In reality, one group might have something special about it that makes the people remember more, irrespective of age, and if the study were performed a second time with different people, the result might be different. This is the equivalent of deciding someone is guilty when they are not, and in hypothesis testing this erroneous conclusion is our friend, the Type I error. We might do the opposite of course, and conclude that the difference in the way the two groups perform is not important. That is, failing to reject the null hypothesis when we should. This is the equivalent of letting a guilty person go, the Type II error. Unfortunately, if we only conduct a single experiment, we may be making an error without realising it. This is why some research is based on replicating the studies already performed in order to spot any errors that previous researchers may have made.

Errors in research decisions of this nature can be controlled for by using probability.

KT

PROBABILITY

Within statistical theory, randomness and uncertainty are modelled by probability theory. Probability is the quantitative description of the likely occurrence of a particular event, the mathematical account of chance. Conventionally we express probability on a scale from 0 to 1: a rare event has a probability close to 0, a very common event has a probability close to 1. You (probably) know more about probability than you think. Coins usually have sides which can be described as 'heads' or 'tails' and if we toss one, in the usual run of things we would be as likely to see one side as the other. If a coin is tossed 100 times, and it is noted whether it fell on the heads or tails side, what we would expect to happen? How many times would you need to see 'heads' before you thought something strange was happening? Most people would say somewhere between 70 and 80 heads out of 100 tosses would not appear bizarre; 50 would certainly not be strange. Well, we might think this is all obvious, but why is it obvious? What we have as part of our knowledge about the world is the idea that a coin that is not 'fixed' has a 50% chance of coming up heads and a 50% chance of coming up tails. From this knowledge we can make inferences that anything other than what we would expect would be unusual. However, where do you draw the line? Suppose that after reflection we decide that the line of bizarre happening falls somewhere in the vicinity of 70%. Anything less than 70 heads out of 100 will not surprise us, but as we get further and further above 70, then we start to think that this is not merely chance operating here. What if the coin tosses totalled only 10, would we still find 7 exciting? That is less likely to be unusual as there is an underlying intuition that a 70% threshold could be much more easily reached or exceeded with only 10 tosses than it could be with 100 tosses.

So, the principles of probability are simply our own intuition expanded and expressed formally in mathematics. Let us look at another concept. Imagine we have taken four pieces of paper, and written on three of them your name, and the remaining one has my name on it. We have then put the paper pieces in a hat, jumbled them up, and then blindly take one out. Of course, we are betting with each other which name we will draw out. In other words, which name has the greater probability of being drawn? If you are blindly drawing one name out of four, and if these four names include three 'you' and one 'Helen', then you have three chances out of four of drawing your name, but only one chance in four of drawing mine. Thus the rational choice would be to bet on your name, as you would have only one chance out of four of losing your bet, but three chances out of four of winning it.

It must be pointed out that these intuitions only represent a simple level of probability theory, but we can build on this and represent it with simple arithmetic. So

Table 5.2

$P_{(me)}$	7/30	0.2333
$P_{(you)}$	12/30	0.40
$P_{(mother)}$	10/30	0.3333
$P_{(father)}$	1/30	0.0333

if we take common-sense concepts such as 'three chances out of four' and convert them into a meaningful numerical form we start to formalise the thoughts we have about events. So our common-sense concept 'this particular event has x chances out of y of occurring,' can be expressed as the ratio of x to y. Thus the probability, P, of drawing your name (with three chances out of four) is

$$P_{(you)} = 3/4 = 0.75$$

and the probability of drawing my name (with one chance out of four) is

$$P_{(me)} = 1/4 = 0.25$$

So, you place your bet on your name, draw the paper and – it's the one with my name on it! Probability values such as $P_{(you)} = 0.75$ or $P_{(me)} = 0.25$ are not reliable predictors of the outcome of a single event, but only in relation to a collection of events: the larger the number of events, the more reliable the prediction. For our names example, the predictive worth of the two probabilities tells us that if we were to perform the name-drawing operation a large number of times we would draw your name in 75% of the cases and my name in 25% of them. If you were to do it only a few times, the observed percentages of your name and mine would perhaps differ markedly from these theoretical values of 75% and 25%, and this is why people lose so much money gambling. However, the more we repeated the operation, the closer they would come.

Let us expand the example to include 30 pieces of paper, of which seven are my name, 12 your name, 10 are your mother's, and one is your father's. If you were to pick one name at random from the hat, what is the probability that the name you select will be yours?

The probabilities are shown in Table 5.2.

These examples illustrate what is known as the relative frequency concept of probability, which defines the probability of an event in terms of the number (frequency) of possibilities favourable to the occurrence of that event, relative to the total number of possibilities. So the probability of the occurrence of a certain event, x, is

$$P_{(x)} = \frac{\text{number of possibilities favourable to the occurrence of } x}{\text{total number of possibilities}}$$

Similarly, if we were to select at random one person from a room full of people, the probability of selecting a woman would be

$$P_{(woman)} = \frac{\text{the number of women in the room}}{\text{the total number of people in the room}}$$

Probability values determined from our intuition are falling somewhere between $P = 0$ and $P = 1.0$ inclusive, as the calculation always involves the division of one number by another number, and the divisor (the bottom number) is in every case equal to or larger than the number it divides.

There are certain kinds of situations where the values for the possibilities of x occurring and the total number of possibilities are known in advance, such as with our names in the hat, where we just know how many of each name is available. This allows us to proceed logically to calculate the probability of something happening. There are other kinds of situations where the probability value cannot be known precisely in advance, but rather must be estimated on the basis of observing a large number of actual instances. So we have meteorological forecasts telling us there is a 40% chance of rain; this has to be merely an estimate, based on observations of the frequency of rain in the past under similar combinations of temperature, humidity, atmospheric pressure and other relevant factors.

Intuitively, we can see that the confidence we can have in probability estimates increases in proportion to the number of observations on which they are based. However, in order to use the theory we have just explored, it needs a little expansion. When we looked at the coin tossing situation, we were actually examining something known as binomial probabilities, where there are two possible outcomes. A binomial probability case is one for which you can specify

p: the probability that the event will occur
q: the probability that the event will not occur
n: the number of instances in which the event has the opportunity to occur

Let us just step it up a notch, and think about two coins and their behaviour. If we toss two coins the possible outcomes are as shown in Table 5.3.

Table 5.3

Coin A	Coin B	Number of heads
Tails	Tails	0
Tails	Heads	1
Heads	Tails	1
Heads	Heads	2

Tossing two coins means that $p = 0.5$ for the outcome of getting a head on any particular one of the coins and $q = 0.5$ for the outcome of not getting a head, so the probabilities for the outcomes are as shown in Table 5.4.

Table 5.4

Coin A	B	Observed probability	Number of heads	Probability	
Tails	Tails	$0.5 \times 0.5 = 0.25$	0	0.25	(25%)
Tails	Heads	$0.5 \times 0.5 = 0.25$	1	0.50	(50%)
Heads	Tails	$0.5 \times 0.5 = 0.25$			
Heads	Heads	$0.5 \times 0.5 = 0.25$	2	0.25	(25%)
Totals				1.0	(100%)

Similarly, if we are considering two days on which it might rain, when the weather forecast has told us that $p = 0.4$ that it will rain and $q = 0.6$ for not raining, the possible outcomes and probabilities are as shown in Table 5.5.

In Figure 5.1 the two sets of probabilities are shown as histograms. In each case, we can think of the total area of the histogram as representing 100% of the total probability that applies to that particular situation.

Table 5.5

Day				
Monday	**Tuesday**	**Observed probability**	**Occurrences of rain**	**Probability**
No rain	No rain	$0.6 \times 0.6 = 0.36$	0	0.36 (36%)
No rain	Rain	$0.6 \times 0.4 = 0.24$	1	0.48 (48%)
Rain		$0.4 \times 0.6 = 0.24$		
Rain	Rain	$0.4 \times 0.4 = 0.16$	2	0.16 (16%)
Total				1.0 (100%)

These sorts of histograms are known as **probability sampling distributions**, because they describe the probabilities for the entire range of outcomes that are possible in the particular situations that are under consideration.

Another way of interpreting a probability sampling distribution would be to say that it describes the manner in which the outcomes of any large number of randomly selected samples will tend to be distributed. The interpretation of central tendency and variability for a sampling distribution is essentially the same as for any other distribution. The central tendency of the distribution describes the average of all the outcomes, and its variability is the measure of the tendency of individual outcomes to be dispersed away from that average.

So why is this important to quantitative measures in psychology? Well, consider what would happen if we had five coins to toss. What would the outcomes look like in probability terms? The lower histogram in Figure 5.1 shows the distribution of heads in the combination of five coins.

The shape is beginning to look a little familiar. If we raised the number of coins the shape would become even more familiar and we would find the distribution getting closer and closer to our old friend, that bell-shaped curve, the normal distribution.

Suppose we want now to know whether the coins being tossed are 'fixed' in order to fall one way or the other, rather than randomly heads or tails. If all our coins fall heads, we know this could have happened by chance, but that is not very likely. What we need to know is the cut-off point, or critical region, where we would accept that something has happened by chance and beyond which we would say that something has affected the outcome. When we set out to test hypotheses about psychological experiments we decide at what point we will accept that we have a chance occurrence.

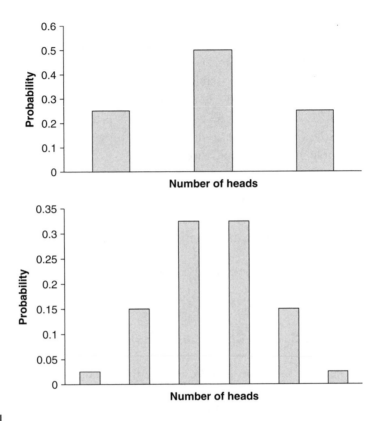

Figure 5.1

HYPOTHESIS TESTING

Hypothesis testing in inferential statistics means making deductions about the nature of a population on the basis of observations of a sample drawn from it. There are several steps we need to navigate in order to do this successfully and, more importantly, rigorously.

Step 1: State the Hypotheses

Well, what do we know about hypotheses already? A hypothesis is a conjecture or a scientific guess about one or more population parameters (see Chapter 3). The hypothesis to be tested is called the null hypothesis and is given the symbol H_0. The null hypothesis is typically the hypothesis of no relationship or no difference. We test the null hypothesis (H_0) against an alternative hypothesis (symbolised H_1), which includes the possible outcomes not covered by the null hypothesis. A null hypothesis is rejected when an observed statistic (e.g. a sample mean) is shown to be highly unlikely if the null hypothesis is true.

So for example we could make the following statements if we are comparing a sample mean to a population mean:

H_0: The mean is not different from the population mean $\bar{x} = \mu$
H_1: The mean is different from the population mean $\bar{x} = \mu$

Or the following would apply in our memory and age example:

H_0: The mean memory score of 25 year olds is not different from the mean memory score of 65 year olds
H_1: The mean memory score of 25 year olds is different from the mean memory score of 65 year olds

Step 2: Set the Criterion for Rejecting H_0

There are three considerations in setting the criterion for rejecting H_0, as follows.

(a) Errors in Hypothesis Testing

Remember: we can make one of two types of errors in hypothesis testing, namely

Type I error – when we reject a true null hypothesis (false positive)
Type II error – when we fail to reject a false null hypothesis (false negative)

In general, we increase the likelihood of one type of error as we decrease the likelihood of the other. Therefore, a judgement must be made depending on the consequences of each type of error. The general approach to hypothesis testing is to argue for the alternative hypothesis by rejecting the null hypothesis. This approach focuses on the Type I error, rejecting the null hypothesis when in fact it is true, and we need to guard against it

(b) Level of Significance

We choose the criterion for rejecting H_0 by determining the **significance level** or **alpha (α) level**. This is defined as the probability of making a Type I error (rejecting

KT

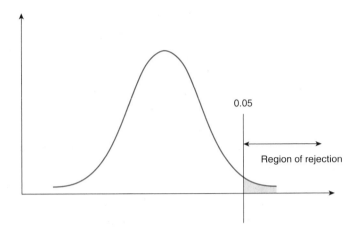

0.05

Region of rejection

Figure 5.2

H_0 when it is true). Researchers usually establish the level of significance before collecting and analysing any data. The most frequently used level of significance is 0.05, a value set by R.A. Fisher in 1925. Statisticians will argue about this level and any alternatives for hours, if you are unwise enough to set them off. However, for our purposes we need to know that, even if it is an arbitrary figure (and, essentially, that is what statisticians argue about!), it has been in use for almost a hundred years, an indication of how practical its use is, at least when we did not have modern computers. In other words, if the 5% level is used, then in most situations where we need to use inferential statistics, it is feasible to set up a study which will be able to pick up those effects which are large enough to be of psychological interest. The convention of using an alpha of 0.05 has been useful to science and would not have stood the test of time if it was not. The alternative alpha level is 0.1%, which means we have to be 99% sure of our result. This would be applicable if we were really worried about the Type I error, such as recommending a new drug treatment on the basis of the difference between it and the old therapy. When using either of these levels, we know that the decision to reject the hypothesis may be incorrect 5% or 1% of the time, respectively. As psychologists that is all we need to know, and you will find that most psychological research will use the 5% in most cases.

(c) Region of Rejection

Remember, in a distribution shown in a graph (Figure 5.2), the area under the curve represents all of the scores we have measured. In our sampling distributions, we can plot the proportion of area that equals the probability of rejecting the null hypothesis if it is true, using the significance level to differentiate between the areas. This area in the sampling distribution that is cut off at the significance level is called the **region of rejection**.

If the result of the statistical analysis is shown to fall within the rejection region then we can assume that we can reject the null hypothesis. If it falls outside the region, then the result is likely to be due to chance and we do not reject the null hypothesis. For example, in our five-coin-toss case the probability of getting all five heads is 0.031 and this is less than the conventionally set level of 0.05. Therefore the probability of five heads by chance is lower than what we would say is the level we would accept chance occurrences, and we reject the null hypothesis that the coins are not fixed.

For all the test statistics of our inferential tests, we have tables to which we can refer and compare. For each level of probability we use as our significance levels, there are critical values related to the sample size (or degrees of freedom, see below). If our calculated test statistic is larger that the tabled critical value then it falls outside the areas we would accept the effect to have occurred by chance, and we reject the null hypothesis.

Step 3: Compute the Test Statistic

The following chapters will look at appropriate statistics for particular situations of design and analysis. For each situation, the application of a statistical test will result in the computation of a test statistic, one number describing the relationship between sets of data. This figure will be computed from various other components including the degrees of freedom (see below).

Step 4: Decide About H_0 (Reject or Not Reject)

The rule for deciding about the null hypothesis is that if the test statistic falls in the rejection region, then we reject H_0. When the null hypothesis is rejected at the 0.05 level of significance, we say that the result, or the difference between the observed statistic and the hypothesised value of the parameter, is 'statistically significant at the 0.05 level'. Essentially, this is saying that the difference between the observed sample test statistic and the hypothesised population statistic is too great to be attributed to chance. In inferential statistics, probability relates to the statistic, which is a measure from the sample. Suppose we reject the null hypothesis; we are not saying that the probability is 0.95 that H_0 is false. Conversely, if we fail to reject the null hypothesis, it is *not* correct to conclude that the probability is 0.95 that H_0 is true. Significance is a statistical term that tells us how confident we can be that a difference or relationship exists, and is only part of the story, but a very important part. If we reject a null hypothesis, we do not automatically accept the alternative hypothesis, because there may be several things preventing us from doing so. This is the realm of the alternative explanation encountered in Chapter 3.

One-Tailed and Two-Tailed Significance Tests

One important concept in significance testing is whether we use a **one-tailed** or **two-tailed test** of significance, and this depends on our hypothesis. When the research hypothesis states the direction of the difference or relationship, then we use a one-tailed probability. For example, a one-tailed test would be used to test the null hypothesis '25 year olds will not score higher than 65 year olds on a memory test'. The null hypothesis indirectly predicts which way the difference lies. A two-tailed test would be used to test the null hypothesis: 'There will be no significant difference in memory scores between 25 and 65 year olds'. The one-tailed probability is exactly half the value of the two-tailed probability. To compute a one-tailed *p*-value, just take the two-tailed *p*-value and cut it in half, and make sure that the effect is going in the direction you hypothesised.

There has been another debate going for about a hundred years on whether or not it is ever appropriate to use a one-tailed test. It is usually safest to use two-tailed tests, and hence keep hypotheses fairly neutral or non-directional, but there may be situations where using directional hypotheses and one-tailed tests is appropriate.

POWER

An increasingly important concept in choosing and carrying out statistical tests is the **power** of a test. The power of a statistical test is the probability that the test will reject a false null hypothesis, or in other words that it will not make a Type II error. As power increases, the chances of a Type II error decrease, and vice versa. The probability of a Type II error is referred to as β. Therefore power is equal to $1 - \beta$. Statistical power depends on the significance criterion, the size of the difference or the strength of the similarity (i.e. the effect size) in the population, and the sensitivity of the data. The significance criterion is a statement of how unlikely a difference must be, if the null hypothesis is true, to be considered significant. The most commonly used criteria are probabilities of 0.05, 0.01 and 0.001. If the criterion is 0.05, the probability of the difference must be less than 0.05, and so on. The greater the effect size, the greater the power. Calculation of power requires that researchers determine the effect size they want to detect. Sensitivity can be increased by increasing the reliability of measures and by increasing the size of the sample. Increasing sample size is the most commonly used method for increasing statistical power. There are no formal standards for power, as with the significance level there is debate about the level to be set, but 0.80 is generally regarded as a standard for adequacy.

Another way of increasing the power of a test is to increase the significance level. As mentioned above, decreasing alpha from 0.05 to 0.01 would mitigate against Type I errors, but would increase the chance of making a Type II error. If alpha was raised (say to 0.1), this would reduce the risk of a Type II error and increase the chance of obtaining a statistically significant result when the null hypothesis is false, but it would also increase the risk of obtaining a statistically significant result and rejecting the null hypothesis when it is true; that is, increase the risk of a Type I error. The probability of a Type II error is symbolised as beta. Beta, and the risk of making a Type II error, increases as the alpha level decreases. The power of a statistical test is its ability to detect a difference when one exists, or the probability of rejecting the null hypothesis when it is truly false. Since the Type II error is the probability of failing to reject the null hypothesis when it is false, power must be $1-\beta$. There are procedures which allow us to estimate the power inherent in experiments and their analysis and we will assess these and the effect size, but there are some things to bear in mind in the next few chapters:

- As alpha gets smaller, power decreases.
- As the difference between the null and alternative hypotheses increases, power increases.
- As the sample size in the experiment increases, power increases.
- Directional hypotheses lead to more power, but may be meaningless psychologically.

Finally, with respect to inferential statistics we need to know something on which power depends. Some tests have more power than others, and these are referred to as parametric tests.

PARAMETRIC TESTS AND ASSUMPTIONS

Parametric statistics are those which assume a normal distribution of the data, a certain level of measurement, and homogeneity of variances when two or more samples are being compared. Most common significance tests are parametric. However, it has long been established that moderate violations of **parametric** **assumptions** have little or no effect on research conclusions in most instances.

All forms of statistical analysis assume sound measurement, relatively free of coding errors. It is good practice to run descriptive statistics on data so that we can be confident that the data is generally as expected in terms of means and standard deviations, and there are no out-of-bounds entries beyond the expected range.

There are several assumptions required by some statistical procedures, referred to as parametric assumptions, and the tests that need them are called **parametric tests**. This means that these tests are dependent on the data on which the tests will be performed having certain parameters associated with them. These assumptions are:

- Normality of distribution
- Homogeneity of variance
- At least interval level data

Normal Distribution

A normal distribution (see Chapter 4 for more details) is assumed by many parametric tests. Some transformations are used to correct non-normally distributed data, but should be used with care. Normality can be visually assessed by looking at a histogram of frequencies, or by looking at a normal probability plot output by most computer programs. There are also some tests that can be performed in computer programs to determine if our distribution is normal.

Shapiro–Wilks's W test is a formal test of normality. A significant W statistic causes the researcher to reject the assumption that the distribution is normal.

 The **Kolmogorov–Smirnov (K–S) test**, or its slightly improved sister, K–S Lilliefors test, is an alternative test of normality for large samples. The K–S test can test **goodness-of-fit** against any theoretical distribution, not just the normal distribution.

Again, a significant result means that the tested distribution is not normal.

An observed distribution may be compared with what would be expected based on the assumption of a normal distribution, using the chi-square goodness-of-fit test. The chi-square test can test goodness-of-fit against any theoretical distribution, not just the normal distribution.

Outliers can radically alter the outcome of analysis and are also violations of normality. Outliers arise from several different causes, requiring different courses of action:

- Errors of data entry: proofread your data for out-of-range entries and other errors.
- Unintended sampling: eliminate non-population members from the sample.
- True non-normal distribution: for a true non-normal distribution with extreme values, choose to analyse extreme cases separately.

Homogeneity of Variances

This means that the variances in the samples of data that are to be compared are not significantly different (equality does not mean exactly the same here).

There are several tests to determine if variances are homogeneous:

- Levene's test of homogeneity of variance is computed to test the assumption that each group has the same variance. If the Levene statistic is significant at the 0.05 level or better, the researcher rejects the null hypothesis that the groups have equal variances. Levene's test is robust in the face of departures from normality.
- Brown and Forsythe's test of homogeneity of variances are recent tests based on criticisms of Levene's test. The former is more robust than the latter when groups are unequal in size and the absolute deviation scores (deviations from the group means) are highly skewed, causing a violation of the normality assumption.
- Bartlett's test of homogeneity of variance is an older, alternative test. It is a chi-square statistic with $(k-1)$ degrees of freedom, where k is the number of categories in the independent variable. Bartlett's test is dependent on meeting the assumption of normality and therefore Levene's test has now largely replaced it.

Level of Measurement

Parametric tests require arithmetic manipulations of the data, and can therefore only be performed on data that can be dealt with in this way. So if the data is interval or ratio there is no problem. However, it is accepted now that some tests are so robust that they can be performed on ordinal data too.

DEGREES OF FREEDOM

One final point before we embark on the quest for the test statistics, and that is an issue about sample size. It has appeared tantalisingly several times above and finally we can look at what we mean by degrees of freedom.

The number of degrees of freedom in a distribution is the number of parameters which may be independently varied. Let us return to our well-worn hat. In it we once again have pieces of paper, 10 of them ($n = 10$) with 10 different names on them, and we are removing one name at a time, perhaps to decide the order in which a group of people take turns at something. If the drawing of the names is truly random, and we are not replacing names after they are drawn, then we do not know which names we are drawing, right up to the last one. However, when we have drawn out nine, we therefore know which name is written on the last piece of paper. We therefore have nine names which were free to vary and one which was fixed. The degrees of freedom in this distribution of names was therefore $n-1$.

Why is this important? Well, degrees of freedom are one of the tools by which we can carry out statistical procedures. When calculating any test statistic, we need to know what is varying and what is fixed. In any distribution of a set of scores there will be one thing that is fixed once we have measured it, such as the mean. So the degrees of freedom are those things that vary minus the things that are fixed. We use this to compare the calculated results with the tabled critical values. Once the statistics have been performed using the degrees of freedom, we need to report the degrees of freedom so that anyone reading our results knows which critical values we have used to determine whether or not our results are significant.

Summary

In this chapter we have looked at how and why we might use statistics to test hypotheses. We test the null hypothesis as we apply the concept of falsifiability and need to understand probability in order to do so. Probability is the mathematical language of chance and is applied to hypothesis testing in order to determine if a null hypothesis can be rejected or not. The ability to do this depends on the power in the design and analysis and this is also connected to whether or not we can use parametric tests, that is when our data does not violate parametric assumptions.

In the next chapter we will look at using inferential statistics to test the results of simple experimental designs.

Sir Ronald Aylmer Fisher (1890–1962)

R.A. Fisher was educated at Harrow and Cambridge, where he excelled in mathematics. However, it was his interest in the theory of errors that eventually led him to investigate statistical problems, while working as the statistician at Rothamsted Agricultural Experiment Station, the oldest agricultural research institute in the UK. There he studied the design of experiments by introducing the concept of randomisation and the analysis of variance, procedures now used throughout the world.

The contributions Fisher made included the development of methods suitable for small samples, and the discovery of the precise distributions of many sample statistics. Fisher published *The design of experiments* (1935) and *Statistical tables* (1947).

In 1933 Fisher was appointed Galton Professor of Eugenics at University College, holding the post for 10 years, before being appointed Arthur Balfour Professor of Genetics at the University of Cambridge in 1943. He was interested in the statistics of genetics, but also made some unpopular and inflammatory comments about natural selection and survival of the fittest, advocating less support for 'weak' members of society. He retired from his Cambridge chair in 1957 but continued to carry out his duties there for another two years until his successor could be appointed. He then moved to the University of Adelaide where he continued his research for the final three years of his life.

CHAPTER 6

SIMPLE EXPERIMENTAL DESIGNS: BEING WATCHED

Contents

Who is watching you?

The analysis of data from experiments with two conditions
The *t* test

Experiments with within-subjects designs
Analysis of data in within-subjects designs

Experiments using between-subjects designs
Analysis of data in between-subjects designs

One-and two-tailed *t* tests

Summary

Simple Experimental Designs: Being Watched

*An unsophisticated forecaster uses statistics as a drunken man uses lamp-posts –
for support rather than for illumination.* (Andrew Lang)

Learning Objectives

- To examine the way in which data can be derived in simple experimental designs, and what those designs might consist of.
- To consider the elements of simple between- and within-subjects designs.
- To explain analysis of data derived from each of these two types of design.
- To explain the alternative analyses for parametric and non-parametric cases.

KEY TERMS

- Between-subjects (independent measures)
- Control condition
- Directional hypothesis
- Experimental condition
- Mann–Whitney *U* test
- One-and two-tailed tests
- Tied ranks
- *t* test (unrelated/independent and related measures)
- Wilcoxon test
- Within-subjects (related measures)

The simplest form of experimentation compares behaviour under two conditions that vary only by one thing; all aspects of the two situations are the same (or as similar as can be achieved), except for one single change. So, for example, people taking part in an experiment, the participants, may carry out some task, but in one condition they are alone (the control condition) and in the other they are being watched (the experimental condition). Any difference noted between the two conditions, all other elements being identical, can be attributed to the manipulation that has been performed. The manipulation here is on the independent variable of being watched, which has two conditions, alone or observed. What we are investigating is the effect of the changes in the independent variable on the dependent variable, the task performance.

WHO IS WATCHING YOU?

Have you ever noticed that you do things differently when you are being watched? You try a little harder, persevere a little longer, especially if it is something at which you are good. This enhancing effect of an audience is called *social facilitation*. Zajonc (1965) suggested a drive theory explanation for the effect of being watched. A 'drive' is a directed need for something, which must be reduced in order to satisfy some internal state. For example, hunger is a drive that can be reduced by eating, and anxiety is a drive that can be reduced by certain behaviours appropriate to the situation. Zajonc's **drive theory** states that, as we never know what an audience's response will be, we need to be in a high state of arousal when performing, or that the heightened arousal is simply an instinctive reaction to the presence of other people. This arousal results in a drive, which is reduced by the dominant response to the situation, utilising skills as best we can. The earliest scientific observation of social facilitation recorded was by Triplett in 1897. He observed that bike racers were more likely to cycle faster when this was against another cyclist than against the clock. This seems to be a nice, simple, clear-cut finding, but hardly explains the sometimes adverse effect of performance anxiety (stage fright). It does appear that social facilitation is not the straightforward explanation for audience effects it was first assumed to be. Later researchers also noted that an audience could have a detrimental effect on performance, particularly when the task is complex and/or unfamiliar. Other possible reasons for this social inhibition can be the perceived evaluation from the audience. Such evaluation apprehension (Cottrell, 1972) means that anxiety about the evaluation should increase arousal, which should increase performance. But Sanna and Shotland (1990) found that if a performer thinks that the audience is going to evaluate

KT

negatively, then this would have a damaging effect in comparison with a perceived positive evaluation. A further complication comes from Baron's (1986) attentional view of social facilitation. He suggested that an audience could have a distracting effect on the performer, with task performance being dependent upon the number of cues or distractions present. We have all seen athletes spurred on by the crowd shouting, but that if we add in inappropriate cues, such as a fan running onto the track, the athletes would not perform quite as well.

So, we appear to have a highly complex social effect that would not lend itself to simple experimentation. However, what Zajonc was suggesting is that it is the dominant response that is affected by the mere presence of an observer. In other words, the things that you already do well or automatically, such as riding a bike, throwing a ball, or dancing a tango, will be enhanced when you are watched. This is now the more up-to-date definition of social facilitation: that there will be strengthening of dominant, or well-learned, responses due to the presence of others. What is important here is not whether the effect of the audience's perceived evaluation will affect performance, but Zajonc's assertion that the mere presence of an audience will have the effect of arousing participants so much that they will at least attempt to perform to the best of their ability. This is the most basic effect of an audience that can be examined, and, if this effect is seen to not be so, the premise on which other theories of social facilitation is based falls down.

The simplest psychological experimental design compares results from two conditions, one in which some manipulation has happened and the other, the control condition, in which no such manipulation has taken place. If the two conditions have resulted in statistically significant different performance, then we can conclude that the manipulation of the independent variable has had an effect. In our social facilitation situation, we would have exactly the same setup for our participants; they will perform the task in the same environment except in one set of trials they will be watched. This is the classical design of an experiment and has certain components.

Firstly, there is direct comparison between two sets of circumstances or conditions; participants are alone or there is at least one other person present.

Secondly, there is control – the two conditions are as equal as we can make them except for the item we are investigating, the presence of another person or other people.

However, there are different variations even of this simple design. The description above of the effect of the audience is termed a repeated measures design as both conditions include data collected from the same person; in other words, any individual is measured both with and without observation. There are other terms for this, such as related measures or **within-subjects design**. The latter is the one we will use throughout the rest of the chapters. It describes measurements made *within* a group of people, whereas **between-subjects design** refers to measurements made *between* two groups of people. This second set of circumstances is also referred to as independent measures or unrelated samples.

So a simple experiment can have a within-subjects or between-subjects design. Usually simple designs refer to experiments in which there are only two conditions, so those with more than two conditions are addressed in a later chapter.

THE ANALYSIS OF DATA FROM EXPERIMENTS WITH TWO CONDITIONS

If the data derived from measures in the dependent variable conforms to parametric assumptions (see Chapter 5) then in order to decide if the means in the two conditions are significantly different a statistical test called a *t* test can be performed. The *t* test assesses whether the means of two sets of data are statistically different from each other. This analysis is appropriate whenever we want to compare the means of two distributions of data, and especially appropriate as the analysis for the two-sample experimental design.

What does it suggest if we say that the means for two conditions are statistically different? Well, if the experiment has been performed properly, we should be confident that it means that the two conditions differ because of something we have done to one to make it different from the other. However, consider Figure 6.1, in which the difference in the means is the same, but the distributions appear very different.

The top graph shows a case with moderate variability of scores within each group of data scores. The second situation shows the high-variability case and the third shows the case with low variability. We would conclude that the two groups appear most different in the low-variability case, as there appears to be relatively little overlap between the two curves. In the high-variability case, the group difference appears least striking because the two distributions overlap so much. So when we examine the differences between scores for two groups, we have to judge the difference between their means relative to the spread or variability of their scores. The *t* test does just this.

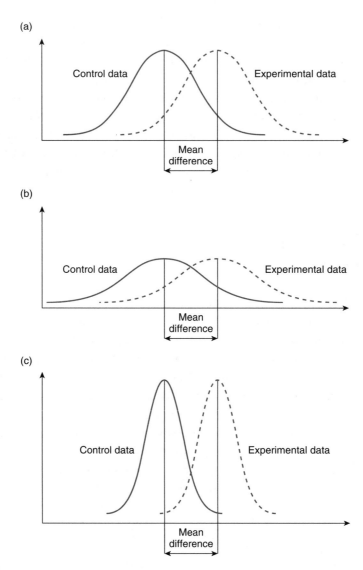

Figure 6.1

The *t* Test

The formula for the *t* test is a ratio:

$$t = \frac{\text{difference between group means}}{\text{variability of groups}}$$

The top part of the ratio is just the difference between the two means or averages, a measure of how different our treatment has made the two groups. The bottom part is a measure of the variability or dispersion of the scores. Essentially what this says is that the value of interest is the difference between the average scores in the two sets of data, but that we need to take into account any variability due to individual differences, the variance.

The *t*-value will be positive if the first mean is larger than the second and negative if it is smaller. Once we have found our *t*-value we need to look it up in a table of significance to test whether the ratio is large enough to conclude that the difference between the groups is not likely to have been a chance finding. To test the significance, we need to set a level at which we will accept that the difference is significant, the significance level or alpha level (α). This level and its use are described in detail in Chapter 5, but conventionally we set this at 0.05 (or 0.01). We also need to determine the degrees of freedom (*df*) for the test. Given the alpha level, the *df* and the *t*-value, we can look the *t*-value up in a standard table of significance to determine whether the *t*-value is large enough to be significant. If it is, we can conclude that the difference between the means for the two groups is different. Fortunately, statistical computer programs routinely print the significance test results and save us the trouble of looking them up in a table.

EXPERIMENTS WITH WITHIN-SUBJECTS DESIGNS

So, we have set up the social facilitation study to measure the dominant response of a group of people in the two conditions, one where they perform alone and one where they are watched by one other person. The dominant response, according to Platania and Moran (2001), is one where the participant is not judged in terms of correct or incorrect responses, but can give responses without the effects of competition, imitation, reinforcement, rewards or punishments. In their experiment the task was a stimulus discrimination task in which stimuli consisted of 11 squares ranging from 22 mm to 52 mm, increasing by increments of 3 mm. The participants were told that they were to distinguish between 11 different-sized squares, calling the smallest square in the trial '1' and the largest '11'. The remaining numbers (2 to 10) were to be assigned to the remaining squares in order of increasing size. In a practice session the participants were shown a guide sheet displaying the 11 squares in ascending order, and then were presented with slides of each square in serial order, from smallest to largest. They were told the correct number to be assigned to the square, and then told that the squares would appear in random order.

The recorded response was the number of times that each participant used his or her two preferred response numbers (responses with the greatest habit strength). A mean of 12 would be obtained if the participant were responding randomly or, alternately, accurately (i.e. two preferred responses, or numbers of particular squares multiplied by six trials). It does not matter if the participant is correct or not. The resulting data was two samples of discrimination responses, A and B.

Analysis of Data in Within-Subjects Designs

Here we are going to use two sets of data from 24 participants, each participant taking part in both conditions, $N_{observed} = 24$ and $N_{alone} = 24$. We are going to treat this data as interval, and assume that the distribution of responses would be normal in the population, therefore we can use a parametric test.

Data Conforms to Parametric Assumptions

Table 6.1 shows the data from each participant in both conditions. The null hypothesis here is that the mean response is unrelated to whether the participant is observed, but, on average, participants produced more dominant responses when observed than when alone. What does this difference mean statistically?

We are concerned only with the *difference* between the observed and alone conditions, so we can treat this as one sample of data described as difference (D). Table 6.2 shows the same data we saw earlier, but now with the calculation of D for each subject. The mean of all these D-values is the same as the difference between the means above, but there is a smaller measure of variability. The square of D is also computed, as we will need that later.

If there were no tendency for people to perform differently under the two conditions, we would expect the mean of the D-values in such a sample to be zero. So is the observed mean difference of 3.16 significantly different from zero? We need only do a simple set of calculations:

$$t = \frac{\overline{X}_{condition1} - \overline{X}_{condition2}}{\sqrt{\frac{(\sum D^2) - ((\sum D)^2/N)}{N(N-1)}}}$$

$$t = (8.7083 - 5.4583) \div \sqrt{[(399.5 - (78^2/24)/(24 \times 23)]}$$
$$= 3.25 \div \sqrt{146/552} = 3.25 \div 0.514288$$
$$= 6.319$$

Table 6.1

Participant	Observed	Alone
1	9.5	1
2	6.5	4
3	10.5	6.5
4	11.5	6.5
5	12	4.5
6	12	4
7	3	3
8	9.5	7
9	12	11
10	6.5	5
11	8	2.5
12	4.5	5
13	1	0
14	10.5	5
15	7.5	4
16	12	8
17	10	9
18	10.5	7.5
19	9	6.5
20	11	8
21	1	1
22	12	7
23	7	6
24	12	9
Mean	8.71	5.46
SD	3.4544	2.7462

Now we need to refer the calculated value of t to the table of critical values of t with $df = N-1$. In our example, $t = +6.319$, $df = 23$, which is well beyond the critical value for t.

Data Does Not Conform to Parametric Assumptions

Like the t test for related samples, the Wilcoxon signed-ranks test applies to two-sample designs involving within-subjects measures. However, this non-parametric test can be

Table 6.2

Participant	Observed	Alone	D	D^2
1	9.5	1	8.5	72.25
2	6.5	4	2.5	6.25
3	10.5	6.5	4	16
4	11.5	6.5	5	25
5	12	4.5	7.5	56.25
6	12	4	8	64
7	3	3	0	0
8	9.5	7	2.5	6.25
9	12	11	1	1
10	6.5	5	1.5	2.25
11	8	2.5	5.5	30.25
12	4.5	5	−0.5	0.25
13	1	0	1	1
14	10.5	5	5.5	30.25
15	7.5	4	3.5	12.25
16	12	8	4	16
17	10	9	1	1
18	10.5	7.5	3	9
19	9	6.5	2.5	6.25
20	11	8	3	9
21	1	1	0	0
22	12	7	5	25
23	7	6	1	1
24	12	9	3	9
Mean	8.7083	5.4583	3.25	16.6458
SD	3.4544	2.7462		
Sum			78	399.5

applied if we conclude that the data may not conform to parametric assumptions. Whilst the t test is robust enough to withstand violations of parametric assumptions, some researchers prefer to use non-parametric tests in smaller samples of data. Smaller samples mean we cannot always be sure that the data will fall into a normal distribution, or that there will be homogeneity of variance. In our sample above, we cannot be certain the distribution is normal even with Kolmogorov–Smirnov results that are not significant (see Chapter 5). Although we have treated the data as interval, we cannot be sure that it conforms to all parametric assumptions, therefore we might want to do a non-parametric test. The **Wilcoxon test** is a non-parametric test that compares two sets of data that are derived from the same people.

KT

The procedure is similar to the *t* test in that we are comparing differences, but once we have worked out the differences, we need to rank them in order, ignoring the sign (positive or minus), and disregarding differences of zero (see Table 6.3).

If there are numbers in *D* that are the same they are given a mean rank, so the ranks of 1, where there are three of them, would normally be given the ranks of 1, 2, 3 and 4, but are assigned 2.5. Similarly the differences of 1.5 would normally have ranks 5, 6 and 7, so are given (5 + 6 + 7)/3.

Once we have the number ranked we need to reassign the plus or minus sign from the original difference. Each of these two groups, the negative and positive ranks, are summed; the smaller one of these summed ranks is Wilcoxon's *T*. The output from a computer program calculation for Wilcoxon's *T* is shown in Table 6.4.

This value is compared with the critical values of *T*. Again we see that this is significant. Note that it is a minus number. This is simply due to the sample in which the highest ranks appeared, but could have implications in a parametric test. See the section on one-tailed and two-tailed tests below.

EXPERIMENTS USING BETWEEN-SUBJECTS DESIGNS

Between-subjects designs are used when the effect of the independent variable on the dependent variable might be such that a within-subjects design is inappropriate. For example, giving a test of memory to a group of people, then giving them alcohol and retesting them, might not show us the effect of the alcohol on memory because the people might have learnt the items on the memory test. So a between-subjects design would be used, and the memory test would be given to a group of people that had not received any alcohol and to one that had. Assuming that we can say that all other aspects are equal, such as age group, intellectual ability, etc., then any difference can be attributed to the effect of the alcohol. If we were to use the between-subjects design in our social facilitation experiment it would be because we thought the task could be learnt between the two sets of conditions. This is unlikely, and it would not be appropriate to use the between-subjects design. However, simply because we have a significant paired samples *t* test result, this does not mean that we can accept without question the effect of observation. There may be other effects

Table 6.3

Participant	Observed	Alone	D	Rank D
1	9.5	1	8.5	22
2	6.5	4	2.5	6
3	10.5	6.5	4	14.5
4	11.5	6.5	5	16.5
5	12	4.5	7.5	20
6	12	4	8	21
7	3	3	0	-
8	9.5	7	2.5	9
9	12	11	1	2.5
10	6.5	5	1.5	6
11	8	2.5	5.5	18.5
12	4.5	5	−0.5	6
13	1	0	1	2.5
14	10.5	5	5.5	18.5
15	7.5	4	3.5	13
16	12	8	4	14.5
17	10	9	1	2.5
18	10.5	7.5	3	11
19	9	6.5	2.5	8
20	11	8	3	11
21	1	1	0	-
22	12	7	5	16.5
23	7	6	1	2.5
24	12	9	3	11

on the social facilitation phenomenon that are dependent on the characteristic of the individual. For example, there may be a sex difference in the way that the performance changes between the observed and alone conditions. According to Steele's (1998) theory of stereotype threat, negative portrayals of individuals belonging to certain groups, such as ethnic minorities or women, can be internalised to such an extent that this state affects scores on ability tests and athletic performance. For example, the commonly held assumption that women are less spatially aware than

Table 6.4

		N	**Mean rank**	**Sum of ranks**
Alone2-observed2	Negative Ranks	21(a)	12.00	252.00
	Positive Ranks	1(b)	1.00	1.00
	Ties	2(c)		
	Total	24		

a   alone2 < observed2
b   alone2 > observed2
c   alone2 = observed2

Test Statistics(b)

	alone2 – observed2
Z	−4.080(a)
Asymp. Sig. (2-tailed)	.000

a   Based on positive ranks.
b   Wilcoxon Signed-Ranks Test

men can lead to lower performance on tasks that require such ability, like our comparative sizing task. It has been shown that when female participants are primed with negative stereotypes, scores on tests are significantly lower than if the women were led to believe the tests did not reflect these stereotypes (Spencer & Steele, 1999; Ben-Zeev, Fein & Inzlicht, 2005).

Fortunately, as seen in Table 6.5, we already were aware of this effect, and had recorded the sex of our participants along with everything else!

Analysis of Data in Between-Subjects Designs

Data Conforms to Parametric Assumptions
Here we need to look at any differences between male and female participants in the difference data. So our data now looks like that in Table 6.6.

There appears to be a bigger change between observed and alone conditions when the participants are male. Is this a statistically significant difference?

Table 6.5

Sex	Participant	Observed	Alone	D
Male	1	9.5	1	8.5
Male	2	6.5	4	1.5
Female	3	10.5	6.5	4
Male	4	11.5	6.5	5
Male	5	12	4.5	7.5
Male	6	12	4	8
Female	7	3	3	0
Male	8	9.5	7	2.5
Female	9	12	11	1
Female	10	6.5	5	1.5
Male	11	8	2.5	5.5
Female	12	4.5	5	−1.5
Female	13	1	0	1
Male	14	10.5	5	5.5
Male	15	7.5	4	3.5
Male	16	12	8	4
Female	17	10	9	1
Female	18	10.5	7.5	3
Female	19	9	6.5	2.4
Female	20	11	8	3
Female	21	1	1	0
Male	22	12	7	5
Female	23	7	6	1
Male	24	12	9	3

The formula for the t test is

$$t = \frac{\bar{x}_1 - \bar{x}_2}{\sqrt{\frac{\left(\sum (x_1 - \bar{x}_1)^2 + \sum (x_2 - \bar{x}_2)^2\right)}{(n_1 + n_2) - 2} \times \left(\frac{1}{n_1} + \frac{1}{n_2}\right)}}$$

This can be broken down into several simple steps. The top line is the difference between the mean change between conditions for the male and female participants:

$$5.0417 - 1.4583 = 3.5834$$

$$n_1 + n_2 - 2 = 22 \text{ and } \left(\frac{1}{n_1} + \frac{1}{n_2}\right) = 0.16667$$

For our data, these calculations become

$$t = 3.5834 \div \sqrt{((47.73 + 21.23) \div 22) \times 0.16667)}$$
$$= -3.5834 \div \sqrt{0.52243} = 3.5834 \div 0.72279$$
$$= 4.9577$$

Levene's test for equality of variances shows that the F-value of the variances of the two samples is 1.585, which is not significant, therefore there can be assumed to be homogeneity of variance. In this case, t is calculated to be 4.958 with 22 degrees of freedom, which is significant at the 0.05% significance level.

Data Does Not Conform to Parametric Assumptions

We need a test as an alternative to the independent samples t test when the assumption of normality or equality of variance is not met. The usual test to use is the **Mann–Whitney U test**. This, in line with other non-parametric tests, uses the ranks of the data rather than their raw values to calculate the statistic. Since this test does not make a

KT

Table 6.6

Female	Male
4	8.5
0	1.5
1	5
1.5	7.5
−1.5	8
1	2.5
1	5.5
3	5.5
2.4	3.5
3	4
0	5
1	3

distribution assumption, it is not as powerful as the *t* test, but we can test similar hypotheses that the data come from different populations. The Mann–Whitney produces a *U*-value that can be compared with a table of critical values for *U* based on the sample size of each group. If *U* exceeds the critical value for *U* at our significance level (0.05) it means that there is evidence to reject the null hypothesis.

The *U* test is easily calculated by hand, especially for small samples. There are two ways of doing this depending on the size of the sample. Having ranked each sample, we call the sample for which the ranks are smaller, sample 1.

Taking each observation in sample 1, we count the number of observations in sample 2 that are smaller than it (count a half for any that are equal to it). The total of these counts is *U*.

For larger samples, a formula can be used:

1   Arrange all the observations into a single ranked series; that is, rank by disregarding which sample they are in.
2   Add up the ranks in sample 1
3   'U' is then given by: $U = n_1 n_2 + \dfrac{n_1(n_1 + 1)}{2} - R_1$

where n_1 and n_2 are the two sample sizes, and R_1 is the sum of the ranks in sample 1.

For sample sizes greater than 8, a *z*-value can be used to approximate the significance level for the test. In this case, the calculated *z* is compared with the standard normal significance levels. The output from a computer program running the Mann–Whitney *U* test is shown in Table 6.7.

ONE- AND TWO-TAILED *t* TESTS

Hypotheses can indicate the direction of effects. In order to test whether a **directional hypothesis** is supported, a one-tailed test would be carried out. A one- or two-tailed *t* test is determined by whether the total area of α is placed in one tail or divided equally between the two tails. The one-tailed *t* test is performed if the results are relevant only if they turn out in a particular direction. The two-tailed *t* test is performed if the results are relevant in either direction. The choice of a one- or two-tailed *t* test affects the hypothesis testing procedure in a number of different ways.

A two-tailed *t* test divides α in half, placing half in each tail. The null hypothesis in this case is a particular value, and there are two alternative hypotheses, one positive and one negative. The critical value of *t*, t_{crit}, is written with both a plus

Table 6.7

	Sex	N	Mean rank	Sum of ranks
D	Male	12	17.58	211.00
	Female	12	7.42	89.00
	Total	24		

	D
Mann–Whitney U	11.000
Z	–3.536
Asymp. Sig. (2-tailed)	.000

and minus sign (±). For example, the critical value of t when there are 10 degrees of freedom ($df = 10$), and α is set to 0.05, is $t_{crit} = \pm 2.228$.

There are really two different one-tailed t tests, one for each tail. In a one-tailed t test, all the area associated with α is placed in either one tail or the other. Selection of the tail depends upon which direction t_{obs} would be if the results of the experiment came out as expected. The selection of the tail must be made before the experiment is conducted and analysed.

If the t-value were positive and over the critical value, then significance would be found in the two-tailed and the *positive* one-tailed t tests. The one-tailed t test in the negative direction would not be significant, because α was placed in the wrong tail. This is the danger of a one-tailed t test.

If t is negative and above the critical value then significance would only be found in the *negative* one-tailed t test. If the correct direction is selected, it can be seen that one is more likely to reject the null hypothesis. The significance test is said to have greater power in this case.

The selection of a one- or two-tailed t test must be made before the experiment is performed. It is not acceptable practice to find that the t-value is over the critical value and then decide to do a one-tailed test. Readers of published articles are sometimes suspicious when a one-tailed t test is done; the recommendation is that if there is any doubt, a two-tailed test should be done.

Summary

We have looked at the analysis of data derived from simple experimental designs, in which there are two samples of data to consider. Data from simple experiments with a between-subjects design and a within-subjects design were considered. When a between-subjects design is employed and the data conforms to parametric conditions, the independent samples *t* test is appropriate and we have looked at how this is done, together with the alternative analysis when the data does not conform to parametric assumptions, the Mann–Whitney *U* test. We have also looked at what happens when the experiment uses a within-subjects design and examined the appropriate analysis for data conforming to the parametric assumption (the related samples *t* test) and the non-parametric equivalent (the Wilcoxon sign test).

Professor Robert Zajonc

Professor Robert Zajonc studied at the University of Michigan, obtaining his PhD in 1955, and gaining a professorship. He held the positions of Director of the Institute for Social Research and Director of the Research Center for Group Dynamics. In 1994 he joined the faculty at Stanford University, where he is currently Professor Emeritus of Psychology. Professor Zajonc has received a number of honours in recognition of his work in social psychology.

Professor Zajonc's contribution to psychology has been the study of basic processes of social behaviour, and his attempts to show that the relationship between emotion and cognition is a strong one. His research demonstrates that affective influences could take place in the absence of cognitive contributions.

CHAPTER 7

SINGLE FACTORIAL DESIGN: THE LEVELS OF PROCESSING EXPERIMENTS

Contents

Models of memory

Designs with more than two groups

Single factor designs

Analysis of variance
Total sum of squares (SST)
Sum of squares between-groups (SS_B)
Sum of squares within-groups
Post-hoc tests in single factor between-subjects designs

Non-parametric tests in single factor designs
Single factor designs with repeated measures
Non-parametric tests in single factor repeated measures designs

Tests of trend

Summary

Single Factorial Designs: The Levels of Processing Experiments

The whole of science is nothing more than a refinement of everyday thinking.
(Albert Einstein)

Learning Objectives

- To understand what comprises single factorial designs.
- To understand factors and levels.
- To understand the difference between simple designs and factorial designs and why the analysis should be different.
- To understand different components of variability in data.
- To examine the analysis of variance for between- and within-subjects factors.
- To explore the use of non-parametric equivalents of the analysis of variance tests.
- To introduce ways of exploring the effects and trends indicated by analysis of variance.

KEY TERMS

- Analysis of variance
- Factor and factorial
- Friedman test
- Kruskal–Wallis test
- Levels
- Partitions
- Post-hoc tests – Tukey, Bonferroni
- Sums of squares/sum of squared deviations
- Variability – total, between and within/error

Carrying out simple experiments means that we can compare two conditions with each other. If the two conditions are only different by one element, then we can say that this element has had an effect. However, very little in psychology can be established, beyond doubt, with one simple experiment. It is usual to find that researchers carry out a series of simple experiments, as we saw with the social facilitation phenomenon in the last chapter, or that they utilise more than two conditions in an experiment. This expansion of the simple two-condition design means that we can compare data from several conditions in the same experiment, but it does change the analysis required. To demonstrate this, let us look at a well-known cognitive event.

MODELS OF MEMORY

Prior to 1972 the accepted models of memory were those that depicted it as several interrelated but separate stores. Such models suggested that the characteristics of a memory are determined by its location. Short-term memory (STM) was a transient, easily disrupted memory trace in a short-term storage location, and long-term memory (LTM) was more durable and stored in a different location. In 1972, Craik and Lockhart suggested that this was too complicated a model and postulated a simpler one of length and type of storage depending upon the amount of processing that a memory had been subjected to on encoding. Items which had received more elaborate processing would tend to be easier to store, and subsequently recall, than those which had undergone less elaborate rehearsal (called maintenance rehearsal). Hence a fragile memory trace is produced by shallow processing, such as that based on superficial characteristics, and a more durable memory trace by deep processing (e.g. based on the meaning of a word). So, according to this framework, information that, for example, involves strong visual images or many associations with existing knowledge will be processed at a deeper level. There is a strong link to theories of attention too, as information that is attended to receives more processing than others. The theory also supports the hypothesis that we remember things that are meaningful to us because this requires more processing and forms more associations. There are many ways that the levels of processing framework has been applied. Perfetti (1976) extended it to language comprehension. He proposed seven levels: acoustic, phonological, syntactic, semantic, referential, thematic and functional. The first levels are normally unconscious, while the fourth level (semantic) is the conscious interpretation of the utterance or sentence. Processing of the last three levels is dependent on context and lack of ambiguity.

The difficulty with the theory, as with many in psychology, is that processing of information at different levels is unconscious and automatic unless we attend to that level. We are normally not aware of the sensory properties of stimuli unless we are asked specifically to identify such information. For example, how hard is the chair you are sitting on? It is unlikely to be something you had even thought about until that moment.

If this process, at many of its levels, is unconscious, how can we go about testing the theory of its existence? When Craik and Lockhart proposed their framework, Hyde and Jenkins (1973) carried out a series of experiments that confirmed the depth of processing hypothesis: 'deeper processing leads to more durable memory traces'. Hyde and Jenkins used a series of classical incidental learning experiments in which they manipulated the characteristics of the orienting task, that is the way in which subjects were directed to focus (or not) on items to be remembered. They found that subjects given tasks that required meaningful or semantic manipulations of the words, but no instructions to learn, recalled lists of words as well as subjects given explicit instructions to memorise the materials.

Let us consider the design of such an experiment if we were to carry it out today (Table 7.1). This may be one of the standard types of experiment students will perform as part of a cognitive psychology module, so it is worth being familiar with it.

Four groups of participants are given different kinds of orienting tasks and then given a surprise recall test. Their performance is compared with a group that was given explicit instructions to memorise the materials. This experiment allows us to test the hypothesis that deeper processing, processing involving accessing and manipulating the meanings of words, leads to recall performance that is equal to the performance of participants given intentional instructions to learn. Intention to learn, therefore, should not determine recall performance. What is critical is the kind of cognitive operations that participants perform on the material.

We would need to collect a list of nouns that have high ratings of concreteness, meaningfulness and imagery. There are several lists available, but a commonly used set is that compiled by Paivio, Yuille and Madigan in 1968, in which concreteness was defined in terms of directness of reference to sense experience, meaningfulness in terms of the mean number of written associations in 30 seconds, and imagery in terms of the word's capacity to arouse non-verbal images.

Table 7.1   Orienting tasks that could be used in a levels of processing experiment

Letter counting (three times through the list)	1 Counting and recording the number of letters in each word 2 Counting and recording the number of consonants in each word 3 Counting and recording the number of letters in each word coming before the letter M in the alphabet
Rhyming (three times through the list)	1 Finding a word that rhymes with each of the words in turn, saying it out loud 2 and 3 Repeat with different rhyme
Adjective adding (three times through the list)	1 Finding a suitable modifying adjective for each of the words in turn, saying it out loud 2 and 3 Repeat with different adjective
Imagery	Attempting to form an image of each of the words in turn. These images are to be rated on 5-point scale, ranging from 1 (no image at all) to 5 (the image is perfectly clear and as vivid as normal vision)
Control (intentional)	Working systematically through the pack, attempting to learn as many words as possible. Repeated three times

So we have a reasonably large (around 30) set of words arranged in random order. We need four orienting tasks. These could be letter counting, rhyming, adjective adding and imagery. Remember that there is also a control condition in which the subjects will intentionally work through the list learning as many words as they can by whatever strategy they wish to use.

So our design is such that we have five groups of subjects, each of whom has carried out different tasks on the same list of words; then the subjects are asked to recall them. Each group comprises different people so the design is between subjects. However, we have five groups of people, and need to compare the scores of each against the other four. This is not the same as the simple design we looked at in the last chapter.

DESIGNS WITH MORE THAN TWO GROUPS

We have looked at experimental designs in which we set up a comparison between two sets of data in either a repeated or independent measures design. However, it may be somewhat simplistic to investigate some of the effects in which we might be interested in psychology in this way. We cannot say that comparing two task groups in the memory performance experiment tells us the effect that levels of processing might have. The depth of processing hypothesis is very clearly much more complex than that – remember, Perfetti suggests a minimum of seven levels! Depth of processing is actually a more complex **factor** than just a comparison of two groups. The more common experimental design in psychology is termed **factorial**, looking at the effect of one or more factors on another variable.

The **analysis of variance** analyses the relation between a dependent variable and one (or more) factor(s). The one-way ANOVA compares means for two or more factor levels taking into account the variance amongst the groups of data. It may seem reasonable just to do several pairs of t tests. However, if we carry out several t tests it is more likely that some of these tests will give significant results just by pure chance. Each test has a certain significance level indicating the probability of making a Type I error. If we carry out more and more tests with an associated alpha, then alpha becomes compounded, and the probability of making a Type I error rises in line with the formula

$$p_{\text{Type I error}} = 1 - (1 - \alpha)^c$$

where α is the significance level, and c is the number of tests we need to carry out. So if we had an alpha of 0.05, and were carrying out three tests, then the probability of making a Type I error would become

$$P = 1 - (1 - 0.05)^3 = 1 - (0.95)^3 = 1 - (0.857) = 0.143$$

This is quite different from 0.05!

In our levels of processing experiment, with five levels to be compared, we would have to carry out 10 tests in order to compare each level with every one of the others, and the probability would become

$$P = 1 - (1 - 0.05)^{10} = 1 - (0.95)^{10} = 1 - 0.5867 = 0.4133$$

Instead of carrying out multiple tests of comparisons of two sets of data, we can do one test that compares all of the groups together. The value of doing this becomes very clear when we have more than one factor to consider, but for now let us look at how we do this analysis with one factor.

Table 7.2 Data from a levels of processing experiment

Orienting task	Control	Counting	Rhyming	Adjective	Imagery
	27	17	20	25	27
	24	11	23	29	25
	22	16	20	23	24
	28	15	17	28	30
	25	14	18	27	28
Mean	25.2	14.6	19.6	26.4	26.8
Variance	5.7	5.3	5.3	5.8	5.7

SINGLE FACTOR DESIGNS

Single factor designs investigate the effect of one factor on the dependent variable. A factor is something which may be thought to have an effect and which has more than two levels. When investigating this effect experimentally we design an independent variable from the factor and manipulate three or more conditions. The test used in ANOVA compares the variation (measured by items related to the variance) *between* the levels of the factor with the variation *within* the groups. Variation within groups can happen simply because we have individual differences, or there may be measurement errors. The ANOVA accounts for this and compares the two types of variation in a ratio. If the between variation is much larger than the within variation, the means of different conditions will not be equal. If the between and within variations are approximately the same size, then there will be no significant difference between the levels.

Therefore, our levels of processing experiment lends itself to this type of analysis (Table 7.2). We have five sets of scores on the recall test, which, if our hypothesis is to be supported, should be different. What we want to know is whether the variation between the levels or conditions is significantly larger than the variation within the groups, namely the variation that is due simply to individual differences or measurement error.

ANALYSIS OF VARIANCE

The ANOVA is a parametric test, which means we need to check if the data conforms to the assumptions. Scores on tests such as a memory recall test can be

Table 7.3 One-sample Kolmogorov–Smirnov test

Most extreme differences	Absolute	0.136
	Positive	0.092
	Negative	−0.136
Kolmogorov–Smirnov Z		0.681
Asymp.sig. (two-tailed)		0.743

Table 7.4 Test of homogeneity of variances

Levene statistic	df_1	df_2	P
0.038	4	20	0.997

regarded as interval, even though they are not strictly continuous. For example, if someone scores 10 on the test, they have scored half as many as someone scoring 20, so we can carry out arithmetic manipulations that are meaningful. Can we also assume that this data comes from a normal distribution? Note that it is not the sample scores which have to be normally distributed, but the population of scores from which they are drawn. There is no data available about the distribution of memory test performance in the population. However, the sample here is normally distributed, as the Kolmogorov–Smirnov test (Table 7.3) comparing it with the normal distribution is *not* significant (see Chapter 4).

The other assumption to be considered is that there is homogeneity of variance (Table 7.4). Looking at the variances of each sample, we can see that they are different from each other, but not too dissimilar. Levene's test for homogeneity of variance would not show that they are significantly different. The analysis of variance is robust enough to withstand violation of this assumption, as long as the sample sizes are equal.

From Table 7.2 we can see that the means are different, but it is not enough simply to state this. We need to take into account the variation in the data, and we do this by calculating the sum of squared deviations usually abbreviated to sum of squares (SS). We need the SS within the groups and between the groups, together with the total sums of squares. The sum of squares is found by the formula

$$SS = \sum (x - \bar{x})^2$$

This may look vaguely familiar. In fact, if we divide the sum of squares by the degrees of freedom we find the variance, which of course is the square of the standard deviation.

There is an alternative formula for the SS which, when the scores are substituted in, gives the same value, and is actually a little easier to calculate by hand, but is intuitively less clear:

$$SS = \sum x^2 - \frac{\left(\sum x\right)^2}{n}$$

KT

The variation in the set of scores, represented by sums of squares, comprises a *total* variation, which is **partitioned** into that for the between and within variation. Partitioning simply means that the amount of variation in a set of data has various sources, and the variance can be separated out into the variation due to different causes.

Total Sum of Squares (SS$_T$)

This is the sum of the squared deviations of each case in the total set of scores from the mean of that set. The total sample mean is calculated by summing all cases and dividing by the sample size, in our example:

$$\bar{x}_{\text{total}} = 563 \div (5 + 5 + 5 + 5 + 5) = 22.52$$

$$SS_T = \sum (x - \bar{x})^2 = (27 - 22.52)^2 + (24 - 22.52)^2 + \cdots$$
$$+ (28 - 22.52)^2 = 670.24$$

Sum of Squares Between Groups (SS$_B$)

This is the sum of the squared deviations of *each* group mean from the total scores mean. Each squared deviation is first weighted by the sample size. Therefore, we calculate four means, one for each condition (Table 7.5).

That is,

$$SS_B = \sum N_G (\bar{x}_G - \bar{x}_{\text{total}})^2$$
$$= 5(25.2 - 22.52)^2 + 5(14.6 - 22.52)^2 + 5(19.6 - 22.52)^2$$
$$+ 5(26.4 - 22.52)^2 + 5(26.8 - 22.52)^2$$
$$= 559.04$$

Table 7.5   Means from each condition

Control	25.2
Count	14.6
Rhyme	19.6
Adjective	26.4
Imagery	26.8

where N_G is the number in each group, and is the weight applied to each squared deviation. $\bar{x}_G$ is each group mean.

Sum of Squares Within Groups SS$_W$

The sum of squares within groups (SS$_W$) is also called SS$_E$ where E stands for error. It represents the variability due to error or variation inside each group rather than between the groups. It is calculated by finding the sum of squared deviations of each case from its group's mean. So each score has the mean of the group to which it belongs subtracted and the result is squared, then all of these are added together.

A point to note at this stage is that SS$_T$ should always be the sum of SS$_B$ and SS$_W$, and you can check your calculations this way. Alternatively, and even better, it means we only need work out two values to find the third:

$$SS_T = SS_B + SS_W$$

Therefore:

$$
\begin{aligned}
SS_W &= SS_T - SS_B \\
&= 670.24 - 559.04 \\
&= 111.2
\end{aligned}
$$

We need to scale our calculated sums of squares so that they can be compared with a standard point of reference, regardless of the sizes of the samples or the numbers of groups we are comparing. This is done by dividing each sum of squares by its associated degrees of freedom. Remember that the degrees of freedom are an adjustment based on the number of items in a calculation. A division by the degrees of freedom produces indices of within- and between-subjects variability unaffected by sample size and number of means being compared. The resulting quantity to be used to test the null hypothesis is the **mean square** (MS):

$$MS = \frac{SS}{df}$$

Dividing by the degrees of freedom serves to standardise the sum of squares.

Each sum of squares of deviations has associated with it a degree of freedom. The three sums of squares we have considered so far have degrees of freedom as follows:

- Between-samples sum of squares: number of samples − 1 ($k-1$).
- Within-samples sum of squares: total number of observations − number of samples ($N-k$).
- Total sum of squares: total number of observations − 1 ($N-k137$).

Note the general rule that the degrees of freedom for the total sum of squares is the sum of the degrees of freedom for its two component sums of squares, in the same way as the partitioned sums of squares add up to the total sum of squares.

So, the next step after calculating the sums of squares is to divide each of the partitioned sums of square by the degrees of freedom to find the Mean Squares. The mean square derived from the SS_W (or SS_E) is also called the Mean Square error (MS_E). MS_E indicates the degree of accuracy with which the means were estimated, and gives an unbiased estimate of the variance, as it is the mean of the squares of all the errors. SS_B is divided by $k-1$ where k is the number of groups, and the SS_E is divided by $N-k$ where N is the total number of cases in the sample.

Here

$$MS_B = 559.04 \div (5-1) = 139.76$$
$$MS_E = 111.2 \div (25-5) = 5.56$$

Now, remember the point of ANOVA: it is to find out whether the variation between the groups is bigger than the variation within the groups. What we are calculating is an F-ratio by dividing the MS_B by MS_E:

$$F = 139.76 \div 5.56$$
$$= 25.137$$

Table 7.6   ANOVA source table

	Sum of squares	df	Mean square	F
Between groups	559.04	4	139.76	25.137
Within groups	111.2	20	5.56	
Total	670.24	24		

Conventionally the results of the ANOVA are summarised into a source table (Table 7.6).

F-values have a sampling distribution in the same way as any other statistic. To find the value to which we are comparing our computed value, we must know the degrees of freedom for the *F*-ratio. The *df* numerator is the degrees of freedom for the effect. The *df* denominator is the error. Therefore, the degrees of freedom for the *F*-ratio for the factor orienting tasks are 4 and 16. Using these, the critical value is found for our chosen significance level. For $\alpha = 0.05$ with our degrees of freedom the critical value is 2.8661 (at $\alpha = 0.01$ it is 4.431). Therefore, our statistic falls well outside the rejection region, so the null hypothesis, that different orienting tasks, representing different levels of processing, do not lead to significantly different scores on the recall test, is rejected. The conventional way of reporting this in research is to give the *F*-ratio and the degrees of freedom, followed by the MS_E and a statement of whether the probability of the finding is greater or less than the significance level:

$$F_{(4,20)} = 25.137, MS_E = 5.56, p < 0.05, F_{critical} = 2.8661$$

This is a clear finding, but does not tell us if any one of the conditions is significantly different from any other. The null hypothesis that the ANOVA tests is referred to as an 'omnibus hypothesis' which simply states that there will be no effect of the factor(s) on the dependent variable. If this omnibus null hypothesis were accepted then we would need do nothing more, but if rejected, we need to examine the omnibus alternative hypothesis, and we might want to do some further investigation of the data, called **post-hoc tests.**

KT

Our levels of processing hypothesis does indeed state that there is not just a difference, but that 'deeper processing leads to more durable memory traces'. The theory goes even further and states that the memory traces resulting from deeper processing will be no worse and possibly better than those resulting from intentional learning with no orienting tasks. So we need to check that our orienting tasks for deeper processing (adjective production and image production) show better recall performance than the more superficial characteristic matching tasks (counting and rhyming) and whether any of these are different from our **control group**. We can examine the means and this does definitely demonstrate the effects we were expecting. We know that the effect of the types of orienting tasks on recall performance is significant, but we do not know which tasks are significantly different from each other.

Post-hoc Tests in Single Factor Between-Subjects Designs

When the analysis of variance is significant and the null hypothesis is rejected, the only valid inference that can be made is that at least one mean is different from at least one other mean. The ANOVA does not reveal which means differ from which others. However, we cannot simply go ahead and perform paired comparisons such as the *t* test, as we are still in danger of making a Type I error. Remember that the probability that a single significance test will result in a Type I error is raised in proportion to the number of comparisons made. This is called the experiment-wise error rate (EER). Statisticians differ in their views of how strictly the EER must be controlled. Some post-hoc statistical procedures provide strict control over the EER, whereas others control it to a lesser extent. When carrying out post-hoc tests on a significant ANOVA it may be best to be quite conservative with respect to the Type I error.

The 'Honestly Significantly Different' (HSD) test proposed by the statistician John Tukey is based on what is called the studentised range distribution. To test all pair-wise comparisons among means using the Tukey HSD, compute the studentised *t*-value (t_s) for each pair of means using the formula

$$t_s = \frac{\text{mean}_1 - \text{mean}_2}{\sqrt{\dfrac{MSE}{\text{mean sample size}}}}$$

The critical value of t_s is determined from the distribution of the studentised range. The number of means in the experiment is used in the determination of the critical value, and this critical value is used for all comparisons among means. Typically, the largest mean is compared with the smallest mean first. If that

Table 7.5 (Repeated) Means from each condition

Control	25.2
Count	14.6
Rhyme	19.6
Adjective	26.4
Imagery	26.8

difference is not significant, no other comparisons will be significant either, so the calculations are halted.

The Tukey HSD procedure keeps the EER at the specified significance level. This is a great advantage. This advantage comes at a cost, however, as the Tukey HSD is less powerful than other methods of testing all pair-wise comparisons.

In our example, the means are as given previously in Table 7.5 and the difference between the biggest mean and the smallest mean is

$$26.8 - 14.6 = 12.2$$

We also know that the MSE is 5.56 and the mean of the sample sizes is 5, 50

$$HSD = \frac{12.2}{\sqrt{\dfrac{5.56}{5}}} = 11.569$$

The critical value of the studentised t for five means and error degrees of freedom of 4 at the 0.05 significance level is 7.0528, so there is a significant difference between the imagery and the counting tasks. We need to carry on and determine the significance of the difference between all pairs of means (Table 7.7).

Table 7.7 Mean differences of the levels of processing

	Counting	Rhyming	Adjective	Imagery
Control	10.6*	5.6	−1.2	−1.6
Counting		−5	−11.8*	−12.2*
Rhyming			−6.8	−7.2*
Adjective				−0.4

Table 7.5a Means sorted into ascending order

Count	14.6
Rhyme	19.6
Control	25.2
Adjective	26.4
Imagery	26.8

Those marked* in Table 7.7 are bigger than the critical value and so indicate a significant difference. Our more complex hypothesis that goes beyond the omnibus hypothesis of effect and specifies the differences between levels can be examined. The control condition has led to better recall than the counting condition, so has the adjective and imagery conditions. Imagery is also better than rhyming. However, neither adjective nor imagery is significantly different from the control condition.

Listing the means from Table 7.5 in size order and interpreting the significant mean differences shows us that the levels of processing hypothesis is supported (Table 7.5a).

An alternative way to carry out post-hoc tests after a one-way ANOVA is to use **Bonferroni's correction** adjustment or, which is used if we want to keep the experiment-wise error rate to a specified level (usually $\alpha = 0.05$). A simple way of doing this is to divide the acceptable α level by the number of comparisons we intend to make. In the above example, if six pair-wise comparisons are to be made and we want to keep the overall experiment-wise error rate to 5%, we will evaluate each of our pair-wise comparisons against 0.05 divided by 6. That is, for any one comparison to be considered significant, the obtained *p*-value would have to be less than 0.0083 – and not 0.05. This obviously makes it harder to claim a significant result and, in so doing, decreases the chance of making a Type I error to very acceptable levels.

Bonferroni's correction is becoming more common with computer programs in which exact probabilities are calculated, as tables rarely allow for very small significance levels.

NON-PARAMETRIC TESTS IN SINGLE FACTOR DESIGNS

The choice between parametric and non-parametric tests is the same as in simple designs. Overall, the *F* test used in ANOVA is highly robust to deviations from

Table 7.8 Ranked levels of processing data

Control	Rank	Counting	Rank	Rhyming	Rank	Adjective	Rank	Imagery	Rank
22	10	11	1	17	5.5	23	11.5	24	13.5
24	13.5	14	2	18	7	25	16	25	16
25	16	15	3	20	8.5	27	19	27	19
27	19	16	4	20	8.5	28	22	28	22
28	22	17	5.5	23	11.5	29	24	30	25
Sum of ranks	80.5		15.5		41		92.5		95.5
Mean rank	16.1		3.4		8.2		18.5		19.1

normality with skewness having little effect. However, very high or low kurtosis in the distribution does tend to inflate or deflate the F-value respectively. It is also assumed that the variances in the different groups of the design are identical. At the beginning of our analysis, we computed the error variance by adding up the sums of squares within each group. If the variances in the two groups are different from each other, then adding the two together is not appropriate, and will not yield an estimate of the common within-groups variance (since no common variance exists). However, statisticians agree that the F statistic is quite robust against violations of this assumption. The only assumption that we cannot violate and continue to use ANOVA with confidence is that the data is interval or equivalent. So, what if we have carried out all the ANOVAs erroneously? In fact, what if we should not have been doing this at all, because all of our parametric assumptions have been violated, particularly the interval-level data need? There are alternatives to ANOVA when we think that we would be better employed carrying out non-parametric tests.

KT

The **Kruskal–Wallis test** is the non-parametric equivalent of the one-way ANOVA. It tests whether several independent samples are from the same population, assumes that the underlying variable has a continuous distribution, and requires an ordinal level of measurement.

We could carry out a Kruskal–Wallis on the data from the levels of processing experiment if we were unsure that the data met parametric assumptions.

The Kruskal–Wallis test is very similar in computational terms to the Mann–Whitney U test (see Chapter 5). The group of data is placed into one set which can be ranked from highest to lowest and tied ranks are dealt with appropriately. The resulting ranks are then replaced into the groups, as shown in Table 7.8.

However, this is where the Kruskal–Wallis starts to diverge from the Mann–Whitney – we need not only the sums of the ranks in each group, but also the mean rank.

Some statisticians call the Kruskal–Wallis test a non-parametric ANOVA or ANOVA by ranks. This is not strictly accurate, but there are some resemblances. In both, the first step is to find an aggregate measure of the degree to which the group means differ. With ANOVA that measure is found in the SS_B, in the Kruskal–Wallis test the group means are based on ranks rather than on the raw measures. So let us call this SS_R. It is equivalent to a sum of squares, but a little less tedious to calculate. In fact all we need to do is to find the difference between the mean rank for each group and the mean of the whole group, square these differences, and add them all together.

The formula for the sum of squared ranks is

$$SS_R = \sum \left(\frac{T_g^2}{n_g} \right) - \frac{T_{all}^2}{N}$$

where T_g is the sum of the ranks of any group and n_g the size of each group, and T_{all} is the sum of all the ranks.

In our example this becomes

$$SS_R = (6480.25/5) + (240.25/5) + (1681/5) + (8556.25/5) - (9120.25/5)$$
$$= 1298.53$$

The null hypothesis that Kruskal–Wallis tests is that in several independent samples of ranked data the mean ranks of the k groups will not significantly differ. We might assume then that if the null hypothesis were true then SS_R would be zero. But, this cannot be so.

! represents 'factorial' – a mathematical function where the main number is multiplied by itself minus 1, by itself minus 2, and so on until we reach 1.

Consider the very simple case where there are three groups, each containing two observations. If you were to sort these six observations into every possible combination of two ranks per group, you would find the total number of possible combinations to be 90:

$$\frac{n!}{n1!n2!n3!} = \frac{6 \times 5 \times 4 \times 3 \times 2 \times 1}{2 \times 1 \times 2 \times 1 \times 2 \times 1}$$

If we worked out all the values of SS_R for these 90 combinations we would have a sampling distribution of SS_R for this set of data. Of these 90 only a few would yield values equal to zero; all the rest would be greater than zero. The mean of this sampling distribution is the value that observed values of SS_R will tend towards if the null hypothesis is true and it is not zero. The mean of the sampling distribution of SS_R is given by the formula

$$(k - 1)\frac{n(n + 1)}{12}$$

For our main example, we therefore know that the observed value of SS_R belongs to a sampling distribution whose mean is equal to

$$(4 - 1)\frac{25(25 + 1)}{12} = 216.67$$

So how do we turn that into an estimate of probability? The Kruskal–Wallis statistic is a ratio symbolised by H: the numerator of this ratio is the observed value of SS_R and the denominator includes a portion of the above formula for the mean of the sampling distribution. That is

$$H = \frac{SS_R}{n(n + 1)/12}$$

We can even break that down a little further. Rather than working out SS_R we can construct it directly from the table of mean ranks, so that the direct formula for H is as follows:

$$H = \frac{12}{n(n + 1)}\left(\sum \frac{R_g^2}{n_g}\right) - 3(n + 1)$$

where R_g is the sum of the ranks of a group of data and n_g is the number of values in that group, and n is the total number of values in the experiment. Thus

$$H = (12/25(26))(80.5^2/5 + \ldots + 95.5^2/5) - (3 \times 26)$$
$$= 18.401$$

When each of the k samples includes at least five observations the sampling distribution of H is a very close approximation of the chi-square distribution for $df = k-1$. We can even be confident enough to use it when one of the samples includes as few as three observations. If we relate our value of H to the chi-square distribution with $df = k-1 = 4$, the critical value is 11.14329, so the value of H is significant and we reject the null hypothesis.

The above example employs a between-subjects design, but we know that this has certain problems associated with it. For example, differences in memory with such small sample sizes might be due to individual differences rather than the conditions. An alternative design would be to employ repeated measures. With the advent of computers the levels of processing experiment is sometimes done this way, as words can be presented randomly with accompanying questions about the word. The random presentation overcomes one of the difficulties with repeated measures design, the **fatigue effect**. The repeated measure design overcomes the issue of individual differences.

Single Factor Designs with Repeated Measures

Repeated measures, or within-subjects designs, means that every participant takes part in all conditions. This reduces the effect of individual differences, but brings about other issues, in that there may be order effects. The order in which conditions are experienced or stimuli are presented may influence the results of the experiment. This could be due to

a) fatigue – the longer participants spend on doing the experiment the more tired they get, or they lose motivation and attention starts to stray
b) practise effects – the more they do something, the better the participants get at doing it.

There are some simple ways of dealing with order effects. The first is **counterbalancing**. Counterbalancing means using every possible combination of orders

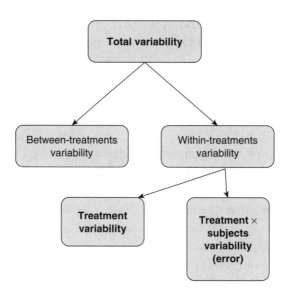

Figure 7.1   Partitioning the sum of squares in a repeated measures design

of the conditions so that every condition can appear equally often in any order. So, for example, an experiment with two conditions, 1 & 2, will be presented to the first participant in the order 1 then 2, to the second participants 2 then 1 and so on. The number of ways of combining the conditions depends on the number of conditions.

The repeated measures ANOVA follows the logic of that for between-subjects quite closely, but with some very important differences. The same participants appear in all conditions so the variance partitioning is slightly different (Figure 7.1). In the between-subjects ANOVA we partition the variance into that due to differences within groups and that attributed to differences between groups, and then compare the ratio. In a repeated measures ANOVA we can calculate the individual variability of participants as the same people take part in each condition, which means we can partition more of the error (or within-condition) variance. The variance due to differences between individuals is not helpful for deciding whether there is a difference between conditions. If we can calculate it we can subtract it from the error variance and then compare the ratio of error variance with that attributed to changes in the independent variable across conditions (see Figure 7.1). So repeated measures allow us to compare the variance in the independent variable to a more accurate error term which has had the variance due to differences in individuals removed from it. This increases the power of the analysis and means that fewer participants are needed in order to have adequate power.

Table 7.9 Another set of conditions in the levels of processing experiment

Condition	Example
Control	No questions
Rhyming	Does mouse rhyme with house?
Synonym	Does mouse mean the same as rat?
Self-referent	Does 'tall' describe you?

In 1986 Solman and Rosen demonstrated that the levels of processing experiment can be carried out using a repeated measures design. They presented words in six levels of orientation (knowledge, comprehension, application, analysis, synthesis or evaluation) and found that their design was a successful way of testing the levels of processing hypothesis. In 1984, Bellezza demonstrated that the self-referent effect, in which participants are asked if words can be applied to themselves, produces much better recall effects than other types of cues. So the levels of processing hypothesis can be further refined from that in our between-subjects design above to include a self-reference condition. A repeated measures (or within-subjects) design overcomes some of the difficulties that a between-subjects design has.

So, let us assume that we have carried out the levels of processing experiment again, but with repeated measures on five participants. Each participant sees 10 words in each condition, randomly presented. Each condition orients the attention to a non-directed learning task, a rhyming task, a task in which the participant is asked if the word is like something else, and in the final one, participants are asked if the word describes them. The answers the participants give are recorded but are not relevant as it is only the amount of processing that they give which is important (Table 7.9).

At the end of the run the participant writes down all the words that can be remembered and the score for each condition is noted (Table 7.10).

Again, we need the sum of squares for each partition of the variability using whichever formula for the SS that you prefer.

Check that you can work out each of the variabilities here. The first partition is due to the levels of the independent variable. The calculation is equivalent to the between-groups variability in a between-subjects ANOVA. So for this data the variability due to conditions is the sum of the variability within each condition. However, this variability is not a measure of error but a measure of the effect of the independent variable, as the participants have remained the same but the

Table 7.10 Data from a repeated measures levels of processing experiment

Participant	Control	Rhyming	Synonym	Self-referent	Mean for each participant
1	5	6	8	9	7
2	2	4	7	9	5.5
3	1	3	6	7	4.25
4	2	3	7	8	5
5	3	4	8	7	5.5
Mean	2.6	4	7.2	8	5.45
Deviation	−2.85	−1.45	1.75	2.55	
Squared deviation	8.1225	2.1025	3.0625	6.5025	19.79

independent variable has altered with the condition. It is the sum of the squared deviations of each participant's mean from the overall mean, multiplied by the number of conditions.

It is also important in the repeated measures design to calculate the variation caused by individual variability; that is, how the five participants in this study differ in the way they give the scores. This calculation was not encountered in the between-subjects ANOVA but the principles remain the same.

To calculate individual variability we still use the sum of squares formula, but now it is the sum of the squared deviations of each participant's score from his or her own mean. We calculate the overall score of each participant and insert that into the sum of squares formula with the participant's mean. This is further partitioned into that due to the error found by subtracting each participant's mean from the score in each condition.

In order to construct the summary table we need to know the degrees of freedom so that we can turn these variabilities into mean squares (MS). The total degrees of freedom is as in the between-subjects ANOVA (Table 7.11). The number of degrees of freedom for individuals is the number of participants minus one, and for conditions it is the number of conditions minus one. The residual degrees of freedom are the total minus the sum of the degrees of freedom from individuals and conditions:

The mean squares are then calculated by dividing the variability by the degrees of freedom (Table 7.12).

To calculate the F statistic we need to discard the estimate of individual variability of subjects. This is part of the error variance which we cannot control for in a between-subjects ANOVA, but which we can measure in a repeated measures

Table 7.11 Degrees of freedom in repeated measures ANOVA

df total	=	$N-1$
df factor	=	$k-1$
df error	=	$N-k$

Table 7.12 Within-subjects ANOVA source table

Source	Sum of squares	df	Mean square	F	Sig.
ORIENT	98.950	3	32.983	68.241	0.000
Error (ORIENT)	5.800	12	0.483		

design. What we are looking for is whether our independent variable which changes on different conditions has an effect on a participant's performance. The F-ratio we are interested in is, therefore,

$$\frac{MS_{\text{conditions}}}{MS_{\text{error}}}$$

Again we need to go to a table of F-values with our degrees of freedom, where we find that the F-ratio is significant at the 0.05 level so we reject the null hypothesis.

There is also a non-parametric equivalent of the repeated measures ANOVA.

Non-parametric Tests in Single Factor Repeated Measures Designs

KT

The **Friedman test** tests the null hypothesis that k related variables come from the same population. For each case, the k variables are ranked from 1 to k. The test statistic is based on these ranks, so the test is used when the data can be order/ranked and the assumptions of the ANOVA may be violated.

The Friedman test is actually a special kind of χ^2 and the resulting statistic is checked against a χ^2 distribution.

If our calculated value were to exceed the critical value derived from the table the null hypothesis would be rejected. Sometimes a non-parametric test returns a significant result when the parametric would not, again reflecting the difference in power of the two categories of test.

TESTS OF TREND

When using ANOVA, we are looking at the case of significant main effects, and often need to examine the data and results a little more closely. However, even tests such as Tukey's HSD do not tell us the whole story. With a main effect on one factor it is sometimes necessary to examine the hypothesis that the means of several sets of data lie in a particular direction, or that they show a **trend**. With interaction effects this becomes even more complicated, and their interpretation can be complex to determine what exactly has happened within the data, and where any effects and/or trends lie. This section will examine other ways we have available to interpret data once a significant result has been obtained in ANOVA.

KT

There are several tests of trend that we can carry out. Page's test is used when we need to carry out multiple comparisons among related data sets to determine if they are in a predicted order. It is also known as Page's trend test or Page's L test and is carried out in the same circumstances as a one-way within-subjects (or repeated measures) ANOVA, when that test has shown a significant main effect of the factor. So, the circumstances under which it would be done are:

- There are three or more levels of a factor.
- The factor has a within-subjects design (the participants are all observed in each level).
- We can predict that the observations will have a particular order.

Let us return to our single factor repeated measures design, testing the depth of processing hypotheses. Remember the hypothesis here is that various orienting tasks lead participants to process words to be recalled in different ways, leading to different levels of processing, and the depth of processing will have an effect on the later recall of those words. We have five participants all of whom have recalled words under all of the different conditions, and we have the mean recall for these conditions and the mean per participant across the conditions (Table 7.13).

Page's test is a test of the significance of the trend across conditions, so it tests the null hypothesis that, for n conditions,

$$\text{mean}_1 = \text{mean}_2 = \text{mean}_3 = \ldots = \text{mean}_n$$

and the experimental (alternative) hypothesis that

$$\text{mean}_1 < \text{mean}_2 < \text{mean}_3 < \ldots < \text{mean}_n$$

Table 7.13

Participant	Control	Rhyming	Synonym	Self-referent	Mean for each participant
1	5	6	8	9	7
2	2	4	7	9	5.5
3	1	3	6	7	4.25
4	2	3	7	8	5
5	3	4	8	7	5.5
Mean	2.6	4	7.2	8	5.45
Deviation	−2.85	−1.45	1.75	2.55	
Squared deviation	8.1225	2.1025	3.0625	6.5025	19.79

Table 7.14

Participant	Control	Rank	Rhyming	Rank	Synonym	Rank	Self-referent	Rank
1	5	9	6	10.5	8	17	9	19.5
2	2	2.5	4	7.5	7	13.5	9	19.5
3	1	1	3	5	6	10.5	7	13.5
4	2	2.5	3	5	7	13.5	8	17
5	3	5	4	7.5	8	17	7	13.5
Mean	2.6		4		7.2		8	
Condition rank	1		2		3		4	
Rank totals		20		35.5		71.5		83
Condition rank × rank total		20		71		214.5		332

To carry out Page's test, the means should be arranged in the order which is predicted by the hypothesis and each of them assigned a rank (Table 7.14), and for each of the participants separately each score is ranked (tied ranks getting the mid-point of the ranks).

Each column of ranks is summed, multiplied by the corresponding condition rank, then each of these products is summed to find L; here this is 637.5, which is significant.

Page's test is most often used with small numbers of conditions and participants. If we had carried out our levels of processing experiment with a between-subjects (or independent measures) design, and needed to see if there was a predicted trend in the result, then the equivalent to Page's trend test is Jonckheere's trend test.

Table 7.15

Orienting task	Control	Counting	Rhyming	Adjective	Imagery
	27	17	20	25	27
	24	11	23	29	25
	22	16	20	23	24
	28	15	17	28	30
	25	14	18	27	28
Mean	25.2	14.6	19.6	26.4	26.8
Variance	5.7	5.3	5.3	5.8	5.7

In order to use Jonckheere's test for trend, the design of the experiment must be between-subjects, and there should be equal numbers of participants in each condition. Additionally the data must be ordinal level or better, and, as with Page's test, we must be able to order the conditions before the experiment. So, let us consider the result of the levels of processing experiment with between-subjects design (Table 7.15).

The first thing to do is to arrange the data in each group in order of the prediction. For each data value the number of scores that are greater than it in each of the following groups is counted and placed in the table, then the totals of the ranked scores for each column are calculated.

As can be seen, this test rapidly becomes quite complex and SPSS only includes it in the more advanced software installations. Interpreting a one-way ANOVA with between-subjects designs is probably best stopped at the pair-wise comparison stage!

Summary

The levels of processing framework was proposed in order to suggest a new, general approach to the study of memory. Craik and Lockhart never intended to refute the idea of different types of storage that the multi-store model proposed, but to suggest different ways of examining it. They did not object to the idea of multi-stores, but were pointing out that the experimentation on memory was so driven by the postulation of different stores and their properties that the area was in danger of becoming unwieldy. Each new experimental finding meant that the theory was expanded to fit the result, and that this is not in fact the way

KT

(Continued)

forward. The best possible solution may be to find a new theory. The levels of processing framework was intended to provide an arena in which theory production could take place (Lockhart & Craik, 1990). In order to do this we must be equipped with the skills of analysis of complex experimental designs.

The purpose of analysis of variance is to test variability among means (for groups or variables) for statistical significance. This is accomplished by analysing the variance, that is by partitioning the total variance into the component that is due to error (i.e. within-groups SS) and the components that are due to differences between means. These latter variance components are then tested for statistical significance, and, if significant, we reject the null hypothesis of no differences between means, and accept the alternative hypothesis that the means (in the population) are different from each other. Further analysis is needed to determine where the difference lies, and post-hoc tests can be applied appropriately. If the assumptions of parametric test use are violated there are non-parametric equivalents available.

The next chapter will examine what happens if we want to study the effects of two factors.

Fergus Craik

Fergus Craik was born in 1935 in Edinburgh, Scotland. He obtained his BSc in Psychology from the University of Edinburgh in 1960. He then worked at the Medical Research Council Research Unit at the University of Liverpool, where he obtained his PhD in 1965. His thesis was on age-related changes in confidence and decision making.

Professor Craik was on the faculty of Birkbeck College, University of London (1965–1971). Since 1971, he has been at the University of Toronto, where he is a Professor of Psychology and holds the Max and Gianna Glassman Chair in Neuropsychology. He is also an Associate Scientist at the Rotman Research Institute of Baycrest Centre. His research work involves the experimental study of human memory processes; a second interest is the effects of aging on learning, attention and memory.

Robert Lockhart

Bob Lockhart received his BA and MA degrees with first-class honours from the University of Sydney in 1961 and 1963 respectively. In 1967 he completed his PhD under the supervision of W.M. O'Neil, and then spent two years as a Fulbright Scholar at Pennsylvania State University.

(Cont'd)

In 1968 he joined the small colony of Australian psychologists in the Psychology Department at the University of Toronto where he has been ever since. In addition to his appointment as Professor of Psychology, he has served as Departmental Chair, as a College Principal and as Director of the University of Toronto's Cognitive Science Program.

Professor Lockhart is best known for his work as a cognitive psychologist, especially in the areas of human memory and problem solving. He considers that the two major factors contributing to his career are the quality of training he received at the University of Sydney and the discipline of psychology itself. In the whole of science, he finds no question is more challenging and fascinating than understanding the achievements of the human mind.

In 1972, Craik and Lockhart proposed a 'levels of processing' framework for human memory research, which had a considerable impact on the field. Memory is characterised as a set of qualitatively different processes rather than as a collection of stores. This approach was supported by experiments showing differences in memory performance as a function of the type of processing carried out during initial acquisition of the information.

CHAPTER 8

SURVEY RESEARCH: WHO IS AFRAID OF CRIME?

Contents

Measuring attitudes using surveys
Attitudes
Attitude measurement
Writing questionnaires
Question format
Scaling
Dimensionality
The major unidimensional scale types
Likert scales
Scoring and analysis
Level of measurement

Sampling
Answers to our crime survey

Ethical considerations of performing surveys

Summary

Survey Research: Who is Afraid of Crime?

I could prove God statistically. (George Gallup)

Learning Objectives

- To learn about construction and data collection of surveys.
- To look at concepts in sampling and sample sizes for surveys.
- To consider ethical questions in survey designs.

KEY TERMS

- Likert scales
- Questionnaires
- Reconstructive techniques
- Reponses formats – unstructured, structured
- Scaling dimensionality
- Surveys

It has been said that we now live in an 'information society', as industrial societies have moved on from the production of the goods and services necessary for survival and comfort to those concerned with entertainment, education and information. This is such an important factor in our world that there is a World Summit on the issues:

> The accelerating convergence between telecommunications, broadcasting multimedia and information and communication technologies (ICTs) is driving new products and services, as well as ways of conducting business and commerce. (WSIS, 2005: 1)

In order to meet the demands of this society we require a prompt and accurate flow of information on preferences, needs and behaviour, and in order to do this many agencies place reliance on surveys. We are all familiar with the 'polls' that are reported by the press. For example, the Gallup Organisation has been gathering public opinion since 1935 and holds responses from more than 3.5 million people. It issues periodic reports that describe national public opinion on a wide range of current issues. The company Market & Opinion Research International (MORI) is a large, independently owned market research company in the UK, and was established in 1969. In 2005, MORI merged with Ipsos UK, and formed a larger company, also incorporating the Social Research Institute and the Reputation Centre. It publishes research on marketing, media, loyalty and public affairs. The major broadcasting networks and national news magazines also conduct polls and report their findings. However, this represents only a portion of the surveys that are carried out, as most are directed to a specific administrative, commercial or scientific purpose. Surveys provide an important source of basic scientific knowledge, and psychologists conduct surveys to study many matters related to everyday life, opinions and attitudes.

The word 'survey' is used most often to describe a method of gathering information from a sample of individuals who are usually part of the population being studied. Surveys can also be conducted in many different ways, including over the telephone, by mail or in person. However, there are certain characteristics in common:

- Surveys gather information from a proportion of a population of interest and the size of the sample depends on the purpose of the study.
- The sample is not selected haphazardly or only from people who volunteer to participate. It is scientifically chosen so that each person in the population will have a measurable chance of selection.
- Information is collected by means of standardised procedures so that every individual is asked the same questions. The survey's intent is not to describe the particular individuals who are part of the sample, but to obtain a composite profile of the population.
- Individual respondents should never be identified in reporting survey findings. All of the survey's results should be presented in completely anonymous summaries, such as statistical tables and charts.

Given the fact that we have spent quite a lot of time looking at experimentation in psychology, why would we use a survey method? Well, surveys are widely used in psychological research because we often we need to ask questions about beliefs, attitudes or emotions. These topics might be related to an aspect of behaviour that is private and the participant might not wish to share in a relatively public way.

Surveys are the preferred method for these types of questions because they involve asking participants about their unique experience or personal thoughts. Surveys, if carried out properly, can yield very good scientific data about thoughts on a particular issue and can tell us about the relationships between beliefs and other matters such as culture or ethnicity, age and sex.

MEASURING ATTITUDES USING SURVEYS

In psychology, a dominant method for studying attitudes is experimentation, with a focus of either attempting to change an attitude by manipulating one or more variables, or measuring individual differences related to attitude change. However, in social psychology, survey research is used extensively in the study of attitudes. This is not the only use we can put surveys to, but it is a very popular one in psychology, and bears some scrutiny.

Attitudes

An attitude is the accumulated information that we hold about 'attitude objects' such as a concrete object, a person, situation, behaviour or an experience, together with the positive, negative or neutral bias towards the object. Allport was one of the first psychologists to study personality, but, rejecting a psychoanalytical approach and a behavioural approach, he emphasised uniqueness of individuals and the importance of the present context. He also suggested that behaviour and attitudes were linked inextricably, because, although attitudes are private, they are formed through a socialisation process and exert a direct influence on how we behave. Allport (1935) suggests that an attitude is a mental, and even neural, state of readiness to behave in a particular way.

A major theoretical model about attitudes is the ABC model (Affect, Behaviour and Cognition model). The affect here is a physiological response that expresses an individual's preference for an attitude object. The behavioural component is the overt behaviour that expresses our attitude. The cognitive response is a cognitive evaluation to form an attitude. For example, a person can be in favour of non-smoking policies but still smoke; this apparent irrationality makes sense if the person enjoys the feeling of nicotine in the bloodstream. There is also a fourth component added to this theory later, the behaviour contention, which is a verbal expression of the attitude and how we intend to behave. For example, someone might hold a racist attitude, and express this verbally in their close social group, but never behave this way in the presence of someone from a different ethnic group.

Attitudes have several functions. They define who we are and what we believe, express our goals or dislike for things that block our goals, therefore they have a utilitarian or adaptive function. Attitudes also allow us to categorise information and manage social situations, so they have an economy function, and also protect us from our fears and rejections and therefore have an ego defensive function.

Attitudes will change with experience, unlike personality, which is seen as stable across the lifespan.

Attitude Measurement

An attitude scale is a questionnaire designed to measure attitudes by producing a score from some form of summing the elements in the scale. The measurement of attitudes by attitude scales arose from psychometrics and educational testing rather than theoretical social psychology. Later theoretical developments attempted to understand the subtlety and complexity of attitudes, and modern attitude scales take into account reliability and validity of the questionnaires used. It is now accepted that attitude scales do not allow us to make subtle insights, they simply group people with respect to a particular attitude and allow us to study the ways in which such an attitude relates to other variables in our survey.

Psychologists and other social researchers are well aware that attitudes are complex and even contradictory, and the outcomes of research can depend on the way in which questions are asked. The attitude to crime, for example, is often revealed as less punitive than policy makers might suppose (Rethinking Crime and Punishment, 2002). This research suggests that public attitudes towards the criminal justice system are indicative of a loss of both confidence and hope for a simple solution to crime. Public attitude towards wrongdoers is that they should be punished, but that the punishment system in place is not effective. Indeed, MORI (2003) showed that only 10% of people asked think that putting offenders in prison would reduce crime, and more than 50% of respondents think that offenders leave prison worse than when they went in. This suggests that the public have a great deal of scepticism about how the criminal justice system meets their needs of effective handling of crime and criminals. Public attitude counts for a lot in terms of policy-making decisions. Firstly, there is the desire of policy makers to be seen to be doing what their electorate want, and to be effective in dealing with difficulties. Secondly, there is the tendency to exaggerate the extent of crime and underestimate the effectiveness of prison sentences and hence the need to correct such misunderstandings as they may lead to erroneous influence on criminal justice policy formation, Therefore, we need to know what attitude the public hold about crime and the criminal justice system in order to correct the misunderstanding and/or find out how it might influence policy.

If we are to use a survey to measure attitudes to crime, how do we go about designing the instrument, the method of using it, the selection of the people to take part in it, and analysing data from it?

The first step is to determine precisely what we want from the survey. If we are looking at public attitudes towards the criminal justice system, and perceived levels of crime, then on what specifically are we focusing? Key issues identified by the UK government have involved: high levels of worry about various forms of crime, confidence in the criminal justice system, the police, the courts, prisons and probation services. Issues have arisen over the rights of people accused of crimes, the effectiveness of the system to extract justice over criminals and for victims, its efficiency and effectiveness in reducing crime. The British Crime Survey is an annual survey carried out for the government in which adults fill in questionnaires about incidents experienced in the previous 12 months. It gives a lot of information about levels of crime and public attitudes to crime in order to inform Home Office policy.

In the year ending June 2006 the representative sample comprised almost 50,000 people (Home Office, 2006). Despite reported levels of crime falling, public perception still appears to be that there are high levels of crime nationally. Part of the survey targets attitudes towards crime and the criminal justice system with the expressed objective of measuring public perceptions of changing crime levels, worry about crime and public confidence. The designers of the questionnaire needed to take these objectives of this part of the survey and transform them into questions. Without clear relationships between the objectives and questions the survey is useless. The main objectives of this part of the survey were to determine the general public's view on the criminal justice system, how people involved in it (the accused, the victim or the witness) are treated, how it deals with crimes and its effectiveness in reducing crime. Given the task of designing this part of the British Crime Survey, how would we go about it?

Writing Questionnaires

KT

When writing a **questionnaire**, it is important to consider who will fill it in, and how the instrument will look to them. We need to include easy, non-threatening questions at least at the start and put any difficult, threatening questions further into the questionnaire, so that respondents will not immediately stop answering. Usually, the earlier questions will request biographical or demographic information.

In any set of questions, we must be sure to ask about only one topic at a time. When a new topic is introduced, it is helpful to leave spaces to signal a change of direction. Sometimes, respondents have a tendency to keep checking the same response, e.g. the neutral or 'don't know' choice. In this case, format and layout of questions can reduce this response set.

Questionnaires must be reviewed to ensure that questions are not too complex or difficult for respondents to answer, and that there are no leading questions that point respondents towards a desired answer. Unless it is the purpose of the questionnaire, emotionally charged questions should be avoided too, as should ambiguity, assumptions of knowledge and burdensome questions.

There are things to be considered, such as thanking the respondent, keeping the survey as short as possible, and what is necessary, being sensitive to the respondents' needs and comfort.

Surveys should be carried out solely to develop a pool of information about a topic. They should not be designed to produce predetermined results or as a ruse for marketing and similar activities. Anyone asked to respond to a public opinion poll or concerned about the results should first decide whether the questions are fair.

It is important to remember that a questionnaire should be viewed as a multi-stage process beginning with definition of the aspects to be examined and ending with interpretation of the results. Every step needs to be designed carefully because the final results are only as good as the weakest link in the questionnaire process.

Question Format

There are two basic formats for questions, open or closed. Open-format questions are those where there is no prompt for the answer. These would be good for finding out subjective data or when the range of responses is not tightly defined. However, there are several disadvantages, such as requiring a higher level of literacy in the questionnaire respondents (if it is a written questionnaire), and it is always possible that respondents will not fill the questions in. It is also much more difficult to code the responses and each one has to be read individually. Such data can be deemed to be qualitative, and will be dealt with in the appropriate sections of the book.

Closed-format questions are quicker to complete and to code, and therefore analyse. We will concentrate on this format in this chapter.

There are several things to bear in mind when constructing closed-format questions:

- Clarity is of paramount importance. Questions must be clear and unambiguous, otherwise mistakes will be made. We must eliminate the possibility that the question will mean different things to different people.
- We must avoid the possibility that the question will force or imply a certain type of answer, in other words be a leading question. For example, the question 'by how much do you think crime has risen in the last 12 months?' certainly implies a particular type of answer! A much less leading question would be 'do you think crime has gone up or down in the last 12 months?' followed by asking by how much.
- Wording as well as focus of phrasing is important too. Two words can have an equivalent meaning, but have very different intent. Consider how different 'negligent' and 'careless' can be.

Scaling

Scaling in questionnaire design is done for scoring purposes. When a participant gives a response to a set of items, we often would like to assign a single number that represents that person's overall attitude. So, in our case, we want to be able to give a single number that describes a person's attitude towards the criminal justice system. A response scale, on the other hand, is the technique used to record responses on an instrument, in our case a questionnaire. For example, we might use a dichotomous response scale like agree/disagree, true/false or yes/no. Alternatively we could use a scored or gradient response scale like a 1-to-5 or 1-to-7 rating. However, all we are doing here is attaching a response scale to an object or statement. Scaling means using procedures independent of the respondent in order to attach a numerical value to the object.

Dimensionality

A scale can have any number of dimensions in it. Most scales that we develop have only a few dimensions. If we want to measure a construct, we have to decide whether the construct can be measured well with one line or whether it may need more. For instance, height is a concept that is unidimensional or one dimensional. We can measure the concept of height very well with only a single number line (e.g. a ruler). Thirst might also be considered a unidimensional concept; we are either more or less thirsty at any given time. It is easy to see that height and thirst are unidimensional. But what about a concept like self-esteem? If we think we can measure a person's self-esteem well with a single ruler that goes from low to high, then we probably have a unidimensional construct. We are probably also misleading ourselves! The way we are going to approach our attitude questionnaire is to assume we have a one-dimensional concept 'confidence in the criminal justice system', but we must be open to the possibility that there may be other ways to measure this.

The Major Unidimensional Scale Types

There are three major types of unidimensional scaling methods. These are similar as they each measure the concept of interest on a number line, but they differ in how they compute scale values for different items. The three methods are Thurstone or 'equal-appearing interval' scaling, Guttman or 'cumulative' scaling and Likert or 'summative' scaling. Here we will concentrate on a very popular method, that of Likert or Likert-type scaling.

Likert Scales

The first thing to do with any scaling process is to define the focus and generate scale items to include. In **Likert scales**, these items are statements which can be expressed in terms of agreement or disagreement with them. It is desirable to have as large a set of potential items as possible at this stage. Our focus here is attitude towards the criminal justice system, and we might end up with 40 statements expressed in such terms as:

> 'I think that the police treat people who come forward as witnesses well.'
> 'I think that the courts deal with young people accused of crime unfairly.'
> 'I am worried about violent crime in my area.'

Once we have a pool of items we need to decide exactly which ones will go in the final form of the questionnaire. We do this by asking a set of judges to rate the items on how favourable each item is towards the concept of attitudes to the criminal justice system:

> 1 = strongly unfavourable to the concept
> 2 = somewhat unfavourable to the concept
> 3 = undecided
> 4 = somewhat favourable to the concept
> 5 = strongly favourable to the concept

It is important to stress here that the judges are not telling us what their opinion is, but rating how each item relates to the concept. Once this is done, there are several pieces of simple analysis we can do in order to decide which of the items will appear in the final form. Firstly, we can compute the intercorrelations between all pairs of items, based on the ratings of the judges. This is done by comparing the sum of all the individual items for each judge. This new variable, the sum, is correlated against each of the other items. What we are looking for here is a lower correlation of item rating against total rating; usually any correlation below 0.6 means the item should be discarded. Another analysis we could do either instead of or after the correlations is to average the top and bottom ratings for each item. A *t* test of the differences between these mean values that turns out to be significant means these items are better discriminators and we may want to keep them in. There are various other analyses, done in order to check the relevance of items, that would lead to validity and reliability checks (see below).

So, we now have our items:

I think the criminal justice system respects the rights of people accused of committing a crime
I think the criminal justice system treats people accused of crime fairly
I think the police treat people who come forward as witnesses well
I think the police are effective in bringing people who commit crimes to justice
I think the courts deal with cases promptly and efficiently
I think the police are effective at reducing crime
I think the courts are not effective at reducing crime
I think the courts do not meet the needs of victims of crime
I think the courts are effective at dealing with young people accused of crime
I am worried about burglary
I am worried about car crime
I am worried about violent crime

Note that some items are expressed positively and some negatively. Respondents will be asked to indicate their level of agreement with the statements:

1 = strongly disagree
2 = disagree
3 = undecided
4 = agree
5 = strongly agree

There are several possible response scales (1-to-7, 1-to-9 and 0-to-4). All of these odd-numbered scales have a middle value that is often labelled neutral or undecided. It is also possible to use a forced-choice response scale with an even number of responses and no middle neutral or undecided choice. In this situation, the respondent is forced to decide whether to disagree or agree, and by how much.

The final score for the respondent on the scale is the sum of the ratings for all of the items (a summative scale score). But remember that we have items that are reversed in meaning from the overall direction of the scale, namely reversal items. If a respondent indicates high agreement (5) with a positively couched item, then that 5 indicates a positive attitude, but a high agreement with negatively couched items means a negative attitude. Therefore, we need to reverse the response value for each of these items before summing for the total: if the respondent gave a 1, we make it a 5, for 2 we make it a 4, etc. Likert scaling measures either a positive or negative response to a statement, and is therefore a bipolar scaling method. Sometimes the middle, neutral option is removed, and this is called a forced-choice method (Table 8.1).

Scoring and Analysis

After the questionnaire is completed, each item may be analysed separately or item responses may be summed to create a score for a group of items. Hence, Likert scales are often called summative scales.

Level of Measurement

Responses to a single Likert item are normally treated as ordinal data, because, with only five levels of response, we cannot assume that respondents perceive the difference between adjacent levels as equidistant. When treated as ordinal data, Likert responses can be analysed using non-parametric tests. However, when responses to several Likert items are summed, they may be treated as interval data measuring a latent variable. If the summed responses are normally distributed, parametric statistical tests can be applied.

The five response categories represent an ordinal level of measurement. The categories represent an order, but the numbers assigned to the categories do not indicate the size of difference between the categories in the way that an interval or ratio scale would. Therefore, when the item scores are summed, the resultant sum is not quite interval, but a so-called **plastic interval scale**.

Likert scale data can be thought of as interval level by applying the Rating Scale Model or Rasch model (see Andrich, 2005), which suggests that the statements reflect increasing levels of an attitude or trait.

KT

Table 8.1 Likert scale items in our crime survey

	Strongly disagree	Disagree	Neither agree nor disagree	Agree	Strongly agree
I think the criminal justice system respects the rights of people accused of committing a crime					
I think the criminal justice system treats people accused of crime fairly					
I think the police treat people who come forward as witnesses well					
I think the police are effective in bringing people who commit crimes to justice					
I think the courts deal with cases promptly and efficiently					
I think the police are effective at reducing crime					
I think the courts are not effective at reducing crime					
I am worried about burglary					
I am worried about car crime					
I am worried about violent crime					

The process for analysing survey data depends on the type of data and the number of items or questions in the survey. In our survey, we have closed-format questions with categorical response options. This type of data requires the use of statistical methods that are appropriate for categorical data. We will also be using a summative scale and therefore will get a scored response. This will require another type of analysis.

SAMPLING

So, we know what questions we are going to ask, we know how we will score them, but now we need to think about who will answer them. Surveys vary widely in sample size and sampling design, from large-scale to small-scale and cross-cultural studies. Large-scale probability surveys are the ideal, and the target population would be a whole country, like the UK. Typical large-scale surveys of a national population use a sample size of 1000 respondents, but can be much larger, as with the British Crime Survey. Small-scale surveys have a typical sample size of 200–300 respondents, although researchers on tight budgets often use smaller samples. Comparative or cross-cultural surveys usually involve 3–6 nations, and sample sizes that typically involve 1000 people per nation.

The sample size required for a survey partly depends on the statistical quality needed for survey findings; this then relates to how the results will be used. However, there is no simple rule for sample size that can be used for all surveys, as much depends on the resources available. Researchers often find that a moderate sample size is sufficient statistically: the well-known national polls referred to in the introduction to the chapter frequently use samples of about 1000 people to get reasonable information about national attitudes and opinions. When we consider that a properly selected sample of only 1000 individuals can reflect various characteristics of the total population, then we appreciate the value of using surveys to make informed decisions. Ideally, we would use the whole population, but it is too large to survey all of its members, and we need to have a small but carefully chosen sample to represent the population from which it is drawn. The first thing we need to determine is if we can construct a **sampling frame**. This is a procedure by which all the potential members of a population can be identified, and a sample then drawn. If our population is all the people in the UK eligible to vote, the sampling frame would be the way in which the electoral register is drawn up, and our sample would be taken from that.

Sampling methods can lead to probability or non-probability samples. When we select a probability sample, each member of the population has a known probability of being selected. Probability methods include random sampling, systematic sampling and stratified sampling. If we cannot employ such methods, then we have to use a non-probability sampling method in which members of the sample are selected on a non-random basis. Such methods include convenient **opportunity sampling**, judgement sampling, quota sampling and snowball sampling. Non-probability sampling means that we cannot calculate a sampling error, the degree to which a sample might differ from the population. When we make inferences about the population based on sample behaviour, we would like to do it in terms of sampling error, but non-random non-probability sampling means that the sampling error remains unknown. Therefore, the sampling method of choice would

KT

KT

Table 8.2 Numbers of respondents in sex, age and socioeconomic class groups

	Upper		Middle		Working	
	male	female	male	female	male	female
18–25	2	2	6	6	7	7
19–30	2	2	6	6	7	7
over 30	2	2	6	6	7	7

always be random sampling if possible. Here we have each member of the population having an equal and known chance of being selected in the sample, reducing **sampling bias**. As an alternative, systematic sampling might be used; this is also called the *N*th name selection technique. Once in a required sample size, and we have a list of population members, every *N*th record is selected (e.g. after every 100 names the next name is selected). If the list of population members does not contain any order, such as being in descending age, systematic sampling becomes as effective at representativeness as random sampling, but is so much simpler.

Answers to Our Crime Survey

Now we have our instrument, our sample and we know what form of data we will gather, let us look at some hypothetical data gathered in our crime survey.

The first things we need to do are check the data and code it, then place it into the analysis software such as SPSS. Once it is in the data file we can examine it for unusual patterns, such as missing data (is there a question that large numbers of people declined to answer?) We can do this by running descriptive statistics on each variable, finding the frequencies of answer types and we could even produce contingency tables to find out if there are particular answers (or missing answers) in one category of responder. If we find that all of our female respondents, for example, said that they were not worried about violent crime, then the data entry would need to be checked! Table 8.2 shows the numbers of respondents to the survey, how many are male and female, in three different age groups and particular socioeconomic class (upper, middle and working class – somewhat crude measures but this is simply for illustration!).

The next step, once we are satisfied that the data represents the answer given correctly, is to analyse variables in conjunction with each other. We have already looked at the frequencies etc. for each variable, and in some cases looked at how these answers correspond to the demographic characteristics of our respondents. However, we have 10 questions about crime, and we have also asked about, age, sex and socioeconomic class. This is 13 variables, and analysing each one in tabular or chi-square format against each other would mean 240 tables, which is rather a lot to analyse. While there may be some variables of particular interest, what we are really concerned with is the attitude to the criminal justice system, and the worry about crime.

Our attitude to the criminal justice system scale comprises 10 questions, some of which could have been reversed, that is, we could have asked respondents to indicate agree/disagree with the statement 'I am not worried about car crime'. When we put them into the data file we will have 'flipped' these around, and can therefore produce a new variable which is the total score on the attitude towards the criminal justice system, and another, which is the total worry about crime. For each of these we can carry out analyses of difference such as an independent samples t test to determine whether there is a difference on worry or attitude scores due to sex, or a one-way ANOVA to see if there is an effect of sex. We can even carry out two-way ANOVAS to see if there is an interaction between the factors.

Table 8.3 shows the mean positive attitude towards the criminal justice system in terms of the demographic factors.

Table 8.4 shows the mean level of worry about crime in terms of the demographic factors.

These tables contain quite a lot of information, and it may be better to display it in a graph. A further way to reduce this would be to carry out statistical analysis. For example, an independent samples t test on the level of worry about violent crime shows that there is no significant difference in the way men and women view violent crime ($t = 1.184$, $df = 88$, $p > 0.05$, $p = 0.239$). Further analysis could be carried out as suggested above.

ETHICAL CONSIDERATIONS OF PERFORMING SURVEYS

The confidentiality of the data supplied by respondents is of prime concern to all reputable survey takers. As in any research method used by psychologists, there are guidelines set out by professional organisations, such as the British Psychological Society or the APA, to govern how we carry out surveys (see Chapter 2 for more details). The recommended policies and procedures for survey data collection include:

Table 8.3

Age	Sex	SEC	Positive attitude to criminal justice system
18–25	Male	Upper	17.0000
		Middle	20.6667
		Working	23.1429
		Total	21.3333
	Female	Upper	24.5000
		Middle	20.3333
		Working	22.0000
		Total	21.6667
	Total	Upper	20.7500
		Middle	20.5000
		Working	22.5714
		Total	21.5000
19–30	Male	Upper	19.0000
		Middle	23.0000
		Working	21.7143
		Total	21.8667
	Female	Upper	23.0000
		Middle	20.1667
		Working	23.5714
		Total	22.1333
	Total	Upper	21.0000
		Middle	21.5833
		Working	22.6429
		Total	22.0000
Over 30	Male	Upper	16.5000
		Middle	24.5000
		Working	19.8571
		Total	21.2667
	Female	Upper	17.0000
		Middle	19.5000
		Working	21.7143
		Total	20.2000

Table 8.3   *(Cont'd)*

Age	Sex	SEC	Positive attitude to criminal justice system
	Total	Upper	16.7500
		Middle	22.0000
		Working	20.7857
		Total	20.7333
Total	Male	Upper	17.5000
		Middle	22.7222
		Working	21.5714
		Total	21.4889
	Female	Upper	21.5000
		Middle	20.0000
		Working	22.4286
		Total	21.3333
	Total	Upper	19.5000
		Middle	21.3611
		Working	22.0000
		Total	21.4111

Table 8.4

Age	Sex	SEC	Worry about crime
18–25	Male	Upper	8.0000
		Middle	9.3333
		Working	9.8571
		Total	9.4000
	Female	Upper	10.0000
		Middle	8.0000
		Working	9.7143
		Total	9.0667

(Cont'd)

Table 8.4 *(Cont'd)*

Age	Sex	SEC	Worry about crime
	Total	Upper	9.0000
		Middle	8.6667
		Working	9.7857
		Total	9.2333
19–30	Male	Upper	6.0000
		Middle	9.8333
		Working	9.2857
		Total	9.0667
	Female	Upper	7.0000
		Middle	9.1667
		Working	9.2857
		Total	8.9333
	Total	Upper	6.5000
		Middle	9.5000
		Working	9.2857
		Total	9.0000
Over 30	Male	Upper	10.0000
		Middle	9.1667
		Working	8.2857
		Total	8.8667
	Female	Upper	8.5000
		Middle	9.5000
		Working	7.2857
		Total	8.3333
	Total	Upper	9.2500
		Middle	9.3333
		Working	7.7857
		Total	8.6000
Total	Male	Upper	8.0000
		Middle	9.4444
		Working	9.1429
		Total	9.1111

Table 8.4   *(Cont'd)*

Age	Sex	SEC	Worry about crime
	Female	Upper	8.5000
		Middle	8.8889
		Working	8.7619
		Total	8.7778
	Total	Upper	8.2500
		Middle	9.1667
		Working	8.9524
		Total	8.9444

- Using only number codes to link the respondent to a questionnaire and storing the name-to-code linkage separately from the questionnaires.
- Refusing to give the names and addresses of survey respondents to anyone outside the survey team organisation, including sponsors.
- Destroying questionnaires and identifying information about respondents as soon as it is possible.
- Omitting the names and addresses of survey respondents from computer files used for analysis.
- Presenting statistical tabulations by broad enough categories so that individual respondents cannot be singled out.

Summary

A correlational design such as that found in a survey is a flexible method that can lead to powerful data that can be analysed quantitatively. However, surveys only access the information that a respondent can remember and therefore are only a reconstruction of experience. The data should therefore be analysed with this in mind.

CHAPTER 9

CORRELATIONAL DESIGNS: THE POOR RELATION?

Contents

Correlational designs and analysis

Correlational analysis with interval-level data

Simple linear regression

Correlation with non-continuous data

Ordinal data

Assumptions made in correlational analysis

Partial correlation

Summary

Correlational Designs: The Poor Relation?

The important thing in science is not so much to obtain new facts as to discover new ways of thinking about them. (W.L. Bragg; extracted from *Genius: The natural history of creativity,* by H.J. Eysenck)

Learning Objectives

- To understand the concepts of quantitative designs other than experimentation.
- To be able to design correlational research.
- To understand simple correlational analyses.
- To be able to identify and calculate correlation coefficients for various types of data.
- To be able to perform simple regression analysis for prediction.
- To understand partial correlation.

KEY TERMS

- Attenuation
- Case studies
- Coefficient of determination, r^2
- Correlation/correlation coefficients
- Correlational designs
- Covariance
- Partial correlation
- Pearson's r
- Questionnaires
- Reconstructive techniques
- Spearman's rho
- Strength of relationship
- Surveys

Many questions in psychology cannot be investigated by experimentation. True experimentation involves the manipulation of at least one variable, the independent variable, in order to assess its effect on (at least) one other variable, the dependent variable. In this way, experimenters seek to control for other variables in order to compare the effect when observing a causal relationship. Some variables that we might wish to define as our independent variables cannot be manipulated, such as sex of the participants. Some may lead to severe ethical implications if we did try to manipulate them, such as illness or poverty. We can still carry out studies using such independent variables, though, one way being to use the quasi-experimental design, and another to use correlational designs. A quasi-experimental design is one that looks like an experimental design but lacks key ingredients of manipulation and random assignment. Probably the most commonly used quasi-experimental design is the non-equivalent groups design. In its simplest form it requires a pre-test and post-test for a treated and comparison group. A correlational design is one in which the purpose is to discover relationships between variables through the use of correlational statistics – the **correlation coefficient** or '*r*'. The square of a correlation coefficient yields the explained variance (r^2), in other words what variability in the dependent variable can be attributed to its relationship with the independent variable. A correlational relationship between two variables is occasionally the result of an outside source, so we have to be careful and remember that correlation does not necessarily tell us about cause and effect. If a strong relationship is found between two variables, causality can be tested by using an experimental approach. The correlational method permits the researcher to analyse the relationships among a large number of variables in a single study. The correlation coefficient provides a measure of degree and direction of the relationship.

KT

These methods are often described as non-experimental, but this suggests that there is something lacking, or that they are a poor relation of the experiment. Common misuse of the term 'experiment' to mean any scientific study tends to lead to the conclusion that 'non-experimental' means non-scientific. This is not so, since these methods do allow us to describe and examine behaviour scientifically. While they do not let us identify the causes or reasons for the behaviour, they are methods in their own right, and may even be thought of as more flexible and allowing us to get closer to real behaviour than experiments can. It is better perhaps to describe quantitative non-experimental designs in other ways – for example, observational designs, correlational designs – rather than lumping them all together. Non-experimental methods do not let us explain why the behaviour occurs, but they do provide scientific data if we execute them correctly and interpret the data properly.

In 1995, Hans Eysenck addressed this question of types of research methods and their value or applicability in investigation of certain types of psychological phenomena. In his paper, Eysenck concentrated on intelligence and the ways it could be examined, but also said that the difficulties that affect experiments on intelligence were also valid for personality studies. He goes further, to suggest that, in fact, some areas of natural sciences, such as physics, have the same difficulties, in that some independent variables cannot be manipulated here either. Hence the 1919 'experiment' to test Einstein's theory of the bending of light was made without manipulating anything, but simply observing the effect of a change in the independent variable from sunlight to eclipse.

Eysenck suggested that there is essentially a continuum from 'pure' experimentation to 'pure' correlation and that the point at which it shifts from one to the other is distinguished by the level of intervention that researchers employ: 'A study is experimental when an intervention occurs to alter the status of the independent variable, and changes in the dependent variable are noted' (Eysenck, 1995: 218). Note that he does not say that the intervention must be a manipulation by the experimenter it could be a natural change in the independent variable such as aging or maturation, or a pre-existing distinction, such as sex. He is suggesting that there is an interrelated set of phenomena which can be investigated in relation to each other and that there should not be a distinction between 'biological' psychology and 'personality' or 'social' psychology that we are sometimes taught there is. Eysenck's biological theories of personality and intelligence are controversial but have made great contributions to our study of human life.

So is Eysenck suggesting that psychological phenomena such as intelligence and personality can be investigated using experimentation? Well, no, not really, but he is saying that correlational studies can be made more scientific, or rigorous, in nature by the application of the process of intervention. So, let us look at correlational designs in more detail in order to assess what he is saying.

CORRELATIONAL DESIGNS AND ANALYSIS

Correlational designs are those which examine the relationship between variables, therefore correlational analysis is the analysis of data from such designs.

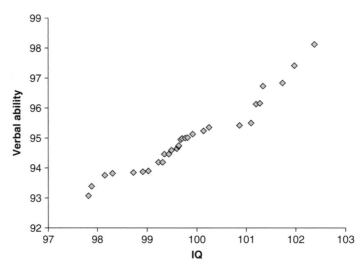

Figure 9.1 A positive correlation between IQ and verbal ability

Correlational analysis is a statistical technique which can show whether, and how strongly, sets of variables are related. For example, IQ and verbal ability tend to be related: people who score high on IQ tests also score highly on verbal ability tests. However, that relationship is not perfect. People of the same IQ score vary in verbal ability, and it is probably easy to think of people of high IQ who are very inarticulate. Nevertheless, the average verbal ability is related to IQ, and could be represented in the graph in Figure 9.1.

The graph shows that, as the scores in one variable rise, so do those in the other. There is a relationship that appears to be represented as a line. This relationship may appear to be very clear and obvious, but there may be more to it than that. There may be other variables that are involved here, such as educational experience or age. The data may contain unsuspected correlations, or at least have some items not included in it. A thorough correlational analysis will involve all of the data of interest and not be interpreted too widely.

The next step in discovering what the relationship between IQ and verbal ability is would be to determine the strength of this relationship that we can see in the graph. We now need to carry out a statistical test to find the correlation coefficient. A correlation coefficient is a number representing the strength of the relationship and can vary from 0 (there is no relationship or the relationship completely random) to 1 (a perfect linear relationship) or −1 (perfect negative linear relationship). A negative relationship might be demonstrated between IQ and errors on a verbal ability test, see Figure 9.2.

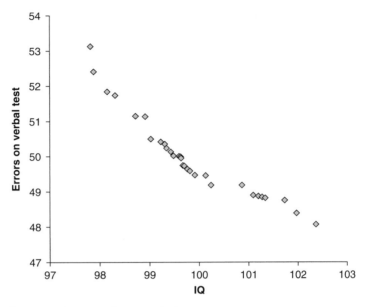

Figure 9.2 Representing negative correlation

Some correlation analyses should only be used to analyse data that represents quantities (such as scores on tests or someone's weight) rather than qualitative or categorical differences (such as sex or someone's favourite music). However, as we will see, there are different types of analysis that can take into account the level of measurement, and also tell us if there is an effect of categorical data.

There are several common pitfalls in using correlational analysis. A correlation does not provide evidence of causation. Correlational designs lack the control that experimental designs strive to contain; therefore, other variables may contribute to the variations in any dependent variable. Any correlation that is found will be assumed to be linear, so that any changes in one variable will predict changes in the other and this relationship can be represented graphically in a line. However, we can also represent correlational relationships numerically by calculating the correlation coefficient.

Correlational Analysis with Interval-Level Data

When the data is of interval level, or can be regarded as such, then the normal analysis is the Pearson product moment correlation coefficient, denoted as **Pearson's *r*.**

For a correlation coefficient we need to examine scores from each person on two variables. Let us take our example of IQ (*x*) and verbal ability (*y*) (Table 9.1).

To calculate *r* we use the formula

$$r = \frac{\sum (x - \bar{x})(y - \bar{y})/(N - 1)}{SD_x SD_y}$$

This is a simplified version of formulae we might find in other texts, but, of course, some of these elements are already familiar. The top line is the **covariance** of the two variables. This is the measure of how much each score on one variable deviates from the variable's mean multiplied by the same deviation in the other variable. So for our first participant this would be

$$(97-100)(92-95) = 9$$

If we repeat that for all the other 29 participants and add all those covariances together we get 47. In order to take into account the sample size, this is divided by the number of people in the sample minus one, so the sample covariance is 47/29 = 1.62. The values for standard deviations for each variable are substituted in the bottom line:

$$1.259 \times 1.414 = 1.78$$

This gives us a value of *r* = 1.62/1.78 = 0.91.

The interpretation of this is relatively simple: there is a strong positive relationship, therefore as IQ increases so does verbal ability. The last information that we can gather from any correlation coefficient is the percentage of variance accounted for in each variable by the other. This is r^2 (the square of the correlation coefficient). It is sometimes called the **coefficient of determination**. For our example, $r^2 = 0.91^2 = 0.828$. This means that the participants' IQ scores accounted for 82.8% of the variance in the scores in verbal ability.

However, we can also test a hypothesis in the same way as we can with other statistical tests, but in this case *r* is used to compute a *t*-value for checking against the *t* distribution. The null hypothesis here is that *r* = 0; the degrees of freedom are *N*−2.

Table 9.1   Measures in a correlational study

Participant	IQ (x)	Verbal ability (y)	xy	x^2	y^2
1	97	92	9021	9409	8649
2	98	93	9114	9604	8649
3	98	94	9212	9604	8836
4	98	94	9212	9604	8836
5	99	94	9306	9801	8836
6	99	94	9306	9801	8836
7	99	94	9306	9801	8836
8	100	94	9400	10,000	8836
9	100	94	9400	10,000	8836
10	100	94	9400	10,000	8836
11	100	94	9400	10,000	8836
12	100	95	9500	10,000	9025
13	100	95	9500	10,000	9025
14	100	95	9500	10,000	9025
15	100	95	9500	10,000	9025
16	100	95	9500	10,000	9025
17	100	95	9500	10,000	9025
18	100	95	9500	10,000	9025
19	100	95	9500	10,000	9025
20	100	95	9500	10,000	9025
21	100	95	9500	10,000	9025
22	100	95	9500	10,000	9025
23	101	95	9595	10,201	9025
24	101	96	9696	10,201	9216
25	101	96	9696	10,201	9216
26	101	96	9696	10,201	9216
27	101	97	9797	10,201	9409
28	102	97	9894	10,404	9409
29	102	98	9996	10,404	9604
30	103	99	10,094	10,609	9604
Sum	3000	2850	285,041	300,046	270,796
Mean	100	95			
SD	1.259	1.414			

Using this formula

$$t = \frac{r\sqrt{N-2}}{\sqrt{1-r^2}}$$

then

$$t = (0.91 \times 5.292) \div 0.828 = 5.816$$

Comparing this with the t distribution for an α of 0.05, we find that the critical value is 2.048, so our value is significant. There is a significant relationship between the two variables.

So, now we know that we have some sort of relationship, it is a strong one and it is statistically significant. However, that is all we know – we cannot predict anything from this, simply that people with high IQs are more likely to have high verbal ability too. But what if we could predict the verbal ability of someone with a particular IQ?

Consider the graph of the data belonging to our 30 participants. One thing that might strike an observer straight away is that this appears to be a line. In fact we can add a line to describe the straightest way through the data points (see Figure 9.3).

This is called the line of best fit, and is found by the application of linear regression.

Simple Linear Regression

Simple linear regression is a technique that enables us to determine the relationship between two continuous variables, one of which is defined as the predictor (x) the other a criterion variable (y). Both x **and** y are related measures and regression describes the way in which one of the measures changes in response to changes in the other. The relationship can be expressed in terms of a mathematical equation for a line, $y = a + bx$, where x is the score on the predictor variable, a is the value where the line cuts the y-axis and b is a measure of the slope of the line; b is also called a **regression coefficient**. The higher the value of a, the steeper the slope of the line; the higher the value of b, the higher up the y-axis the line cuts. What we want to know is how to work out a and b.

KT

KT

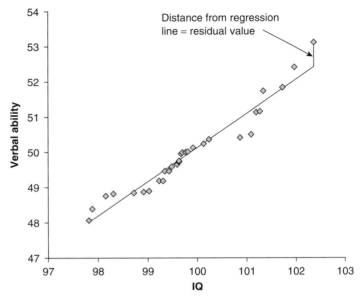

Figure 9.3 Correlation between IQ and verbal ability – the line of best fit

The formulae for working out each of the regression components are as follows:

$$b = \frac{\sum xy - \left(\frac{\sum x \sum y}{n}\right)}{\sum x^2 - \frac{(\sum x)^2}{n}} \qquad a = \bar{y} - b\bar{x}$$

By now these should hold no fear! Substituting values we see that $b = 1.022$ and using this we see that $a = -7.174$. Our regression line equation is then

$$y = -7.174 + (1.022x)$$

So, for any value of x, the corresponding y-value can be found by multiplying x by 1.022 then subtracting 7.174.

We can now predict by extrapolating (looking at x-values beyond those included in the sample) or interpolating (making a prediction within the range of values of the predictor). Interpolation makes sense, but only for values of x which might be expected to appear. Imagine if our sample did not include anyone with an IQ of 99. Then we could find a predicted value of verbal ability for that case:

$$\text{verbal ability} = -7.174 + (1.022 \times 99) = 94.004$$

which is very close to what we observe.

Extrapolation is making a prediction outside the range of values of the predictor in the sample used to generate the model and carries a risk which rises as the value of x examined gets further beyond the limits of the sample. Extrapolation needs to be done with care, especially in regression models describing variables' relationships that could not hold negative values. For example, if we looked at an IQ value of 6 the verbal ability would be predicted as -1.042 which is ridiculous, for two reasons: no one can have a negative verbal ability, and why did we even consider that a person would have an IQ of 6 in the first place?

Regression is a more useful technique if we have more than one predictor, as the relationships among several variables are more difficult to examine. The next chapter will look at regression for several predictors.

For variables which do not contain interval/continuous data there are alternative ways of calculating correlation.

Correlation with Non-continuous Data

Frequency/Nominal Data

KT

We can find relationships between variables that contain frequency data using a test called the **chi-square test** (χ^2, pronounced 'kai-square'). This is known as an enumeration statistic, which means it does not measure the value of a set of items, but compares the frequencies of various categories of items in a random sample with the frequencies that are expected if the population frequencies are as hypothesised by a researcher. It is also often used to assess the 'goodness of fit' between an obtained set of frequencies in a random sample and what is expected under a given statistical hypothesis. For example, chi square can be used to determine whether to reject the hypothesis that the frequencies in a random sample are as expected when the items are from a normal distribution.

In the following equation, O and E are the observed and expected frequencies in each category:

$$\chi^2 = \sum \frac{(O - E)^2}{E}$$

Table 9.2 Contingency table

Smoking * Lung cancer				
		Lung cancer		
		no	yes	Total
Smoking	no	34	16	50
	yes	5	75	80
Total		39	91	130

Table 9.3 Expected frequencies

Smoking * Lung cancer			
		Lung cancer	
		no	yes
Smoking	no	15	35
	yes	24	56

There are some assumptions to be met before using the test:

1 The sample must be randomly drawn from the population.
2 Data must be reported in raw frequencies (not percentages).
3 Measured variables must be independent.
4 Values/categories on independent and dependent variables must be mutually exclusive and exhaustive.
5 Observed frequencies should be greater than 5.

So, for example, if we want to test the hypothesis that there is an association between smoking and lung cancer, we would look at a sample of people who did or did not smoke and who had developed or not developed lung cancer. We might see the values in Table 9.2. The calculation for the χ^2 runs as follows.

Firstly, we need to work out the expected values for each cell. They are found by multiplying the row total and the column total relevant for each cell and dividing by the table total. These are shown in Table 9.3.

Secondly, we then need to work out the differences between the observed and the expected frequencies, as shown in Table 9.4.

Thirdly, χ^2 is then all over the differences squared and divided by the expected frequency as seen in Table 9.5.

Table 9.4 Differences between observed and expected frequencies

		Lung cancer	
		no	yes
Smoking	no	34–15 = 19	16–35 = –19
	yes	5–24 = –19	75–56 = 19

Table 9.5 Squared differences divided by expected frequencies

		Lung cancer	
		no	yes
Smoking	no	24.06667	10.31429
	yes	15.04167	6.446429

The chi-square value then becomes 24.06667 + 10.31429 + 15.04167 + 6.446429, which is 55.86905. If this is significant it means there is an association between whether or not the members of the sample smoked and whether or not they developed lung cancer. There is a probability distribution for chi-square in the same way as there is for other tests, and we need to know the degrees of freedom for the value. The degrees of freedom are the product of the number of rows minus one and the number of columns minus one. Both the columns and rows number two, so $df = (2–1)(2–1)$ which is 1. Degrees of freedom are calculated this way because the expected values in each cell are computed from the row and column totals of each cell. All but one of the expected values in a given row or column are free to vary. Thus, the value of over 55 with 1 degree of freedom is significant, so the law on not smoking in public places was brought in just in time.

Ordinal Data

With ordinal data we can use Spearman's rho, Kendall's tau, polyserial correlation or polychoric correlation.

Spearman's Rho

This is the most common correlation for use with two ordinal variables or an ordinal and an interval variable. Rho for ranked data equals Pearson's r for ranked data. The formula for Spearman's rho is

Table 9.6   Ranked data

Participant	x	x-rank	y	y-rank	d	d²
1	97	1	12	1	0	0
2	98	2	13	2	0	0
3	100	5	50	4	1	1
4	100	5	53	8.5	−3.5	12.25
5	100	5	54	10	−5	25
6	100	5	53	8.5	−3.5	12.25
7	100	5	50	4	1	1
8	101	8.5	50	4	4.5	20.25
9	101	8.5	52	6.5	2	4
10	103	10	52	6.5	3.5	12.25

$$\Sigma d^2 = 88$$

$$\rho = 1 - \frac{6 \times \sum d^2}{n\left(n^2 - 1\right)}$$

where d is the difference in ranks

What if we asked 10 of our people in the IQ sample to rate the level of discomfort in taking the verbal ability test (variable y)? This data is not interval, so we can treat both variables as ranks (taking into account tied ranks within each variable), see Table 9.6:

$$\rho = 1 - [6 \times 88 \div 10(100 - 1)] = 1 - (528 \div 990) = 1 - 0.533 = 0.467$$

A positive relationship, but not necessarily a strong one. If we had carried out a Pearson correlation on the data, r would be 0.803 and significant, but here we do not have a significant value. Spearman would appear to be the more conservative analysis, but possibly leading to a Type II error. An alternative view would be that using Pearson with an inappropriate level of data opens us to the risk of a Type I error. The caveat here perhaps should be 'know your data'!

Point–Biserial Correlation

This is recommended when we have an interval variable and a dichotomous variable and want to examine the correlation. There are some anomalies with these, though, as even when it appears that the two are perfectly ordered together, r will be less than 1.0. In other words, r will only have a maximum of 1.0 if the data-sets contain only two cases. When one or both variables are dichotomies then the calculation of the relationship can be found by performing a chi-square calculation.

ASSUMPTIONS MADE IN CORRELATIONAL ANALYSIS

As with other types of analysis, correlation makes some assumptions. Firstly, in order to use Pearson analysis the data should be interval-level data, which of course does not apply to the non-parametric alternatives. Carrying out a correlation assumes there is a linear relationship and that there is the same error variance along this linear relation-

ship (referred to as **homoscedasticity**). In other words, we have to be able to represent the relationship, even theoretically, by a line, and correlation is a measurement of covariance between two variables, so must also assume minimal measurement error. A lack of reliability in the measurement reduces the reliability of the correlation coef-

ficient, as it artificially lowers it. This lowering is called **attenuation** and can be corrected for. Most computer programs would give a corrected r-value.

Correlational analysis uses covariance of the variables to be compared as an essential element of the calculation. There would therefore appear to be a relationship between correlational analysis and analysis of variance. In fact the significance level of a correlation coefficient for the correlation of an interval variable with a dichotomy will be the same as for an ANOVA on the interval variable using the dichotomy as the only factor. In the next chapter we will see how that close relationship can be used to advantage in the analysis of multiple variables. However, let us just consider what might happen if we include a third variable in our correlational analysis.

PARTIAL CORRELATION

KT

Partial correlation is the correlation of two variables while controlling for a third variable. Partial correlation still requires all the usual assumptions that need to be met for the Pearson correlation.

If we carried out a partial correlation we would compare the correlation with the other variables controlled for with the original, and if there is no difference we can infer that the control variable has no effect. However, if a partial correlation is close to 0 we would infer that the original correlation is unfounded and that there cannot be such a link between the two variables.

For example, in our IQ/verbal ability data we might wonder if there was an effect of age on the result. Our Pearson correlation coefficient was 0.91 remember, but if we add age to the data we obtain Table 9.7.

Carrying out a Pearson correlation calculation on all three variables in pairs gives us the matrix in Table 9.8.

Age does seem to be correlated with both of our other variables, but not very strongly. We can carry out a partial correlation using the formula

$$r_{\text{partial}} = \frac{r_{xy} - (r_{xz} \times r_{yz})}{\sqrt{\left(1 - r_{xz}^2\right)\left(1 - r_{yz}^2\right)}}$$

Our partial correlation coefficient is 0.9073, not very far away from the original of 0.91. In fact, considering the original and the partial coefficients, we know that 82.8% of the variability on verbal ability is accounted for by IQ, but that age only accounts for $(0.245^2 \times 100) = 6.0025\%$ of the variability in verbal ability (and 3.497% of that in IQ). Partial correlation calculations remove the part of the variability in age that accounts for the variability in verbal ability and that in IQ. The variability that is left, that will account for the variability in verbal ability due to IQ, is therefore $0.9073^2 \times 100 = 82.32\%$ when controlling for age. The tiny difference between this and the original correlation coefficient suggests that age does not have any effect on the relationship between IQ and verbal ability.

So, we now know how to determine *if* there is a relationship between two or three variables, and what the strength and direction of that relationship might be, and even how to predict some of the values of one variable from those of another. But where does all that knowledge take us? Not very far into determining the way variables affect each other, as we have neither the causal inferences drawn from experiment nor the richness of information derived from qualitative methods. This was Eysenck's question: does the fact that correlation does not appear to lead to an examination of cause mean that we can never use the results of such designs to make inferences?

Table 9.7 Adding a further variable to the correlational design

Participant	x	y	Age (z)
1	97.00	12.00	28
2	98.00	13.00	24
3	100.00	50.00	31
4	100.00	53.00	36
5	100.00	54.00	36
6	100.00	53.00	45
7	100.00	50.00	19
8	101.00	50.00	29
9	101.00	52.00	35
10	103.00	52.00	25
11	97.00	12.00	27
12	98.00	13.00	22
13	100.00	50.00	21
14	100.00	53.00	26
15	100.00	54.00	26
16	100.00	53.00	20
17	100.00	50.00	27
18	101.00	50.00	28
19	101.00	52.00	31
20	103.00	52.00	28
21	97.00	12.00	28
22	98.00	13.00	28
23	100.00	50.00	44
24	100.00	53.00	30
25	100.00	54.00	29
26	100.00	53.00	27
27	100.00	50.00	42
28	101.00	50.00	34
29	101.00	52.00	47
30	103.00	52.00	27
Sum	3000	2850	900
Mean	100	95	30

Table 9.8 A correlation matrix

	IQ	Verbal ability
IQ		
Verbal ability	0.910	
Age	0.187	0.245

Eysenck refutes the idea that there is this clear distinction between correlational and experimental designs. In a 1983 paper he suggests that the measurement of intelligence can be done by means of electrophysiological recordings, such as **evoked potentials**. High correlations exist between these psychophysiological indicators and orthodox IQ tests. Eysenck suggests that these biological measures are less influenced by cultural, educational and other environmental variables than by genetic make-up. If this is the case then using these to examine intelligence has advantages as they can be manipulated experimentally. His argument throughout this type of research is that correlation, if used properly, can be a very strong method and analysis in the investigation of psychological phenomena. His argument makes us examine why correlational studies might not have been as conclusive as many had hoped – firstly, that they utilise poor measurement and, secondly, that, for example, different personalities might have different profiles on different tests due to their nature. So we should treat correlational studies just as scientifically and rigorously as we approach experimental ones.

KT

Summary

We started this chapter with the distinction between experimental and non-experimental designs, but are ending it with the knowledge that correlational designs can be just as valuable as others. Eysenck's contribution here has been to show us that the fields of psychology should be interrelated, that biological mechanisms can be used to examine more socially related aspects such as intelligence and personality, and that there is no real distinction between these facets of human life. Therefore there should not be the distinction between the methods of investigation that many psychologists seek to make.

This chapter has explained some of the simpler analyses that can be carried out in correlational designs. These include correlation coefficient calculations, and there are several available dependent on the nature of the variables included, and simple linear regression. Such analyses can be used in correlational designs such as surveys and questionnaire production, but such simple analyses are often used in an exploratory way in psychology, in much the same way as simple experimental design analysis is used. The next chapter looks at more complex analyses in order to explore more closely the arguments in Eysenck's discussion of correlational research.

Hans Jurgen Eysenck (1916–1997)

Hans Eysenck was a British psychologist born in Germany. The son of German film and stage celebrities, he was encouraged to pursue acting as a career. After graduating from high school, however, he left Germany in opposition of the Nazi regime and eventually completed his PhD in Psychology at the University of London. He wrote over 50 books on such diverse topics that he seemed to have an interest and expertise in everything. He was more a theorist than a researcher, and although much research has supported his theories since, there are some that have been attacked.

Best known for his theory of human personality, Eysenck suggested that personality is biologically determined and is arranged in a hierarchy consisting of types, traits, habitual responses and specific responses. A staunch critic of psychoanalysis, Eysenck maintained that the recovery rates of the emotionally disturbed were approximately equal for treated and untreated individuals, though the accuracy of his studies on the subject have been questioned in recent years.

As can be seen from his criticism of psychotherapy, Eysenck was known as a controversialist. He has received acclaim and criticism from colleagues and seemed to strive more from the latter. His theories have inspired many and, although controversial in many aspects of his career, he remains a celebrity. He died on 4 September 1997, from a brain tumour.

PART III

COMPLEX QUANTITATIVE DESIGNS

In this part, we will look at experimentation that is more complex and how to analyse the data that is generated. This is explained in terms of experiments on memory and placed in the context of eyewitnesses. We will also examine more complex correlational designs in terms of investigating murder.

CHAPTER 10

FACTORIAL DESIGNS WITH MORE THAN ONE FACTOR: A CLOSER LOOK AT MEMORY

Contents

Alternatives to the levels of processing framework
The principles of encoding specificity

Analysis of factorial designs with more than one factor

Reporting factorial results

Mixed designs

Post-hoc analysis
Simple effects
Simple main effects for between- and within-subjects contrasts

Non-parametric tests
Transformations
Friedman's test

Summary

Factorial Designs with More than One Factor: A Closer Look at Memory

Do not worry about your difficulties in Mathematics. I can assure you mine are still greater. (Albert Einstein)

Learning Objectives

- To examine designs with more than one factor.
- To examine multi-factorial designs with two between-subjects factors, two repeated measures factors and mixed designs.
- To examine the analysis in multi-factorial designs.
- To examine the interpretation of main effects and interaction effects.

KEY TERMS

- Interaction/interaction effect
- Main effect
- Multi-factorial ANOVA

Factorial designs allow us to examine more complex effects of variables on each other. However, it is unlikely that a simple one-factor design is going to encompass all the effects in a psychological phenomenon. Memory, for example, is a very complex and wide-ranging psychological process, and examining one element of it is never going to give a rounded picture of what happens when we encode items for storage.

In a previous chapter we examined a framework for studying memory called the levels of processing, proposed by Craik and Lockhart. This was a big step forward from the idea of separate 'locations' for memories and was very influential in memory research. The levels of processing framework suggests that the deeper the processing during a study phase, the more effective the learning and the better the subsequent recall. This is tested by a recall test after subjects have carried out tasks to manipulate the processing made. Tasks could be orthographic (dealing with physical characteristics of words presented), phonological (dealing with the sound of words, such as rhyming) and semantic (asking questions about the meaning of words).

Results from levels of processing experiments do show that these tasks lead to differences in performance, so the framework does distinguish between learning that takes place under different cognitive conditions and between incidental learning (learning without being warned) and intentional learning (learning that takes place when the subject is warned of a test). However, there are difficulties with what appears to be a simple and effective explanation for differences in recall performance. The levels of processing framework suggests that a deep processing task forces participants to think about more than one aspect of the stimulus, so that a more complex or elaborate memory trace was formed. A more elaborate trace of this nature would have more potential cues to use when trying to retrieve it, and would be more distinct. But the first problem we encounter is a definition of 'deep'. If we say it is the processing that produces the best memory we are in danger of making a circular definition. If we say it is the processing that results from doing a difficult task we cannot be right, as some of the orthographic tasks can be quite difficult and have long reaction times, but do not lead to better traces. It would be possible to define the deeper processing as that resulting from a semantically based task, but there are cases where this does not happen, such as asking semantic questions that require a negative answer. Deeper processing might also happen because we are integrating the stimulus item with prior knowledge, which explains the high recall rates when the questions are 'self-referent', for example 'does this word describe what you are like?' (Symons & Johnson, 1997). This might be the best explanation/definition of deeper processing, but there is an alternative explanation for why this happens.

ALTERNATIVES TO THE LEVELS OF PROCESSING FRAMEWORK

Imagine an experiment in which the subjects experience a study phase, and they are asked whether

Eagle rhymes with legal
Peach rhymes with book
Train has an engine
Pen is used to drink with

and so on, very much like the levels of processing experiment.

They are then asked to pick out words they saw before from a list containing target words and others. Well, as the levels of processing hypothesis predicts, there is better recall of the words that have been subjected to a semantic question. However, if we give them another test in which they are asked to pick put words that rhyme with the words they saw, they will pick out more words subjected to the rhyming task: levels of processing cannot explain this! However, an alternative perspective, transfer appropriate processing, can. This experiment was carried out by Morris, Bransford and Franks in 1977 to demonstrate that we cannot attribute recall performance only to processes happening at encoding, as any effect is not independent of the type of memory test used for retrieval. The levels of processing model is limited due to an overemphasis on encoding and the best recall does not depend on the depth of the processing but could be related to the type of learning that is most relevant to the retrieval task. Under some circumstances phonetic learning can result in better recall than semantic learning. So what we remember will depend on what we will be tested on and memory performance at the test stage will depend on the match between encoding and retrieval conditions, with retrieval cues needing the encoding conditions. This framework is known as transfer appropriate processing and central to this is the *principle of encoding specificity* examined in a series of experiments by Endel Tulving and associates.

The Principles of Encoding Specificity

What is learned depends on the learner's focus of attention and the context of the learning episode. Successful retrieval occurs when the cues at retrieval match what was learned.

There are many items available as retrieval cues, so that successful retrieval might depend on context.

The principle is clearly demonstrated in an experiment by Tulving and Osler in 1968. They presented participants with lists of words that they would be asked to recall under a free-recall condition. Each to-be-remembered (TBR) word was accompanied by weak associate A or weak associate B at encoding, by both of these (AB), or by neither. At recall, cues A, B, AB or no cues were provided for retrieval. When a particular cue was present at both encoding and retrieval, performance was good. But a cue at retrieval which had not been present at encoding was completely ineffective. This led Tulving and Osler to propose that a retrieval cue will facilitate recall if, and only if, its relationship with the TBR item was processed at encoding.

There is a wealth of evidence that supports this, including the idea that change in context is harmful to memory. For example, Emmerson (1986) gave amateur divers lists of 16 words to study either underwater or in a boat, and then gave them a recognition test with a list of 100 words that included the studied words. Recognition was best when the context was the same as it had been at study. Thus words studied underwater were best recognised there and vice versa.

Further evidence for encoding specificity is the effects of weak and strong cues on recall. A suitable hypothesis would predict that even cues which strongly elicit the target item in an association test will not be effective if they were not encoded with the study items. Tulving and Thomson (1971) initially thought that if a study word was paired with a weak associate, then recall was better when the weak associate was used as a cue rather than a strong associate. In fact, the strong associate appeared to give no benefit compared with a situation in which no retrieval cues at all were given. This is further supported by a study carried out by Roediger and Payne in 1983. Their participants studied lists of four words from each of 20 categories, with the critical items being the last word on each list. Then some participants were given a free-recall test, others a 'congruous' cue (the name of the relevant category) and others 'incongruous' category cues that were strongly associated with the target items but inconsistent with the encoding category. The congruous cue elevated performance over free recall, but incongruous cues led to significantly lower levels of performance even than free recall. Therefore no matter how strongly associated with the target, a cue will be ineffective if encoding was incongruent with the cue, and can even inhibit recall performance.

According to Tulving's encoding specificity principle, the recollection of an event depends on the interaction between the properties of the encoded event and the properties of the encoded retrieval information. In other words, whether an item will be remembered at a particular time depends on the interaction between the processing that occurred during encoding and the processing that occurs at retrieval. This principle has important implications for investigating memory. As it is the interaction of both encoding and retrieval that is important, it means that we cannot make any statement about the mnemonic properties of an item or a type of processing or a cue unless we specify both the encoding and the retrieval conditions.

Testing the Framework

We now have a new theoretical framework to test. The encoding specificity principle allows us to think of experiments for investigating how contextual information affects memory. Specifically, the principle states that memory is improved when information available at encoding is also available at retrieval. For example, the encoding specificity principle would predict that recall for information would be better if subjects were tested in the same environment they had studied in versus having studied in one environment and being tested in a different one, such as under and above water. It would also predict that the context of the information provided is important, in that strong, but incongruous, cues are no better, and possibly worse, than weak but congruous cues. So we now have two factors to consider rather than one as in the depth of processing hypothesis: that context affects recall, and so does congruity of cues. How could we test such a hypothesis generated from consideration of the effects of these two factors?

ANALYSIS OF FACTORIAL DESIGNS WITH MORE THAN ONE FACTOR

We have examined the one-way ANOVA but this only analyses one factor at a time. We are now going to move up a level in complexity and consider two factors simultaneously. These two factors can be both between-groups designs, both repeated measures designs, or used in a mixed design. The two-factor mixed design has one between-groups factor and one within-groups factor. If a significant *F*-value is found for one factor, then this is referred to as a significant **main effect**. However, when two or more factors are considered simultaneously, there is also always the need to discover if there is a significant **interaction** between the factors. Often the best way of interpreting and understanding an interaction is by a graph. A two-factor ANOVA with a non-significant interaction can be represented by two approximately parallel lines, whereas a significant interaction results in a graph with non-parallel lines. Because two lines will rarely be exactly parallel, the significance test on the interaction is also a test of whether the two lines diverge significantly from being parallel.

REPORTING FACTORIAL RESULTS

If the interaction is not significant (note the use of *not significant* or *non-significant*, rather than *insignificant* which means something entirely different!) we can then examine the main effects without needing to qualify them because of the interaction.

If the interaction is significant, we cannot only examine the main effects because they do not tell the complete story. Most statistics texts follow this line. However, it may seem to make sense to tell the simple story first and then the more complex story. The explanation of the results ends at the level of complexity that we wish to convey to the reader. In the two-way case, many researchers prefer to examine each of the main effects first and then the interaction. If the interaction is not significant, the most complete story is told by the main effects. If the interaction is significant, then the most complete story is told by the interaction. One consequence of the difference in the two approaches is if, for example, we did run a four-way ANOVA and the four-way interaction (i.e. $A \times B \times C \times D$) was significant, we would not be able to examine any of the lower order interactions even if we wanted to! Describing a four-way interaction is exceedingly difficult and would most likely not represent the relationships we were intending to examine and would not hold the reader's attention for very long. With the other approach, we would describe the main effects first, then the first-order interactions and then the higher order interactions only if they are likely to add anything to the explanation. We can stop at the level of complexity that is the most useful to describe our results.

Another point about two-way ANOVA is related to the number of subjects in each **cell** of the design. If the between-groups factor has equal numbers of subjects in each of its levels, then we have a **balanced design**. With a balanced design, each of the two factors and the interaction are independent of each other. Each factor can be significant or non-significant and the interaction can be significant or non-significant without any influence or effect from one or the other effects.

When there are different numbers in the levels of the between-groups factor, however, this independence starts to disappear. The results for one factor and/or the interaction will depend somewhat on what happened on the other factor. Therefore, as much as possible we should try to keep the numbers of subjects in each level of the factor as close as possible to each other. There is no strict rule about how disparate the cell numbers have to be before the results become invalid, but in practice most researchers would agree that if the largest cell number is greater than three times the smallest cell number, the results would start to become too invalid to interpret.

The two-factor ANOVA has three distinct hypotheses associated with it, concerning the main effect for factor A, the main effect for factor B and the interaction ($A \times B$, expressed by cell means). These are still omnibus hypotheses and do not indicate the direction of any finding.

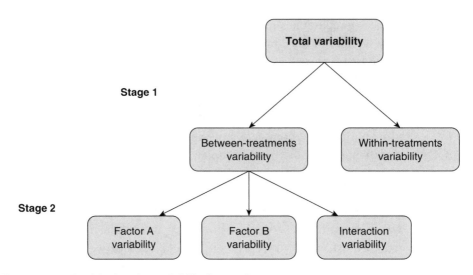

Figure 10.1   Partitioning the variability in two factors

In each case the treatment effect will be evaluated by an *F*-ratio which is the ratio of the variance for between treatments to the variance expected by chance. As we have a more complex hypothesis testing situation here, the structure of the analysis is a little more complex than that of one factor, as we have to take into account the variability due to any interaction between the two factors. In a two-factorial design with completely between measures, the between-treatments variability is partitioned into that corresponding to each of the factors and the interaction (Figure 10.1).

The following examples are drawn from the hypotheses associated with the encoding specificity principle. We are going to examine a situation where participants have their recall tested either in the context in which they learned the target words or not, and where they have congruous cues, incongruous cues or no cues. At this stage we will not examine the *strength* of the cues or any combination of contexts.

The calculations we need to do are shown in the structure in Figure 10.2.

As we have looked very closely at the calculation in the previous chapter, and the vast majority of researchers use computer programs to perform calculations today, there is little point going through all the calculations number by number.

So we have participants given a list of 50 words to learn, and 10 participants recall in the same context with congruous cues and 10 with incongruous cues and

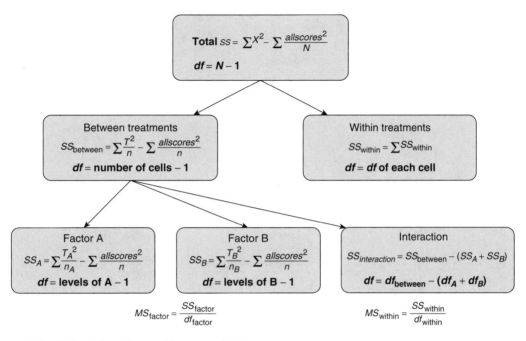

Figure 10.2   Calculations for partitioned variability

similarly in the different context conditions, 40 participants in all. Table 10.1 shows the means in each of our cells in this experiment and the overall means. We can already see the trend the results are indicating: that the same context leads to better recall than changing the context, and that congruous cues are better than incongruous ones. However, there is something more complex happening than that, because if we look at the cell means, there appears to be an interaction, as different context but congruous cues show a better performance than same context but incongruous cues, see Table 10.1.

Table 10.1

	Same context	Different context	
Congruous cues	48.1	40	44.05
Incongruous cues	30	8.5	19.25
	39.05	24.25	31.122

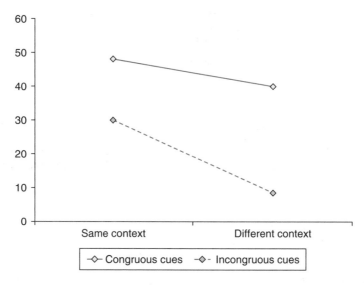

Figure 10.3 Context versus cues

Let us have a look at the graph in (Figure 10.3) to see whether that effect can be clarified.

There is a main effect of context as the height of the lines changes between the two levels, and there is one in cue type, which can be seen by the distance between the lines. However, the lines are not strictly parallel, suggesting that one factor is affecting the other. In other words, the effect of context is different depending on the cue type given.

What we need to know now is whether any of these effects are significant. Running a general linear model univariate (one dependent variable) ANOVA we obtain the source table (Table 10.2).

Table 10.2 Source table

Source	Sum of squares	df	Mean square	F	Sig.
CONTEXT	2190.400	1	2190.400	63.521	.000
CUES	6150.400	1	6150.400	178.359	.000
CONTEXT* CUES	448.900	1	448.900	13.018	.001
Error	1241.400	36	34.483		
Total	50100.000	40			

The degrees of freedom for the total variability is always equal to the total number of data points or scores in the analysis minus one. The number of degrees of freedom for the main effect of a factor is always equal to the number of levels of the factor minus one. The degrees of freedom for an interaction are equal to the product of the degrees of freedom of the variables in the interaction, namely $df_A \times df_B$.

As in the case of a one-factor design, each mean square is equal to the sum of squares divided by the degrees of freedom. The F-ratio for an effect is found by dividing the mean square for the effect by the mean square error. To find out whether the F-ratio is significant we need the degrees of freedom for the components used to calculate it. Using these in tables of an F-distribution we can find out the critical value. However, most computerised statistical analysis packages will supply a probability value, and we can check whether that given for the sample is less than the significance level chosen. Note that this will only be the probability value for the sample only.

Our source table for this simple investigation of cues and context shows us that the hypothesis generated by the encoding specificity principle can be supported. Not only are there main effects of context and cue type, but the two interact and we find that congruous cues can allow the effect of the different context to be overcome.

An alternative design for our two factors would be repeated measures or within subjects. When using within-subjects factors in **multi-factorial ANOVA** designs, for one or all the factors, each main effect or interaction effect is compared with the corresponding error variance based on the interaction of the subjects factor with that effect or interaction (Figure 10.4). Hence each within-subjects effect will have a *different* error term for calculating the F-ratio. As with any within-subjects design, the two-factorial design has two advantages over the between-subjects equivalent. It is a very economical design, as it minimises the number of participants used. It should be very sensitive to the effects of our experimental manipulations because, by using the same people throughout, we control many potential confounding variables.

There is a major problem with using within-subjects design in memory experiments, however. The same participants cannot be shown or tested on the same material twice as there will be learning effects to take into account. So we need different, but equivalent, sets of recall material. We can carry out the above experiment using only 10 participants but each person takes part in each of the four combinations of levels, so each cell has 10 pieces of data in it, but derived from

KT

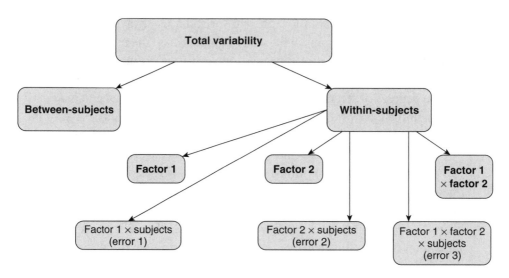

Figure 10.4 Partitioning in a within-subjects factorial design

the same people. Table 10.3 shows our means again, but with the assumption that the data came from a within-subjects design.

Requesting a fully repeated-measures design (see SPSS output in Appendix B) we get the source table (Table 10.3).

Table 10.3 Source table and means

Source	Sum of squares	df	Mean square	F	Sig.
CONTEXT	2190.4	1	2190.400	79.780	.000
Error (CONTEXT)	247.1	9	27.456		
CUES	6150.4	1	6150.400	196.220	.000
Error (CUES)	282.1	9	31.344		
CONTEXT* CUES	448.9	1	448.900	15.098	.004
Error (CONTEXT CUES)	267.6	9	29.733		

	Mean
same context congruous cues	48.1
same context incongruous cues	30.0
different context congruous cues	40.0
different context incongruous cues	8.50

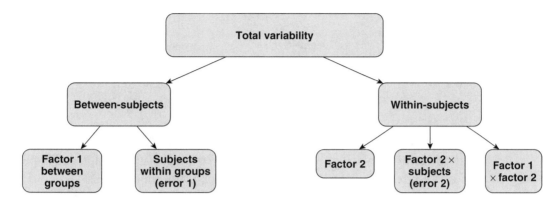

Figure 10.5   Error terms in within-subjects factorial designs

Here we see that each factor or interaction has its own error term, which is used to determine the *F*-ratio for each effect. This minimises the effect due to any individual differences within the group.

Interpreting a repeated design means examining how the within-subjects variability can be partitioned (see Figure 10.5) into that due to the effect of the different levels of each factor and the interaction between the variables and the variability due to the participants which comprise the error variabilities.

For the degrees of freedom,

factor = number of levels −1
subjects = number of subjects −1
error of each factor = *df* of factor × *df* of subjects
interaction = product of *df* of each factor

So the *MS* of each variability is the *SS* divided by the *df*.

The *F*-ratio is the comparison between the *MS* for the factor (or interaction) and the *MSE* for each factor (or the interaction).

There is another issue to be considered with fully repeated-measures designs, and that is **sphericity**. There is a need to have **homogeneity of variance** among different scores; this is much more a requirement in repeated measures ANOVAs than with between-subjects designs. Samples that are drawn from the same population should have a large proportion of their variance in common (their covariance). Many computer programs will give the results with an assumption of sphericity, but the

KT

Table 10.4

Context	Congruous cues	Incongruous cues	
Same	48.1	30	78.1
Different	40	8.5	48.5
Total	44.05	19.25	

more popular ones will provide different adjustments. What we really need to know about this is whether we can assume we have sphericity or not, and a quick glance at a printout will tell us this (see Chapter 17 for more details).

There is one final, non-statistical point to be considered when using a fully within-subjects design like this. It is a human point: people get tired. In this design we are asking 10 people to do a quite intellectually demanding task four times. We need to consider not only in which order they do them etc., but also how tired they will be by the time they have finished. This is quite a commitment from our participants. There is a type of design that falls partway between the uneconomic between-subjects design and the tiring within-subjects design, one which uses elements of both.

MIXED DESIGNS

Designs with at least one between-subjects factor and at least one repeated-measures factor are called mixed designs or sometimes split-plot designs. The partitioning of variance in a two-factor mixed design is, as we might expect, somewhere between that of a fully between-subjects and a fully within-subjects design and the summary table consists of the between-subjects factor effects and the within-subjects together with the interaction. For our encoding example, we could make our cue-type factor a within-subjects with the context factor a between-subjects one, see Table 10.4.

Many computer programs separate out the within-subjects and between-subjects effects, so there are two tables to examine: see Tables 10.5 and 10.5a.

POST-HOC ANALYSIS

If a significant main effect or interaction is found, then we can only conclude that there is a significant difference amongst the levels of our independent variable(s) somewhere. We still have to isolate exactly where the significant differences lie. If

Table 10.5   Tests of Within-subjects effects

Source	Sum of squares	df	Mean square	F	Sig.
CUE	6150.400	1	6150.400	201.396	.000
CUE*CONTEXT	448.900	1	448.900	14.699	.001
Error (CUE)	549.700	18	30.539		

Table 10.5a   Between-subjects effects

Source	Sum of squares	df	Mean square	F	Sig.
Intercept	40068.900	1	40068.900	1042.707	.000
CONTEXT	2190.400	1	2190.400	57.000	.000
Error	691.700	18	38.428		

an independent variable has only two levels then the significant F-value is sufficient to tell us that the two levels are significantly different from each other. If, however, we have three or more levels for an independent variable we need to follow up the significant F-value with Tukey's HSD post-hoc test. The method for doing this is the same as that encountered in the previous two chapters and is illustrated in the examples following.

If we find a significant interaction, we also need to follow up that finding with post-hoc tests. Even though a graph illustrates the relationship between the two independent variables, a graph is open to 'scale abuse'. That is, by choosing an appropriate scale *any* difference can be made to look like a large difference on a graph. We need to have a numerical way of objectively deciding if a certain difference is actually significant or not. The main thing to remember is that when examining a significant interaction with post-hoc tests, it is actually the individual cell means that are being compared, so that in a 2×2 ANOVA there are four cell means to be compared, in a 2×3 ANOVA there are six cell means to be compared, etc. The number of means being compared is important for determining the q-value in the HSD formula.

Simple Effects

Let us consider the inspection of the interaction as calculated by the ANOVA, see Figure 10.3.

Table 10.6

	Same context	Different context	
Congruous cues	48.1	40	44.05
Incongruous cues	30	8.5	19.25
	39.05	24.25	32.122

If we relate that back to the cell means, this suggests that there is an effect of giving incongruent cues, but this affects participants more in a different context. The best performance comes in the same conditions and congruous cues but the worst is in different context and incongruous cues; however, there is better performance with congruous cues overall.

We can test the cell means against each other with Tukey's HSD, but we can also carry out a simple main effects analysis. In this procedure the main effects of one variable are analysed within each of the levels of the other variable. Here we have a 2×2 design (see Table 10.6), therefore we can analyse the difference in means between the congruous and incongruous cues for the different context condition, and then for the same context condition. If these analyses turn out to be different we can interpret the effect of cue type on context. As we have two levels of cue type we need only carry out a t test. The t test for cues under the same context gives the value $t = 22.374$, $p < 0.05$, with a mean of 18.1, and for the different context condition $t = 8.69$, $p < 0.05$, with a mean difference of 31.5. If we then analyse the means for the context under each condition of cue type for the congruous cues $t = 11.732$, $p < 0.05$, with a mean difference of 8.1 and for incongruous cues $t = 5.892$, $p < 0.05$, with a mean difference of 21.5, each set of means is significantly different from each other in this analysis, so the two factors are exerting influence over each other.

If there had been three levels of one factor the t test would not have been applied and a one-way ANOVA, followed by pair-wise comparisons, such as with the HSD, would be appropriate.

A simple main effects analysis of an interaction can be viewed from either of the perspectives described above, from the simple main effects of variable A within variable B, or vice versa, and whichever you choose will depend on the theoretical basis for the study. However, although simple main effects are becoming more widespread in the psychological literature, there is a problem. Interactions occur because the effects of one variable are not the same across the levels of the other variable, which can be shown graphically when we have a set of non-parallel lines, as in Figure 10.3 (earlier) for the cues versus context analysis. Computationally, a simple 2×2 interaction is the difference of differences. For example, the following formula

$$A \times B \text{ interaction effect} = (A_1B_1 - A_2B_1) - (A_1B_2 - A_2B_2)$$

describes the interaction as the difference of the differences between A_1 and A_2 within each level of B. In our example we have all the differences as significant, therefore the simple effects analysis has not really got us very much further forward. If one set had been significant and not the other, this would have aided us more, but here the graph is actually the more useful piece of interpretative analysis.

Simple Main Effects for Between- and Within-Subjects Contrasts

In mixed design ANOVAs with both between- and within-subjects factors, simple main effects comparisons may require two different types of contrasts. If B represents a repeated measure, and A represents a between-groups measure, simple main effects contrasts will represent very different types of effects depending on the type of effect examined. For example, a contrast of A_1B_1 versus A_1B_2 is a within-subjects contrast, whereas a contrast of A_1B_1 versus A_2B_1 is a between-subjects contrast. It is usually found that between-subjects differences are larger than within-subjects differences, and the error term needs to be adjusted accordingly.

NON-PARAMETRIC TESTS

The widely used **non-parametric tests** do not extend beyond one-way designs. This is part of the problem with non-parametric tests, so they have not been developed to a level similar to the parametric ones. Alternative procedures include transforming data or employing a test that does not require the normality assumption to be met. Transforming data means correcting non-normality and unequal variances by transforming all the data values by applying a single mathematical function to all values in the data.

Transformations

Transforming all the measurements to remedy non-normality often results in correcting **heteroscedasticity** (unequal variances), and in eliminating interactions.

However, a transformation that corrects non-normality may create interactions where none existed before. In many statistical procedures, transformations include changing all the values to their logarithmic equivalent, or standardised scores.

Friedman's Test

For the two-factor factorial ANOVA, the most common non-parametric alternative test is Friedman's test. This test is designed for the case where we have exactly one measurement at each possible combination of values for the two factor levels. When there are replications, the values in each cell are replaced with their mean or median. Although Friedman's test does not assume normality of the distributions for the factor populations, it does assume that the populations have the same distribution, except for a possible difference in the population medians. Thus Friedman's test will not address the problem of inequality of variances. Also, as with the two-factor factorial ANOVA, it is assumed that the measurement errors are identically distributed and independent of each other. In addition, Friedman's test assumes that there is *no* interaction present anywhere in the data.

If the measured values do indeed come from populations with normal distributions, then the two-factor factorial ANOVA is the most powerful test of the equality of the means; no other test is more likely to detect an actual difference among the means. If the population distributions are not normal, however, Friedman's test may be more powerful at detecting differences between the factor-level medians.

Summary

In this chapter we have looked at a range of two-factorial designs and the analysis of the resultant data. The concepts and procedures for two factors can be applied to designs with more than two, but it is not recommended that designs with more than three or four factors should be carried out as the resultant higher order interactions are very difficult to interpret. The next chapter will examine what happens in designs with other types of factors and variables incorporated into them.

Endel Tulving

Endel Tulving was born in Estonia in May 1927 but moved to Germany when he was 17, then to Canada to attend the University of Toronto. He received his B.A. in 1953 and his M.A. in 1954. He then went to Harvard University and earned a Ph.D. in experimental psychology in 1957. Tulving's contribution to Psychology is in suggesting that memory comprises different forms. One of these he called episodic memory, that which allows us to recall our own experiences and he suggested that this is distinct from other forms of memory. This difference attributes to a feature called autonoetic consciousness, i.e., when we remember our own past we have a knowledge about this mental experience that we recognise as 'remembering', and this is different to other types of experience.

Professor Tulving remains an active reseacher at the Rotman Research Institute near Toronto.

CHAPTER 11

MULTIVARIATE STATISTICS

Contents

Analysis of covariance

Multivariate analysis of variance

Summary

Multivariate Statistics

With many calculations, one can win; with few one cannot. How much less chance of victory has one who makes none at all! (Sun Tzu, Art of War)

Learning Objectives

- To examine design and analysis in studies with covarying continuous independent variables.
- To examine design and analysis in studies with more than one dependent variable.

KEY TERMS

- Analysis of covariance
- Centroid
- Covariance
- Multivariate analysis of (co)variance

The preceding chapters on experimental and correlational design and analysis all have one thing in common, the idea that we can only look at one dependent variable at a time. The essence of the experimental approach is control, and the ultimate controlled experiment will look at the effects of psychological factors on one variable. However, in certain situations this is not enough and several dependent variables can be seen to act together. This chapter will examine how we can analyse data derived in such circumstances.

There are several instances when the analysis of variance is inadequate as a tool to decipher the meaning in our data. We might have to take into account the effects of a variable for which we cannot control, such as age or IQ, or we may need to look at the interaction between two or more dependent variables, such as the prediction that memory scores are affected by anxiety or a combination of the two situations. These designs would be analysed by the analysis of covariance (ANCOVA), multivariate analysis of variance (MANOVA) and multivariate analysis of covariance (MANCOVA) respectively.

ANALYSIS OF COVARIANCE

A covariate is an independent variable of continuous (interval-level) data that is not manipulated by the experimenter but may still affect the response. This effect is assessed by the analysis of covariance, which is used to assess the statistical significance of the variability of means among experimental groups adjusting for differences on one or more covariates. ANOVA focuses on F tests of significance of variability among group means. We need to know if the difference in sample means is enough to conclude that the population means differ. This depends on the size of the variability of group mean, the sample sizes in each group (as larger sample sizes give more reliable information and even small differences in means may be significant if the sample sizes are large enough) and the variances of the dependent variable scores. The formulae for the tests of variability in mean differences such as ANOVA therefore reflect three sets of difference: those in the means, the group sample sizes and the group variances. That is, ANOVA is a function of the variance of the set of means, and the variances of the scores in each group in relation to sample size: the larger the difference in means, the larger the sample sizes, and/or the lower the variances, the more likely a finding of significance.

ANCOVA is used to test the main and interaction effects of independent variables, whose levels are expressed as categories, on a continuous dependent variable, controlling for the effects of one or more continuous variables which covary with the dependent one. The first stage of an ANCOVA is a regression analysis (see Chapter 12) using the covariates to predict the dependent variable scores. There will be a difference between the predicted scores and the actual scores; this set of differences is termed 'residuals'. The analysis then does an ANOVA on the residuals to see if the factors are still significantly related to the dependent variable after the variation due to the covariates has been removed. Covariates are commonly regarded as variables. For example, for a recall word list test, we have some research evidence to suggest that IQ will affect performance, so the IQ score can be used as a covariate to control for initial group differences on recall ability. So, in ANCOVA we look at the effects of the categorical independent variables on an interval-dependent variable, after effects of interval covariates are controlled. Note that the independent variables must be a mixture of categorical data (those that can be split into categories such as male/female, young/middle aged/older or control condition/treatment 1/treatment 2, etc.) and interval-level (such as IQ, age, etc.) data. If only categorical variables are entered, this will result in an ANOVA;

if only interval-level independent variables are entered then this will be run as a multiple regression (see next chapter). However, the covariate effect in an ANCOVA can be interpreted in the same way as for a regression model.

There are several assumptions related to ANCOVA, which should be strictly observed, as ANCOVA is more sensitive to violations than ANOVA:

1   The higher the number of covariates, the lower the number of degrees of freedom, and the less effect each covariate will have. Hence the explanatory power of the analysis is being lowered.
2   There should be low measurement error of the covariate(s). Poor measurement reduces the statistical power of ANCOVA with an increased probability of Type II errors (false negative).
3   There is a linear relationship between the covariates and the dependent variable.
4   For any group formed by the categories of the independent variable(s) there is homogeneity of the regression coefficients of the dependent variable scores.
5   There are no outliers in the covariates.
6   There is low correlation between the covariates. High levels of correlation between covariates is known as multicollinearity and is discussed in detail in the next chapter. However, if covariates are highly correlated it can be assumed that one is redundant and need not be added.
7   The error term should be independent of the covariates and the independent variable(s). This is assured by using randomisation.
8   There must be homogeneity of variances in each group formed by the categories of the independent variables. Heteroscedasticity refers to a lack of homogeneity of variances, meaning that the covariate should be withdrawn.

So, how would we apply this technique? Remember that, in the introductory chapters about quantitative designs, we talked about memory and how it might be affected by age. There, it was suggested that 25 year olds and 65 year olds would perform differently in recall tests, but then the following chapters on experimental design went on to test participants without reference to their age. For example, in Chapter 8 we looked at the levels of processing framework, which suggests that items which had received more elaborate processing would tend to be easier to store and recall than those which had undergone less elaborate encoding. This leads to the depth of processing hypothesis, 'deeper processing leads to more durable memory traces'. We then examined how to test this hypothesis using different orienting tasks, that is the way in which subjects were directed to focus (or not) on items to be remembered. Our analysis showed that participants given tasks that required meaningful or semantic manipulations of the words, but no instructions to learn, recalled lists of words as well as subjects given explicit instructions to memorise the materials. We had 25 people in five different conditions, but suppose we carry out the levels of processing experiment with 100 people, and we are now concerned that age may be having an effect on our results. However,

Table 11.1

Orienting task	Mean age	N	Std. deviation	Minimum age	Maximum age
Control	40.1000	20	9.59660	26.00	55.00
Counting	45.1500	20	12.90155	27.00	64.00
Rhyming	40.3000	20	9.78775	27.00	59.00
Adjective	45.1000	20	11.27130	27.00	62.00
Imagery	48.3500	20	9.23537	26.00	63.00
Total	43.8000	100	10.90362	26.00	64.00

Table 11.2

Source	Type III Sum of squares	df	Mean square	F	Sig.
Corrected Model	290.540(a)	4	72.635	2.517	.046
Intercept	42477.210	1	42477.210	1472.078	.000
Orient	290.540	4	72.635	2.517	.046
Error	2741.250	95	28.855		
Total	45509.000	100			
Corrected Total	3031.790	99			

a R Squared = .096 (Adjusted R Squared = .058)

we are unable to get equal numbers of participants in each age group between 25 and 65, so instead we simply note our participants' ages, and we get the results shown in Table 11.1.

This would indicate that we do not have an equal spread, or not as equal as we would like, of ages across all conditions. Therefore we cannot simply use age as a fixed factor; it must be treated as a covariate. The univariate ANOVA results in the source table shown in Table 11.2.

This shows a significant effect of orienting tasks on recall. An interesting analysis here would be to carry out the Pearson correlation coefficient calculation between recall and age, and this turns out to be a non-significant value of −0.043, suggesting that recall performance dips slightly with age but not significantly. But we still need to take into account the effect this might have on the effect of the orienting task. Adding age as a covariate gives us the source table in Table 11.3.

Table 11.3

Source	Type III Sum of squares	df	Mean square	F	Sig.
Corrected Model	312.740(a)	5	62.548	2.162	.065
Intercept	2713.944	1	2713.944	93.823	.000
Age	22.200	1	22.200	.767	.383
Orient	307.005	4	76.751	2.653	.038
Error	2719.050	94	28.926		
Total	45509.000	100			
Corrected Total	3031.790	99			

a R Squared = .103 (Adjusted R Squared = .055)

This demonstrates that, even if we take age into account, the effect of the orienting tasks remains significant, and there is no significant effect of age as an accompanying variable.

We thought previously that age might have an effect, so this result, while heartening to those of us who are aging, is surprising. It might be that something is mediating any effect aging might have. What could it be?

We know from research on eyewitness memory that the confidence someone has in their accuracy of recall affects the recall performance. Brewer and Wells (2006) showed that eyewitnesses are an important part of the criminal investigation process, and the memory after witnessing a crime has been the subject of a great deal of psychological study, both *in situ* and in the lab. Failure to identify suspects may lead to a change in police investigation strategy, and a positive identification may lead to the police concentrating on one person, possibly the wrong person (Wells, Small, Penrod, Malpass, Fulero & Brimacombe, 1998). Eyewitness testimony is often the key piece of evidence in a criminal trial, and will convince juries of the guilt of the defendant like no other evidence will. One piece of contributory evidence is that the witness's confidence in the accuracy of the memory is crucial to the outcome of evaluating that evidence (Potter & Brewer, 1999). Studies using a mock-juror setup have found that confidence has a major influence on participants' assessment of witness credibility and verdicts (Brewer & Burke, 2002). However, several studies such as that done by Memon, Hope and Bull (2003) suggest that there is little real relationship between the confidence in recall accuracy and the actual accuracy. Research in memory other than in eyewitness identification also suggests that there are other variables that exert an influence on confidence and accuracy, such as personality (Furnham & Thomas, 2004). Some theories of memory suggest that recollection-based processes, including the effect of familiarity of the cue, vary with memory trace strength (Wixted & Stretch, 2004). So, a measure of confidence is possibly indicating the strength of the memory trace that the participant possesses. This may be even more important in older people. A study by Lachman and Andreolotti (2006) suggests that the older the participant, the more likely it is that confidence in their ability to recall will strengthen the accuracy of the memory. This is due to the amount of control the participants believe they have over their own cognition, as the belief that you can retain, or have retained, a good memory is crucial to actually having one. If we believe we can control our memory then we are more likely to use mnemonic strategies and use them more effectively. Lachman and Andreolotti go on to say that young people do experience memory problems despite the research evidence, but they attribute it to distraction or other external factors, unlike older adults who attribute forgetfulness to aging. So, the mediating effect here, and a contributory factor in the older participants' being as good at recalling as the younger ones, may be confidence in their ability leading to the use of better mnemonic strategy. This would be seen as a second dependent variable in any study on memory rather than a covariate, because it would need to be measured while the experiment was being performed. Therefore analysis of covariance is not appropriate, and we would need to analyse this design using a multivariate analysis of variance, a MANOVA.

MULTIVARIATE ANALYSIS OF VARIANCE

KT

Multivariate analysis of variance (MANOVA) is an extension of ANOVA to cover designs where there is more than one dependent variable and where the dependent variables cannot simply be combined. There is also a possibility of multivariate analysis of covariance, in which two or more dependent variables are analysed together to determine the effect of one or more categorical factors together with an interval-level independent variable or covariate. MANOVA would show the main and interaction effects of categorical variables on multiple dependent interval variables. We could have one or more categorical independents as predictors, like ANOVA, but more than one dependent variable. ANOVA tests the variabilities among the means of the interval dependent for various categories of the independent(s), whereas MANOVA tests the differences in the **centroid** of means of the multiple interval dependents, for various categories of the independent(s).

KT

Multiple analysis of covariance (MANCOVA) is similar to MANOVA, but interval-independent variables may be added as covariates. These covariates serve as control variables for the independent factors, serving to reduce the error term in the model. MANOVA and MANCOVA are found under the General Linear Model in statistical analysis packages, and produce similar output to ANOVA. However, coefficients or parameters are created for all categories of each factor. These are not interpreted in linear fashion unfortunately: that is, a unit change in an independent variable does not correspond to an equivalent change in the dependent variable.

There are several assumptions of MANOVA, in addition to those for parametric tests, which must be met:

1   Observations must be independent of each other, as MANOVA loses robustness if variables depend on other. This would be the case of pre- and post-test scores in repeated measures designs, for example, and it would be better to test time 1 and time 2 as a repeated measures factor, or to take the difference between them as the dependent variable.
2   The independent variable(s) must be categorical.
3   The dependent variables are continuous and interval level, as are any covariates.
4   As with ANCOVA, there must be low measurement error in the covariates. Imperfect measurement reduces the statistical power of the F test for MANCOVA giving increased probability of making a Type II error. Any covariate that may give rise to doubt in the measurement should really be treated as a dependent variable. For example, we can measure age with little error, as people usually know how old they are, but weight might vary from hour to hour given someone's metabolism.
5   Equal group sizes.
6   There should be data in every cell in the design. A 2×3 design will have six cells.
7   Residual data is randomly distributed.
8   There should be low homoscedasticity – so there needs to be homogeneity of variances and covariances. Within each group formed by the categorical independent variables, the variance of each interval dependent should be similar. For each of the groups formed by the independent variables, the covariance between any two dependent variables must be the same.
9   In repeated measures design (unusual cases for multivariate analysis) sphericity should be examined. A spherical model implies that the assumptions of multiple univariate ANOVA are met, that the repeated contrasts are uncorrelated. When there is a violation of this assumption, we should use MANOVA rather than multiple univariate ANOVA tests. If Bartlett's and Mauchly's tests of sphericity are significant, the sphericity assumption is violated.
10 No outliers.

When we look at all of this, it might be thought that it would just be simpler to carry out multiple ANOVA tests, one for each dependent variable. This might be the case, but multiple univariate ANOVA tests are susceptible to Type II errors as ANOVA is looking for differences in means under assumptions of independence, whereas MANOVA does not require such an assumption to be met. The next question to ask naturally then is 'how many dependent variables can MANOVA cope

Table 11.4

	Minimum	Maximum	Mean	Std. Deviation
score	10.00	30.00	20.6100	5.53391
age	26.00	64.00	43.8000	10.90362
confidence	0	100	46.66	27.751
Orient		**score**	**confidence**	**age**
Control	Mean	20.3000	47.35	40.1000
	Std. Deviation	5.42023	25.656	9.59660
Counting	Mean	17.9500	50.70	45.1500
	Std. Deviation	5.55807	28.514	12.90155
Rhyming	Mean	19.9000	43.20	40.3000
	Std. Deviation	4.44735	31.770	9.78775
Adjective	Mean	22.2500	48.85	45.1000
	Std. Deviation	5.90161	26.081	11.27130
Imagery	Mean	22.6500	43.20	48.3500
	Std. Deviation	5.42193	28.352	9.23537
	Std. Deviation	5.53391	27.751	10.90362

with?' There is no real limit, but the more that are included, the higher the likelihood of them being correlated, and the more difficult the result is to interpret. This also holds for adding covariates.

So, let us look at our situation now in the levels of processing experiment. We have the experimental factor of orienting task and its effect on recall performance, but we also have age, and now we are adding in the self-rated confidence the participants give in their ability to recall, or their confidence in having recalled accurately. Say the confidence in accuracy of recall is rated on a 0–100 scale, 100 indicating that participants are 100% confident that they have recalled accurately and to the best of their ability. The descriptive statistics might look something like those in Table 11.4.

Using confidence and recall score as dependent variables would give the source table for the MANOVA in Table 11.5, showing that confidence has no effect on whether the orienting task has a significant effect or not. Also adding in the covariate age gives us the result in Table 11.6, which indicates that there is no effect of either the confidence or the age of the participant on whether the orienting task is having an effect on the recall of words.

Table 11.5

Source	Dependent variable	Type III Sum of squares	df	Mean square	F	Sig.
Corrected Model	score	290.540(a)	4	72.635	2.517	.046
	confidence	910.740(b)	4	227.685	.287	.886
Intercept	score	42477.210	1	42477.210	1472.078	.000
	confidence	217715.560	1	217715.560	274.566	.000
Orient	score	290.540	4	72.635	2.517	.046
	confidence	910.740	4	227.685	.287	.886
Error	score	2741.250	95	28.855		
	confidence	75329.700	95	792.944		
Total	score	45509.000	100			
	confidence	293956.000	100			
Corrected Total	score	3031.790	99			
	confidence	76240.440	99			

a R Squared = .096 (Adjusted R Squared = .058)
b R Squared = .012 (Adjusted R Squared = −.030)

Table 11.6   Tests of between-subjects effects

Source	Dependent variable	Type III Sum of squares	df	Mean square	F	Sig.
Corrected Model	score	312.740(a)	5	62.548	2.162	.065
	confidence	1657.689(b)	5	331.538	.418	.835
Intercept	score	2713.944	1	2713.944	93.823	.000
	confidence	6555.763	1	6555.763	8.263	.005
Age	score	22.200	1	22.200	.767	.383
	confidence	746.949	1	746.949	.941	.334
Orient	score	307.005	4	76.751	2.653	.038
	confidence	953.863	4	238.466	.301	.877
Error	score	2719.050	94	28.926		
	confidence	74582.751	94	793.434		
Total	score	45509.000	100			
	confidence	293956.000	100			
Corrected Total	score	3031.790	99			
	confidence	76240.440	99			

a R Squared = .103 (Adjusted R Squared = .055)
b R Squared = .022 (Adjusted R Squared = −.030)

Summary

This chapter has looked at the case of experimental data in which there are more variable types to take into account than in the simpler experimental designs. Here we have encountered designs in which covariates may be having an effect on the dependent variables in conjunction with the categorical factors. Additionally there may be cases in which there are several dependent variables which cannot be separated from the design. These must all be taken into account in the analyses, and we have looked at the variations on the ANOVA model that we can use.

CHAPTER 12

COMPLEX CORRELATIONAL DESIGNS AND ANALYSIS: STATS CAN BE MURDER

Contents

Murdering stats

Multiple linear regression
Multicollinearity
Selection methods

Getting away with murder
Logistic regression

Summary

Complex Correlational Designs And Analysis: Stats Can Be Murder

There's the scarlet thread of murder running through the colourless skein of life, and our duty is to unravel it, and isolate it, and expose every inch of it. (Sir Arthur Conan Doyle, *A Study in Scarlet*)

Learning Objectives

- To learn about analysis in cases of complex relationships in data.

KEY TERMS

- Criterion
- Linear regression
- Logistic regression
- Logit
- Multiple regression
- Predictor
- Regression

In Chapter 9, we encountered the concept of regression. This is a technique whereby we can express the relationship between a predictor and a criterion variable in terms of a line, the equation for which is $y = a + bx$ where x is the score on the predictor variable, a is the value where the line cuts the y-axis and b is a measure of the slope of the line. Here a is referred to as a constant, this doesn't mean it will always be the same figure, but once it has been calculated for this model it remains the same and the higher the value of a, the steeper the slope of the line.

The figure *b* is referred to as a *regression coefficient* and the higher the value of *b* the higher up the *y*-axis the line cuts. This is fine if we are only interested in one predictor variable, but there are cases where we might have several, and need to use a technique in which multiple variables and their effect on the criterion can be examined. When the criterion variable is continuous, we can use a technique known as multiple regression, which examines the relationship between several predictor variables and a criterion variable.

The general analytical problem that needs to be solved in multiple regression analysis is to fit a straight line to a number of points. When we have only one criterion and one predictor, then the scatterplot approach is fine, as we saw in Chapter 9. However, multiple predictors cannot be expressed in this simple two-dimensional space, but it can be expressed mathematically. Where we have a number of predictors, numbered from 1 to *n*, the equation would be

$$Y = a + b_1X_1 + b_2X_2 + ... + b_nX_n$$

Each regression coefficient represents the independent contributions of each independent, predictor variable to the prediction of the criterion or dependent variable. Let us look at an example using our old friend, the question of age and memory. In our experimental setup explored in Chapter 11 we discovered that age was a covariate for the effect that orienting task condition had on recall, but there was also only a very small negative correlation between age and recall ability overall. This might be surprising as anecdotal evidence and research evidence suggest that memory does decline with age, and we would therefore expect that the negative correlation would be a larger figure. However, if we then add in a person's level of confidence in their ability to recall, and possibly other factors such as occupation, we might find that recall performance is predicted by many factors, not just age, explaining why age might not have the debilitating effect research would suggest. The relationship between the factors can be examined using the ANCOVA, described in Chapter 11, but it can also be explored with multiple regression analysis, because there may be things that do not fall into a straight factorial design. These facts may be hinting that there is a relationship between ANOVA models and regression models that we have not yet encountered, so watch this space!

Here we have a line in regression analysis, if one could be drawn, that represents the best prediction of the values of the dependent (criterion) variable, *Y*, given the values of the independent (predictor) variables, *X*. However, we saw in the scatterplot with one X variable that there is quite a lot of variation around the line, and this becomes more complex with several predictor variables. The deviation of any actual value of Y from the regression line is called its **residual** value. The smaller these are, the better prediction we are making. If there is no relationship between the predictor and criterion, then the ratio of the residual variability of the criterion variable to the original variance is 1. If the variables are perfectly related then there is no residual variance and the ratio of variance would be 0.0. In most cases, this ratio is somewhere between 0.0 and 1. The calculation of one minus the ratio is known as **R-square** or the coefficient of determination. If we have an R-square of 0.5 then we know that the variability of the Y-values around the regression line is 1–0.5 times the original variance; in other words, we have explained 50% of the original variability, and are left with 50% residual variability. The higher the value of R-square, the better the model fits the data. The square root of R-square is, naturally enough, R, which is the correlation coefficient that tells us the degree to which the predictors are related to the criterion. In multiple regression, R can be between 0 and 1, and in order to interpret this we look at whether the beta (β) coefficients are negative or positive. The beta value tells us how much each predictor influences the criterion, and is measured in units of standard deviation. So, a beta value of 1.5 suggests that one standard deviation change in the predictor variable will result in a change of 1.5 standard deviations in the criterion variable, and the higher the beta value, the greater the impact of the predictor. With one predictor variable in our model, then beta is equivalent to the correlation coefficient between the predictor and the criterion, but with more predictors we cannot compare the contribution of each predictor variable by simply comparing the correlation coefficients. The beta regression coefficient is computed to allow you to make such comparisons and to assess the strength of the relationship between each predictor variable to the criterion variable. If a β coefficient is positive, then the relationship of this variable with the dependent variable is positive; if negative, then the relationship is negative. So, in our age and memory example, we would expect that the β coefficients of the age variable to be negative, as age rises memory performance goes down, but we might have a positive β coefficient for confidence in memory, so the higher the confidence, the higher the recall.

All this is a very technical way of talking about whether some variables have effects on others. By now we have encountered several ways of looking at quantitative data, using experimental designs or correlational designs, analysing the data by *t* tests, ANOVAS, correlation and regression. Perhaps you feel like murdering someone? In fact, we can examine our regression models a little more realistically by examining exactly that – whether someone would murder another person if they thought they could get away with it.

MURDERING STATS

Murder is when a man of sound memory, and of the age of discretion, unlawfully killeth within any country of the realm any reasonable creature in rerum natura * under the king's peace, with malice aforethought, either expressed by the party or implied by law, so as the party wounded, or hurt die of the wound or hurt within a year and a day after the same. (Edward Coke) *an independent being born of its mother and alive at birth.

So, if someone asked you if you would commit the above crime, what would you say? Of course the answer would be no. What if you could get away with it, and the person to be murdered was someone you detested, and you would be paid a huge sum of money for doing it? Would you think again? Of course not, the answer would still be no! Hm, remember the Milgram study in Chapter 2. Those participants were just ordinary folk like you and me, yet they went further than they thought they would, thinking they were really hurting another person. In 1996, Russell and Baenninger set out to discover what would predict how likely it is that someone would say yes to the above question, they would murder someone, and the answers surprised everyone.

Their participants were students at North American Universities, and 14% of the men and 7% of the women answered 'yes' to the question 'If it was arranged that you could never be identified nor arrested and there was no possibility of retaliation, would you personally kill someone you knew and thoroughly hated?'

The idea that people will, at least in their imagination, commit quite serious crimes, or even terrible crimes such as murder, is a recently researched one. In 1981, 35% of male Canadian students, asked in a study by Malamuth, said there was a possibility they would rape a woman if they knew they would get away with it. Again in Canada, 47% of ice hockey fans said they would take part in a fight if one broke out at a game (Russell & Arms, 1995). It has been suggested that these figures are indicative more of the spirit of boasting than actual behaviour, but the fact remains that at least a proportion of people are saying they would carry out quite serious crimes and only the thought of prosecution or social censure is stopping them! The validity of studies such as these are severely questioned in the commentary literature, but if we examine Milgram's study, a large proportion of psychological experts did not think the participants would go as far as they did. Perhaps we are so shocked by the thought of whether we would behave badly, if given the opportunity, that we cannot imagine others feeling the same way. In fact, the desire to respond in a socially desirable way to questions of situations such as these may be underestimating the extent to which people really respond to this. Russell and Baenninger attempted to overcome this question of validity by developing a questionnaire designed to overcome any inflation or deflation of responses status, and examining the responses in the light of several demographic and psychological characteristics. Their measurements included a scale of social desirability, and subscales of a hostility inventory designed to measure likelihood to commit physical assault, together with irritability, and guilt subscales and a scale to measure faith in people (or misanthropy). The dependent measure was the score on a six-item scale developed for the study that the authors called the Limits of Behavior Scale (LOBS). This was a set of six questions about behaviour, answered yes or no, to test how far someone would go in altruistic, criminal or undesirable behaviour. Remember: this was an American study and the terminology may not be familiar:

Limits of Behavior Scale (Russell & Baenninger, 1996)

1. Would you be willing to walk 2 blocks to the store as a favor for someone if you knew it was 40 below zero?
2. If it was arranged that you could never be identified nor arrested and there was no possibility of retaliation, would you personally kill someone you knew and thoroughly hated?
3. Would you be willing to donate one of your kidneys to save the life of a child?
4. Would you be willing to help out a beginning knife-thrower by volunteering to be his/her practise target?
5. Would you agree to be carried across Niagara Falls on the shoulders of an expert tight rope walker?
6. Would you eat monkey brains in a restaurant if the dish had been ordered for you by your host?

All of the participants were psychology students, some studying at Lethbridge in Canada and some in Philadelphia, USA. Their sex was noted, but the universities would not allow the researchers to record race, though it was noted that the ethnic composition at each university was different. Russell and Baenninger hypothesised that men would score higher on willingness to murder than women, as violent crime statistics do indicate a sex difference in physical aggression

(Baron & Richardson, 1994). It was also expected that non-religious participants would be more likely to say they would commit murder given that religions usually support non-violent solutions to problems. Also, those who scored high on scales or irritation and 'assaultiveness' were predicted to be more likely to endorse violent behaviour in the LOBS, as trait aggression has predicted involvement in violent events (Russell, Arms & Robert, 1995). Finally, low scores on the faith in people scale, indicating less adherence to social control, were expected to endorse the murder element. Once this data was collected from 513 (205 male and 308 female) participants in Canada and 248 (100 male and 148 female) American participants, the researchers submitted it to various quantitative analyses to test their hypotheses. A chi-square analysis showed that men were more likely to express willingness to murder than women in both universities. Correlational analysis showed that some variables correlated more strongly than others with the dependent measure of willingness to murder.

MULTIPLE LINEAR REGRESSION

The data then underwent a multiple regression analysis with nine predictor variables including sex, age, religiosity, visa status, social desirability scores, guilt scores, assaultiveness scores, irritability scores and faith in people scores. The two universities were separated, as the researchers were not allowed to give the faith in people questions to participants in Canada. The results showed that there were negative correlations between the criterion variable of willingness to murder and sex, age, religiosity and scores on social desirability, faith in people and guilt but quite strong relationships between assaultiveness and irritability. So what does all this mean? Well, what will predict whether or not someone is going to harbour murderous thoughts appears to be whether they are male, not religious, have low levels of social desirability, sense of guilt and faith in people, and high scores on assaultiveness and irritability. Here we begin to get the sense of where offender profiling started. High levels of the ability to predict the likelihood of committing violent crime would certainly add to the profiler's understanding of offenders.

As such, multiple regression is a very useful tool in the psychological analysis kit. The Russell and Baenninger study shows that some variables account for 12% of the variance in the endorsement of violent behaviour such as murder. Obviously there is a large step between the endorsement of murder and actually carrying it out, but when we consider that statistics suggest we are more likely to fall victim to a serial killer than win the National Lottery (1 in 1 million compared with 1 in

13 million against six numbers coming up; Hicky, 1991), anything casting light on murder is welcome. Knowing that someone's level of irritability might predict whether they would think positively about murder is revealing.

We have already discovered that multiple regression and ANOVA have some sort of relationship. ANOVA tells us how much of the variance in participants' scores is accounted for by our manipulation of the independent variables, and possibly we can add a covariate. But it is still a relatively limited and controlled way of examined variance in data. In multiple regression there is no direct manipulation of variables but the measure of naturally occurring variability is added to the model to aid prediction on the criterion.

Multiple regression then is used when we want to explore linear relationships between the predictors and a continuous data criterion. The predictor variables should be measured continuous or ordinal. Nominal predictors are acceptable, but then they are called dummy variables. An example of this would be sex, where items can be coded as 0 or 1. Dummy variables usually would have only two values, but more can be included if this is justifiable. There are other items about the data which must be complied with, such as large numbers of cases (or participants). Tabachnik and Fidell (2001) state that sample sizes should be greater than eight times the number of predictor variables plus 50 ($N \geq 50 + 8m$, where m is the number of predictors). This means that the minimum number for a regression analysis is 58.

There are several other design issues to take into account when using multiple regression.

Multicollinearity

The concept behind multiple regression is that we need to determine whether the predictor variables are correlated with the criterion, but a problem arises when the predictor variables are correlated together. This is known as **multicollinearity** and cause an instability in the model. In fact, if two variables are highly correlated, the removal of one does not cause as many problems as leaving it in as they will rule each other out. Imagine that we have our irritability predicting willingness to murder design, and we considered adding in an anger measure. The likelihood would be that irritability and anger are highly correlated so the second measure is simply adding another measure of irritability to the mix, and is redundant. We would also need to find at least another eight people to be measured on all of the variables if we left it in.

Selection Methods

There are several methods of calculating the relative contribution of each predictor variable to the model. The first way that SPSS offers is called the Enter method and it requires a set of predictor variables to be specified, but the whole set is measured against the criterion, with no weighting or any particular order of preference. Other models are known as hierarchical methods in which the variables are entered into the model in a specified order that reflects the theoretical considerations or research findings. These are only used if we suspect that some variables will have a more important effect than others because each variable's effect is assessed before the next is entered. If the variable does not alter the model significantly, it is dropped. In other words, those that we hypothesise are going to be more salient to the criterion are added, the regression is calculated, then another added. If the second does not add to any predictive power =, then it is removed and the next added, and so on. These methods are called forward selection, backward selection and stepwise selection, depending on the way the predictors are added:

> **Forward selection**   Enter the variables into the model one at a time in an order determined by the strength of their correlation with the criterion variable.
> **Backward selection**   Enter all of the predictor variables into the model, then remove the weakest predictor variable and recalculate the regression. If the model is weakened, then the predictor variable is re-entered, and so on.
> **Stepwise**   Enter each variable in sequence and assess its effect: if it contributes, it remains; if not, it is removed. This method ensures that the smallest possible set of predictor variables is included in the model, called the parsimonious model.

So, in our example above we have examined what might predict whether someone was willing to murder if they could get away with it. The next obvious question is whether they would get away with it.

GETTING AWAY WITH MURDER

This can only be answered by examining how effectively police forces deal with murder cases. In 2005, Lee suggested that many factors beyond those strictly regarded as 'legal' should be taken into account when analysing homicide clearance rates. Lee suggested that allocation of public resources is not decided on an equitable basis, but with a gender, race and social bias. This also applies, she argues, to the investigation of a murder. She cites Baldus et al. (1990) who showed that when a murder case involves a white female victim, the suspect(s) is (are) more likely to be charged with the more serious crime and to receive the most severe penalties. In the USA this would mean being charged with first-degree murder and subsequently receiving the death penalty in some states; in the UK this would be murder with a potential life sentence. Many researchers have commented that there appears to be a bias hinting at higher 'value' placed on the life and murder of some types of victims than others. There may be a social trend indicated here too. In the USA clearance rates have dropped from 94% in 1961 to 67% in 2002 (Bureau of Justice Statistics, 2002). In the UK the figure remains stable at around 80% (Francis et al., 2004) but the overall number of homicides in the UK is considerably smaller (Flood-Page & Taylor, 2003). Given that there is a proportion of murders that remain unsolved, it is surprising that there is very little research on what factors contribute to the likelihood of homicide clearance. In 1976, Black suggested that some victims receive 'More law' than others and that this predicts whether or not their murder will be solved. Black suggested that 'the law' (patterns of reporting or non-reporting of crime, and the techniques used to investigate it) acts as a form of social control. The law and its response depend on the cultural and organisational characteristics of those involved, and victims who occupy social positions perceived as lesser receive poorer responses from the law (Black, 1976). He suggests that if such things can be quantified, then the patterns of arrest can be judged as inversely proportional to the social status of the victim. Hence, cases where the victim is not white, is not female and is at the extreme ends of the age demographic are less likely to be investigated to the point where a suspect is charged. Lee therefore set out to address this question and examined why and how quickly murder cases were solved in Los Angeles, concentrating on crimes committed between 1990 and 1994 when 9442 murders took place. She used event history analysis (how much time is needed to clear a case) and a specialised form of multiple regression called logistic regression.

Logistic Regression

Logistic regression follows the same overall logic as multiple linear regression but is applied when the criterion variable is binary or dichotomous, such as answers to a question 'if I was murdered would the case be solved?' There are cases when the criterion can take more than two values, in which the analysis becomes multinomial logistic regression.

KT

Logistic regression is used to predict values of a dichotomous variable from continuous and/or categorical predictor variables and to determine the proportion of the variance in the criterion explained by the predictors. It will also rank the importance of predictors, assess any interaction between them, and between them and any covariates. The calculation transforms the values of the criterion variables into their logit equivalents. This means the natural logarithm of the odds of the criterion variable occurring or not. We do not need to worry about what a logarithm is, simply that what we are looking at is the likelihood of an outcome: in other words, what is the probability of the murder being solved or not? Logistic regression will apply this transformation for us, then apply a maximum likelihood estimation of the outcome. When we apply all of these transformations in a computer program such as SPSS we get logit coefficients, which are equivalent to beta in multiple linear regression. However, logistic regression does not assume that the relationship between the predictors and the criterion is linear, or that the variables are normally distributed, and therefore can be applied in many different cases. So,

KT

continuous variables can be transformed to dichotomous and then such variables and naturally occurring dichotomous variables are transformed into logit variables. Predictor variables can be continuous, ordinal or dichotomous and the program transforms them all into binary. Additionally there can be interaction terms such as continuous covariates.

Interpreting Logits

Logit coefficients (logits) are called parametric estimates in SPSS, and can build prediction equations and generate predicted values (logistic scores). The model will be interpreted in similar ways to multiple regression except that where linear regression predicts a score, logistic regression predicts the odds of something occurring.

Summary

This chapter has examined what forms of analysis can be applied when considering whether several variables can jointly predict the outcome of another variable. The predictor variables can be a mix of continuous or categorical, and the criterion variable can be continuous, in which case multiple linear regression is applied, or categorical, in which logistic regression is applied and the outcome is the probability of one of two or more events occurring.

Sir Edward Coke (1552–1634)

An early English legal specialist, Coke was appointed to Speaker of the House of Commons in 1593, and was the prosecutor in such famous trials as that of Sir Walter Raleigh and the Gunpowder Plot conspirators. He was an early advocate of human and civil rights, interpreting the Magna Carta to include rights for all citizens, not just nobles. This did not make him very popular with the king, who removed him as Chief Justice in 1616, and had him imprisoned in 1620. However, Coke returned to public life unbowed and was instrumental in guaranteeing rights against arbitrary search and seizure, and was the first author of the concept of blind justice. He is seen as the very first instigator of rights for all subjects of the Crown, and his writings eventually became the basis of the US Bill of Rights. His writings are also regarded as the best examples of good legal practice from the early days of application in civil and criminal court, and lawyers across the world are now trained using his principles.

PART IV

BEGINNING QUALITATIVE RESEARCH

In this part, we will address some theoretical issues in qualitative approaches to psychological research that need to be examined before starting, the theory and design of qualitative research. We will explore the paradigms and philosophies of alternative worldviews and look at issues of why and how qualitative research can be performed.

CHAPTER 13

THEORY IN QUALITATIVE RESEARCH

Contents

The alternative paradigm?
Qualitative versus quantitative research paradigms

Theoretical viewpoints in psychological qualitative enquiry
Phenomenology
Ethnomethodology
Symbolic interactionism
Semiotics
Hermeneutics
Modernism, post-modernism

Psychological approaches to qualitative research

Summary

Theory in Qualitative Research

I have no data yet. It is a capital mistake to theorize before one has data. Insensibly one begins to twist facts to suit theories instead of theories to suit facts. (Sir Arthur Conan Doyle, *A Scandal in Bohemia: The Adventures of Sherlock Holmes*)

Learning Objectives

- To understand the different forms of paradigm available to researchers.
- To examine the range of theoretical viewpoints in qualitative research.

KEY TERMS

- Critical psychology
- Discursive psychology
- Ethnomethodology
- Feminist psychology
- Hermeneutics
- Naturalistic observation
- Paradigm
- Phenomenology
- Semiotics
- Symbolic interactionism

THE ALTERNATIVE PARADIGM?

In the quantitative approach to psychological investigation and research, a psychologist will take measurements of variables and look for patterns within the data, in order to test hypotheses. We already know that we do not seek to verify these hypotheses, but to falsify them, thereby advancing knowledge by proving something cannot have happened by chance. Scientific advance in quantitative approaches means the accumulation of certainty in facts. This approach has been challenged as denying the exploration of, or even the existence of, an alternative view of reality. A more interpretive approach would allow us, as researchers, to access descriptions of viewpoints other than in controlled experimental and artificial environments.

Qualitative Versus Quantitative Research Paradigms

In Chapters 1 and 3, we looked at the way that different paradigms in psychology lead to different forms of investigation. A paradigm represents a position or viewpoint that defines how we interact with and understand the world around us. Qualitative research uses a naturalistic approach that seeks to understand phenomena in context-specific settings, whereas quantitative research uses experimental methods and quantitative measures to test hypothetical generalisations. Each is a function or product of fundamentally different paradigms, with researchers acting on the underlying assumptions of each paradigm. In psychology, and many of the social sciences, a major shift away from experimentation has been experienced as more people are turning towards a richer way of investigating and interpreting psychological phenomena. This means that the boundaries of interpretation have been pushed a little further out, and we need alternative forms of enquiry in order to provide data, evidence and information that we can examine. When we do step into a richer, broader form of data and interpretation of that data, we open up for ourselves different issues than those encountered in experimentation or other strictly quantitative forms of research. The inherent criticism of quantitative enquiry that qualitative research implies means that there needs to be a viable alternative. This alternative also means that researchers are exploring not only the reality of their participants' world, but their own, and there needs to be an acknowledgement of that contained within the paradigm.

Qualitative research, according to Lincoln and Guba (1985), allows us to take into account effects of social settings, accepting that the complex and dynamic quality of the social world will fundamentally affect the findings of research carried out with people. They also suggest that the ability of qualitative research to provide a rich description of psychological events is important from the perspective of the reader as well as the researcher/writer. Therefore, the reader becomes an integral part of the research interpretation.

Therefore, we arrive at certain characteristics that are important for, or indicative of, qualitative research: the naturalistic setting as the source of data with the researcher as central to the data collection, using a predominantly inductive process to provide rich descriptions with expressive language, and acknowledging their input and place in the context of interpretation. This allows the theory and design to *emerge* instead of being predetermined and will therefore be judged on different criteria to quantitative research. This emergent nature of qualitative approaches is important. As qualitative researchers we observe and interpret meaning, so cannot finalise the strategy by which this will be done before we have discovered anything. Instead, we need to specify questions that will be addressed.

We already know that qualitative research seeks a depth of understanding that is distinct from quantitative research. Instead of testing a large sample drawn from a population, we seek to gain intimate information about a small group of people. What we try to do here is learn how people behave and think and how they make meaning of the world, rather than generalise on a large scale. So qualitative research is neither micro level nor macro level, and can therefore examine small processes at the human or social/societal level. It also means that qualitative research is about discovery and not necessarily about confirmation of a theoretical stance. This can cause a problem for researchers, as quantitative research seeks to confirm or verify or support hypotheses drawn from observation or the literature; qualitative research does not have that level of theoretical support. While such a position frees qualitative research from hypothesis-driven foci, this lack of reliance on previous research can leave researchers feeling alone and unsupported. For this reason, qualitative research should not be chosen simply as an alternative to qualitative, but as a deliberate choice towards freedom and stepping into the unknown, and a desire to contribute to the process of theory emergence.

Quantitative research is often termed 'positivistic' in nature, because the methods allow observations and knowledge to be duplicated in order to find rules and patterns. It is deductive in nature; that is, theories are examined by falsifying hypotheses through prediction or experimentation. An alternative viewpoint to this is naturalistic, in which the researcher enters the world of those being studied and interacts, asks questions and formulates emergent theoretical positions based on **naturalistic observations** and inductively scrutinises and reformulate those theories. Popper suggested that it is impossible to prove scientific theory by induction, as contrary evidence could always be found to refute the theory. However, naturalistic methodologists reject the idea of the *need* for proof. Here, we are looking at drawing theory from data, rather than testing theory by data. This 'grounded theory' approach, proposed by Glaser and Strauss in 1967, and known as the

KT

KT

Chicago School, became very prominent, as qualitative research became more prevalent and researchers turned away from **positivism** and towards an alternative epistemology. Here, our own orientations both as researchers and as people become part of the process of doing research. Our own worldview becomes part of the research and its findings and must be made explicit when we are reporting the result of our investigation. This of course means that there is a huge range of orientations and epistemologies that can be used in qualitative research, causing major differences of opinion. These differences can lead to isolation of the researcher and possibly a tendency towards suppression of research that does not conform to the reviewer's position.

In some areas of qualitative research, the Chicago School is seen as still too objective for some people's taste. Such researchers suggest that qualitative writing is still socially constructed and will reveal hidden constraints located in the use of style and voice. Here we are encouraged to identify our own characteristics, and perspectives, and how they influence investigation and reporting. A major focus in this approach is a feminist perspective, in which a major aim is to attempt to explain cultural position and experiences of women by using methods that are consistent with female/feminine/feminist values. This can include grounded theory, symbolic interactionism, critical psychology or post-modernist approaches, while seeking to acknowledge that any researcher has a social position that influences his or her approach and interpretation of data, and that we do not do research in a cultural vacuum (Haraway, 1988; Smith, 1990). This element of exclusion can be applied to other areas of research, and we are urged to reframe established theories to include race, class, culture, ethnicity as well as sex and gender (Dilworth-Anderson et al., 1993).

So, we find ourselves in the position where different qualitative methods have different methodological underpinnings. We might also mix different methods on the same project on the same data or even mix qualitative and quantitative methods. This is extremely confusing for someone setting out for the first time in qualitative research. Not only are we set free from the boundaries of positivistic deduction, we are set adrift without any moorings! We must attempt to understand the different epistemologies and choose from a variety of theoretical approaches that we are now offered. If it is confusing to attempt to choose an approach in quantitative research, and subsequently the form of analysis and number manipulation, how scary is it to be faced with a choice, when we can be criticised simply for making the choice, the way we make the choice, and the way we express our choice? Qualitative and quantitative research therefore are not merely different ways of approaching data, they are different ways of thinking about the world. Qualitative research allows for multiple realities placed in context instead of an external reality that is context-free. The realities can be accessed in natural settings rather than in controlled conditions and not through examination of preceding theory, which is perceived as limiting.

As qualitative researchers, we approach our enquiry assuming reality is socially or personally constructed by every individual from a unique contextual interpretation. This means we can be attacked for using undisciplined methods and subjective observations, without rigour, and approaching our interpretations without guidance from theoretical stances. Lincoln and Guba would suggest that this is not the case because the criteria used to judge quantitative research (internal validity, external validity, reliability and objectivity) do not apply. They assert that validity criteria are inappropriate measures for evaluating qualitative work; instead, it is 'trustworthiness' and 'credibility' that are important together with an understanding of the epistemological viewpoint of our own reality. Thus, there are several theoretical approaches in qualitative research that can guide the method of enquiry.

THEORETICAL VIEWPOINTS IN PSYCHOLOGICAL QUALITATIVE ENQUIRY

Popper's viewpoint is that knowledge is theory-laden and that methods are theory-driven, but this raises questions when we approach theory in qualitative research. Can qualitative research enhance understanding and expand theoretical knowledge or is it purely inductive with its validity divorced from preconceived theory? The various viewpoints are reflected in the theoretical positions that inform us how to approach qualitative enquiry. Here we will look at some of the positions that have had major impacts on psychological research. These are not the only viewpoints by any means, but they have had a major influence on shaping the qualitative approach.

Phenomenology

Phenomenology draws heavily on the work of Edmund Husserl (1910), who suggested that we focus attention on the ways in which people construct their views of everyday life. We should not concentrate on theories about the world, but only on generate descriptions. According to Husserl, human consciousness is separated into two elements, the act of consciousness and the phenomena we encounter via discovery of the world. This approach is phenomenological because it only allows for certain data, the appearance of objects or events, to be interpreted. So there is an ontological shift from reality being interpreted to phenomenological assumptions of objectivity, providing systematic strategies to follow in order to access or generate scientific comprehension of lived experience. These strategies are dominated by the need to be aware of preconceptions held about what is being studied, and allowing the grouping or clustering of data about it to provide isolation and cohesion.

Ethnomethodology

This can be seen as an extension or variant of phenomenology, but we are not required to suspend our notions when we are investigating the world ethnomethodologically. Here we focus on the everyday practices of 'social actors', which allow us to make sense of, rationally account for and construct our behaviour. Both ethnomethodology and phenomenology are built on the principles of eidetic science, the definition of objects, relationships and events via themselves (Lindlof, 1995). For example, for an ethnomethodological understanding of 'love' we would need to conduct interviews with people on what love means and consists of, but then we would have to strip away those interpretations to reveal the essence of the concept. Thus, ethnomethodology looks at both people and the essence of the phenomena and experiences in order to construct understanding.

Symbolic Interactionism

In a personally constructed world, meanings are produced by objects or events via their interaction with the representational symbols. According to Blumer, **symbolic interactionism**

KT

> does not regard meaning as emanating from the intrinsic makeup of the thing that has meaning, nor does it see meaning as arising through a coalescence of psychological elements in the person. Instead, it sees meaning as arising in the process of interaction between people. The meaning of a thing for a person grows out of the ways in which other persons act toward the person with regard to the thing. Their actions operate to define the thing for the person. Thus, symbolic interactionism sees meanings as social products, as creations that are formed in and through the defining activities of people as they interact. This point of view gives symbolic interactionism a very distinctive position, with profound implications (1969: 4).

This view of meaning as socially constructed realities sits really well in our own, psychologically oriented, understanding of the qualitative paradigm. If there are no objective or inherent meanings embedded in a text or a conversation or an action, then any meanings construed are socially constructed creations, and they create meaning by interacting with others or their writings. Blumer suggests several levels to this:

1. Human beings act toward things on the basis of the meanings that the things have for them. These things can be objects, people, or representations and we attribute meaning by what they mean to us, not their intrinsic attributes of themselves.
2. The meaning of such things is derived from, or arises out of, the social interaction with others, because we are social beings.
3. These meanings are handled and modified via an interpretative process that is continuously revisited.

These levels and the ways in which we traverse them are applied to qualitative research in that we seek understanding of phenomena within context, which needs to be re-evaluated after change.

Semiotics

KT

Semiotics, according to Denzin and Lincoln (1994), is a systematic analysis of symbols and their systems within a set of assumptions. Using semiotics, or a semiotic approach, we would investigate signs and meaning making and how this produces a meaningful world. Therefore it is not simply the use of signs and their interpretations (as in symbolic interactionism), but the strategies by which people engage in discourse within themselves and via signs. Semiotics accepts the view that meaning is not inherent in any sign but by continual reconstruction of personal and social meaning held within them. Signs are incomplete until they find an 'interpretant' context in which the interpreter can create meaning from the content of the sign.

Hermeneutics

Broadly speaking, hermeneutics is the theory of the interpretation and understanding of texts, originally biblical text, now widened to include all text and systems of meaning. A hermeneutic is a specific system or method for interpretation, or a specific theory of interpretation. In a hermeneutic approach we would need to have the ability to understand events from another's point of view, including understanding the cultural and social forces influencing it. The scope of hermeneutics is not only the interpretation of textual and artistic works, but also human behaviour (language and speech patterns, social groupings and ritual behaviour).

All of the above theoretical stances include the broader social science definitions of naturalistic, interpretative approaches to investigating the world, but there are some more radical schools of thought that have influenced the ways in which social research and its underpinning philosophy have changed. The theories above suggest that the ways in which we interact with our world and our own worldview are the most important topics for investigation, or at least they must be taken into account. Some philosophers would suggest that this viewpoint itself must shift, and that it cannot take into account the real structure of the social world.

Modernism, Post-modernism

Modernism is a philosophical movement loosely associated with the age of Enlightenment, an intellectual movement of eighteenth-century London and Paris, whose members set out to enlighten others, by the fostering of progress through the principles of rationality. Post-modernism then is usually regarded as the movement succeeding modernism, although there are many similarities in the way they are expressed. Post-modernists suggest that it is impossible to gain absolute and total knowledge; therefore positivist pursuit of knowledge is redundant. Philosophers such as Kierkegaard and Nietzsche argue against objectivity and scientific scepticism and led more recent thinkers such as Sartre and Derrida to favour subjectivity in viewing the world, rejecting rationalism. Deconstruction is a term that is used to denote the application of post-modern ideas of criticism, or theory, to a 'text' or 'artefact'. A deconstruction is meant to undermine the frame of reference and assumptions that underpin it. A discussion of this radical movement would not be complete without mention of Foucault. He rejected any association with post-modernism, but many commentators think he embraced a form of critique of research and thought that is post-modern in its rejection of rationality and the Enlightenment.

Where does this leave us as researchers? There is a little hope left, as Chomsky has suggested that post-modernism is meaningless as it cannot add to empirical knowledge, and post-modernists have no answer to questions about their principles and theories.

These deep philosophical notions often serve to confuse the researcher, particularly those who are concerned with the individual rather than a large social context. Psychology is often criticised for being too inward looking, and for forgetting the social world in which the individual must act; however, there are some specifically psychological approaches we can consider.

PSYCHOLOGICAL APPROACHES TO QUALITATIVE RESEARCH

KT

Critical psychology is a branch of psychology that is aimed at critiquing mainstream psychology and attempts to apply psychology in more progressive ways. One of critical psychology's main criticisms of conventional psychology is how it fails to consider the way power differences between social classes and groups can impact on the mental and physical well-being of individuals or groups of people. Parker (1999) suggested that critical psychology should include an examination of how some accounts of psychology (such as positivistic methods) dominate academic and professional work in psychology. He criticised psychological research conducted in such methods for paying little attention to 'power differentials' such as that between lecturers and students, or doctors and patients, thereby implicitly condoning the difference in power and the abuse of it. His criticism focuses on language and meaning and he suggested that we can use **discursive psychology** to discover the ways in which we use language, and what hidden meaning it has for us. Discourse analysis does exactly this, attempts to analyse hidden meaning and examine how people present identity through spoken interactions with others. This can lead to many different identities belonging to one individual – leading to the idea that there is no such thing as true self.

KT

There is strong opposition here to biological theories of psychological experience, such as personality or sexual orientation. For instance, a discursive psychology would suggest that the impression of masculinity (and its identity) comes through social cues such as a low voice and a lack of emotional expression (a somewhat simplified version, but go with it!). These are socially constructed traits of masculinity, but they are also cultivated by interaction. This means that if you viewed someone as masculine, but encountered them speaking in a high soft voice about how delightful it was to be in love, you would either reassess your view of masculinity, or of your friend. Discursive psychology can be used to understand the way people use language in many different contexts, from friends talking to each other to government propaganda.

Feminist psychology has also had an enormous influence on the way psychological methods have moved on from a strictly objective viewpoint. Feminist psychologists have led much of the effort to refocus psychology and the underlying theoretical assumptions, research methods, professional practices and ethical guidelines. Feminism radically challenges society so it is not surprising that psychology, looking at the place of people within society, has been challenged too.

Summary

In this chapter we have encountered the idea that there are several theoretical viewpoints in qualitative research. This does not mean that theory drives the research, but that the philosophical positions inform the approach to research and human positions within it. All of our theories stress the importance of context in meaning and interpretation. As such, symbolic interactionism, semiotics, phenomenology and ethnomethodology embrace an ontology that assumes the only reality that exists is the one we interpret through our interactions with symbols, culture and ourselves. They also accept that knowledge is not gained through discovery of objective facts, but created through understanding of phenomena within a particular context, and this understanding is flexible and changing. Thus, when designing qualitative research we must approach our study from a chosen ontological viewpoint that is clear. The next chapter considers some general issues in designing qualitative research.

CHAPTER 14

DESIGNING QUALITATIVE RESEARCH

Contents

Features of qualitative research

The role of the researcher

Research design

Sampling strategies
Data collection techniques
Analysis of data
Credibility of qualitative research

Summary

Designing Qualitative Research

This is the rock solid principle on which the whole of the Corporation's Galaxy-wide success is founded – their fundamental design flaws are completely hidden by their superficial design flaws. (Douglas Adams, *So Long, and Thanks for All the Fish*)

Learning Objectives

- To examine the features of qualitative design.
- To understand the role of the researcher in qualitative studies.

KEY TERMS

- Confirmability
- Credibility
- Dependability
- Purposeful sampling
- Reflexivity
- Transferability

In quantitative research there are such very clear-cut choices about design and subsequent analysis that they almost seem like the result of navigation through a set of rules. In qualitative research we are not bound by these strict rules and have more freedom, but nevertheless must base our decisions about the way we carry out research on rational and justifiable sets of choices, otherwise the research becomes meaningless.

There are several matters to take into consideration when choosing to use a qualitative research methodology. Firstly, we may decide to use such a method if we are trying to understand a phenomenon we know little about as there is little previous research. As theory and data emerge through the process of qualitative research, they can be used to guide us towards knowledge of psychological events. In addition, we may wish to examine items about which a great deal is known, but from fresh perspectives, which is where qualitative research also excels. So, qualitative methods can be used to identify the variables that might be examined quantitatively in future research, or where quantitative measures cannot be used to describe or interpret observation. In both these cases research questions are open-ended in order to allow us to discover new information. This leaves us with a lot of scope and a lot of freedom in choosing and designing the approach, but unfortunately not much guidance. In order to identify the approach and not leave researchers floundering in a mass of choices, there are several features which might lead us down particular paths towards the best method for our questions.

FEATURES OF QUALITATIVE RESEARCH

There are various characteristics of qualitative, naturalistic research that we can identify:

1 Qualitative research uses natural settings in which to gather data.
2 The researcher is an integral part of data collection.
3 Analytical techniques are predominantly inductive.
4 Reports are richly descriptive, interpretive and expressive providing a voice for those involved.
5 There is an emergent focus in addition to focus on the product of research.
6 There is less of a focus on validity/reliability than on trustworthiness and credibility.

It is important to stress the emergent nature of qualitative research design, as we seek to observe and interpret meanings in context. Due to this, it is often not possible or indeed appropriate to finalise a strategy for investigative process before data collection has begun. Many feel uncomfortable with this, but it is this very freedom which is also most attractive. The design of qualitative studies depends on the objectives with judgements about usefulness and credibility being left to the researcher and the reader.

THE ROLE OF THE RESEARCHER

As the researcher is a fundamental component of the research and its design, there are several things we must do before embarking on the research itself.

Firstly we must put ourselves in the frame of mind appropriate to the naturalistic paradigm. Secondly we must determine, identify and acquire the necessary skills to allow ourselves to be a research instrument. Thirdly we must find what Strauss and Corbin (1990) call a sensitivity to theory, a readiness to gather and interpret qualitative data appropriately. This is an interesting point, as the authors are referring to a personal quality of the researcher. Such things are never mentioned in quantitative research beyond an acceptance that a quantitative researcher will be objective and detached. This reflects the subtlety of extracting meaning from data in other ways than with what some think is the sledgehammer of scientific viewpoint and statistical analysis. So, a qualitative researcher, instead of detachment, needs insight, understanding and subtlety, crucial if the researcher wishes the reader to trust the legitimacy of the data and its interpretation.

RESEARCH DESIGN

Lincoln and Guba (1985) suggested a set of steps for the design of naturalistic investigations:

1　Determining a focus.
2　Determining the appropriate research paradigm.
3　Determining the sources of data.
4　Determining the stages of the enquiry.
5　Determining instruments required.
6　Planning data collection and recording.
7　Planning data analysis procedures.
8　Planning how to evaluate the trustworthiness of the enquiry, data and interpretation.

Determining a focus means we need to establish any boundary for the study, what inclusion/exclusion criteria will be applied to the sample and to the data. We then have to ensure that the goals of the research study can be met through a qualitative paradigm. Such an approach may not be suitable for every question we are asking in psychology. Once we know how we will ask the questions, we need to know who will be approached to provide the answers and how we can sample from our population. There will be several stages to the study and this is only one of them, so we need to identify what the phases of the enquiry will be, and whether we will move from more open-ended to more focused approaches as we gain more insight into the issue(s). We also need to think beyond ourselves and the place of the researcher to what other instrument of enquiry might be needed. We also need to think through how this will be handled and how data will be recorded and analysed, and how the credibility of the data and its analysis will be determined.

Sampling Strategies

The most popular sampling technique is purposeful sampling, in contrast to probability sampling in quantitative research. Purposeful sampling is an attempt to provide cases relevant to the research question which are rich in information and will give in-depth insight. There are several varieties of purposeful sampling, Patton (1990) identifies 16, but perhaps the most useful and most used is maximum variation sampling. This strategy allows us to capture and describe central themes or principal outcomes from the greatest variation of participants. However, such variation can be seen as a problem, but if the intention is to gain maximum variation, then the sampling strategy is turning an apparent weakness into a strength. This is because common patterns that emerge from maximum variation will be those of interest in observing core, shared experiences and aspects of the sample (Patton, 1990).

Data Collection Techniques

The dominant forms of data collection are dealt with in subsequent chapters on interviews, focus groups and observation, together with text-based data in Chapter 17. Interviews with open-ended questions are the most popular way of gathering data, as they are deemed to give insight into a participant's thoughts and feelings, but they can also be used in conjunction with other methods. The major questions to be answered are how to record data and how to transcribe it if it is a spoken record. This issue becomes even more evident when attempting to record data from observation. One way to overcome this is to use written data from the participants, but the act of writing can affect the data as it makes the participant focus on the issue, and may prevent some points being made explicit. All of these questions are addressed in the relevant chapters.

Other sources of data include other documents that have been produced by the population of interest, such as journals/diaries (research diaries are slightly different and dealt with in Chapter 17), official records, letters, newspapers, etc. Hermeneutics, for example, uses text-based documentation as data, originally religious texts such as the Bible, but it has also come to include other types of literature.

Analysis of Data

Qualitative data analysis means organising it into meaningful and manageable units in order to search for patterns. This is the same as quantitative data analysis: each set of numbers must be reduced and re-synthesised in the same way, but here we have a complex, rich and non-numerical set of data to be examined. Usually this process is inductive in qualitative research, meaning that the patterns or themes will emerge from the data. This is very challenging, and much more difficult than statistical analysis. Here we need to be creative and look at the whole set together in order to place it into meaningful categories, a daunting task with piles of interview transcripts or field notes. The following chapters deal with some forms of analysis in qualitative research.

The final point to consider about designing qualitative research is how to ensure and determine its quality. In qualitative research there are the concepts of reliability and validity to consider: can we replicate this finding, and are we sure it measures what we think it should? Can we generalise to other parts of the population? In qualitative research we do not have these concerns, and do not set out to suggest that we have findings that will be found again, or that they apply to everyone in a similar way. What we do have is a relatively inductive process that we must try to make explicit to the reader in a plausible way.

Credibility of Qualitative Research

In naturalistic research we assume that there can be multiple realities, and that what we have discovered represses these adequately. One way of doing this is to triangulate the data. This means either testing the data we have under various analytical techniques, or attempting to gather the same data in several different ways. If we cannot generalise to other parts of the population, can we at least transfer the findings to another situation or another form of data gathering with the same people? This means that we cannot predict as we aim to do with qualitative research, but we do attempt to gain transferability of the results and conclusion we draw from it. We also need to be assured of the dependability of the findings in some way, whether such results will endure over time or, if not, why not.

Finally we need to address the question of lack of objectivity. We have already determined that this lack is not necessarily a bad thing: if the researcher can acknowledge the influence on the findings in some way, and even minimise this influence, then the findings do not need to be seen as objective. Instead Lincoln and Guba (1985) suggest it requires 'confirmability', which is how much neutrality can be seen in the interpretation of the data. Keeping notes of the process of analysis and induction, the ways in which several judges make sense of the data, and so on, can allow a reader to confirm whether or not the findings are ones which others would have found by the same process.

Summary

In this chapter we have learnt how to design studies utilising qualitative methods. These methods have as their strength the flexibility that comes from working outside the constraints of previous theory, in order to achieve greater understanding of the phenomena of interest. While they may lose in generalisability, they gain in detail and complexity of data. In the following few chapters we will discover how to gather qualitative data and how to analyse it.

PART V

COMPLEX QUALITATIVE RESEARCH

This part looks more closely at the issues of qualitative research, how it can be performed and how the data can be analysed. We will examine some popular forms of qualitative data collection using market research as a forum for examining interviews and focus groups, and female gang violence to look at how participant observation is carried out. Next, we need to examine data analysis and we will look at some research on music in public places and on police interrogations to navigate our way through some analytical techniques. The final chapter in this part looks at evaluation, a set of research techniques that can be brought together to provide information on organisations or programmes.

CHAPTER 15

INTERVIEWS AND FOCUS GROUPS

Contents

Market research

Qualitative interviews
Conducting interviews

Focus groups in qualitative research
Use of focus groups
Questions for focus groups

Analysis of interview and focus group data

Summary

Interviews and Focus Groups

I think that the undecideds could go one way or the other. (George Bush, 1988)

Learning Objectives

- To explore the use of interview and focus group techniques for gathering data.
- To examine the different forms of interviews.

KEY TERMS

- Consumer behaviour
- Focus group
- Interview
- Market research
- Probes
- Questions

 Interviews and **focus groups** are probably the most widely used techniques of data collection in qualitative research. Such techniques provide a depth and breadth of information if used effectively, and can be used alongside other methods of data collection. Interviews and focus groups are very flexible methods of data collection and have been used in a wide range of research in psychology. One major user of these methods is the market research industry.

MARKET RESEARCH

Commercial qualitative research is a relatively new development in psychology, but is rapidly becoming an accepted part of business life. Such research needs to meet a lot of demands, not only to do with the quality, reliability and validity of research and its findings, but also in terms of commercial needs for brand identity and consumer satisfaction (Sherlock, 2005). The psychology of consumers examines how people select different brands or products and how a consumer will be affected by the environment, how he or she makes decisions, what information is available to him or her about products, etc. Consumers have changed during the period in which consumer psychology has developed, and those whose business is keeping consumers happy and therefore buying their goods are aware that they must change to meet this shift in tastes and behaviour (Gavin, 2006).

Shopping behaviour has changed over the last 50 years, and we now spend most of our money in supermarkets and shopping malls. Some think that this has dehumanised our shopping experience, and that consumers are demanding a return to older values of good service as well as convenience (Fletcher & Morgan, 2000). This also means that there are changes to ways that goods are marketed, as companies respond to the changes in information technology and the mobility of the consumer. As such, branding has to work harder for the manufacturer and retailer, as consumers need reassurance that well-known brands provide in terms of product quality and after-sales care, as well as the choice and competitive pricing that a range of brands can offer. Increasingly this means finding out what will attract time-hungry consumers to the retailer's brand, and psychologically based market research is the way they discover this.

Market research is a systematic process of recording and analysing information about consumers and the market from which they buy particular goods. It can assist in the development of products or enhancing the marketability of existing products (Burns & Bush, 2000). This can include the analysis of how a particular product or brand appeals to different demographic characteristics of potential customers, how the product is evaluated against its closest competitors, and how well the advertising campaign is going. Market research follows the same basic steps of all research in that we must define the research problem, design how we are going to carry out the research, collect and analyse data, then disseminate the findings. Insight into consumer motivations and emotions is crucial to the business world, and market research is the fundamental tool for manufacturers and retailers to gain that insight. The depth of information that can be garnered from qualitative approaches is important to market researchers attempting to match consumer motivations to products at deep non-verbal levels. For example, Fletcher and Morgan (2000) observed that potential buyers of stereo audio equipment tend to press the eject button of the CD deck when viewing the hi-fi. They followed this up with in-depth questioning, which revealed that this was a form of evaluating the quality of the system in comparison with others, and in conjunction with other tactile and visual cues. Hence the focus of market research should be multidimensional, multimodal and multi-level. This is not easily achieved but is reached more readily by using psychological theories and a qualitative approach to information gathering. The difficulty lies in the fact that market researchers are often not trained in psychology but business fields. Market research does have its roots in psychology or allied social sciences, but the focus of those in the industry is towards business, with the danger of an application of psychology being more naive than the understanding of implicit psychology needed to understand the modern consumer. Let us take a simple example. A sales assistant in a shop where there is a range of stereo music systems on display may notice the tendency to push various buttons on the display models, and have decided that this is the way that customers check out the system. However, we might notice that male customers do this immediately, and then read the information sheets in front of the display, but female customers will look at the displays for some time, and will read the information before they press the buttons. It might be possible to say that there is a sex difference in the way customers decide on the quality of the item, and that women will gather information before touching the display, but male customers use more tactile information first. This is a rather superficial conclusion to draw from the observation, and would require more in-depth study before determining which strategy male and female customers use to decide what to buy. This can be done via quantitative dearth, such as using the Consumer Styles Inventory (Sproles & Kendall, 1986); however, Mitchell and Walsh (2006) discovered this may not have high construct validity for men, making it unfruitful to carry out research into sex differences in buying behaviour. A quick review of the literature in this area also suggests that there are few if any sex differences in the effect of various promotional strategies on buying intention or behaviour. So how can we account for the simple observation of differences in information-seeking behaviour between men and women and will this possible difference affect any purchase intention? What else might mediate this difference? This is where the qualitative commercial research into the consumers' motivations, feelings and intentions will be more rewarding.

There are three major forms of interview: structured, semi-structured and unstructured. The more structured forms are close to the questionnaire format discussed in the chapter on survey design, and should really undergo the checks on reliability and validity discussed there. Bakken (2006) suggests that market researchers employing such techniques are guilty not only of superficially applying psychological theory, but also of misapplying methods of scale construction such as the Likert technique. He points out that market research questionnaires are seeking measurements of judgement rather than of fact as Likert scales should be applied. For example, imagine a questionnaire on microwave oven design, in which the respondent filled in his or her agreement to statements such as 'I like this button layout'. This would be a correct application of Likert techniques, whereas 'I think this button layout is more user-friendly' is not. However, it is the latter type of answer that market researchers are seeking as they wish to know why someone likes the button layout better than another. The constraints of structured quantitative application of psychological theory and social research method are too restrictive here, so another method is needed. In quantitative research, we must examine the reliability and validity of measurement of concepts and follow a clearly operationalised set of research questions. In qualitative research, there is an emphasis on greater flexibility, focusing on discovering the interviewee's point of view. In order to examine people's views about brands, products, promotional elements, or to explore the psychology of how people make purchase decisions and are influenced by the environment, market research can use a range of interview types, or focus groups. Each technique has a slightly different application.

QUALITATIVE INTERVIEWS

In using unstructured interviews we have perhaps one main question and the interviewer uses a set of prompts in order to keep the interviewee focused on the topic. However, the interviewee is then allowed to respond freely, with the interviewer prompts used for following up any points that arise. So, for example, let us think about our new microwave oven button layout interviews. In a fully unstructured format the interviewee would simply be asked something like 'what do you think of this layout?' The interviewees would then give their opinion while the interviewer recorded what they said in some way. There would be no other question asked directly, but the interviewer might urge the interviewee to expand on some detail, and so on. There might be an aide-memoire for the interviewer to check all the items needed to have been discussed, such as number of buttons, spatial configuration, clarity of icons, etc., but no questions would be directly written. In addition there may be **probes** given to the interviewer, if the previous research has demonstrated that certain areas would need to be coaxed out of the interviewee. There are three basic ways in which the unstructured interview can proceed:

KT

1   In an informal conversational interview, the interviewee can become relaxed enough to forget it is an interview, as it seems simply like a chat. This is very useful for talking about something important to the interviewee, or something in which he or she is closely involved.

2   The guided interview involves a basic checklist of relevant topics, but the interviewer has freedom to explore, probe and ask subsequent questions. This is the most useful approach for highly specific topics, but where the interviewer needs to move around the topic freely. This is probably the most used for commercial qualitative research, next to the completely structured questionnaire used in street surveys.

3   Finally the standardised open-ended interview uses a prepared set of open-ended questions carefully worded and arranged so that there is minimal variation in the way questions are posed to the interviewee. This method definitely provides less flexibility and is best used when there is more than one interviewer involved or the interviewers are relatively inexperienced. This method is also called a semi-structured interview, and the set of questions or topics is known as an interview schedule, but the questions are open-ended and the interviewees are free to answer how they wish. There is also flexibility in the order in which the questions are covered, and the interviewer can 'probe' if necessary. So, for our microwave evaluation, the main question might be the same, but the interviewer would also have the checklist and specific question to ask. Such a schedule might look like this:

Please look at the layout of the buttons on this microwave and tell me what you think of it.
Are the buttons clear?
Can you tell what each one is for?
Are they spaced appropriately?
Would this be easy to use?
Why do you think this?
Etc.

Conducting Interviews

Whichever technique is used, there are several steps in conducting interviews that it is wise to follow:

1   Establish rapport. Without some preliminary introductory moments, no interview will proceed in a comfortable manner. This stage should be conducted in a polite and friendly but professional manner.

2   Describe the purpose of the interview and how it fits into the project, how long it is expected to take, ask permission to record the interview in some way (notes, tapes, video) and ask for informed consent to use the information gathered in the project.

3   Conduct the interview, getting the interviewees to open up and express their views clearly and fully. Interviewers should ask for clarification if needed and reflection on what has been said. This can also mean pursuing lines of thought, and even challenging some ideas in order to get more information.

4 Ending the interview is as important as starting it, being sensitive to the interviewee's needs, such as time limits. Summarising what has been said is useful in several ways – it allows the interviewer to check everything has been asked, it allows the interviewees to add anything they want to, and it signals the end of the interview. Further – always thank interviewees.
5 Write down notes or transcribe tapes as soon as possible.

Kvale (1996) suggested that there were several attributes that a good interview should possess:

- Familiarity with the topic and a high level of knowledge about it.
- The ability to structure a discussion.
- Clear and gentle manner of speaking without jargon or aggression.
- Sensitivity and empathy shown through listening attentively.
- Openness to respond to interviewee and flexible enough to change direction if necessary.
- Focused enough to steer the interview towards its objectives.
- Critical enough to challenge what is said and to deal with inconsistencies in replies.
- Have a good memory and the ability to relate what is said to what has gone before.
- Have the ability to interpret without imposing meaning.
- Know when to be quiet and when to speak.

One characteristic that is invaluable is the ability to probe, sensitively and carefully, but thoroughly.

One of the key techniques in good interviewing is the use of probes. There are three types of probes identified by:

- Detail-oriented probes are used to follow up issues and are the kinds of questions we naturally use in conversation, such as 'where were you when this happened?' These stem from the natural curiosity between people having a conversation.
- Elaboration probes are used to encourage the interviewee to reveal more. This can vary from non-verbal encouragement such as head nodding, or even remaining silent and attentive. However, there may be times when it is appropriate to say something, such as 'tell me more about this' or 'can you give me an example?'
- Clarification probes are used when the interviewer has misunderstood something, and interviewers should always make it clear that the interviewee is not at fault for this. So 'I'm having trouble understanding these terms you are using' is fine, 'you are using difficult-to-understand terms' is not.

FOCUS GROUPS IN QUALITATIVE RESEARCH

The focus group probably has its origins in work done by Merton in 1941, who was evaluating radio audience response to programmes. He applied what he had learnt about gathering data to army training in the Second World War. Modern focus groups are much more sophisticated than those used in the early part of the twentieth century, and have been extensively modified as a data collection technique. In market research they are used to gauge consumer perceptions and opinions on products and promotional material, in order to understand thinking and decision making by potential buyers. This has the same limitation that Bakken raises about questionnaires: that the interview technique is applied rigorously and the psychological theory applied appropriately (Merton, Fiske & Kendall, 1990).

A focus group then is, at first view, a group of people talking about a particular subject, in a relatively structured way. This should not be confused with group interviewing, which means that a small group of people have a discussion on a topic, but that there is the opportunity for genuine discussion, and group members are empowered enough to talk, or the group members know each other well enough not to be intimidated by each other (Smith, 1954). A focus group is also a small group of people, but the make-up of the group is different to a group interview. The format is also more structured as the interviewer will have very specific questions to be answered because some research has already taken place (Denzin & Lincoln, 1994). Kreuger (1988) defines a focus group as a set of people entering into a discussion that is designed to gather the perceptions of the members in a way that is inclusive and non-threatening. Focus groups have been used to gather information on a wide variety of topics and are particularly useful in market research. The interviewer (sometimes called the moderator) must direct the interaction and have a very clear technique for recording the data and the way in which it is generated by the group and the dynamics of the group.

Use of Focus Groups

Focus groups can be used in any research that requires discussion of the topic under investigation. They are useful for obtaining background information about a topic, generating research hypotheses for future stages of the research, stimulating ideas and concepts, identifying problems with products, etc., or simply learning how people talk about certain things (Stewart & Shamdasani, 1990).

In order to select participants for a focus group, convenience sampling can be used, but in order to obtain a representative sample this might need to be quite large. Most groups appear to be between 6 and 12 – any larger and the data will be difficult to analyse and the management of the group become unwieldy, any smaller and the group might not generate enough discussion (Merton et al., 1990).

A smaller group, fewer than six, might be appropriate if a particular group of people have a lot to say about the topic. It is also possible to run more than one focus group on a topic, particularly if there are different demographic groups involved and researchers do not wish to mix them.

In order to gather data from focus groups it is usual to use audio or video recording techniques, and this in itself can cause problems. Firstly, researchers must be sure they know how to work this technology! Secondly, recording can really affect some interviewees adversely, so interviewers must be alert to such problems. The moderator should try to get participants to speak one at a time or the recording can be too messy to analyse, and each member of the group should identify themselves at least once in the discussion. Notes are really only useful as a backup to the recording, and perhaps as an aid to subsequent analysis.

Questions for Focus Groups

It is usually best to keep the number of questions small, because, as moderators, we do not want to be hopping all over the place. Generally, focus group research will have between 6 and 12 questions. Using open-ended questions allows the group to answer from several different dimensions, but they must be focused on the topic carefully. Stewart and Shamdasani (1990) suggest that the way the questions are phrased will elicit different types of discussion: for example, including 'how' or 'why' questions suggests that the research is about complexity and participants' own opinions are important, hence allowing the moderator to probe more deeply to the issues. Some researchers are reluctant to use such 'depth' questions, though, as they are more open to answers reflecting social desirability. As such we can see that the role of the interviewer/moderator is crucial here. Moderating a focus group is a highly developed skill, and should really only be attempted by someone who has experience of interviewing individual interviewees. Once in the focus group, the moderator must keep order, keep focus and keep time! It is important that the group establishes some form of rapport; in the same way as with the individual interviewee, this must be with the participants, but they must also establish a relationship with each other. Often this is a group of strangers brought together to talk about something which may be controversial, such as the experiences of prison, or something commercially important, such as evaluating a new product. The moderator must be alert to the group dynamics as well as able to record the information being generated. Moderators need to be good listeners, but also to know when to interject if the group is going off track or the discussion is becoming too heated. Glesne and Peshkin (1992) suggest that a good moderator anticipates what is happening in the group whilst simultaneously analysing, reacting, directing and probing.

ANALYSIS OF INTERVIEW AND FOCUS GROUP DATA

In the following few chapters we will look at some ways of analysing qualitative data in detail. Such data is likely to have been generated from interview or focus groups, however, and therefore it is worth looking at some general items of analytical technique that will be useful.

We need to remember that all the data gathered in such types of discussion is raw data, in the same way that scores on a test or blood pressure changes under stress are quantitative raw data. Our task as researchers is to transform this raw data into something meaningful to report about the topic of interest.

Firstly we need to transcribe data; this means the entire set, the words spoken, the passes made, and the non-verbal utterances or even gestures. We must provide a complete record of the interview in order to analyse it properly and comprehensively. We cannot examine the content without this, because we will be looking for trends, patterns or themes that occur repeatedly, but also for idiosyncratic instances of just one thing. Doing this effectively will also allow us to record the emphasis the participants give to their answers or the intensity with which they speak.

Summary

This chapter has examined the ways in which qualitative data can be derived in the applied setting of a market research focus. The issues and problems with verbal qualitative data have been explored and the analysis of this has been introduced. The following chapters will look at alternative ways of gathering qualitative data and how to analyse it.

CHAPTER 16

PARTICIPANT OBSERVATION: GIRLS, GANGS AND AGGRESSION

Contents

Observing violence

Violent women

Observation as method

Access

Time

Recording data

Analysing data

How to be a participant observer

Summary

Participant Observation: Girls, Gangs and Aggression

In violence, we forget who we are. (Mary McCarthy, American novelist and critic, 1912–1989)

Learning Objectives

• To examine the issues and methodology of research as a participant and as an observer.

KEY TERMS

- Access
- Covert
- Observation
- Overt
- Records

Observing the behaviour of a group by participating in the group is a well-established form of ethnographic study. Observation can give a different form of data to interviews, as it can lead to in-depth understanding of a group's behaviour beyond that which the group members themselves are aware. A good observer can monitor both verbal and non-verbal behaviour in context, once immersed in the group's activities either passively, from outside the group, or interactively, as a member of the group with either a hidden or known identity.

Observation does of course bring its own challenges, whether the observer is in the group or outside it. Observation distorts the observed no matter how unobtrusively it is carried out. Even hidden non-active observation changes the group, as the observer brings his or her own interpretation to what he or she is viewing, which may or may not be accurate. Hidden or covert observation may also be unethical, as the group members may not have carried out certain behaviours if they knew they were being observed. This highlights the ethical and research-based dilemmas that researchers encounter when choosing observational techniques. Overt observation, in which the observer is known to the group members as a researcher, must distort the behaviour, but it allows the observed to exert some control over what is recorded. Covert observation, in which the researcher observes from a hidden vantage point outside the group, or participates fully as a group member with the research objective hidden, is necessarily deceptive. There are other problems, such as being accepted by the group, and attempting to share the characteristics of the group members. There is also the problem of becoming so much part of a group that a researcher no longer observes the group objectively. Even if this does not happen the researcher must somehow record his or her observations, and writing a field research diary while participating in some activities may not be exactly feasible! However, an inaccessibility of field note taking may lead later readers to question the data's reliability and validity. In his well-known study 'A view from the boys', Parker (1974) attempted to examine the life of late adolescent boys in Liverpool. He had been involved in a youth project in the area and had become a trusted associate of the group. He discovered that the boys' lives were centred on overcoming the poverty and high unemployment in a depressed area in the northwest of England in the early 1970s. The boys rejected school as a strategy for improving their lot, and started their own successful, if nefarious, business of stealing and selling on car radios. Parker's report becomes one of a description of transition between levels of delinquency, and could have led to legal action against some gang members. However, he chose to withhold some data from publication and left the final decision whether to publish some information with the group. His main ethical stance was that the research did no harm to gang members, resolving ethical issues and gaining the trust of the group, but is questionable in terms of whether it is a full account of the behaviour studied.

OBSERVING VIOLENCE

Participant observation is an interesting and useful research method when attempting to study cultural aspects of life, in which some lifestyles cannot be studied by other means. In recent years socio-psychological research has turned to examination of female violence, the rise in which seems, to some commentators, to represent a societal decay. In addition, street gangs and the violence they are perceived as perpetrating have been of major concern to law enforcement agencies and social commentators.

A gang is a loosely organised group that controls a territory through violence. Klein (2005) goes further and defines a street gang as a durable group, whose members spend most of their time outside their home (streets, shopping malls, cars, etc.) and whose identity includes involvement in illegal activity. This necessarily is a negative view, but members do adopt the phrase in terms of identity or defiance of authority. Much of the research has been in the USA, where street gangs are seen as a growing menace by the police, and it is also where our view of them originates, particularly through the media portrayal of news, social commentary and crime drama. Almost exclusively, modern gangs are portrayed as comprising predominantly young African American men. In such representations, if women or girls are involved in the gangs, they are shown as the sexual property of the male members of the gangs, or as satellites of male groups. The media representation and the research appear to have trivialised female gangs (Campbell, 1991). Why might this be the case? Is it that women do not participate in violent behaviour? Are young women and girls less likely to be violent than young men or boys? This appears to be an overriding impression, both in law enforcement agencies and in the general public's perception.

VIOLENT WOMEN

What is clear is that violent crime carried out by girls is on the increase, but so is that by boys (Chesney-Lind & Brown, 1999). Statistics on this trend are very difficult to find, and even more difficult to interpret. We know that female arrests are less than a quarter of all arrests for under-18s, and that violent crime constitutes a small percentage of that. Police data also suggests that the nature of girls' violent crime is different, in that knives rather than guns are involved, and that the assaults happen during conflict rather than the commission of another crime (like rape or burglary) as with boys. However, even if the proportion of female arrests in comparison with male arrests is low, the actual numbers are not insignificant. It is clear that the number of arrests for violent crimes or weapon carrying is rising overall, and the number of girls involved in such crime is therefore rising with the trend. Early research suggested that delinquency and gang activity were strictly male pursuits with girls as sexual associates of the gang members. However, in the latter parts of the twentieth century, attention turned to female violence, possibly because of the increases mentioned above, and because of the shifting nature of social research to include more women academics. Even then the questions centred on why women were 'under-represented' in violent crime (Artz, 1998). A popular explanation for violence was that it was the result of biological and socialisation factors. Conventional roles for women are still viewed as passive and nurturing, with men/boys as the aggressive hunting members of the tribe. It was thought that this difference was due to social conditioning and biological factors, with testosterone being the main culprit in male violence. Olweus, Mattsson, Schalling and Low (1988) found that behaviour involving a response to provocation and threat had the clearest correlation with plasma testosterone levels with a clear assumption that testosterone somehow causes aggressive behaviour. While this is now accepted to be a flawed conclusion, it remains clear that there is a differential number of men and women indicted for violent offences, and there must be some sex-based differences in violent behaviour. That it might be the type of aggression was only first examined in 1986, when Eagly and Steffen found that the difference was for aggression that produces pain or physical injury, and that men were more likely to behave in this way than women, whose aggression tended to result in psychological or social harm. Such results are supported by Lagerspetz, Bjorkqvist and Peltonen (1988) who looked at 11/12 year olds and their social structures. The authors discovered that the social interactions of the girls were more ruthless and aggressive than previously suggested, because this study found that indirect social aggression was the norm for girls rather than physically violent behaviour. Lagerspetz et al. concluded that the girls were behaving as mini-adults, and mimicking the social interactions of their parents, whereas boys were still using immature social strategies.

Female violence then is seen as either a practice session for adulthood or a direct result of the adoption of masculine characteristics due to feminist rejection of feminine conventions. According to commentators, the women's movement was to blame for women becoming assertive and wanting to drink, steal and fight (Adler, 1975). Fortunately, later research demonstrated that things were a little more complex than this. According to Chesney-Lind and Pasko (2003), there appears to be a number of risk factors that are implicated in girl violence, such as physical and sexual victimisation, negative attitudes towards school, lack of academic success, perceived lack of opportunities, low self-esteem, severe family problems such as poverty, divorce, parental death, abandonment, alcoholism and frequent experiences of abuse. There is a very clear correlational relationship between experience of physical and sexual abuse with female criminal activity and violence with reportedly 50% of incarcerated women having a history of abuse, compared with 12% of male prisoners (Artz, 1998). The hypothesis here is that women subjected to violence in the home learn that power and control in the family is bound up with physical force. As such, domination of the weaker members of a family or group equates with survival. Additionally, sexual abuse of girls leads to low self-worth and negative views of other women (Trickett & Puttman, 1993) with an internalised belief in women's inferiority being a rationalisation for violence.

Estimates of female involvement in gangs vary between 4% and 30% depending on the agency carrying out the estimates, and the way in which gang membership is viewed. Numbers then are meaningless here; what is clear is that young women are becoming more prevalent in violent crime and gang culture, and the question should be not 'how many?' but 'why?'. In her research into female gang culture, Campbell (1984, 1991) explored the lives of several African American and Latin American girl gangs in New York. Her research technique, in addition to case studies and interviews, was that of participant observation. She acknowledges that the data gathered in this way may serve both to clarify and mystify at the same time, but nevertheless the information gathered has been enlightening, in terms of the opportunity to view the lives of these women and to highlight how difficult such lifestyles are to examine. Campbell discovered acute hardship in the lives of the young women she talked to and followed in their activities. The gang, she concluded, served a social function and was a replacement familial connection: 'family' was where the women were abused, 'gang' was where they were accepted. They participated in violence because it was a survival strategy and a way to provide status and protection for themselves and the other female gang members. Joining the gang is an adaptive solution to hardship, lack of educational or financial opportunity, social isolation and economic marginalisation. She also discovered a rejection of the typical roles available to women, such as the 'good wife' and 'sex object', although the women's interpretation of these stereotypes is atypical. For example, Campbell suggests that the gang members define 'sex object' as procuring sex for male counterparts and seducing men in other gangs in order to accuse them of rape.

OBSERVATION AS METHOD

Participant observation as a method to examine youth culture and, in particular, gang culture appears to be the research method of choice for many researchers. In 2000 Eggleston gained access to a gang comprising young men in New Zealand, having gained trust through a previous youth programme contact. He chose such a method as it allowed a broader perception of the environment before settling in to the exploration of specifics and it allowed him to experience at first hand the social and emotional concepts of living the life, providing, he claims, a reflexive validity not available from other methods.

While it has much to commend it as a research method that gives insights not available elsewhere, participant observation does bring its own difficulties, most notably in gaining access, time spent in the field, recording data and analysing data.

If a researcher immerses him–or herself in the subject being studied, in true ethnographic style, then it is assumed that a deeper understanding is being gained. The idea is that we gain information 'from the horse's mouth', giving higher validity to the data. The corollary to this of course is that a certain amount of objectivity is lost and we see distortion of the information happening. The deep immersion into the group or lifestyle studied that is required means acceptance of the researcher at various levels, and negotiating this access and acceptance means more than simply following a group of people around. The group may be suspicious of and/or uncomfortable with the researcher's presence.

There are also different levels of access in that observers may choose how to engage with the observed. A complete participant engages fully with the activities of the group, but hides his or her true identity and intentions, thus making the observation covert. While possibly more accurate, this has many ethical implications to consider, as well as potential danger to the researcher: if the group infiltrated in this way is one with violent intentions, then exposure of the observer exposes him or her to reprisals from group members. The less dangerous position is patient as observer, in which the researcher adopts an overt role with identity and notations revealed to the group. While it may be more difficult to establish rapport, the observer does not have to take part in illicit activities and does not expose him- or herself to as much danger. Even more detachment means that the researcher is simply an observer and no more, and records behaviour passively and at a distance.

TIME

Participant observation cannot be rushed – from first contact to analysing findings can take months or even years if we are to do justice to the subject and the participants' voices are to be heard properly. The more time taken, the more detailed an observation can be made, but a good researcher will also know when to stop and withdraw. Taking time means that we can discover whether there are any inconsistencies between what the participants say and believe overtly and what they do covertly.

RECORDING DATA

The most difficult aspect of participant observation, after access, has to be making field notes, which are running descriptions of the things observed. These could include a multitude of items such as notes, maps, drawings, tapes, photographs, etc. Lofland and Lofland (1984) recognise how difficult this is and suggest writing notes that will allow jogging of the memory when the researcher has the opportunity to write something more extensive. They also recognise that this can take a very large period of the researcher's day or evening and can be boring. The second step is also to annotate the notes for further use, such as highlighting items of interest, or adding explanatory or even analytical notes. There are also aspects of the note-taking process to be borne in mind. The first is that the notes might be either too general or too selective, which will affect the validity of the observation. Lofland and Lofland identify this as subjective adequacy, and suggest that this can be raised by spending more time in the setting and making notes, concentrating on the physical setting of the observation (such as drawing a map to aid memory), to take as much opportunity as possible to interact with the group, to become familiar with the language used, to raise personal involvement, and to reach as much shared understanding with the group as possible.

ANALYSING DATA

There are various approaches that can be taken to analysing the data gathered in participant observation. A phenomenological approach emphasises shared understanding of behaviour, goals and needs. In general the researcher must seek the meaning of the experiences shared with the group and the range of perspectives represented. An empirical approach, on the other hand, would emphasise the systematic study of the frequency of observed behaviour, the establishment of norms or rules with the observed, and to detail illustrative incidents. Many researchers feel uncomfortable with the idea that these two approaches are incompatible, so there is a third position, known as definitional mapping. This is the in-depth and systematic decapitation for a set of terms inherently used in the group. For example, in Campbell's work, the girls used various derogatory terms for other gang members, whether male or female, and described themselves in similar ways, but non-pejoratively. Such an examination of the labels and language used can give insights to the way the group is structured and the dynamics of personality and power within it.

HOW TO BE A PARTICIPANT OBSERVER

As we can see from all of the above, participant observation is more than simply writing down what people say when the researcher is following them around. It is a personally and physically demanding and high-risk way of carrying out research. It can lead to a great deal of insight into a group's behaviour and beliefs, but can put researchers at risk of threat from the group, and a great deal of criticism to readers of the research. Critics of Campbell's work, for example, said she was highly selective in the information she chose to analyse and, in fact, is guilty of the prurient interest in sexual activities that she accuses other observers of pursuing (Kornhauser & Hirschi, 1986). These commentators go on to describe the work as contradictory and confused (p. 514) and making no distinction between what she has observed and what she has interpreted. Horowitz (1986), on the other hand, suggests that Campbell has exposed a subculture that is surprisingly conservative and aspirational, refuting a stereotypical view of women involved in a violent lifestyle. For all the criticisms of style and design, it is agreed that the participant observer has opened out the topic for discussion, and included the voice of the participants in ways that had not been done before.

Summary

In this chapter we have discovered that participant observation of whatever level of access and analysis is a flexible and insightful technique if used properly and responsibly. Witnessing actions in natural settings and hearing views from a group's own voice are the deepest levels of understanding a social researcher can achieve.

Anne Campbell

Anne Campbell's research is concerned with sex differences in aggression with special emphasis on female aggression, both as an end in itself and because it may illuminate the more physically dangerous nature of male aggression. She has employed a variety of methods and populations including ethnographic work with gang members in New York, interviews with British inner-city teenagers, development of a psychometric instrument to measure differences in the representations which people hold about the causes and consequences of their own aggression, and larger scale analyses of criminal justice, employment and mortality trends. She is currently a professor of psychology at the University of Durham, but has previously held academic posts at Rutgers University and the University of Teesside.

CHAPTER 17

THEMATIC ANALYSIS

Contents

Research diaries

The effect of recording experience

The analysis

The outcomes

Summary

Thematic Analysis

Silence is more musical than any song (Christina Rossetti, 1830–1894)

Learning Objectives

- To learn about a popular way of analysing qualitative data derived from interview, observation or text.

KEY TERMS

- Conditioning
- Diaries
- Emergent themes
- Quotes

KT

In Chapter 15 we looked at interviews and focus groups and in Chapter 16 we encountered participant observation. These two methods of data collection usually generate qualitative data, and we need to make sense of it in some way. A hugely popular analytical technique is **thematic analysis,** which is used widely in psychology (Boyatzis, 1998; Roulston, 2001). It can be used to analyse data from both the interview situation and that gathered by observation, but yet another form of data collection that generates data suitable for thematic analysis is written material, such as that generated from the research diary.

RESEARCH DIARIES

A diary format is selected in order to gain real-life experiences from personal accounts. Diaries can be either historical documents, or newly produced accounts focused on a particular topic. In the latter, participants are directed to record accounts of episodes of interest during their day-to-day lives, and possibly any effects these episodes have on them. This is a well-established method in social research as identified by Robinson and Nicosia (1991) when they reviewed studies where diary use was the prevalent method. Harvey (1990) investigated leisure behaviour by using time diaries, which allow participants to record the total flow of activities and perceptions. Analysis is carried out at both macro and micro level. A micro-level analysis examines time points, individuals and events, such as the activity of a participant at any one time. This provides a detailed sense of the activities or emotions etc. of each participant. A macro-level analysis examines subpopulations, bundles of time and aggregated events.

There is also evidence that diaries can be used to record emotional content. In a study of male inmates of a high-security prison, Kette (1990) asked 30 men to record, in structured diaries, whether they felt good or bad, and a description of mood. The study was to examine coping strategies for long-term incarceration and whether that was affected by personality characteristics. In addition to the outcomes of the study, Kette concluded that the diary method was an extremely rich form of such data and that this could be invaluable alongside other quantitative measures.

THE EFFECT OF RECORDING EXPERIENCE

As a research method, diary research involves the participant writing a daily (or other time unit) journal of his or her day-to-day behaviour relevant to the research question. Each participant is provided with a paper leaflet in which the pages are printed in advance with pertinent points or questions. Formats of diaries can vary from open format to highly structured, where all activities are pre-categorised. The advantage of free-form is that it allows greater flexibility of expression, but is highly labour intensive both for the diarist and the researcher in preparation and analysis. It is also possible that diaries are highly error prone (Silberstein & Scott, 1991). The source of error can be conditioning, incomplete recording of information and under-reporting, inadequate recall, insufficient co-operation and sample selection bias. These can be minimised by ensuring that the diary-keeping period is of optimum length (overcoming co-operation difficulties and under-reporting or inadequate recall), ensuring the literacy level of all participants (although this may exclude some sections of a population from participation), and personal recruitment of participants and collection of the diaries. Conditioning is a particular problem specific to diary methods, and it means that participants can be observed to change behaviour as a result of keeping the diary, and the first day is atypical of the rest of the diary. In other words, the method itself is affecting the data. It can be minimised by visiting diarists during the period of the diary keeping, which encourages good record keeping and focuses the diarist on the topic.

This conditioning was seen quite clearly in research carried out using diaries to catalogue the experience of intrusive music. In 2006, Gavin looked at the question of how music is used in retail outlets, and what effect it has on the listener, namely the potential consumer and the assistant in the shop, pub, café, etc. Music is a powerful focus for emotions and mood. It plays a huge part in the business world, in terms of both the performance and sale of music and players itself, but there is a pervading use of music in retail outlets such as shops, gyms, bars and restaurants. The retail and advertising trade uses music to manipulate and influence the consumer. Gardner (1985) discovered that music is a major influence in changes in buying behaviour. This would seem to indicate that the public accept the presence of music and that the retailers accept that music is a permanent, necessary fixture. However, research suggests that there is little attention paid to the quality or appropriateness of music or the effect that it is having on the consumer (Bruner, 1990). Although it appears to be accepted that there is a link between the store's atmosphere in its home in financial performance (Shapiro, 2004), there appears to be little understanding that the music must be appropriate and of good quality. There are potentially negative effects of music (Ramos, 1993), and comments from customers suggest that a mismatch between client intentions and the perceived intent of music is a major factor in loss of custom. Arnold et al. (2005) also discovered that loud music has been identified as giving 'terrible retail experience'. These findings must be addressed when music is used prominently in commercial settings and advertisements. Research was needed to discover the extent to which music is regarded as welcome or unwelcome by the consumer. Therefore, in this research (Gavin, 2006) the researcher set out to address these issues. Participants were asked to keep a diary of situations in which they found themselves where music was not the primary focus, such as in a concert, but where it accompanied other behaviour, like shopping, going to the gym, having a meal, etc. The participants were equipped with a printed notebook containing aide-memoires for the pertinent points and space to record date, time, place, status (alone or otherwise), type of music and volume, and asked to write about each experience of music that was outside their personal control. This was to ensure a certain level of consistency in the report for comparison, but the format was deliberately open. The diary was to be completed for a period of 10 consecutive days.

The Analysis

Thematic analysis is a process of making explicit the structures and meanings that the participant or reader embodies in a text. The diaries were subjected to thematic analysis by two readers who highlighted text and noted regularly occurring and/or atypical themes. This resulted in a thematic overview (see Figure 17.1) in which each reader had identified forms of response highlighting the occurrence on each diary with different colours, each colour indicating a source of the emergent theme.

These were exchanged and each other's commentary was read to indicate agreement or otherwise. This process went on in several iterative instances, until agreement was achieved. At the end of this, three overarching forms of behaviour had been identified (emotional reaction; characteristic of music; consequent behaviour). The examples of these behaviours were further analysed using what was termed a selective sub-categorisation (see Figure 17.2).

The text that contained comments about the experience and effect of music was sub-categorised under more specific headings.

It is worth noting here that making explicit the thematic elements of experiences is a complex process, which will be necessarily inductive. Themes are not objects but expressions of phenomenological experience and therefore the process of discovering them cannot be wholly explicit. It is important to acknowledge the reflexive nature of this type of research. The researcher was driven by a desire to discover if her own feelings about musical experience were mirrored by others, but the background literature was ambiguous. Data must be gathered in as open a way as possible, and analysed in conjunction with someone who did not necessarily share the same experience or perception of the retail setting. This allows a check on accuracy of analysis and minimises the effect of bias. It is accepted and welcomed in qualitative analysis that subjective views will form part of a researcher's process (Brown, 1996), but that there is a responsibility to manage this influence. Assistance from another person not involved in the process is seen as a suitable measure towards reducing the input of bias (Mehra, 2001). As the analysis proceeded it was discovered that there was little disagreement about how the text should be categorised and the way in which it should be used as evidence of the emergent themes. An interesting point of disagreement was about something that seven participants mentioned, namely the experience of 'goosebumps' (the involuntary raising of skin at the base of body hairs experienced during cold or strong emotions). Was it a reaction to the music or a consequent piece of

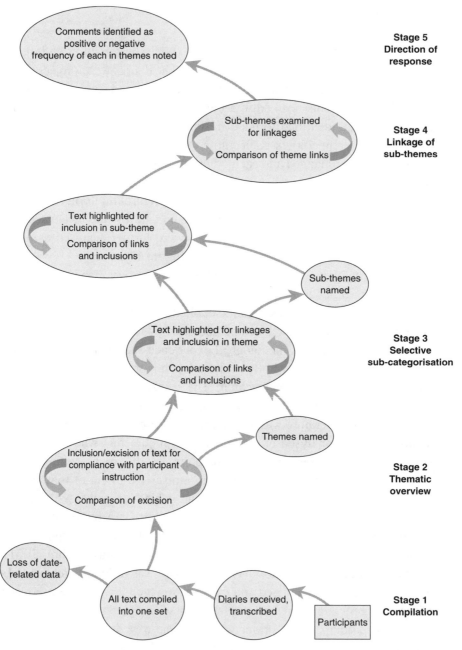

Figure 17.1 Stages of thematic analysis from diaries to themes

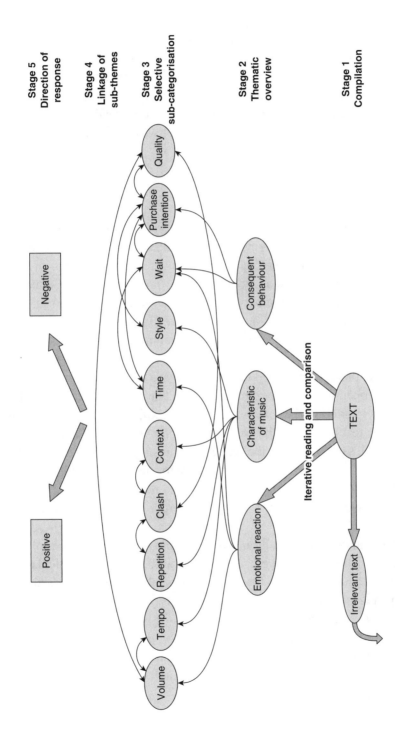

Figure 17.2 Development of themes and sub-themes

behaviour? In the end it was decided that it indicated strong positive emotional reactions, on the basis of Panksepp's (1995) discovery that music with emotive meaning for a listener will produce clear physical reactions.

Once such reactions or behaviour had been identified they were linked to characteristics of the behaviour or the situation recorded, leading to a fourth level of analysis as seen in Figure 17.2. The final level was whether these instances were positive or negative.

The Outcomes

The findings were discussed in terms of several of the sub-categorisations and what the participants were saying that led to these emerging. For example, 'context' indicated that there were right and wrong contexts for types of music to be used in. So music described as 'cool' would definitely encourage someone to visit a well-known chain of coffee bars again: 'it was so cool the first time. The music was different but really good, and I felt just really chilled, happy to be there and wanted to stay', but badly played music at inappropriate times can produce very negative feelings.

Therefore, this research used thematic analysis to explore participants' text in a focused but open way. The researcher involved an accuracy check in asking a colleague to help analyse the text, and has made explicit the process by which they analysed the text and re-synthesised the thematic view of it. Finally the researcher has used quotes directly from the participants to support her analysis and acknowledge the input of her own bias and perception of the world in this framework. The conclusion of the work addresses the previous research and the theoretical positions, and suggests some ways forward in order to achieve attractive consumer environments.

So, from interviews, focus groups observations or written records of life, we can collect information about people's thoughts and feelings on a particular topic, then examine this data for patterns that occur across all the data, or ideas that are peculiar to one person. Such ideas can be examined by a thematic analysis focusing on identifiable themes and patterns of living and/or behaviour. Each thematic analysis will develop in its own way, each one led by the needs of the research and the input of the researcher. However, once we have the data and know that themes will emerge, there are stages consistent in all thematic analysis:

- Examine the data for the emergent themes.
- Identify all data that relates to these themes.
- Combine related patterns into sub-themes, units derived from patterns that can be brought together.
- Check that the sub-themes are truly representative, by referring back to the data and/or the participants or checking with a co-researcher.
- Identify the argument for choosing the themes, possibly by relating to the literature. In this way the reader can identify the process by which the researcher has developed the themes.

Summary

In this chapter we have seen how to apply a popular technique for analysing qualitative data to data derived from research diaries. Thematic analysis is a procedure whereby emergent themes are drawn from the data in order to describe a particular aspect of the world. In the next chapter we will look at how to analyse the data derived from interpersonal communication such as conversation.

CHAPTER 18

DISCOURSE ANALYSIS: POWER AND CONTROL

Contents

Language structure

Syntax – relation of signs to each other
Semantics – relation of signs to objects

Definitions of discourse analysis

Assumptions of discourse analysis

Issues of reliability and validity

How do we perform discourse analysis?

Gathering data for discourse analysis

Natural discourse

The method of discourse analysis

Summary

Discourse Analysis: Power and Control

What can't be said can't be said, and it can't be whistled either. (Ram Tirtha, quoted in *Be Here Now*)

Learning Objectives

- To introduce the examination and analysis of language in conversational situations.
- To examine the ways in which underlying meaning in interpersonal communication can be made explicit.

KEY TERMS

- Discourse
- Illocution
- Natural discourse
- Perlocution
- Pragmatics
- Semantics
- Syntax
- Text

During recent years, research in psychology has undergone a shift in emphasis away from observing behaviour to attempting to discover meaning in experiences. One way of doing this has been to examine language, both written and spoken, but at the level beyond the sentence. The way people describe and express their experience is by using language, and discourse analysis is the analysis of large pieces of language taking into account the context in which the language arose. Let us first examine some concepts in **psycholinguistics**.

KT

LANGUAGE STRUCTURE

Syntax – Relation of Signs to Each Other

Spoken language is made up of small pieces of sound and meaning: phonemes and morphemes. Phonemes are the smallest functional acoustic units. They are not necessarily directly associated with letters or syllables. The word 'rat' has three phonemes, 'r', 'a' and 't', but so does mouse 'm', 'ow' and 'ss'.

Morphemes are the smallest functional units of meaning. They are not necessarily directly associated with words. The word 'rat' is a morpheme, but the word 'rats' has two morphemes, the meaning of 'rat' and the suffix 's' which pluralises it.

There are a limited number of phonemes in human speech, but a much greater variety of sounds that can be made. English contains about 40. If we put together all the phonemes of known languages, we get only some of the sounds that human speech contains. In every language, phonemes and morphemes form the larger units via a hierarchical structure.

In addition, all languages are fully developed, and can express all the ideas that the cultural group needs to communicate. Just because a language does not express the concepts of higher order philosophical analysis, it does not mean that the language or the cultural group to which it belongs is cognitively underdeveloped or primitive, it is simply that the group may have more important things to talk about.

We normally speak in constructions such as sentences. What is, and is not, an appropriate structure for constructions is the syntax of a language.

It has been argued that the sentence is an artificial unit created by the advent of writing. Written text is a fairly recent development, and there are still cultures that do not rely on it. Even in 'literate' cultures, speech often does not entirely consist of complete sentences (Brown & Yule, 1983). Analysis of speech, in which we use pauses and filler (such as 'er', 'you know' and so on), suggests that the real unit of language is the clause. We tend to use the fillers just before clauses, er, which are parts of sentences that can, you know, stand alone.

However, whatever level of construction we use must be understandable, and there are rules which everyone uses, albeit unconsciously. It is also clear that **syntax** is inextricably bound up with meaning. When we have something to say, we do not start with the structure of the sentences and then say it, we start with the meaning we wish to convey.

KT

Semantics – Relation of Signs to Objects

KT

Semantics is the study of the meaning of words alone and in longer constructions. Words (or, in psycholinguistic terms, lexical items) designate things, people, abstract concepts, actions, events and properties of objects. If words are meaningless, then the object of language is lost. Communication, either by speaking or writing, is central to cognitive functioning, so it is very important for us to study semantics. Native speakers of a language have a store of words giving knowledge of pronunciation, function in linguistic constructions (e.g. as a noun) and meaning. This store is referred to as a **mental lexicon**. The way this is used is the subject of much study. The psycholinguistic approach proposes several theories of how meaning is represented, such as feature theories in which lexical items are stored in the mental lexicon in terms of shared features (but this is only viable for concrete items) and procedural semantics in which items are stored in terms of procedural operations.

KT

Sentences and phrases, on the other hand, are combinations of words that allow us flexibility in expressing thoughts. But sentences do not stand by themselves, they link to each other, and to the sentences spoken by other people. Conversation is about using the language in particular ways, but also about understanding the intention and meaning of other people's use of it. Verbal interaction is about using the language in particular ways, but also about understanding the intention and meaning of other people's use of it. Semantics is the study of what words and sentences mean, whereas **pragmatics** is what users mean when speaking or writing. For example, the sentence 'I am now over here' can mean that the speaker wishes to impart some information, or can be an indirect request to join him or her. The major question is 'how does the person being addressed identify the intended meaning?' Studies in pragmatics suggested that there are three things extracted from utterances: reference, speech actions and implicatures (what is implied). These are analysed in terms of shared perceptual experience, previous conversations and shared culture. So if a friend mentions 'the man in the red car', your friend is assuming that you will identify this man as the most salient man in a red car in your current common experience.

KT

Reference is used and subsequently extracted in many ways. Demonstrative reference is accompanied by perhaps pointing when saying 'this is my friend with the red car'. Anaphoric reference refers to something mentioned earlier, 'my friend with the red car drove it round the block, then put it away in the garage'. The 'it' here is being used anaphorically. Language use is active, involving utterance, **illocutionary** and **perlocutionary** acts. Utterance acts are the action of speaking, perlocutionary acts are the intent of the utterance. For example, if you asked your friend 'where is your car?' the utterance act is the act of speaking; the perlocutionary act is trying to get your friend to tell you where his car is now. The illocutionary act here is directive, the attempt to get the addressee to do something. Other illocutionary acts include assertives (expressions of belief), commissives (promises and offers), expressives (thanking, apologising, congratulating or greeting) and declarations. The addressee not only must hear the utterance, but must understand the illocutionary content. We do this by deriving the implicatures, that is what is implied from the utterance, by interpreting it against current purpose or direction of the exchanges, and the assumption that the speaker is co-operative. In other words, the context of exchanges is **discourse**, and cannot be separated from the comprehension and context of language. The comprehension of language is the ability to respond appropriately to messages in natural language. However, there is also the act of acquiring new knowledge, and in conversation we may learn of things not in our own personal experience, and through text learn of things in the past and distance. Language comprehension is inseparable from our knowledge banks, both in the use of language and in the hearing/reading of it. The study of comprehension is important as a major aspect of cognitive functioning, and for artificial intelligence.

To understand utterances, the person hearing or reading them must relate the linguistic content to knowledge stored. Language use then is a highly complex cognitive and social process, involving both the knowledge of a language and the general knowledge of the world. Language comprehension is a perceptual, analytical and representational process. Its use, however, is directly related to the underlying knowledge. Context will always differentiate between pieces of language. For example, suppose you and I look at the sky, and see a cloud. We would think 'Oh, a cloud, I wonder if it will rain today?' A meteorologist would look at the cloud and decide its type, estimate its size, direction and doubtless hundreds of other variables, and decide whether or not it will rain today. A glider pilot, on the other hand, would look at the cloud and think 'A mountain wave – rising air and good lift for flying today.' Context and knowledge determine the use of the concept of cloud. Models of language assume that it is the currency of thought, and indicate role and culture.

Discourse analysis then is concerned with these elements of language and the context in which they are placed. Let us look a little more closely at what discourse analysis can do to lay bare the meaning of language and what assumptions underlie its use. There are some underlying assumptions that we also need to be familiar with.

DEFINITIONS OF DISCOURSE ANALYSIS

The term 'discourse analysis' was first used in connection with psychology by Potter and Wetherell in 1987, when they said that discourse analysis was concerned with the study of linguistic and rhetorical devices rather than the behaviour of the language user. Definitions of discourse analysis vary from this and can be very ambiguous and confusing, but researchers generally agree on several points. Firstly that discourse analysis is concerned with language use beyond the boundaries of a sentence/utterance; secondly that it is concerned with the relationships between language and the wider context; and thirdly that it is concerned with the interactive or dialogue properties of everyday communication.

Conversation analysis provides a systematic account of talk-in-interaction, such as the rules of turn-taking when talking with others (Schegloff, 1992). It is related to discourse analysis in that it allows a general understanding of the minutiae of interaction. Conversation analysts allows a rich description of the format of a conversation. Discourse goes beyond this to look at the implications of the interaction and the dynamics of the social context. This brings us to another allied position, that of critical linguistics and critical discourse analysis, in which the central issue is around social conditions as opposed to discursive action. What such a position means is that the analyst is examining the ways in which power is exerted in language and its use (van Dijk, 2001). So it is the context, not the language itself or utterances themselves, which is the unit of analysis (Kress, 2001). Here, in this type of research, we range from the psycholinguistic analysis of words and pauses to the examination of the shared and global environment in which these exchanges happen.

ASSUMPTIONS OF DISCOURSE ANALYSIS

These are as follows:

1   The basic unit of discourse analysis is 'text'. This can be written or spoken (and transcribed) text.
2   Text is structured. Structure here means the rules that keep it together, and refers to the syntactic or grammatical structure underlying language. Discourse analysis also assumes that there are semantic relations maintaining cohesive ties between pieces of text.

3   Texts are meaningful language units that primarily derive their meaning from their context. The meaning we give to a text depends on how we connect it to the context. People attribute meanings differently because we all hold expectations about discourse based on our world-knowledge. This becomes difficult the less formalised the discourse becomes – the more conventionalised the speech act, the clearer our expectations are. Expectations differ depending on culture, speakers' relationship, situation, etc., and formalising the discourse can clarify these somewhat.

4   The text must be authentic.

The first issue we encounter when attempting to perform discourse analysis is choosing the language to be analysed. This involves a certain amount of subjectivity and is open to researcher bias as discourse is sensitive to the wider context of cultural norms, knowledge, beliefs and values. The danger here is that researchers project their own values. For this reason it may be best to have more than one person choosing and analysing the text, and to determine the amount of agreement between the two judges.

Discourse analysis is, then, a heuristic methodology for the analysis of texts, a qualitative and interpretive, but systematic, approach to understanding why a given piece of language appears as it does. There are several types that can be employed.

ISSUES OF RELIABILITY AND VALIDITY

Discourse analysis is basically a matter of interpretation. No hard data can be provided through discourse analysis, so the reliability and the validity of findings depend on the logic of the analyser's arguments. These in turn are subject to their deconstruction and counter-interpretations. Even so, well-founded arguments remain convincing over time and have concrete applications. We may not have repeated testing and comparison to use as we do to establish the reliability of quantitative data, or the opportunity to test the congruence between sets of data to ascertain validity, but Potter and Wetherell did start the discussion about understanding and trusting the data and interpretations that come from discourse analysis. They suggest that there are several ways of establishing the credibility of data and interpretation from discourse analysis:

- Discourse analysis often examines phenomena with the aim of establishing patterns. However, deviations from the pattern are interesting in that they, instead of disconfirming the pattern, confirm it. This is known as deviant case analysis.

- When examining discourse a major contribution should be from the participant's understanding of the interpretation. This is not always possible, especially if the data is derived from a source not in the analyst's remit, but the understanding that is made clear should be addressed.
- Each new analysis should build on the previous ones in that area in order to provide coherence as a further check.
- Finally, the analysis should be made available to readers whose own evaluations can assess this interpretation in the light of other similar studies, and in terms of their own cultural perspectives.

HOW DO WE PERFORM DISCOURSE ANALYSIS?

So, we now understand something about how language is constructed and something about how it is interpreted. We understand that there are various ways to interpret the disclosure in terms of patterns or context, but how do we do it?

The best way of learning how to carry out discourse analysis and what it shows is to examine the ways it has been applied.

One particular way that researchers apply discourse analysis is to examine the dynamics of the exchange and the relationships formed within it. The dynamics of the discourse mean that each participant has a role and function within the exchange that may go beyond the particular time and place of the conversation, but which are brought to bear within it. So, for example, the exchange between a parent and child about schoolwork may centre on whether the child is happy at school and what the child is deriving from going to school, and whether any homework needs to be done, but this will be different from an exchange between the parent and child about food, and will also be different from an exchange between a school teacher and the child about schoolwork. The factors that become significant here are the relative relationship between the participants, the realities of power each has in the relationship, the control over the exchange and the form of the exchange about the topic.

According to French and Raven (1960), power is always evident in interpersonal communication and there are various ways that any differential possession of power can be expressed. So, for example, if we are talking with someone who appears to have more power, we would be more polite, back down from arguments, allow interruptions and use titles of authority, and they even suggest that specific clothing choices can suggest change in power.

There are also six different forms of power in interpersonal communication:

- the power to coerce someone to do something against their will, through physical, non-verbal or verbal threats;
- the power to reward someone in order to provide a service, or to withhold reward in order to punish;
- the power invested in a role, such as monarch, police officer, teacher, manager;
- the power derived from someone liking another person, or wanting to emulate them;
- the power of the celebrity and the leader;
- the power of the expert, one who possesses knowledge and skill that others need.

In interpersonal discourse, the more inherent power, derived from his or her role or expertise, a contributor has, the more influential or in control of the discourse he or she should be. Analysing discourse in terms of power and control exerted and the shifts they undergo is very valuable in understanding how different roles are handled and outcomes achieved. In 2006 Haworth carried out a study of police interviewing and the language used, together with an analysis of the use of power and control by investigators and a suspect. She was particularly interested in the way that power and control was 'negotiated' and used in the interviews and the interactions, how this demonstrated the status of each participant, and how these issues were challenged and resisted. In order to analyse the transcripts of the interviews, she integrated conversation analysis, critical discourse analysis and pragmatics. This was a particularly distinctive analysis, because of the context of the interviews, why they were conducted and who took part. In this regard, her participants are worthy of note, and there needs to be an explanation of why they are not completely anonymous. Haworth had access to the investigative interviews undertaken with Dr Harold Shipman, who was convicted of the murder of 15 of his patients. It is estimated that he is implicated in the death of more than 260 patients over 27 years. He maintained his innocence throughout the investigation, subsequent trial and imprisonment, right up to his suicide, by hanging, on 13 January 2005. The interview analysed by Haworth took place early in the investigation of the death of Kathleen Grundy, an energetic and healthy woman. Mrs Grundy died on 24 June 1998 and had apparently made a new will bequeathing her entire estate to Shipman. Her daughter, a lawyer, was suspicious and informed the police.

Haworth outlines the background to her research in several ways. She is ostensibly interested in the way in which the British police use power and control when interrogating/interviewing murder suspects. However, she has looked at the ways in which interviews with 'built-in asymmetry between participants in terms of prescribed discursive roles' (p. 740) are conducted. This asymmetry and prescription seems to describe police interviews very well, as roles are clearly defined yet unequal, but there is little research into such discourse. Heydon (2005) has defined such interviews as institutional discourse, because there are legal procedures controlling interaction and the expectations of the participants. For example, the police caution ('you have the right to remain silent') has a particular perlocutionary force as it creates a certain state, attracting special attention. There are necessarily formalised structures to police interviews with the beginning and ending easily identifiable, and more variety in the information-seeking sections. Heydon also suggests that there are typical roles undertaken by the participants and standardised forms of question and answer interactions. The control of the interview would seem to be in the hands of the police, as the officers control the setting and make decisions based on answers to questions. However, the interviewee has control over what he or she reveals and the objective of interviews is for the interviewer to gain information. Haworth also points out that although the police have a clearly defined institutional role to play, this *particular* interviewee has a powerful role in a different institution, and therefore the asymmetry may be of a different nature to the more regular interrogative setting.

Turning then to how Howarth has analysed the Shipman interview, it is clear that she has concentrated on the dynamics of power and control and she has identified four features which demonstrate these shifts: topic, question type, question and answer sequence, and references to institutional status. In each of these cases it is expected that the police interviewer has control. For example, the syntactic form of the questions asked requires a particular form of answer, as they signal the requirements of the questioner. The role of questioner is also the way in which the interviewer exerts power, as the interviewee's experience is that the format of turn-taking in the conversation is imposed upon him or her. The most interesting aspect that Haworth identifies, and one that differs from other interviews that may have been analysed, is the institutional status. As police interviews commence, each contributor identifies him- or herself in terms of the reason they are participating. In this way the status of each is exposed or reinforced, with implications for how the interview is conducted.

Haworth suggests that each of the four features she identifies have manifested themselves in the interview and that the shifts in power and control emerge when the topics change. For example, right after the opening sequence of police caution and legal forms of identification, the interviewer attempts to open the questioning with a particular topic, but Shipman responds with a change of topic, namely a clarification of how he came to witness Mrs Grundy's will. The interviewer lets him continue, which is actually a deviation from the expected question and answer sequence, but does acknowledge that this deviation is taking place, and reasserts control. As Shipman attempts to explain the events surrounding Mrs Grundy changing her will, it appears that the interviewer is allowing him even more discursive freedom. However, the interviewer's overall aim is to get the suspect to talk, if he is willing to do so, so why not allow him to have that freedom? It is also clear that the interviewer does not allow Shipman to assert power or control. For example, Shipman implies criticism of the interviewer in not allowing him previously to clarify this situation, but the interviewer clearly dismisses this challenge.

Once this exchange has finished, the interviewer moves on to his main topic, the medical records. Here Shipman appears to conform to the interview format and comply with the questioner's intentions, but several times uses his expertise as a shield to deflect the questions. For example, he claims to have followed standard practice when taking a blood sample and recording that he has done so. The interviewer has no choice but to defer to this expertise, and is placed in a weaker interrogative position than would be wished. The interviewer chooses to change the topic again, but with more restrictive questioning, in order to divert Shipman from his tactic of using institutional power to avoid questioning about blame. This then moves swiftly to a set of questions about Shipman's access to dangerous drugs, which Haworth identifies as an unusually weak section of the interview and which is dispensed with quickly. The matter of the forged will is then introduced, and here Haworth suggests that the interviewer is moving into his area of expert power, as it involves forensic evidence. Shipman is less communicative here, and the interviewer is allowed to dominate, with a large number of declarative statements. For example:

> as I mentioned earlier, for your information it's not a question, there was an existing will … made out in 1986 which was held at Kathleen Grundy's solicitors, her daughter's firm in Warwickshire. This document is actually marked D24 is a copy of the will received at Hamiltons … have you seen that will form before?

Haworth expands on this by explaining that the interviewer is giving information and seeking explanation throughout this section, and that this is largely successful. Hence the acquisition and maintenance of control is a successful strategy for the interviewer. However, it is clear that the dominance shift is what interests Haworth as she continues to give examples of how the power transfers back and forth. It becomes even more apparent that Haworth's analysis is moving in this direction when she comes to the exchange about the cause of Mrs Grundy's death. Here the two roles are almost directly equal to each other as the police officer has forensic evidence at his service, but this is of a medical nature, the very type of information that Shipman holds in his expert power. The interviewer declares that the autopsy has revealed fatal levels of morphine in Mrs Grundy's body, but then hands the initiative to Shipman by asking him to comment. This allows Shipman to dominate the exchange and Haworth illustrates this by quoting examples where he interrupts the interviewer and criticises the investigative procedure of house searching that was carried out.

As the analysis of the interview turns to the summary and closing sequence, we see Haworth's own summary emerge, as the interviewer is allowed to summarise the whole interview, so Haworth uses the analysis of this to describe the 'discursive pattern of the interview reproduced in microcosm' (p. 752).

Haworth moves into a full analysis of the discourse after her description of the course of the interview is concluded. She has explicated her thesis about power, dominance and control by illustrating the points she is making with examples from the exchange. This serves to evidence the ways in which she has concluded what is happening. The major objective of this interview was to build a case against Shipman and the interviewer has achieved this, but in ways that another officer might not have used. The fact that this interview material was entered into the prosecution case shows that, even though some portions appear to have been given into the control of Shipman, the evidence gathering was still successful and Shipman's answers, even when resistant and challenging, allowed anomalies in his account to be used against him. For example, Shipman attempted to explain the high levels of morphine found in the body by implying that Mrs Grundy, a healthy 81-year-old pillar of society, was a drug user, Secondly, he also denied that he had easy access to dangerous drugs such as diamorphine. Both of these pieces of testimony arise from sections of the interview that Haworth describes as discursively weak for the officer. These simple answers allow the prosecution to point out logical inconsistencies in Shipman's testimony and strengthen the case against him.

Haworth suggests that it is too simplistic, therefore, to look at only the discursive, linguistic elements of the discourse, but that the wider context is equally as important. She concludes by considering how such analyses can help police interviewers and enhance the way such evidence is used in court.

The analysis presented by Haworth is certainly interesting and worthy of note by police officers and court officials who need to gather and use such evidence. Where we might take issue is that Haworth does not present any evidence that may be contradictory to the approach she is taking in relation to power and control dynamics in the interview. This is not a major criticism, however, as she does state clearly at the outset that this is what she is examining.

So, given that we have examined the process that Haworth followed in her analysis of this discourse, there are some general procedural elements we can draw on in order to carry out our own such analysis. Firstly, read research that has used discourse analysis and discover why the researchers used it and how. Here we have examined Haworth's intentions, but also seen how she has drawn on research in dominance dynamics in discourse. Secondly, in order to carry out the analysis, there must be text of some nature to examine, so we must decide on the best form of data collection – documents, transcripts of interviews, transcripts of conversations. Here Haworth acquired a tape of an interview and transcribed it carefully, allowing her to see patterns emerging through the exhaustive reading and rereading of the data. While she was intuitive about what she saw emerging, she also was highly systematic in recording the illustrative examples of discourse.

Potter and Wetherell's description of discourse analysis as the study of talk and texts as social practices (1987), and the use of resources that permit those practices, is clearly central to the way Haworth has steered her way through the transcript of Shipman's interrogation. Even though the elements of psycholinguistics aid the discourse analyst, there is also a rejection of strictly cognitive interpretations of the exchanges, and a turning to examining how mental processes are constructed in discourse. Hence discourse analysis will be an ever-changing procedure for examining human interaction. The danger here is that analysts might try to provide a discourse analytical explanation for every psychological phenomenon, which would not be possible. It would only be feasible to explore issues that lend themselves to examination in this way, and it does not allow the examination of inherently visible processes that cannot be expressed linguistically.

GATHERING DATA FOR DISCOURSE ANALYSIS

The Haworth study demonstrates effectively that interview data can be used for discourse analysis and even data that has not been directly gathered by the analyst. The difficulty with interviews, or perhaps the value, is that they are constructed in particular ways, question and answer sequences are not the most natural way in which people interact. They have been used extensively because of this value: they allow a standardised range of material to be covered and the interviewer/analyst is looking for and expecting several thematic patterns to emerge.

Much of the work by the major researchers in the psychological discourse arena, such as Billig (1992) and Potter and Wetherell, used interviews. However, there are issues of extrapolating the practices of interviews and their analysis to the more 'natural' interaction of everyday conversations. The discourse appears to be packed with the categories constructed by the interviewer and the turn-taking is much more artificial than might be seen naturally. The Haworth analysis is valuable for such insights to police techniques as it provides, but does appear more artificial than natural.

NATURAL DISCOURSE

Here natural is still not quite as we imagine it to be. **Natural discourse** is not naturally recorded, taping a conversation instantly makes it something other than straightforward, and it becomes intrusive. Neither is the transcription a straightforward transition onto paper of what the participants have uttered. In many cases the participation will fail to capture nuances of interaction such as body language or accent. So, it must be accepted that discourse analysis will not capture natural discourse even when we set out to do so.

THE METHOD OF DISCOURSE ANALYSIS

While qualitative methods should not have prescriptive methods and procedures attached to them, there are several rules to follow once the research question is decided:

- Sampling data should be carried out in strict accordance with the research question and how it may manifest itself in discourse.

- Collecting data should be as accurate as possible, with the best recording strategy available.
- Data collection techniques should be decided well in advance of starting. Is it by interview? Then these need to be set up and the questions decided. Is it natural discourse? Then the recording technique must be considered together with the effect of its intrusion.
- Thought should be given to transcription: exactly what is it that is to be transcribed? Full transcription might record the pauses, alterations to sentences, accent, etc.
- Once transcribed, will the data be coded in some way? Coding might be iterative with several passes over the material.
- Preliminary analysis may occur during coding, or even when deciding on the coding mechanism. However, discourse analysts suggest that nothing should be ignored and everything should be analysed, even the way in which we read the material. There is also no prescription for this stage, but a rule of thumb might be to look for consistencies and then look for anomalies.
- The next stage must be – do it again! What remains unexplained? Are the preliminary explanations still valid?
- Write up the analysis and let someone else read it and then, do it again!

Summary

In this chapter, we have defined discourse as language that occurs in situations such as conversation, interview or narrative. We have encountered ways in which to examine this language and the methods by which we can explore the language rigorously. We have also looked at the ways in which this has been applied to examining the dynamics of power and control in an investigative interview.

Jonathan Potter

Jonathan Potter is Professor of Discourse Analysis in the Social Sciences Department at Loughborough University. He has studied topics such as scientific argumentation, current affairs television, racism, relationship counselling and child protection helplines. His main focus recently has been on the study of professional–client interaction in a variety of settings. He is an international authority on qualitative methods and has written on discourse analysis and discursive psychology, focus groups, the study of psychological issues, and he has taught short courses on analysis in 10 different countries. He has recently edited a book on the relationship between cognition and interaction (*Talk and Cognition*, Cambridge University Press, 2005, with Hedwig te Molder) and a three-volume collection *Discourse and Psychology* (Sage, 2007).

Margaret Wetherell

Margaret Wetherell is Professor of Social Psychology at the Open University and currently Director of the ESRC Identities and Social Action Research Programme. She has written extensively on discourse analysis (theories and methods) and has applied that thinking to the empirical study of masculinities, majority white group identities and, most recently, in a grant from the Department of Health, to the process of deliberation in Citizen Councils. She is an authority on discursive psychology and discourse analysis, which examines natural language use and the implications of patterns in people's talk for the study of self and identity, psychological states such as emotion and memory and the study of ideology or collective sense-making.

CHAPTER 19

EVALUATION RESEARCH

Contents

Evaluation of treatment programmes

Sexual offending, the research, the theory

Biological and evolutionary explanations of sexual aggression

Social and psychological explanations for sexual aggression

Treatment of sexual aggression and sexual offending

Evaluation study design

Effectiveness of therapy

Summary

Evaluation Research

Whenever a system becomes completely defined, Some down fool discovers something that either abolishes the system or expands it beyond recognition. (Brooke's Law)

Learning Objectives

- To understand the process of evaluation when applied to research or programmes.
- To examine different forms of evaluation.
- To examine in detail the evaluation of one programme.

KEY TERMS

- Descriptive evaluation
- Field experiment
- Impact evaluation
- Normative evaluation

Evaluation is a relatively new method to the social sciences, and uses slightly different methodological stances. In psychology, evaluation is usually carried out for organisational analysis rather than individual or group analysis of people, and is therefore thought of as a course of action that leads to decision or policy making rather than predictive or investigative questions or models. Due to this objective, carrying out evaluation requires a great deal of skill, such as high levels of sensitivity to political positions and the management of more than simply data or ethics, therefore evaluation is usually carried out by skilled and experienced researchers. However, it is possible that evaluation research is included in topics in which new researchers are interested, so it is worth some examination of the technique in order to understand it.

Evaluation research is carried out systematically to provide information and analysis that can lead to critical or diagnostic feedback about an object or a process. This feedback may be sought by a range of people, organisations or stakeholder groups. The major objective is to influence decision making or policy making by the provision of assessment, based on empirically derived evidence. Evaluation research questions can be descriptive, normative, or impact. In descriptive studies researchers simply describe the way a process functions and what its outcomes are, but with attention paid to the detail of how well the programme itself is communicated and understood. In contrast, normative studies need to arrive at the evaluation of the process for other reasons than merely describing them. It should be possible to decide if the goals are unrealistic or unhelpful or not communicated successfully enough. It should also be possible to determine if the objectives by which the goals are to be met are behavioural or attitudinal. An impact study would take the normative study one step further and look at the outcomes (intended or realised) in order to determine short- and long-term impacts and direct and indirect cost and benefits on the client or stakeholder.

Evaluations can include survey research, case studies, field experiments and secondary analysis of archived data. Field experiments would usually be used for impact designs. They have the same elements as laboratory experiments in terms of control and manipulation of independent variables, but are performed *in situ*, not in a laboratory.

A large proportion of evaluation research is carried out using a scientific–experimental model. This means the evaluation research needs to be impartial and objective and validate the information generated. It utilises experimental designs or the elements of these that are applicable together with cost–benefit analysis and they are theory-driven. There are, however, three alternative modes to this scientific experimental position:

1 Management-oriented systems models which emphasise comprehensive analysis within a large framework of organisational function.
2 Qualitative/anthropological models, which are based on observation from a phenomenological perspective and value of subjective interpretation. These are the naturalistic or 'fourth-generation' approaches to evaluation using critical theory and grounded theory.
3 Participant-oriented models place fundamental importance on the participants, who can be the clients of the evaluation or users of the system under evaluation.

Formative evaluation is done with the intention of improving what is being evaluated by examining the way something is carried out, or the technology that is being used to do the process, or the quality of product or input. For example, students are often assessed formatively before their course is finished so that they can receive feedback on the way in which they are learning and communicating that learning. In this way they can find out what level of performance they are achieving before the final examination which counts towards the qualification. Summative evaluations will examine the effects or outcomes of some object in order to describe what happens after the programme is finished. In the case of our students being examined, the summative assessment will predict their final grade and their subsequent performance in using what has been learnt. Organisational evaluation would use summative evaluations to determine the impact of the object being evaluated beyond the immediate outcomes.

Formative evaluation is carried out in order to define and describe the process, identify problems and how they might be addressed, and how well they are being addressed. There are several ways in which this can be done:

- Needs assessment to determine who needs the process, the extent of the need and the way the need might be met.
- Structured conceptualisation involves stakeholders to define the process and the possible outcomes for them.
- Implementation or process evaluation is a procedure of monitoring the processes/or its delivery and considering alternatives.

Summative evaluation is carried out to determine the feasibility of the process, its effectiveness and its net impact. The ways in which this can be done include:

- outcome evaluations investigating whether the process results in measurable effects, usually within specifically defined targets;
- impact evaluation assessing the overall or net effects;
- cost-effectiveness and cost–benefit analysis addressing questions of efficiency;
- secondary analysis re-examining data already gathered within a context or organisation but by new methods;
- meta-analysis integrating the results of multiple studies to make an overall summary judgement.

This is not by any means a full list of evaluative techniques, but covers a large number of those that will be found in the social science literature. One area in which evaluation is an invaluable tool is in assessing the effectiveness of treatment programmes. Mental health is a highly complex issue, with variations in perception, attitude and models of treatment. Unlike some physical illnesses that are relatively easy to diagnose and treat, and also do not usually carry social consequences, difficulties in mental health have many causes, and even more consequences. When the psychological difficulty results in individuals exhibiting deviance away from societal norms, the consequences are very harmful indeed, not only to the person carrying out deviant behaviour, but to victims of that behaviour too. The victim will have been harmed in some way, either mentally or physically, or both, and society demands that someone take responsibility for that. Therefore a major consequence for the person responsible for the deviant behaviour is punishment and possibly incarceration. Sexual offending is one crime from which society clearly sees a victim and a perpetrator, with offenders often receiving custodial sentences. In today's penal system, offenders are often offered the opportunity to reflect on their behaviour and to take part in treatment programmes. The next section will examine the ways in which treatment programmes can be used effectively and evaluated soundly.

EVALUATION OF TREATMENT PROGRAMMES

Treatment programmes used with offenders are designed to aid understanding of the causes and consequences of deviant behaviour, therefore a successful outcome is behaviour change. The evaluation of a treatment programme should measure the clinical impact in a number and range of those treated via psychometric data before and after treatment; and measure how subsequent behaviour change persists – that is, provide a framework for investigating the relationship between short-term change achieved through treatment and subsequent longer term recidivism. A final outcome should be to make recommendations as to how programmes might improve their efficacy in the future and how this might be achieved. The British Sexual Offender Treatment Programme (SOTP) is used in several prisons that house the most violent and persistent sexual offenders in the UK.

SEXUAL OFFENDING, THE RESEARCH, THE THEORY

Sexual offending includes rape, sexual abuse and rape of children, forced prostitution of adults or children, paraphilic behaviour that results in harm, sexual assault, sexual violence, abduction or kidnap with sexual motives and murder with sexual motives. Within the academic and research literature there are a variety of theories that attempt to explain sexual offending. The variety arose as there is no such thing as a typical sexual offender, and consequently no such thing as one set of attributable causes as to why some sexually offend. However, the theories can be grouped together under various schools of thought we are familiar with from other areas of psychological research, biological/medical explanations, evolutionary theories, and sociocultural explanations and psychological function.

BIOLOGICAL AND EVOLUTIONARY EXPLANATIONS OF SEXUAL AGGRESSION

Biological perspectives of sexual behaviour and dysfunction centre on hormonal and nervous system processes. Male hormones such as testosterone are linked closely to sexual development and hence to sexual aggression, so an early model of treatment was castration, and, later medication that leads to chemical castration. When treated with drugs designed to block the action of androgens, reoffending rates in male sex offenders are significantly lowered (Bradford, 1995). Other studies have shown that neurotransmitters such as dopamine, noradrenaline and serotonin play an important role in sexual motivation and drugs that affect them will affect sexual behaviour. All of this suggests a very clear association with biological function and sexual behaviour. Neurotransmitter dysfunction can be linked to sexual deviance or hypersexuality and Greenberg and Bradford (1997) found strong compulsions towards violent sexual urges can be lowered by the use of Selective Serotonin Reuptake Inhibitors (SSRIs), a class of antidepressants including fluoxetine (marketed as Prozac). Such clear biological and biochemical underpinnings for sexual deviancy have led some researchers to suggest that sexual aggression is part of our evolutionary make-up, not just a biological dysfunction

Thornhill and Palmer (2000) argue that rape has evolved as a procreational strategy, despite strong contradictory evidence that there is little reproductive success in forced copulation (Tang-Martinez & Mechanic, 2000). Thornhill and Palmer's position would suggest that sexual aggression is driven by sexual desire, when in fact, power and violence are the more likely motivations (Knight & Prentky, 1990), and easier to explain when we consider the fact that victims are often not women of childbearing age. Also, an evolutionary perspective would mean that men are predisposed to coerce women into sex in order to mate and reproduce, and this motivation is very difficult to treat. A medical model suggests that sexual offending is pathological: that is, it is a disease which can be treated with pharmacological or surgical means.

However, it is clear that many medical treatments for sexual dysfunction are not effective for the majority of sex offenders. Surgical treatments such as castration and neurosurgery do indeed directly affect a sex drive, but they are viewed as drastic measures with possible outcomes of suicide or other violent crimes (Bradford, 1990). The difficulty here is that many sexual crimes do not have a sexual motive (Coleman et al., 1992), therefore reduction of sexual drive and interest will not reduce the urge to commit sexual offences. Emory et al. (1992) suggest that treatments which combine surgical or pharmacological interventions with behavioural treatments might be more effective. The biological–medical model suggests that there are biological urges that must be subjugated, the evolutionary model suggests that an aggressive sexual urge is somehow of benefit to the species. A more fruitful argument lies in psychological explanations of sexual aggression, and this leads to the potential of therapeutic models.

SOCIAL AND PSYCHOLOGICAL EXPLANATIONS FOR SEXUAL AGGRESSION

It is clear from a great deal of research evidence that early parental bonding experiences affect the sexual development and hence later sexual behaviour of the individual. It is thought that attachment difficulties can lead to sexual dysfunction (Baker & Beech, 2004), and an acknowledgement of this and a therapy designed to work through such problems can be an effective treatment for sex offenders. An inadequate social environment combined with early abuse is a common factor found in sexual killers, as this appears to lead to violent fantasies and distorted attitudes as coping strategies for neglect and/or abuse. Psychological models of the developing abused child and the resultant violent and/or sexual criminal recognise a complex set of psychological factors such as distorted cognition and affect resulting socially deviant behaviour. The psychological approach to intervention is one of personality and functioning, with sex offenders seen as exhibiting large variations in personality characteristics, but with some forms more prevalent, such as psychopathic or anti-social personality types. In addition to this, there are several psychological deficits and dysfunctions which are seen as associated with sexual offending:

- Low self-esteem is a typical finding possibly stemming from childhood relationship dysfunction, and this is a high-risk factor for reoffending (Marshall et al., 1999).
- Social skills deficits are often seen, particularly in child sex offenders, social confidence is very low (Ward et al., 1997), and rapists show tendency to misinterpret rejection as positive interest, with aggression deemed an appropriate response (Marshall et al., 1995).

- Again the result of childhood relationship problems, and poor parenting, intimacy is a problem for sexual offenders. Emotional loneliness and poor intimacy skills lead to relationship difficulties in adult life, with the possibility of developing distorted perceptions of other people. Such distortions can lead to deviant sexual fantasies, again a high-risk factor in sexual reoffending (Marshall and Anderson, 1996).
- Rapists typically exhibit a difficulty of recognising emotions in other people. This is an identified empathy deficit, which suggests that there is also a deficit in emotional response and viewing things from an alternative perspective (Marshall et al., 1995). This empathy deficit is most prevalent in offenders who are the most violent (Hanson & Scott, 1995).
- Sexually aggressive behaviour often has as its basis and its justification distorted thinking and reasoning (Ward et al., 1997). Such cognitive distortions can be seen in sexual aggression against both adults and children (Bumby, 1996; Ward et al., 1995). Cognitive distortions are reinforced by rationalisation and internalised justification for any form of offending (Gavin & Hockey, 2007).
- High levels of deviant sexual arousal appear to result from associating abusive and violent fantasies with repeated masturbation (Burgess et al., 1986), which contributes to the maintenance, repetition and escalation of sexual offending (Hanson & Bussiere, 1998).

Most of the above difficulties must be taken into account when developing treatment programmes for sex offenders.

TREATMENT OF SEXUAL AGGRESSION AND SEXUAL OFFENDING

Marshall et al. (1999) suggest that there are several risk factors that contribute to the likelihood of sexual offending, and that these can interact. So, for example, having low victim empathy can contribute to cognitive distortions about offending, and such distortions might lead to violent sexual fantasies. If one factor is treated, therefore, the others can be affected without being primary parts of the treatment.

Successful treatment of sex offenders has always been directed towards assessing and attempting to modify deviant sexual interests in the hopes of reducing the probability of sexual offending. However, early treatment was directed at suppressing deviant sexual interests via such tactics as aversion therapy and, if possible, raising non-deviant sexual interests via orgasmic reconditioning and systematic reduction of anxieties about adult sexuality. Such sexual preference modification techniques when used alone were unsuccessful in producing sustained reduction in offending behaviour. The review of programmes by Perkins et al. (1998) suggested that if sexual deviance led to maintenance of sexual offending, then its reduction is of paramount importance, and the most effective way of doing this was to use behaviour modification techniques and/or anti-libidinal medication on the primary target of sexual deviance. Later programmes have expanded into a broader range of therapeutic techniques which include a more cognitive position for developing acceptance of responsibility, increasing self-esteem, improving social skills, reducing cognitive distortions, enhancing empathy for victims. These are used in conjunction with therapy to deal with unresolved issues in an offender's early life which contributed to the development of sexual offending behaviour (Marshall et al., 1999).

The SOTP was initiated in 1991 in order to integrate assessment and treatment of sex offenders. There are 26 sites at which the group programme is running with treatment of over a thousand men. The SOTP comprises a core and an extended programme. The core programme aims to challenge the cognitions used by offenders to justify behaviour, in order to develop new attitudes and change behaviour (there is a core-adapted programme for offenders with learning disabilities). The extended SOTP is a longer, highly intensive programme of work for high-risk and high-need sexual offenders who have completed the core programme (Hollin & Palmer, 2006). The programme is designed to increase motivation to avoid reoffending and develop self-management skills. Comprehensive assessment is also part of the programme. Currently there are 86 sessions of assessment, therapy and role-play, with the group seen as an essential element, whereby the offender publicly acknowledges his need to change and normal social interaction is reinforced. This treatment approach is known as a cognitive–behavioural–therapeutic (CBT) programme and it appears to be efficacious in the treatment of child abusers. It involves a cognitive aspect in which the offender recognises patterns of distorted thinking. This could include contemplation of illegal sexual acts and recognising the impact of abusive behaviour on the victim. There is also a behavioural component of treatment, which can involve production of sexual arousal to inappropriate images or fantasies.

Professionals concerned with the incarceration, rehabilitation and treatment of sexual offenders are in agreement that there are a range of psychological and even medical difficulties with which they present, but that there is a shared 'core' of problems. The treatment programmes reflect this range of problems with core elements in the therapeutic approach.

Entry to the programme is via extensive psychometric measurement of the highly prevalent, psychological difficulties identified above, followed by a targeted therapeutic programme of the CBT nature. The measures typically include such scales as the Multiphasic Sex Inventory, which has various subscales which measure:

- admitted sexual drives and interests (MSI: social and sexual desirability);
- fantasising, manipulation and coercion (MSI: sex deviance admittance);
- justifications for sexual deviance (MSI: justifications);
- level of sexual obsessions (MSI: sexual obsessions).

Additionally there are measures of level of denial of victim harm, planning, future risk and overall denial; distorted thinking about sexual contact with children and children's sexuality; level of denial of the impact of sexual abuse on victims and level of fixation on children.

Once the levels of sexual deviance are established as above, each offender is entered into the programme in order to increase victim empathy, reduce distorted thinking and denial, and develop an awareness of the pattern of offending. In this way he will learn about strategies to deal with deviant arousal, about alternatives to offending, and acquire coping skills to use when encountering situations where an offence is more likely to occur.

Programme evaluation is carried out via measures designed to detect change in 'primary treatment' targets (such as admittance or denial of sexual interest and behaviour and relapse prevention skills as included in the core programme) and 'secondary treatment' targets, which are more general aspects of dysfunctional personality that can lead to offence behaviour

These measures include:

Primary:

- Awareness of risk situations.
- Generation of sensible strategies to deal with such situations.
- Recognition of future risk (Relapse–Prevention Questionnaire).

Secondary:

- Social competence.
- Personal distress (self-esteem, emotional loneliness, under-assertiveness and inability to deal with negative emotions).
- Acceptance of accountability for behaviours.
- Locus of control.
- Control over own behaviour (MSI: cognitive distortions and immaturity).

In addition to all of this, detailed personal histories are also included, in order to collect demographic details, offence history and own victimisation experiences. Also, it is established that sex offenders often lie about their offending and are susceptible to attempting to show themselves in a socially desirable light (Gannon &

Polaschek, 2005), so the assessment also includes measures to indicate this, such as 'lie scales' and social desirability measures inserted into some of the scales. In this way the assessors avoid the element of 'faking good' and allow the reliability and consistency of the subjects' responses in pre- and post-testing.

In 1998, an evaluation of the prison SOTP was carried out for the Home Office, by Beech, Fisher and Beckett (1999), in order to determine the efficacy of treatment of sex offenders in category C prisons. This study had six major objectives:

1 To examine how the core programme is implemented.
2 To analyse psychometric data before and after treatment.
3 To evaluate treatment delivery.
4 To evaluate behaviour change over time.
5 To establish a framework whereby the relationship between short-term change and long-term change can be examined.
6 To make recommendations on the improvement of efficacy.

So this study was an impact study using a scientific–experimental model, because, in addition to examining the programme itself, the researchers were commissioned to evaluate the impact of the programme on a number of prisoners, how the programme is delivered and make recommendations for improvement, and used analysis of before- and after-treatment measures in order to achieve this.

The researchers, all forensic psychologists, visited seven prisons in order to discuss the study with the managers and followed this up by interviewing group leaders and sitting in on group sessions, to collect data. A total of three sessions for each group were observed: an introductory session, a session in which affect, cognition and behaviour were explored, and a victim-empathy role-play session. Other measures were taken, these allowing researchers to identify the environment in which an established group was working.

Participants were seen prior to treatment, during treatment and after treatment. A follow-up study included men in the treatment groups and those who had finished. The post-treatment group included men who had left prison and were in the care of the probation service, which meant that probation officers could also be included.

Beech et al. had already established by reviewing the literature (Marshall & Pithers, 1994; Perkins et al., 1998) that features of successful treatment programmes include:

- identification of deviant sexual arousal and fixation then addressed via behavioural modification techniques and/or medication;
- CBT to increase motivation and offence-reduction skills;

- development of relapse prevention plans geared to the individual offender, monitored after the offender returns to the community.

The evaluation of the prison SOTP included:

- examining the effect on offender readiness to admit to behaviour;
- reduction in pro-offending attitudes, such as thoughts about having sexual contact with children;
- reduction in levels of denial of the impact that sexual abuse has on victims;
- increase in levels of social competence.

The evaluation study concluded that 67% of those treated showed a treatment effect and that the longer term treatment showed better results for post-release reduction in recidivism than short-term therapy for highly deviant offenders.

So, how did the evaluators go about doing this?

EVALUATION STUDY DESIGN

The researchers selected six prisons and then two groups inside each. The full sample comprised 100 men, of which 82 were child sex offenders. A large set of psychometric data was gathered at the start of the study and then at the end of the study, by which time five men had either failed to finish treatment or refused to be seen again. Some of the offenders were on the core programme and some on the extended programme

A nine-month follow-up was also included in which 56 men from the original took part; they were reinterviewed and given further psychometric testing.

EFFECTIVENESS OF THERAPY

The psychometric tests administered before and after treatment were designed to measure change in four main areas:

- The readiness to admit to sexual fantasising and victim manipulation together with denial of victim harm.
- Cognitive distortions about sexual contact (especially with children) and justification of deviant behaviour.
- Personality factors which might predispose to offending.
- Relapse prevention skills.

Significant improvements were found in nearly all of the measures used. The major findings were that the programme was more effective with low-deviancy groups, and that the effectiveness of long and short programmes was the same for these groups. For high-deviancy groups the longer programme was more effective. The therapeutic groups were cohesive and task oriented, and the levels of this were related to the effectiveness of treatment, as indicated in much of the literature about CBT. The evaluators found that there was a high likelihood of the treatment effect being maintained, but that was significantly related to reduction in pro-offending attitudes.

So, the men in the sample showed significant change in level of denial, pro-offending attitudes, social competence and acceptance of accountability, and both the shorter and longer treatment programmes were effective. The second finding of the evaluation was that sex offenders could acquire by the end of the programme a 'treated' profile. In other words, offenders could show overall treatment effects in the variables of interest which meant they were indistinguishable from a non-offender in terms of attitude and sexual deviance. The researchers concluded that the programme led to over 65% of the sample showing a 'treated' profile and this is particularly likely in low-deviance cases in which the men were open about their offending. However, even 43% of high-deviance offenders were successfully treated. The study also found that these treatment gains were maintained even after the offenders were discharged to the community.

The evaluation researchers therefore concluded that the SOTP is an effective programme and made several recommendations:

- To identify high-deviance offenders and to complete a programme aimed at reduction of denial before entering the SOTP.
- That the high-deviancy offenders do not exhibit a treated profile by the end of the programme due to low social competence (low self-esteem, under-assertiveness, emotional isolation) and that these men are given priority for admittance to an extended programme.
- To identify men who do not show reduction in pro-offending attitudes by the end of the programmes and are required to repeat it.
- Higher emphasis is given to acquiring social competence.

There were other recommendations including placement of prisoners in vulnerable units, and so on.

The study described was therefore a scientific–experimental examination of a programme that had a range of objectives and outcomes. The study has identified that the mode of treatment is effective, and identified where improvements might be made. Hence it was an impact evaluation, as it assessed the impact on those treated, the therapists and the likely outcome of discharge and lower likelihood of reoffending.

Summary

In this chapter we have looked at the research technique known as evaluation, which is the systematic and rigorous examination of an organisation, process or programme, in order to provide feedback and suggestions for improvement where necessary. Evaluation can be descriptive, normative or impact depending on need, and can include survey research, case studies, field experiments and secondary analysis of archived data. We have examined in detail the evaluation of a programme for rehabilitation of sex offenders.

PART VI

COMMUNICATION OF RESEARCH

Once we have carried out research we need to communicate our findings and this part looks at how this is done, and how to find out more about research in our area of interest.

CHAPTER 20

COMMUNICATING RESEARCH

Contents

Journal articles

Conference proceedings

Books

Government/corporate reports

Newspapers

Theses and dissertations

Internet

Research paper sections

Abstract

Introduction

Method and research design

Results

Statistical results

Qualitative results

Discussion

Summary

Communicating Research

He who knows only his own side of the case, knows little of that. (John Stuart Mill)

Learning Objectives

- To understand the purpose of communicating research.
- To understand the forms of research communication.
- To understand the format for research reports.

KEY TERMS

- Abstract
- Books
- Conclusions
- Conference proceedings
- Confidential reports
- Discussion
- Internet
- Introduction
- Journal articles
- Literature review
- Methods and design
- References
- Results
- Theses

It may be possible to think of the performance of research as an end in itself, but knowledge does not progress without letting other people know what has been found out and allowing criticism and discussion of the findings. Any findings that have not been independently evaluated are of questionable value, so they are presented in the form of formal papers and published in journals. This means we must be familiar with this communication format in order to conduct research, for two reasons: to understand what has been found in an area and also to communicate what we have found.

Papers must be understandable and meaningful. There is little value in writing papers using language that is so obscure that it will confuse and complicate the issues. A paper is designed to tell somebody something, not show how many big words the writer knows. This chapter will describe how to find papers that are relevant to the topic we are researching, and how to write an acceptable paper to describe research findings.

Before even carrying out a piece of research, a researcher should examine the literature in the area. If students are required to perform research as part of classes, the tutors will have done this too. There are several sources of information about the topic.

JOURNAL ARTICLES

Journals are the best source for recent information that has been peer reviewed and accepted by the research community. The review process means that journal editors only accept the most relevant research for publication. However, due to the review and editing process that journals undertake, it might be up to two years before a piece of research is published. So a more up-to-date source might be conference proceedings.

CONFERENCE PROCEEDINGS

Conferences are arenas in which the latest findings are presented to colleagues interested in a research area, in the form of papers or posters. The proceedings are the published papers or abstracts of the conference. They can be useful in providing information on the latest research, or on research that has not been published. They are also helpful in providing information on which people are currently involved in which research areas, and so can be helpful in tracking down other work by the same researchers.

BOOKS

Books tend to take longer to be published than a journal article, so usually do not contain the most recent research, but may be collections of research in the topic. Textbooks are unlikely to be useful for including in your literature review as they are intended for teaching, not for research, but they do offer a good starting point from which to find more detailed sources.

GOVERNMENT/CORPORATE REPORTS

Many government departments and private corporations commission or carry out research. Their published findings can provide a useful source of information, depending on your field of study. However, many tend to be confidential reports, so you may not have access.

NEWSPAPERS

Newspapers are generally intended for a general audience, and the information they provide will be of very limited use for a literature review. Often newspapers are more helpful as providers of information about recent trends, discoveries or changes, for example announcing changes in government policy, but you should then search for more detailed information in other sources.

THESES AND DISSERTATIONS

A research thesis is usually written by a candidate for a doctoral or other postgraduate qualification, but some libraries may hold well-written undergraduate theses. They will contain up-to-date research, particularly the doctoral ones. However, there are disadvantages in that they can be difficult to obtain since they are not published, and the student who carried out the research may not be an experienced researcher and therefore you might have to treat the findings with more caution than with published research.

INTERNET

The fastest growing source of information is the Internet. While this is a valuable asset in any researcher's world, there are some very important difficulties to be aware of:

- Anyone with access to a computer and the relevant authoring software can design a website, and just about anyone can post information on the Internet, so the quality may not be reliable.
- The information posted may be intended for a general audience and so not be suitable for inclusion in your literature review.

It is very easy to place information on the Internet and those who do may have various motivations for doing so. Some people may have a political agenda to meet; some may simply be posting up their own opinions without any reference to other viewpoints. It is safest to view each website with more than a little scepticism until the information can be verified by another source. Sites such as Wikipedia have been shown to be unreliable, and in 2005 the founder of Wikipedia admitted that the quality of the information placed on it was suspect at best, and possibly unreliable garbage! However, many of the articles on such sites are invaluable to readers new to a topic. These can be viewed as useful introductions to the topics in easily readable and accessible forms before moving on to more reliable sources of data.

Many refereed electronic journals (e-journals) are appearing on the Internet – if they are refereed it means that there is an editorial board that evaluates the work so the quality should be more reliable (depending on the reputation of the journal).

Most academic libraries now provide access to databases of abstracts and on-line subscriptions to some journals. This is a very valuable tool in searching for the information you need, so be sure to get the password your library will provide.

Carrying out a search of the literature in the area provides the context for the current research and will also provide clues about how to write up work. There are some conventions about writing up research papers and every researcher should be aware of them.

RESEARCH PAPER SECTIONS

Abstract

The first section of a research paper is the abstract, which is a short summary of the research. Some journals or conferences specify a length for the abstract, usually 120–500 words.

The purpose of an abstract is to establish the topic of the research, indicate the methods used, and present the main findings and conclusions. When searching on-line databases you will need to use key terms, so an abstract should include all those relevant. It should not be too detailed, though, and should not contain detailed explanations or present statistical results, unless specifically requested.

The abstract in the box is 226 words long, places the study in context, describes the method undertaken, and discusses the main findings and the conclusion.

Example of abstract

This paper describes research investigating the perception of intrusive music, that is music heard when choice, volume and occurrence are not under the control of the participant. [*Main theme and context introduced*]

A diary study was carried out into the effects of hearing music that the participant had not chosen to listen to. Participants were directed to record accounts of episodes in which music was played in instances when they were not in control of the decision to play the music, and to record various items about the music, together with any effects on themselves. [*Method described*]

A number of themes arose from analysis of the diaries, particularly relating to strong reactions. Characteristics such as music tempo, repetition, context, style and quality appeared consistently in the reports. Strong negative responses were experienced from inappropriate volume levels, poor sound qualities, unexpected contexts and unpopular styles. Results showed that mood, desire to stay or return and intention to purchase were all influenced by the presence of intrusive music. Conversely, beneficial effects included an increase in energy and motivation levels, distraction from menial tasks and induction of a relaxed and content state even from unexpected music. [*Main analysis technique and findings*]

Consumer behaviour does appear to be manipulated and influenced by the presence of music. However, the negative effects must be addressed, and the implications of these for commercial practice are discussed along with the everyday effects of intrusive episodes of music. [*Conclusion*]

Introduction

The introduction gives the background to the research carried out, presents the research problem and the rationale for doing the current research. The rationale is crucial for a reader to understand the significance of the study, but must be placed in the context of previous research. This might be a useful checklist for writing an introduction, as it should answer all these questions:

- Why is this research important?
- Who will it benefit?
- Why do we need to know these things or improve the current understanding?
- What is the gap in our knowledge this research will fill? (Rationale)
- How will this study fill the gap in the knowledge? (Objectives)

There is no need to make the introduction too long, as too much detail will cloud the issues. There should be a clear statement of the research problem and a well-organised discussion of how it can be approached. Organisation means that the discussion of the topic should move from the general (theoretical perspectives perhaps) to the specific (previous findings). For example, from the general:

Music plays an important role in consumerism, not just the multi-billion-pound industry it represents in its own right, but the increasing use of it in shops, bars and restaurants, where it is intended to have beneficial effects on customers and their likelihood to spend.

to the specific:

Kotler (1994) first introduced the concept of 'store atmospherics' to account for the efforts involved in the design of purchasing environments in order to create specific emotional influences of the consumer.

The first part of the introduction defines the field and the problem,

Music has a profound effect on the listener. However, it is suggested that it has become such a part of everyday life that music psychology is failing to address these effects, and that our listening behaviour is so contextualised that we have yet to examine and explain the effects of musical stimuli on the listening situation.

but the second part must provide a potential solution to the problem – a suggestion as to how the research gap could be filled. Aims and objectives can be outlined in the introduction so that the reader has a clear idea of what the study attempted to accomplish.

This study's aims were to highlight natural music exposure and identify important factors and outcomes within personal experience of listening to music when we have no choice in the matter.

Additionally the introduction will include a literature review – a critical examination of existing research that is relevant to the present study. The review will summarise and evaluate the work, and show how it is relevant to the present study and how the methodology relates to the study to be carried out. In other words, it provides the context for the research we are currently writing about. Do not read or include everything in the area, just that which is relevant, and remember to keep all the bibliographic references for that which is read!

A short literature review

It has long been established that the presence of music in a working environment can increase productivity and reduce errors (Gardner & McGehee, 1949). However, further investigations show that the type of music is very important, with 'up-beat' music increasing arousal levels (Fisher & Greenberg, 1972). These effects do not appear to map directly onto commercial use of music. Englis and Pennell (1994) discovered that there are many negative effects that can be identified, with their major finding being that meaning in music, and therefore its effect, is highly dependent on the individual consumer. However, when a popular piece of music is used for advertising the result is often a dislike for the music or the product. Use in advertising has the effect of cheapening the music, although this is possibly the disapproval found when widening access to elitist constructs (Englis & Pennell, 1994). Individual differences account for a large proportion of music preference. Rawlings and Ciancarelli (1997) found correlations between music preference and elements of the five-factor measure of personality. Excitement seekers, for example, like rock, but not classical music, whereas those 'open to experience' liked a diverse range of styles.

Remember: if your report is being written for a class assignment you will probably have had some references provided by the tutor, but these are for guidance only and not the full literature in the topics. Newer or alternative reference material will be available, and you can find these by searching your library resources with 'key words'.

A word is in order here about the 'voice' in which a report should be written. Verbs take voices which can be passive or active. An active verb is used in the sentence 'the cat scratched the dog' but passive in 'the dog was scratched by the cat'. In the passive sentence the main focus is the dog, even though it does nothing; something is done to it, and we could leave out the cat altogether. In the active sentence the cat is the focus. The reader is more interested in the research than the researcher so that is where the emphasis should be.

'An experiment to investigate the effect of inverting illusory stimuli was carried out ...' passive voice. 'We carried out an experiment to investigate the effect of inverting illusory stimuli ...' active voice with 'we' as the focus.

It also makes the writing sound far more objective. The only real exception to this is where the method is one where reflexivity is required (see the chapter on qualitative methods) and the text is written in the first person.

Method and Research Design

A method section should explain how the data was collected and analysed as this affects the results and their presentation. The method section should make it clear why a particular method or procedure was chosen and why it was appropriate to the question. There should also be enough information for other researchers to replicate the work. There is no need to include irrelevant details, such as the computer program used to store and analyse the data, but enough, such as the equipment and calibration of machinery, or the validation of a questionnaire or interview schedule.

Results

A diary format was selected in order to gain real-life experiences and personal accounts. Participants were directed to record accounts of episodes in which music was played in instances when they were not in control of the decision to play the music, and to record various items about the music, together with any effects on themselves. Diary methods have a long history in psychology; particularly relevant in this case are investigations of leisure behaviour (see Harvey, 1990) and consumer behaviour (see Robinson & Nicosia, 1991).

Participants were directed to keep accounts of encounters in which music is not the primary focus (as would be the case in, for example, a concert), but where it is an accompaniment to non-music-focused behaviour such as shopping, visiting the gym, cafes, etc.

Participants gave informed consent after an explanation of the objectives of the data collection was provided, together with assurances of anonymity and confidentiality. Participants were also informed of their right to withdrawal from the study and of their data at any time. In addition to demographic data, a request was made to identify preferred musical style. The participant was then equipped with a blank notebook and asked to write about each experience of music that was outside his or her personal control. The diary was to be completed for a period of 10 days, and should include date, time, place, status (alone or otherwise), type of music and volume. This was to ensure a certain level of consistency in the report for comparison, but the format was deliberately open.

This section is to present the findings after analysis in a way that is meaningful to the reader. There should be a statement of results in which they are presented in accessible formats (graphs, tables, diagrams with accompanying annotation in the form of written text). Raw data should not be included in a research report, but summarised in an appropriate way dependent on the method and analysis used.

The text should not include too much detail that simply repeats information presented in graphs, tables, etc., without making the results meaningful. Note that the results should be interpreted giving enough information for the reader to understand them, and direct attention to significant parts, but not too much detail, as full discussion should be kept for the next section.

Statistical Results

In quantitative research a clear presentation can be given by starting with descriptive statistics summarising the data, then using these to describe and justify the choice of inferential statistics. After all, if the means of the groups are not different, for example, there is little need to carry on and perform t tests or ANOVAS! Graphs can be used either descriptively or to aid the interpretation of complex quantitative analyses.

There are several conventions in presenting statistical results, including how each statistic and its significance is presented. Conventionally we choose a significance level and stick to that throughout the results section. So for example in our simple experiment on social facilitation, the t test for independent samples returns a t-value of $t=+5.2$ with 46 degrees of freedom. The p-value is given as 0. Therefore the results would be written

$$t=+5.2, \mathit{df}=46, p<0.01$$

Qualitative Results

Qualitative reports are slightly different. While the same standards should apply, a logical flow of reasoning from introduction, methodology, findings and conclusion, researchers will often find that the results and discussion will start to merge, as the interpretative nature of the method and analysis means that consideration of findings and their interpretation start to emerge in a different way to quantitative research. The presentation of findings that are plausible and provide enough context for readers to make their own interpretations is a very suitable aim in writing up qualitative findings. Many researchers who are new to qualitative research, and who have often approached it from an academic environment in which quantitative research dominates, find it challenging to transform large amounts of data and its potential interpretation to a written form. As we have encountered in the chapters on qualitative research, the difference between carrying out a quantitative method, in which large databanks can be reduced to a few numbers, and a qualitative one, where the analysis often means a recombination of data, is that explaining the qualitative findings can be bewildering to the researcher, never mind the reader. Therefore good organisation during analysis is needed if the report is to read in an organised, logical fashion.

Discussion

The discussion section starts with an explanation of the results and comments on whether or not the results were expected. References to previous research should compare the results with the results of the other studies and tell the reader whether the results can be used to support a hypothesis or similar claim.

A deduction of whether the results can be applied more generally should be given too, or whether further hypotheses could be generated. A discussion should not simply supply more detail about the results or reiterate them, but explain them and place them in context. The discussion section is also for explaining what the methodological limitations of the study are, but should not simply be a list of faults. Future research suggestions should be made – not simply improvements to the study, but real progression from it.

Participants in this study have reported an increased awareness of intrusive music, suggesting that some form of priming has occurred. As a direct result of participation, perception of music has been heightened and thinking has been shaped by the diary-keeping task. This suggests that unconscious desensitisation is the normal state with respect to environmental music, due to its prevalence and our exposure, and that we must maintain a certain amount of indifference.

Data also suggests that when music is experienced in the home, but out of our control, we regard this as particularly intrusive. Homes are regarded with higher degrees of value, control and privacy, and such 'confrontations' are deemed more offensive.

In addition, the study shows that participants are ready to air personal opinions with regard to how music should be used. Strong views were expressed, to the extent of suggesting that music should be avoided completely in certain contexts. High-volume, strong bass-line and poor quality were generally not appreciatred, particularly in the daytime. Volume is a major factor in discouraging consumers from returning to particular venues, and therefore from spending money.

(Cont'd)

Applications of findings

This study would appear to indicate that some thorough market research is required to ensure that, where music is used, it can be more consistently structured towards meeting consumer needs and preferences. There are various strengths and weaknesses in the way music is utilised commercially, and the implication is that this should be addressed more directly in order to achieve a more attractive consumer environment. It is clear that the intention, in using music, is to satisfy the consumer in some way, but, in fact, that it is detracting from any pleasurable experience. The aim of retailers and service providers, in the use of music, should be to reflect the atmosphere of stores, products and services, generating a comfortable experience. This is a challenging objective, but common ground must be established if retailers are to take advantage of the positive influences of music. Konecni (1982, 500) has suggested that music is 'embedded in the stream of daily life', but his study would seem to suggest that when attention is paid to this stream, attention is also paid the possibility of 'disembedding' from the stream, and more elements of choice are brought to bear. If individuals make choices based on personal preferences, then larger groups may too, and retailers may find they are using the supposed environmental persuasion techniques in the wrong way.

One further warning about the study is appropriate too. The keeping of the diary had the effect of making the participants pay more attention to the music around them, with thinking about music being shaped by the diary keeping. If, as listeners of no choice, we start to pay more attention to what is embedded in our stream of life, then perhaps those who inflict music of poor quality and uncontrollable volume upon us had better pay heed, since we may vote with our ears, followed by our feet.

The final part should be a list of all the references used in the report. Referencing is also referred to as citing or documenting. There are several widely used formats for referencing such as author–date and numbering. It is the researcher's responsibility to find out which referencing system should be used. Journal and conference editors specify particular styles, and, if writing for assessment, tutors will specify a form too (and students may lose marks for referencing incorrectly!).

All work/words belonging to other writers must be referenced and the reader must be able to ascertain the source of all the work used to present the information. Items that are general or common knowledge do not need to be referenced. Using other people's work is not a sign of weakness of the researcher's own idea, in fact the opposite is the case as reports without references appear to be out of context or the writer appears to be unfamiliar with the work in the area. Good use of other people's writing, properly referenced and acknowledged, is to be encouraged. Check the format of the required referencing system in order to avoid ignoring any author and to avoid any accusation of plagiarism.

Summary

This chapter is an introduction to how to write up research and how to find what research is relevant to our current area. However, this is only an overview and specific requirements of assessment or publication must always be taken into account. Excerpts taken from Gavin, H. (2006) Intrusive music: the perception of everyday music explored by diaries. *The Qualitative Report, 11* (3), September.

APPENDIX A

CHOOSING A STATISTICAL TEST

The following flowcharts are designed to assist in the choice at statistical test. First decide whether the study was experimental (chart 1) or correlational (chart 2). Start at the top and follow the arrows by answering the questions about your data, design, independent variable, etc.

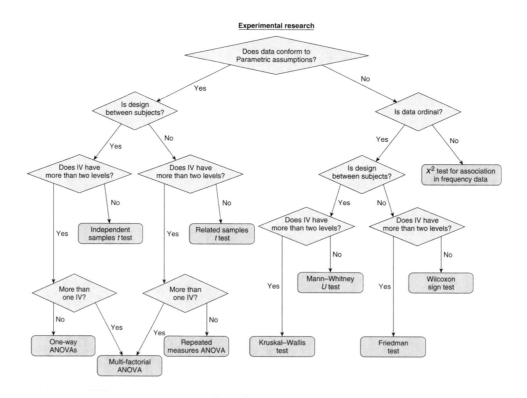

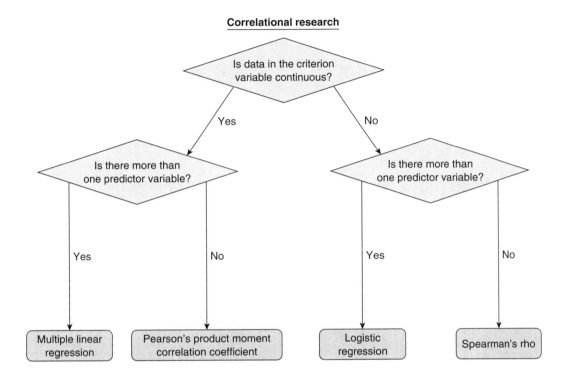

APPENDIX B

SPSS OUTPUT FOR DATA AND ANALYSIS DISCUSSED IN CHAPTER 6

Figure B.1 shows the data in the repeated measures case, in which the participants have carried out the task alone and observed. Note that each condition has its own column, and each participant their own row.

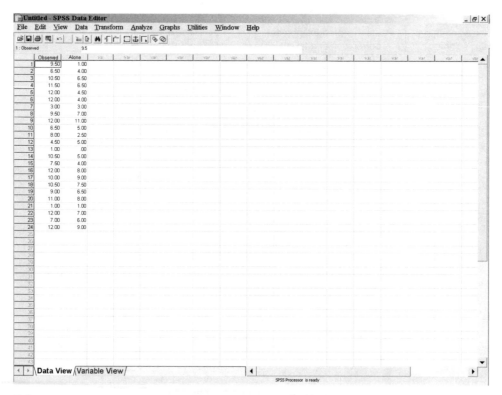

Figure B.1

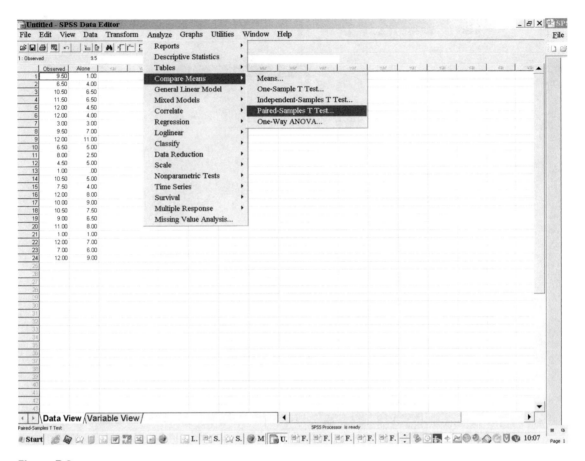

Figure B.2

Figure B.2 shows the process of choosing to carry out a repeated measures *t* test. The menu choice are Analyze–Compare Means–Paired-samples *t* Test.

Once the *t* test is selected we need to indicate the pair of data sets we are using, as in Figure B.3.

Figure B.3 Clicking OK generates the output in Figure B.4.

Here we seem to have quite a lot of information. We are given the descriptive statistics for the pair of data sets, that is the conditions, always handy, together with the correlation between the two sets. The high positive correlation tells us that the conditions vary in much the same way. This means that each participant is

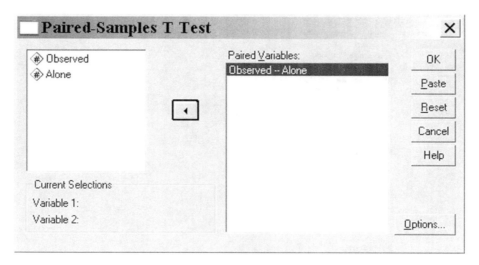

Figure B.3

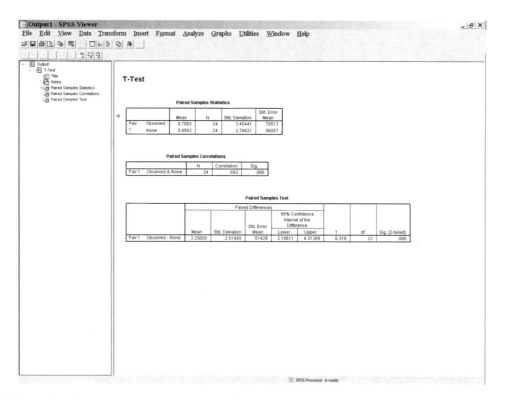

Figure B.4

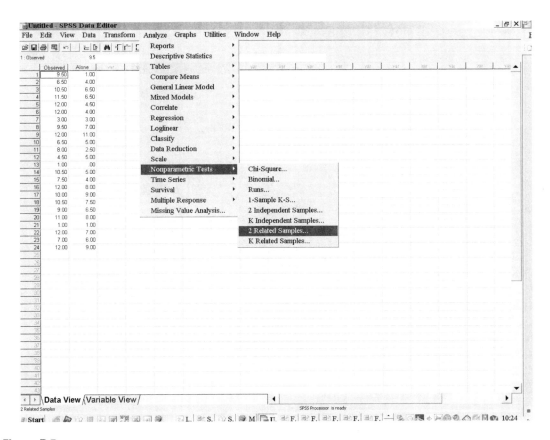

Figure B.5

being affected in the same way. Moving to the *t*-value, we can see it is significant (the significance value in the right hand box is lower than our significance level), therefore the means are significantly different to each other. We can now reject our null hypothesis that the means of the two performance scores are not different in the two conditions of being observed or alone. We can now return to our research question with the null hypothesis rejected and determine whether or not our alternative hypothesis is supported. Here we cannot simply accept our alternative hypothesis, but must examine our experimental situation to see if there are other explanations for the effect we have seen.

An alternative analysis would be the Wilcoxon test. This is selected via the Nonparametric Tests menu option (Figure B.5).

Again setting up the pairs as in Figure B.6 and pressing OK generates the output in Figure B.7.

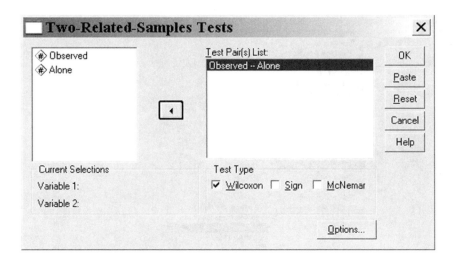

Figure B.6

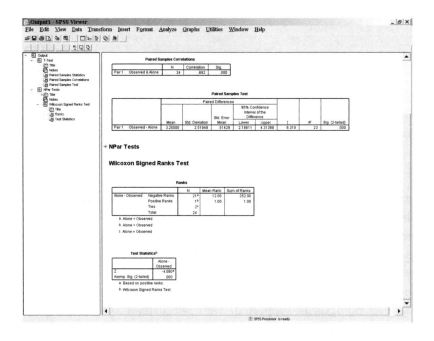

Figure B.7

Again, the test shows a significant difference.

Moving to the between-subjects case then, the data is in a different layout (Figure B.8).

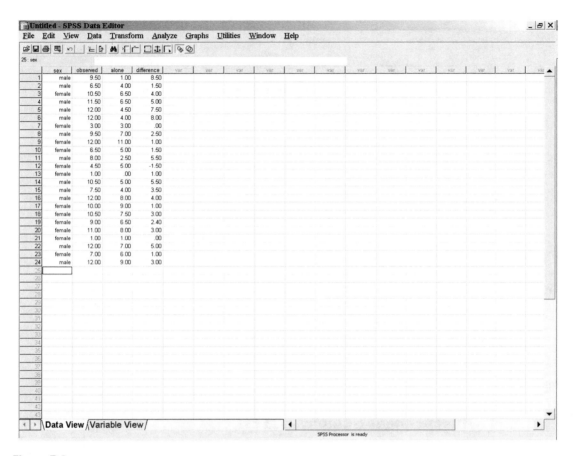

Figure B.8

The participants now have their sex recorded and the difference between the two conditions computed (Figure B.9). The choice of independent samples *t* test is through the same menu until the choice of test (Figure B.10).

When setting up the data for comparison, we need to define the groups, in this case male and female, which in the data are designated 1 and 2 respectively (Figure B.11).

This time the output (Figure B.12) gives us descriptives but no correlation. The *t*-value is significant here, and we can use the equal variances assumed figures, as they are exactly the same as those when not assumed.

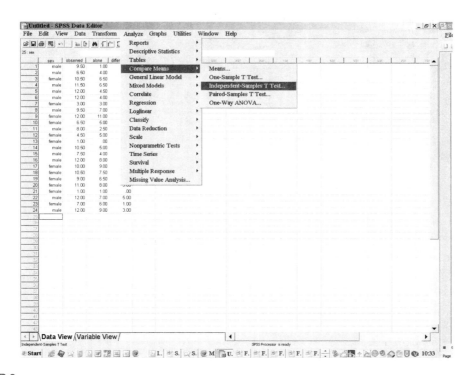

Figure B.9

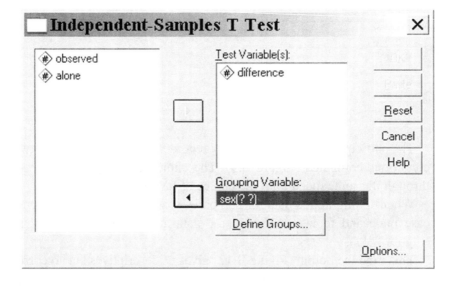

Figure B.10

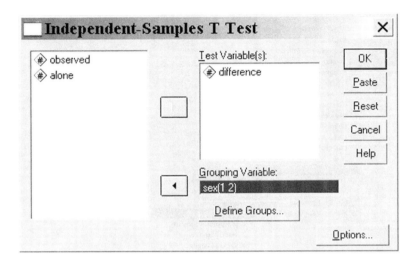

Figure B.11

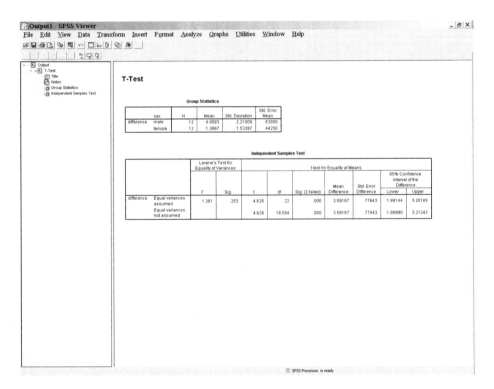

Figure B.12

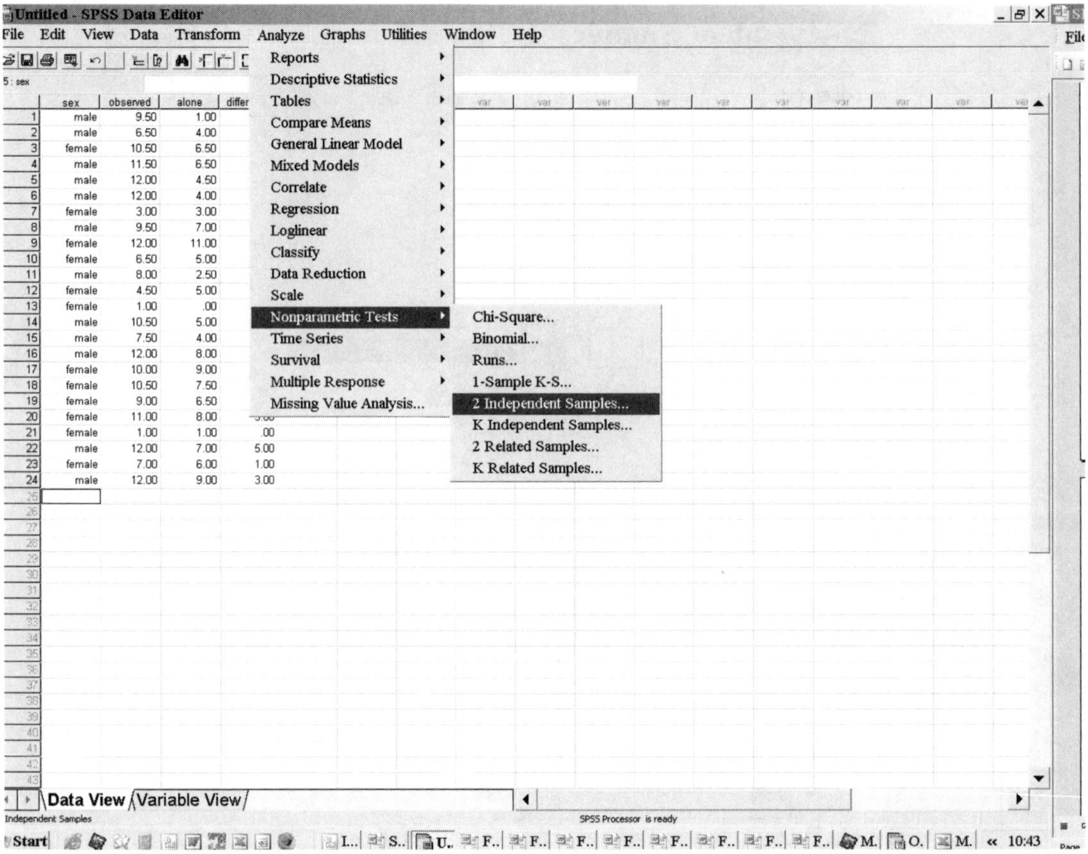

Figure B.13

As always, our statistical output is only half of the story, and we must refer back to our hypothesises for interpretation. The null hypothesis was that there would be no sex difference between the effects of the observation.

Choosing the non-parametric alternative is the same procedure as before, but the choice is for two independent samples (Figure B.13).

And the groups and data are defined as before (Figure B.14), with the output generated as in Figure B.15.

We can see that the Mann–Whitney test turns out to be significant too.

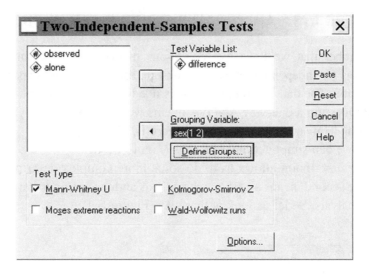

Figure B.14

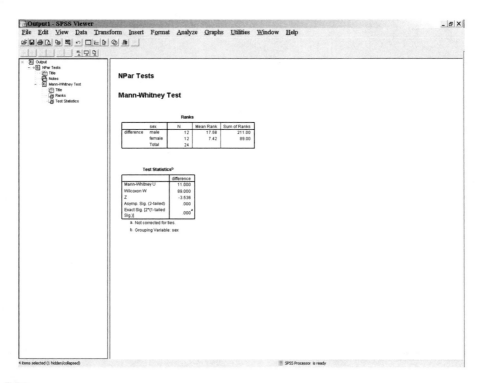

Figure B.15

SPSS OUTPUT FOR DATA AND ANALYSIS DISCUSSED IN CHAPTER 7

Remember that we have five conditions of orienting task, and in the between-subjects (or independent measures) design, each participant experiences a different condition. The data file therefore looks like that in Figure B.16.

Requesting a one-way ANOVA means we can use the Analyze–General Linear Module–Univariate mean option (Figure B.17).

Or we can simply compare means (Figure B.18).

The first option allows us to do some more complex description of the model, but the second means a very quick analysis and the option to carry out simple post-hoc analysis. So let us look at that way (Figure B.19).

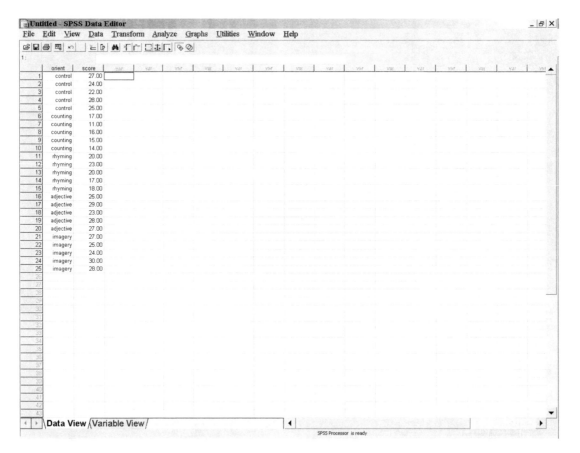

Figure B.16

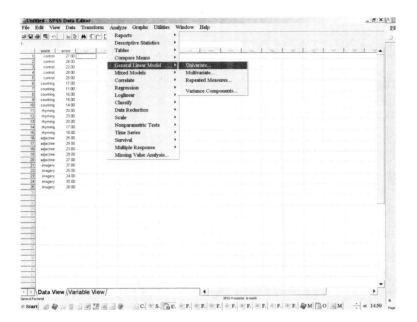

Figure B.17

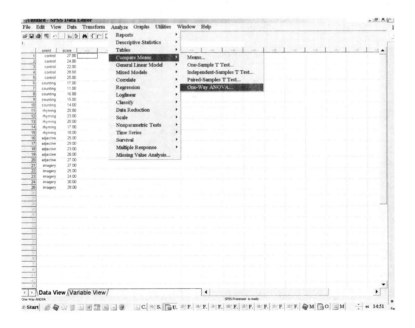

Figure B.18

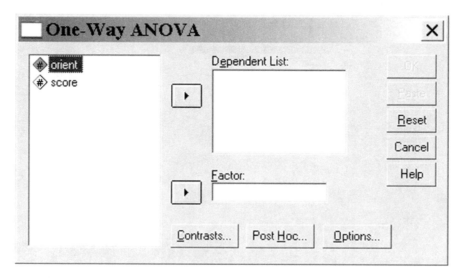

Figure B.19

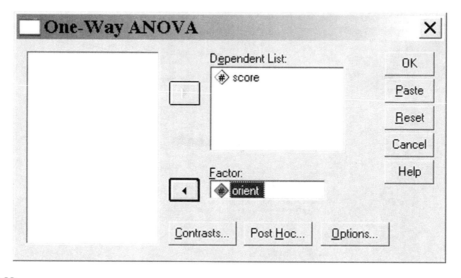

Figure B.20

We need to place the score in the dependent list box and the orient in the factor box using the arrows as in Figure B.20.

We can choose post-hoc tests now (Figure B.21)

Then click Continue and then OK, and we get the output in Figure B.22 and B.23.

Figure B.21

Oneway

ANOVA

score

	Sum of Squares	df	Mean Square	F	Sig.
Between Groups	559.040	4	139.760	25.137	.000
Within Groups	111.200	20	5.560		
Total	670.240	24			

Post Hoc Tests

Multiple Comparisons

Dependent Variable: score

	(I) orient	(J) orient	Mean Difference (I-J)	Std. Error	Sig.	95% Confidence Interval Lower Bound	95% Confidence Interval Upper Bound
Tukey HSD	control	counting	10.60000*	1.49131	.000	6.1374	15.0626
		rhyming	5.60000*	1.49131	.010	1.1374	10.0626
		adjective	-1.20000	1.49131	.926	-5.6626	3.2626
		imagery	-1.60000	1.49131	.818	-6.0626	2.8626
	counting	control	-10.60000*	1.49131	.000	-15.0626	-6.1374
		rhyming	-5.00000*	1.49131	.023	-9.4626	-.5374
		adjective	-11.80000*	1.49131	.000	-16.2626	-7.3374
		imagery	-12.20000*	1.49131	.000	-16.6626	-7.7374
	rhyming	control	-5.60000*	1.49131	.010	-10.0626	-1.1374
		counting	5.00000*	1.49131	.023	.5374	9.4626
		adjective	-6.80000*	1.49131	.002	-11.2626	-2.3374
		imagery	-7.20000*	1.49131	.001	-11.6626	-2.7374
	adjective	control	1.20000	1.49131	.926	-3.2626	5.6626
		counting	11.80000*	1.49131	.000	7.3374	16.2626
		rhyming	6.80000*	1.49131	.002	2.3374	11.2626
		imagery	-.40000	1.49131	.999	-4.8626	4.0626
	imagery	control	1.60000	1.49131	.818	-2.8626	6.0626
		counting	12.20000*	1.49131	.000	7.7374	16.6626
		rhyming	7.20000*	1.49131	.001	2.7374	11.6626
		adjective	.40000	1.49131	.999	-4.0626	4.8626
Scheffe	control	counting	10.60000*	1.49131	.000	5.5506	15.6494

Figure B.22

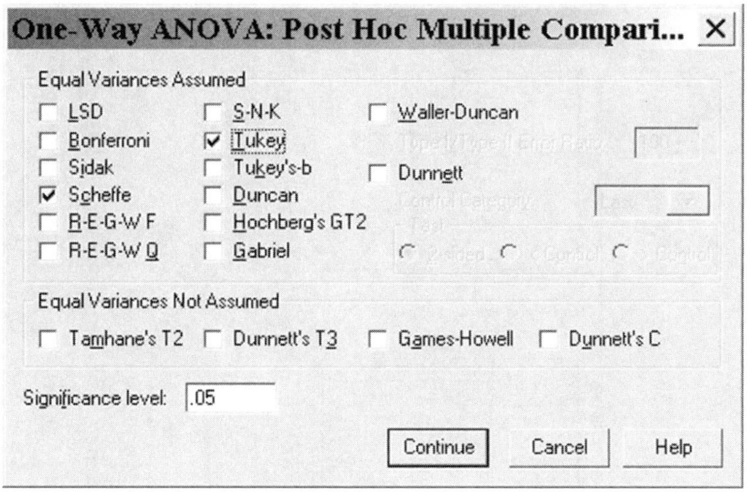

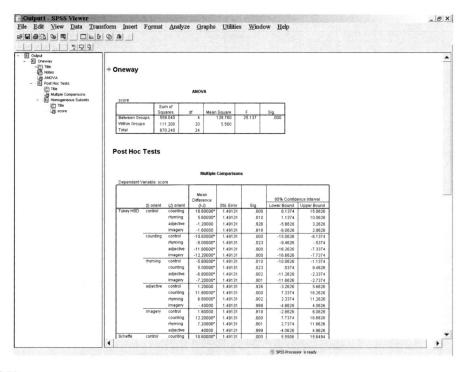

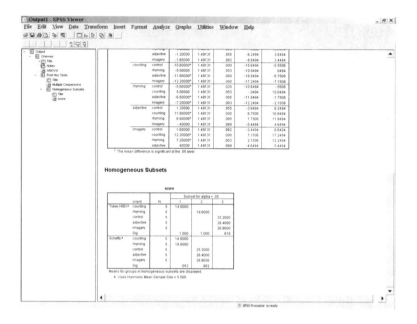

Figure B.23

There's an awful lot of trees here, so where's the forest?

Well, again we are looking for the nitty-gritty of the *F*-value and its significance, and we can see that it is indeed significant. What does this mean for our hypothesis? Well, we can reject the null hypothesis that there will be no effect of orienting task on recall scores.

An alternative analysis would be the non-parametric Kruskal–Wallis test, accessed through the Analyze–Nonparametric Tests 5 menu options (Figure B.24.)

With a window for identifying the test variable and the grouping variable, together with the latter's levels (Figure B.25).

Clicking OK gets us the output in Figure B.26, with a significant test result.

Figure B.27 shows the data for the levels of processing experiment in a repeated measures design. Note that each condition has its own column.

In order to run a repeated measures ANOVA we choose the Analyze–General Linear Model–Repeated Measures menu options (Figure B.28).

Then the window shown; Figure B.29 opens.

We can name the factor; in the next screen in Figure B.30 it has been named 'orient' to signify orienting task. Then we need to specify the number of levels, in

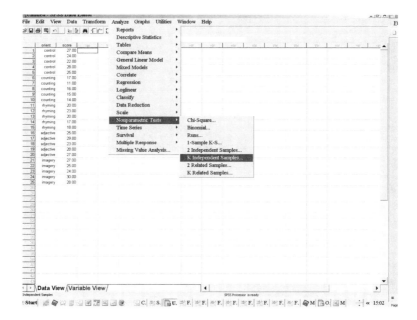

Figure B.24

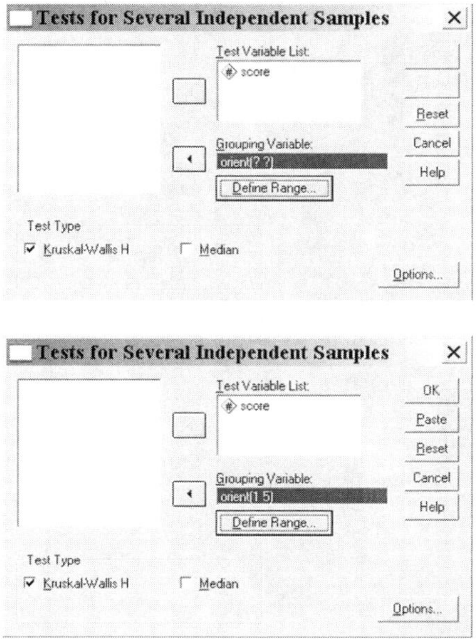

Figure B.25

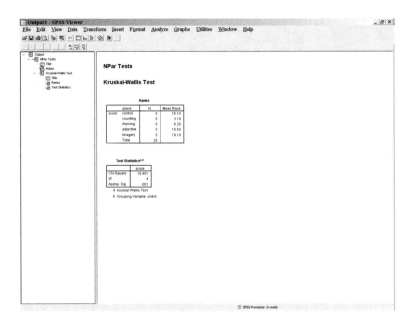

Figure B.26

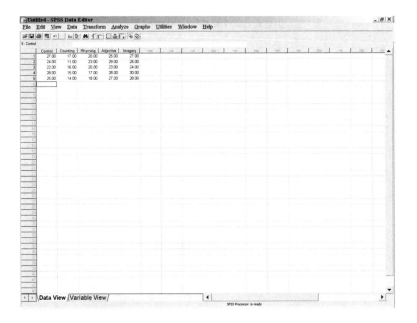

Figure B.27

Figure B.28

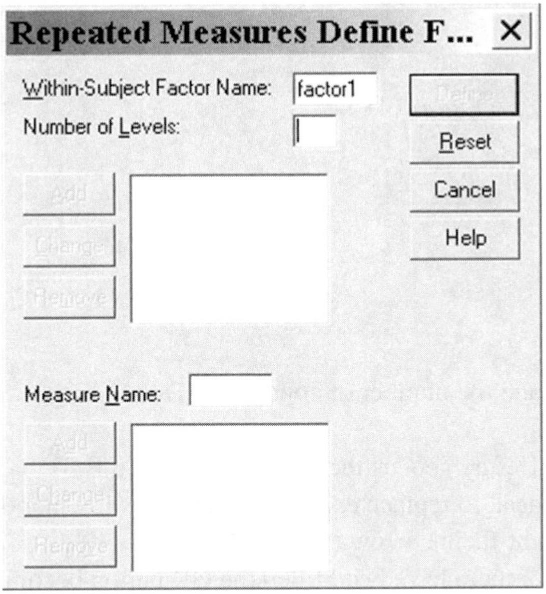

Figure B.29

this case 5, and the number of conditions. Do not forget that we need to 'Add' this to the model.

Clicking Define gets us the window in Figure B.31.

Here we need to replace each one of the question marks with a name of a level, using the right-facing arrow (Figure B.32).

Once all of them have been filled the OK button becomes available, we have no between-subjects factors or covariates and can therefore click to get the output shown in Figures B.33 and B.34.

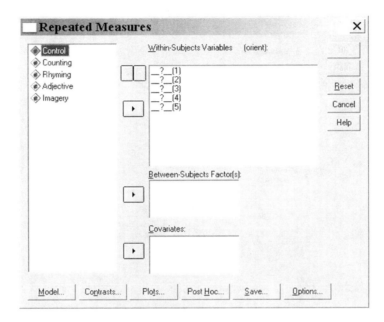

Figure B.31

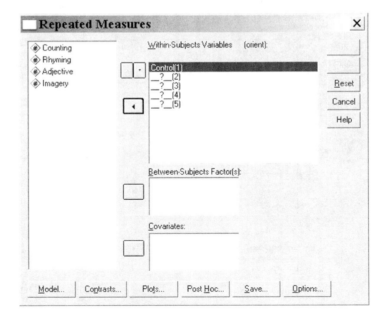

Figure B.32

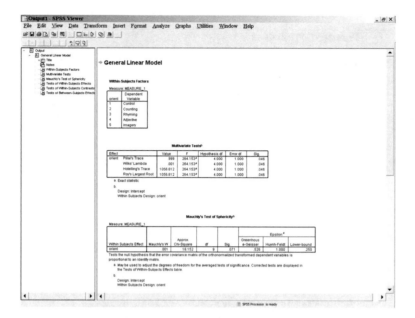

Figure B.33

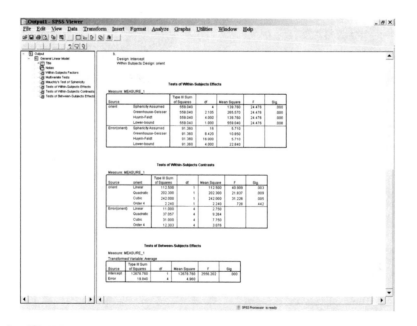

Figure B.34

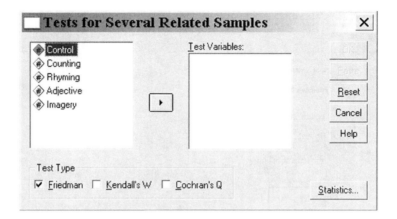

Figure B.35

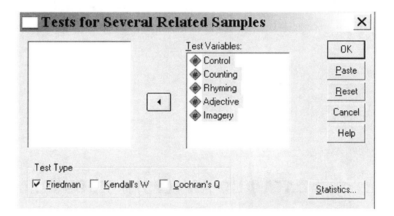

Figure B.36

Two pages this time! However, we are really interested in the tests of within-subjects effects, where we can see that the F-value for the 'orient' factor is significant.

A non-parametric alternative is the Friedman test, accessed via the Nonparametric Tests option on the Analyze menu, then K Related Samples. Doing that sequence gets us the window in Figure B.35.

Again we need to move the names of the levels over into the test variables box (Figure B.36) and click OK, which gives us a neat little output this time, and a significant value (Figure B.37).

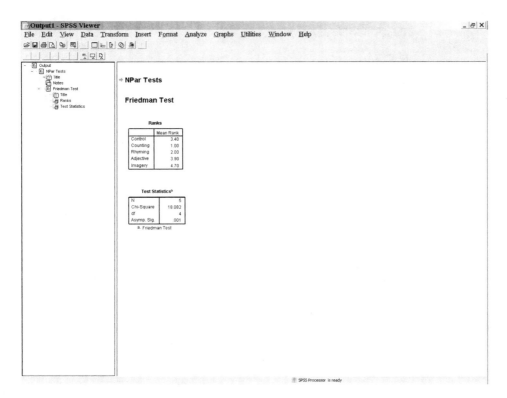

Figure B.37

SPSS OUTPUT FOR DATA AND ANALYSIS DISCUSSED IN CHAPTER 9

Here in Figure B.38 we have the data file with two columns of data each representing one variable in the correlational analysis.

In order to specify a Pearson correlation analysis we use the Analyze menu and choose Correlate and Bivariate (Figure B.39), because we have only two variables.

To specify the correlation elements each variable must be placed in the variables box using the right-facing arrows (Figure B.40).

Pressing OK generates the output for a Pearson correlation (Figure B.41). The table shows the correlation coefficient and whether it is significant, which it is.

If we want to perform a regression analysis, again we use the Analyze menu but click on Regression (Figure B.42).

Figure B.38

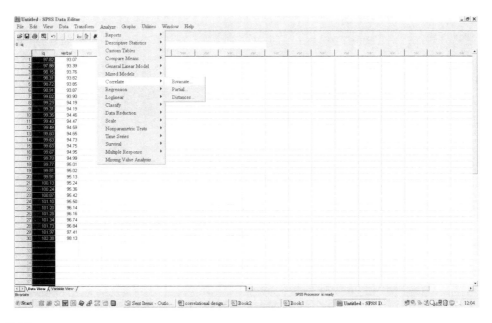

Figure B.39

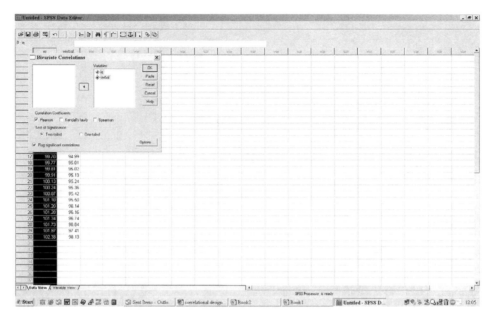

Figure B.40

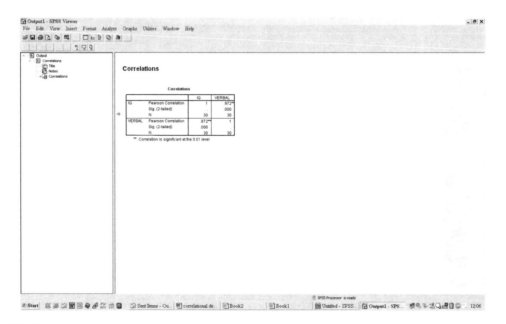

Figure B.41

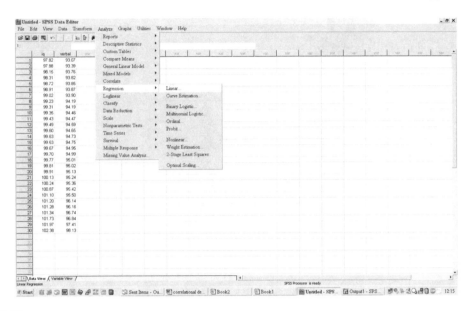

Figure B.42

To specify the regression model, in which one variable must be identified as dependent and one as independent (Figure B.43), we choose IQ as the independent variable as this is relatively stable.

The output from regression (Figure B.44), in addition to the expected coefficients telling us the contribution of each predictor variable and the R^2, tells us how much the variability in the predictor variable contributes to the variability in the criterion. Note that we are also given an analysis of variance. The relationship between regression analysis and ANOVA is discussed in the chapter on complex correlational analysis. An alternative form of bivariate correlation for non-continuous data is a Spearman's rho correlation.

Examining the correlation of more than two variables means that we need to use partial correlation. Figure B.45 is the data file with another variable added, one which we want to determine whether there is an effect on the correlation between the other two.

Requesting partial correlation is again through the Analyze–Correlate menu choices, but this time (Figure B.46) we request Partial.

Specifying the components is similar too, but for partial correlation we have the third variable in the box marked 'controlling for' (Figure B.47).

The output (Figure B.48) tells us that removing the effect of age lowers the strength of the correlation slightly.

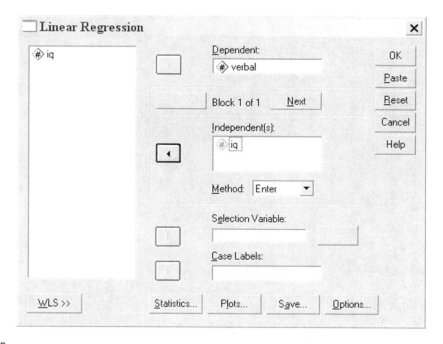

Figure B.43

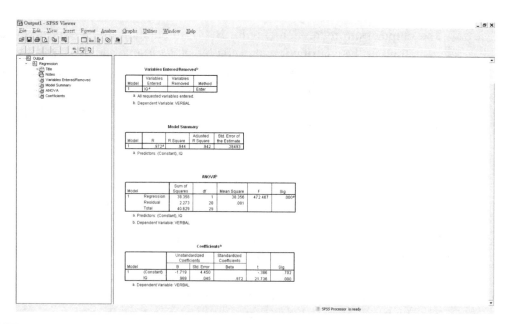

Figure B.44

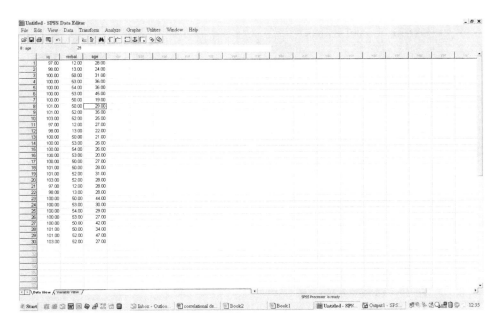

Figure B.45

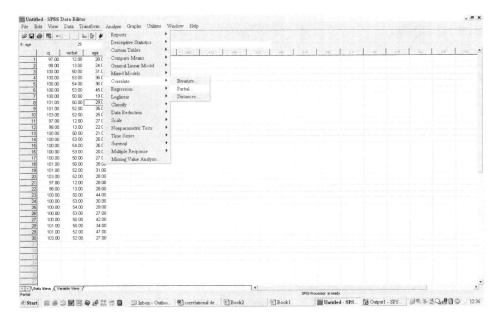

Figure B.46

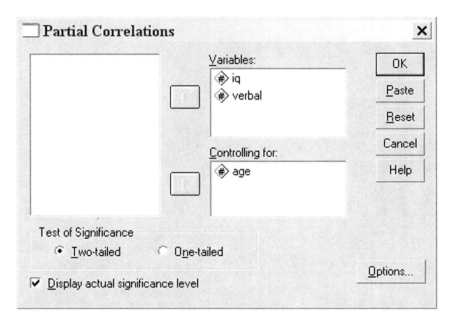

Figure B.47

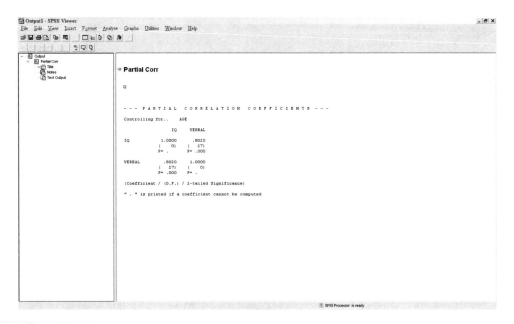

Figure B.48

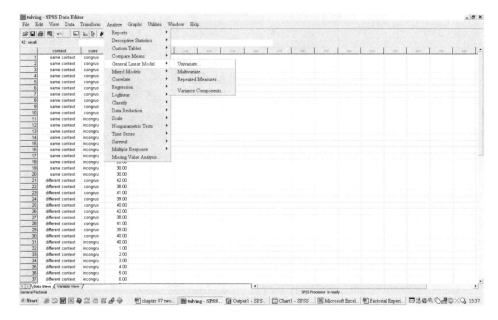

Figure B.49

SPSS OUTPUT FOR DATA AND ANALYSIS DISCUSSED IN CHAPTER 10

Here we see in Figure B.49 the data file for the two-factor design on the encoding specificity experiment. Each participant has their own data row, which describes which set of conditions they experienced; that is, whether they recalled under the same or different context to that in which they learnt the stimuli and whether the cues given for recall were congruent or incongruent. The third column is the recalls score. This design is fully independent measures and therefore we want to carry out a two-way impendent measures ANOVA. This is accessed through the Analyze menu (Figure B.50).

Clicking OK generates the output in Figure B.51.

We can see that both factors result in significant effects and there is a significant interaction. We can interpret this through the graph shown in Figure B.52. Or by using a post-hoc test for simple effects (see Chapter 10).

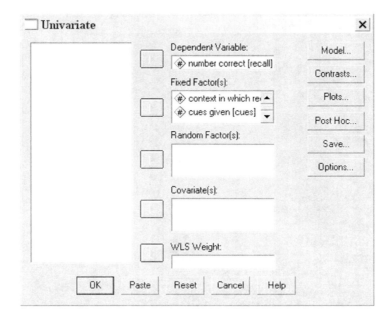

Figure B.50

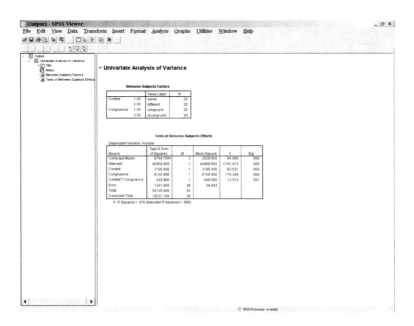

Figure B.51

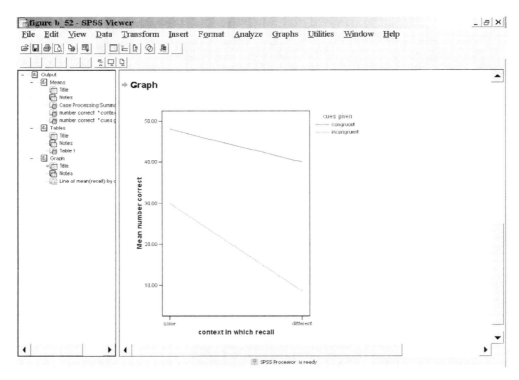

Figure B.52

Essentially, the simple effects test would carry out a *t* test on the context factor using only the congruent group, and then on the incongruent group, or the reverse with the congruency data.

This is the same data but in a repeated measures setup (Figure B.53). Each combination of factors has its own column and then each participant (now only five are needed) will have their own row.

We use the Analyze menu again, but we are requesting a repeated measures ANOVA (Figure B.54).

Again we define the factors (Figure B.55) and specify how many levels each has.

Then each combination of levels has its own slot, so the first is the combination of the first level of factor 1 and the first level of factor 2, and so on (Figure B.56).

Once again the output (Figure B.57) is generated by clicking the OK button and we see that there are significant main effects of both factors and the interaction effect again (Figure B.58).

The graph (Figure B.59) again allows us to interpret the effects.

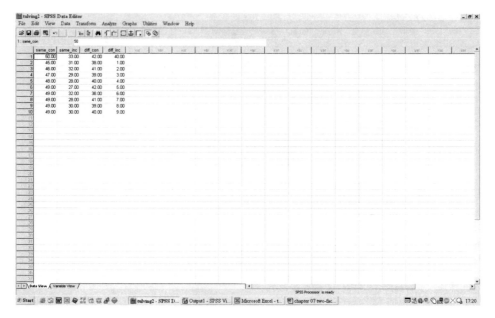

Figure B.53

Figure B.54

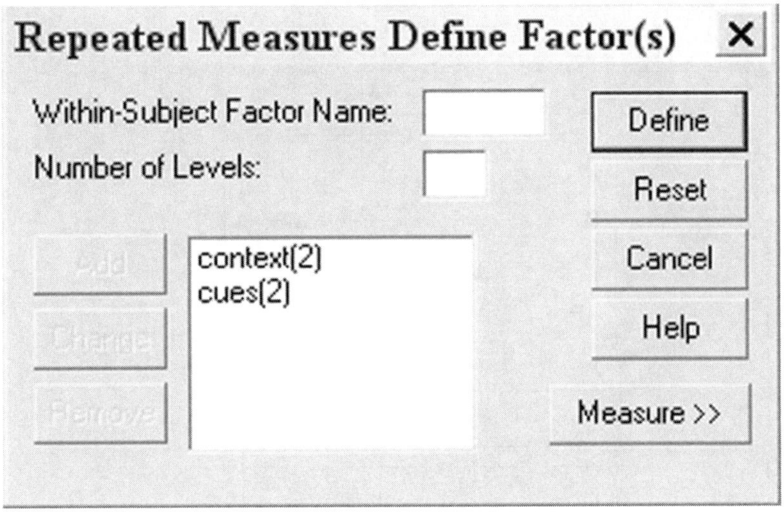

Figure B.55

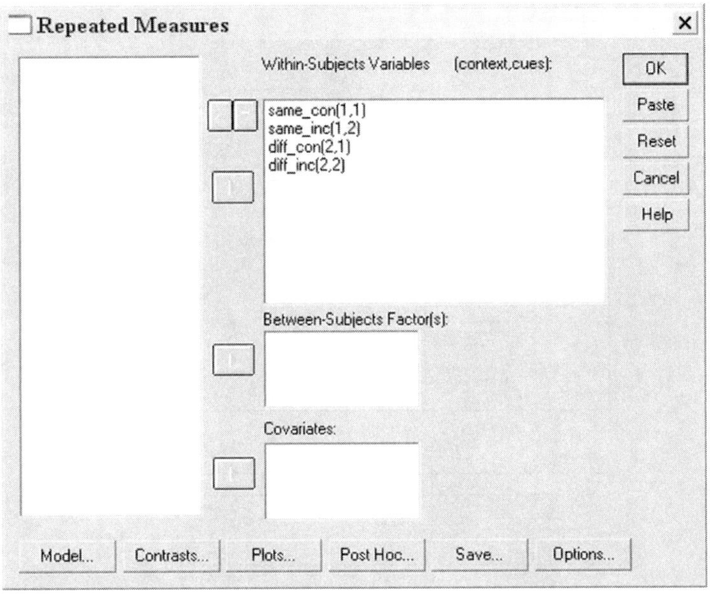

Figure B.56

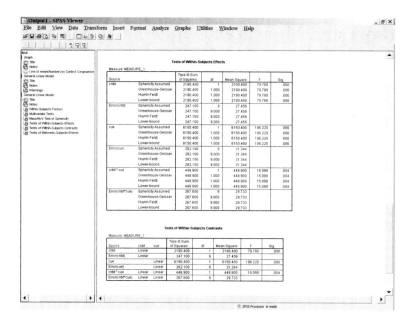

Figure B.57

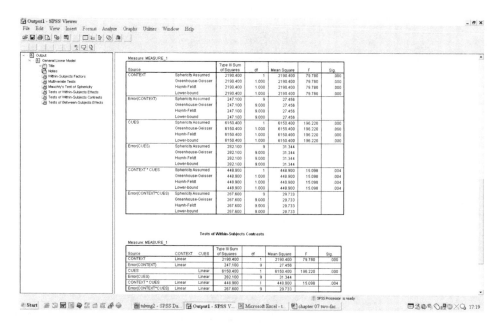

Figure B.58

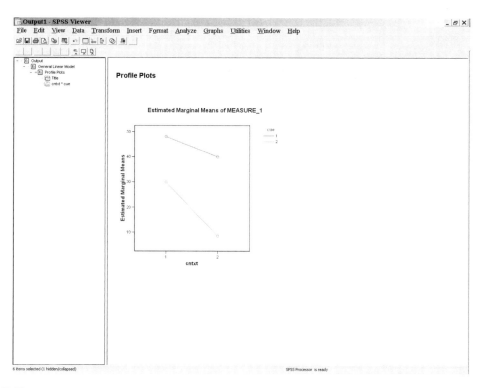

Figure B.59

SPSS OUTPUT FOR DATA AND ANALYSIS DISCUSSED IN CHAPTER 11

Here we are again, setting up in Figure B.60 the model to analyse a two factor design, but this time we will be adding a covariate age to the analysis, so the specification will be slightly different from that seen in Chapter 10 (Figure B.61).

Our output (Figure B.62) is the ANOVA result with age added in as a factor.

This is demonstrating that we cannot say that age has a significant effect on the effect of the orienting task on recall. In Chapter 11, we suggested therefore that here was something else that might mediate the effect of the task, and that was confidence in the recall ability, so adding confidence in as a second dependent variable brings up a different type of specification for the model, the multivariate analysis (Figure B.63). With a model specification like that in Figure B.64).

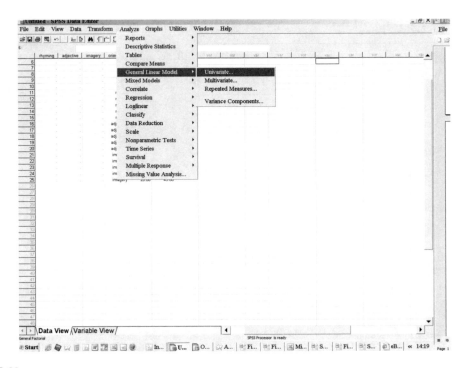

Figure B.60

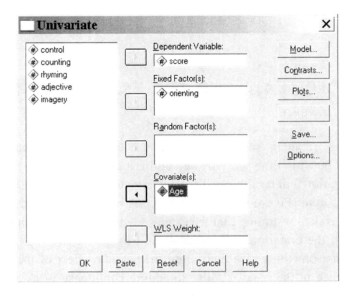

Figure B.61

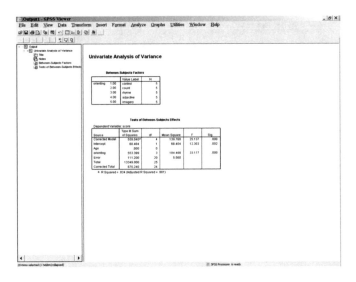

Figure B.62

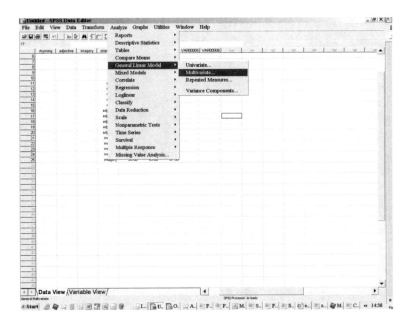

Figure B.63

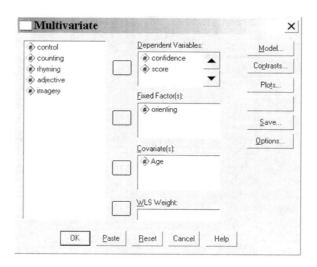

Figure B.64

GLOSSARY

Alpha Level (94): See significance level.

Analysis of Variance (ANOVA) (126): A statistical test to analyse the effect of categorical factors on a response variable. It partitions the variability in the response variable among the different factors. It may also analyse the effect of a continuous factor, an analysis of covariance (ANCOVA), or the effect on several response variables, a multivariate analysis of variance (MANOVA) or covariance (MANCOVA).

Attenuation (182): The lowering in reliability of the correlation coefficient due to errors in measurement corrected for by statistical procedures.

Balanced Design (195): When the between-groups IV has equal numbers of subjects in each of its levels.

Beta Level (222): The probability that a statistical test will generate a false-negative error and defined as 1-power.

Between-Subjects Design (independent measures, unrelated measures, unrelated samples, etc.) (107): A research design in which different participants are allocated to each condition.

Bonferroni's Correction (135): Adjustment to the significance level required when a single hypothesis is investigated using multiple statistics. The *p*-value, the probability of a Type I error, increases with every new statistical procedure. The solution is to recalculate the multiple *p*-values into a single adjusted *p*-value.

Briefing (26): Telling research participants what the research is about (*see* deception), giving them the opportunity to withdraw their consent to take part, as required by the codes of practice.

Case Study (60): An in-depth examination of a typical or atypical example of an issue. For example, the study of the childhood of a serial murderer.

Causality (13): The cause-and-effect relationship between variables.

Cell (195): If each factor in a two-factor design has two levels, then the design has four cells, or combination of levels:

	Factor B, level 1	Factor B, level 2
Factor A, level 1	Cell A_1B_1	Cell A_1B_2
Factor A, level 2	Cell A_2B_1	Cell A_2B_2

Central Tendency (70): A measure of where the centre of a given distribution lies with reference to its lower extreme and upper extreme. Graphical displays of central tendency include box-and-whisker plots; computed measures are mean, median and mode.

Centroid (214): A point which is representative of all of the measures of central tendency of several sets of data. It is a hypothetical centre about which the data points are scattered and the point of intersection of all geometric planes. For a centroid of means, this would be the point at which the lines connecting the means on a graph would intersect.

Chi-Square Test (178): A statistical analysis for frequency data. Given an array of observed cell frequencies, the statistical procedure computes an expected distribution if the null hypothesis were true, and then tests whether the observed–expected difference could have occurred by chance.

Coefficient of Determination, r^2 (222): The proportion of variability in a data set that is accounted for by a statistical model.

Coefficient of Determination (r^2) (174): The proportion of variability in a data set that is accounted for by a statistical model. Variability is defined as the sum of squares.

Coercion (33): Compulsion to behave involuntarily in a certain way due to pressure.

Concurrent Validity (16): Is demonstrated when a test correlates well with a measure that has previously been validated. The two measures may be for the same construct, or for different, but related, constructs. It is also the ability of a test to distinguish between groups that it should theoretically be able to distinguish between.

Conditions (9): Procedures that are varied in order to measure a variable's effect by comparing the outcome of each different set of circumstances.

Confederate (23): A person who acts a part in a research procedure designed to deceive participants.

Confounding Variable (44): An independent variable *not* formally designed into a piece of research, and which, by not being controlled, is likely to affect the course of hypothesis testing.

Construct Validity (16): The agreement between the theoretical concept to be measured and a specific measurement device.

Contingency Tables: Tables that record and present the relationship between two or more variables, usually categorical.

Continuous Variable (229): A variable of interval/ratio data.

Control (44): Part of a scientifically valid experiment, designed to show that the experimental treatment being tested is responsible for the effect observed.

Control Group (133): A subset of a research sample that does not receive the experimental treatment and is a baseline comparison with an experimental group. The control group provides an observation that is not attributed to the variable being manipulated.

Correlation (46): The observation of whether variables vary in the same direction and proportion at the same time.

Correlation Coefficient (170): The mathematical index that measures the strength of the amount of covariance between two or more variables. The coefficient ranges from -1 (a perfect negative correlation) to $+1$ (a perfect positive correlation).

A coefficient of 0 indicates no relationship at all. Common ways of calculating are using Pearson's product moment (r) or Spearman's rho.

Counterbalancing (139): An aspect of research design intended to minimise order effects in experimental manipulations. Participants are exposed to the required experimental conditions in different sequences, so that the effects of practice or fatigue are lowered.

Covariance (174): The measure of how much two random variables vary together.

Criterion Validity (16): A measure of how well one variable or set of variables predicts an outcome based on information from other variables, and will be achieved if a set of measures from a test relate to an agreed behavioural criterion.

Critical Psychology (259): A branch of psychology that is aimed at critiquing mainstream psychology's aim of progressive ways of applying research findings.

Data Audit (56): An examination of systems and procedure in order to determine their efficiency and effectiveness.

Debriefing (35): A short summary of what the participants have contributed to the study, and revealing any intentional deception.

Deception (34): The deliberate concealment of the true purpose of a piece of research, which may be necessary to avoid demand characteristics, reduce experimenter effects, or otherwise control confounding variables.

Degrees of Freedom (*df*) (76): The number of components of a variable or model that are free to vary. Usually in statistical calculations the degrees of freedom are

$n-1$, the number of scores minus one. We derive the population variance from the sample mean and the deviation of each score from the sample mean, but we need to be able to calculate it if any of this information was missing. So, for n scores only $n-1$ of them are free to vary when we know the mean and we could calculate the missing one; $n-1$ is therefore the number of *degrees of freedom* of our data.

Demand Characteristics (11): The case of factors affecting the motivational state of participants during studies which may make the observed behaviour unnatural.

Dependent Variable (44): The variable in which the values may depend on changes in an independent variable.

Descriptive Statistics (66): Statistical procedures designed to present research data in summary form, including central tendency, dispersion, graphical displays.

Design (9) The way in which a research study is set up.

Deviation (74): A measure of difference between the observed value and the mean. The sign of deviation, either positive or negative, indicates whether the observation is larger than or smaller than the mean.

Diary (60): An account of real-life experiences, in research terms, participants record accounts of episodes of interest to the researcher.

Directional Hypothesis (118): A hypotheses that predicts that the results will lie in a certain direction.

Discourse (286): The language of interpersonal communication.

Discursive Psychology (242): An approach in psychology that seeks to discover how language works.

Dispersion (74): A measure of how tightly clustered a distribution is around its mean.

Distribution (67): The spread of scores on a variable; the arrangement of values of a variable showing their observed or theoretical frequency of occurrence.

Drive Theory (105): The suggestion that an organism has an internal state of tension that motivates it to engage in activities that will reduce this tension.

Ecological Validity (11): The degree to which the behaviours observed and recorded in a study reflect the behaviours that actually occur in natural settings.

Emic (57): An approach to an ethnographic study which takes the perspective of examining the way that the members of the given culture perceive their world.

Empirical (5): Making decisions about the world based on observations and measurements of reality.

Encoding Specificity (principle) (192): Refers to a general theoretical framework for understanding how contextual information affects memory. The principle states that memory is improved when information available at encoding is also available at retrieval.

Epistemology (52): Concerned with the nature, sources and limits of knowledge.

Errors in Research Decisions (87): Type I error – rejecting a null hypothesis incorrectly; Type II error – accepting a null hypothesis when false; α – the probability of making a Type I error; β – the probability of making a Type II error.

Ethics (24): The code of practice for researchers developed by their professional body and the study and evaluation of human conduct in the light of moral principles. Moral principles may be viewed either as the standard of conduct that individuals have constructed for themselves or as the body of obligations and duties that a particular society requires of its members.

Ethnography (17): Research that deals with the scientific description of specific human cultures. It can be carried out from an etic or emic perspective – an approach to research focusing on meaning through close field observation of sociological and psychological cultural phenomena.

Etic (57): An approach to an ethnographic study which takes the perspective of examining the way that non-members perceive and interpret behaviours and phenomena associated with a given culture.

Evaluation (17): Research involving systematic appraisal of organisations, processes or programmes leading to feedback on improvement or performance.

Evoked Potential (185): The electric response evoked in the central nervous system by stimulation of sensory receptors or some point on the sensory pathway leading from the receptor to the cortex. The evoked stimulus can be auditory, somatosensory or visual, although other modalities have been reported. Event-related potentials are sometimes used synonymously with evoked potentials but are often associated with the execution of a motor, cognitive or psychophysiological task, as well as with the response to a stimulus.

Experimental Group: A subset of a research sample that receives the experimental treatment. In comparison with a control group, the experimental group should provide an observation that can be attributed to the variable being manipulated.

Experimental Methods (15): A class of research design intended to approximate to the ideal of the true experiment, and characterised by systematic observation of the effects of one or more independent variables on dependent variable (s), while the effect of other possible causation is controlled.

Experimentation (146): A research approach in which attempts are made to identify causal relationships among variables under controlled conditions.

Experimenter Effects (12): The potential of experimenters to bias their research, for example by failing to prevent demand characteristics.

Extrapolate (55): Inference or estimation by extending or projecting known information to a larger context.

Factor, Factorial (126): Aspects of the environment that can affect dependent variables, usually operationalised as independent variables. Research designs that involve more than a simple comparison between two sets of data are termed factorial, and the analysis is to examine the effect of the factor under investigation. It is therefore equivalent to the independent variable. Each factor has a certain number of levels, which in an experimental design are manipulated by the experimenter. These levels are therefore the equivalent of conditions.

Falsifiability (9): Popper's (1959) assertion that the scientific method is ultimately based on our ability to prove an assertion is false (by finding a counter example to it), but *not* to prove one is true.

Fatigue Effect (139): A potential source of error in an experiment due to a prolonged or physically demanding research procedure, and in which performance on the later items will be different to the earlier ones. Fatigue effects may be controlled for by counterbalancing.

Focus Group (254): A discussion group focusing on one topic for research purposes.

Frequency (45): The measurement of the number of occurrences of a repeated event per unit of time, or the number of units contained in a closed environment, e.g. either the number of times a pigeon presses a lever in response to a light, or the number of people taking part in an experiment.

Frequency Data (82): Nominal data.

Friedman's Test (143): Used to test the null hypothesis that several sets of data come from the same population when the data does not conform to parametric assumptions.

Gaussian Distribution (70): Another name for a normal distribution.

Generalise (11): To draw inferences from specific cases to the general.

Goodness of Fit (99): How well a statistical model fits a set of observations. Measures of goodness of fit typically describe any discrepancy between observed values and the values expected under the model in question.

Grounded Theory (58): The generation of theory by examining data, and subject to debate and disagreement among its founders. It is a systematic, iterative process that allows the researcher to develop theory about phenomena. An iterative process is one that repeats itself using the result of the previous process.

Hermeneutics (57): The development and study of theories of the interpretation and understanding of texts, originally religious texts, but broadened to include any form of text.

Heteroscedasticity (205): See homoscedasticity.

Homogeneity of Variance (201): All variances in each of the populations are equal. Also referred to as homoscedasticity, the opposite being heteroscedasticity.

Homoscedasticity (182): Random variables in the model being tested have the same variance. This is also known as homogeneity of variance. The opposite is heteroscedasticity.

Hypothesis (9): A statement of the relationship between two (or more) variables.

Hypothesis Testing (86): The application of statistical analysis and logic to data gathered to determine the answer to a research question. Conventionally, an attempt to disprove the null hypothesis and by showing the results found are not due to chance.

Illocutionary (286): The intention of a speaker in using the words spoken, rather than the meaning of the words themselves.

Independent Measures *t*-test (or between subject t-test) (XX): A statistical test for a research design that delivers two sets of scores from a between-subjects design.

Independent Variable (43): The variables whose categories are manipulated in an experiment.

Inferential Statistics (86): Statistical procedures designed to establish the probability of a causal relationship existing between sets of empirical observations. These can be correlational statistics or tests for difference/variance.

Interaction/Interaction Effect (194): When two factors examined by analysis of variance act together on the dependent variable such that the effect of one would be different if the other were removed. There is an interaction between two factors if the effect of one factor depends on the levels of the second factor. When the two factors are identified as A and B, the interaction is identified as the A × B interaction.

Interval-Level Data (81): Continuous data where differences can be calculated, but where there is no 'natural' zero.

Interviews (59): A conversation between two or more people where questions are asked in order to obtain information about the interviewee.

Introspection (6): The consideration of the contents of one's mind, and the reports of that consideration. Example of an introspective technique – a verbal protocol.

Kolmogorov–Smirnov Test (often called the K–S test) (99): Used to determine whether two probability distributions differ, or whether a probability distribution differs from a hypothesised distribution, such as a normal distribution.

Kruskal–Wallis Test (136): A test of variability among three or more sets of unrelated ordinal data.

Kurtosis (81): A measure of whether the data are peaked or flat relative to a normal distribution. Higher kurtosis means more of the variance is due to infrequent extreme deviations.

Levels of Measurement (45): Nominal, ordinal, interval/ratio are the different forms that data can take. The level of measurement is the relationship among the values assigned to the attributes of a variable.

Likert Scales (157): A form of constructing questionnaire items in terms of the agreement with statements.

Logit: Predicted values in logistic regression, the natural logarithm of the odds of the value of the criterion variable occurring or not.

Logistic Regression (229): A regression model for binomially distributed dependent variables. Used to model the probability of an event occurring as a function of other factors.

Main Effect (194): The effect of one factor on the dependent variable.

Mann–Whitney _U_ test (117): A statistical test examining the differences between two sets of ordinal data.

Mann-Whitney *U* test (also called the Mann–Whitney–Wilcoxon, Wilcoxon rank-sum test, or Wilcoxon–Mann–Whitney test) (117): A non-parametric test for assessing whether two samples of observations come from the same distribution.

MANOVA (209): *See* analysis of variance.

Mean (74): The sum of the observations divided by the number of observations in a data set.

Mean Square (131): (in ANOVA) An estimate of the population variance based on the variability among a given set of measures. Within Mean Square is an estimate of the population variance based on the average of all sums of squares within the several samples. Between Mean Square is an estimate of the population variance based on the sums of squares of the sample means multiplied by *n*.

Measurement Error (56): Discrepancies between the observed value of measurement and the true value, due to error contained in the measuring instrument.

Median (71): The score midway between the lowest and highest score in a distribution.

Mental Lexicon (285): A language user's knowledge of words including the meaning, pronunciation and syntactic characteristics.

Mixed Design (202): A factorial design that includes both between- and within-subjects variables.

Mode (73): The most common score in a distribution.

Multicollinearity (226): The existence of a high degree of linear correlation amongst two or more explanatory variables in a regression model, making it difficult to distinguish their effects dependent (criterion) variable.

Multi-factorial ANOVA (199): Analysis of variance with more than one factor.

Multivariate Analysis of Variance (214): Analysis of variance with more than one dependent variable measures.

Natural Discourse (295): Discourse that occurs naturally in everyday life, as opposed to interview discourse.

Naturalistic Observation (236): The recording of behaviour as it occurs in a natural setting.

Naturalistic Paradigm (252): Assumes that there are multiple interpretations of reality and that researchers should attempt to understand how people construct their own reality within their personal context.

Non-parametric Tests (205): Statistics derived from less powerful tests, and usually performed on data that is ordinal or nominal in nature.

Normal Distribution (70): A distribution in which the scores are spread evenly around the mean, with fewer scores in the extremes. It is described as a bell-shaped curve when plotted on a histogram.

Null Hypothesis (49): A statement of no effect, for example memory is not affected by age. The principle of falsifiability will mean that statistics are set up to test the null hypothesis for rejection. Once this is rejected, the alternative hypothesis of effect can be examined in order to determine if that can be accepted.

One-Tailed Test (97): Testing of a directional hypothesis. *See* two-tailed test.

Ontology (52): Investigates and explains the nature and essential properties and relations of all beings and concepts.

Operationalised (49): Assigning a particular dimension as a measure of a research variable. For example, aging may have an effect on memory can be operationalised as two or more age groups and a score on a memory test; the transformation of abstract psychological constructs into specific, concrete, observable and measurable components of a hypothesis.

Opportunity Sampling (161): Selecting a research sample according to who is available to take part rather than any other more precise criteria.

Outlier (75): An observation that is numerically distant from the rest of the data. Statistics derived from data sets that include outliers will often be misleading.

Paradigm (15): A set of assumptions or values that constitutes a way of viewing reality in an intellectual discipline. A model forming the basis of a theory or a methodology, or the description of the relationship of ideas to one another in the philosophy of science forming a conceptual framework within which scientific research is carried out.

Parametric Assumptions (99): Assumptions about the data sets to which parametric tests can be applied such as normality of the distribution of the population with respect to the variable(s) the level of measurement of the data and homogeneity of variance in the sets being compared.

Parametric Tests (99): Statistical tests applied to data that conform to parametric assumptions.

Partial Correlation (182): The correlation of two variables controlling for a third.

Partitioned (129): Splitting total variance into components.

Pearson's *r* (173): A correlation coefficient demonstrating the relationship between two sets of continuous data.

Perlocution (286): The effect that a speaker's words have on somebody's emotions and responses.

Phenomenology (57): A philosophy or research approach that is directed towards exploration of what presents itself to conscious experience.

Plastic Interval Scale (159): A form of interval scale, where the intervals between units are numerically equal but they are not, in reality, the same size.

Populations (42): All the members of a uniquely definable group of people or things. A statistical population is a set of entities about which statistical inferences are to be drawn, often based on a random sample taken from the population. The term 'population' is also used to refer to a set of measurements or values.

Positive Correlation: *See* correlation coefficient.

Positivism (237): A philosophy that states that scientific knowledge leads to positive confirmation of theories through the application of strict scientific method.

Post-hoc Tests (132): Tests carried out after a significant effect has been found in order to determine the source of the effect.

Power (97): The probability that a test will not lead to Type I errors.

Pragmatics (285): The study of how language is used and its intention.

Predictive Validity (16): The extent to which one measures predicts scores on some other agreed measure.

Predictor Variable (15): An optional name for the independent variable in correlational designs.

Probability (86): The mathematical expression of chance (or gambling!). In any set of circumstances such as we encounter in an experiment or a card game, there are certain possible outcomes and the set of all possible outcomes is called the sample space of the experiment. For each element of the sample space (i.e. each possible outcome) there is a probability measure between 0 and 1 inclusive.

Probability Sampling Distribution (92): A distribution containing all of the probabilities for the entire range of outcomes that are possible in a particular set of circumstances.

Probes (257): Follow-up questions in interviews.

Psycholinguistics (283): An interdisciplinary subject in which psychology and linguistics combine to examine language behaviour. This includes such areas of investigation as language structure, language development and acquisition, conversational analysis, and the sequencing of themes and topics in discourse.

p-value (97): *See* alpha level.

Questionnaire (154): A research instrument consisting of a series of questions and other prompts.

R (235): Indicates correlation between the observed value and the predicted value of the criterion variable. *R*-square is the square of this indicator correlation and indicates the proportion of the variance in the criterion variable which is accounted for by our model; in other words, all of the predictor variables acting together. This tells us how good a prediction of the criterion variable we have made measuring the predictor. *R*-square is an overestimate of the success of the model, so adjusted *R*-square value is used.

Range (74): The distance between a distribution's lower and upper extremes.

Reconstructive Techniques (15): Research techniques that allow participants to reconstruct experience rather than observing experience directly.

Reflexivity (54): The process of critical reflection on the research, the role of the researcher. An awareness of theoretical assumptions and how they shape and limit the research is critical to qualitative research, together with an awareness of how the methods used impact on participants. A reflexive researcher is also critical about his or her own self-involvement and how that shapes the research.

Region of Rejection (96): The area of a distribution in which the null hypothesis would be rejected if the statistic fell within it.

Regression Analysis: Examines the relation of a dependent variable (response variable) to specified independent variables (explanatory variables). The mathematical model of their relationship is the regression equation (see regression coefficients).

Regression Coefficients (176): Elements in a regression equation, which describes a line as $Y = a + bX$. The Y variable can be expressed in terms of a constant (a) and a slope (b) times the X variable. The constant is also referred to as the intercept, and the slope as the regression coefficient or B coefficient.

Reliability (48): The consistency of a measurement over time.

Replicability (11): The ease with which findings of a study can be repeated.

Residual (222): An observable estimate of unobservable error.

Sample (42): The subset of the target population of objects or participants that is selected for research investigation. A sample is the part of a population that is observed. A sample must be selected in such a way as to avoid presenting a biased view of the population. A biased estimate is one that for some reason overestimates or underestimates what is being measured.

Sampling: The selection of individual observations intended to yield some knowledge about a population. Random sampling, or probability sampling, means that every member of a population has a known (and usually equal) probability of being included in the sample. This form of sampling leads to the most representative sample as the sampling error can be computed. Systematic sampling means selecting every nth occurrence in the population. Convenience sampling, or opportunity sampling, means choosing items for the sample arbitrarily and without a structure, snowball sampling is similar as existing study participants recruit more participants.

Sampling Bias (162): Bias arising from flawed sampling, resulting in a sample which is not representative of the population.

Sampling frame (161): The enumeration of all members of a population, in order to allows a sample to be drawn (randomly).

Self-reports (6): The gathering of data by having the participants report on their own behaviour or thought; a research technique used to study problem solving and knowledge representation, including methods such as verbal protocols, self-ratings and focused diary keeping.

Semantics (285): The meanings of words and sentences, or the study of meaning.

Semiotics (240):   The study of signs, and how meaning is constructed.

Shapiro–Wilks's W test (99):   A test to determine whether or not the sample in analysis was drawn from a normal distribution.

Significance Level (94):   The criterion used for rejection of the null hypothesis, i.e., the level at which a researcher would accept that a result is due to chance. The significance level is the probability that the null hypothesis will be rejected in error when it is true (Type I error). Alpha indicates the value of the significance level to be accepted, conventionally 0.05 or 0.01. This is determined before the data is analysed. The p-value on the other hand is a probability, with a value ranging from zero to one, indicating that if samples are drawn from the same population, what is the likelihood that the effect observed is due to chance.

Significant (85):   In quantitative research the description given to a mathematical measure of difference or relation between groups. The difference/relationship is said to be significant if it is greater than what might be expected to happen by chance alone. Note that, if an effect is found not to be significant, it is described as 'not significant' or 'non-significant' and not as 'insignificant' which means something else entirely!

Skew or Skewness: (73):   The degree of asymmetry of a distribution.

Social Facilitation: The tendency for people to attempt better performance on tasks when they are observed.

Sphericity (201):   The level to which data is not correlated in an ANOVA model. ANOVA assumes homogeneity of variance across conditions but is robust against violations of this assumption if the data are uncorrelated. Sphericity means that data are uncorrelated and violations of sphericity require strict homogeneity of variance.

Standard Deviation (75):   The measure of the spread of values in a data set. Defined as the square root of the variance, the average of the squared differences between data points and the mean.

Standard Error (77):   The estimated standard deviation of the error in a measurement. It is the standard deviation of the difference between the measured or estimated values and the true values. The standard error of the mean of a sample from a population is the standard deviation of the sampling distribution of the mean.

Standard Score (z-score) (80): A score derived by subtracting the population mean from an individual (raw) score and then dividing the difference by the population standard deviation. The z-score reveals how many units of the standard deviation a case is above or below the mean, and allows us to compare the results of different normal distributions.

Structured Interview: *See* interview.

Student's *t* Test: *See t* test.

Sum of Squares/Sum of Squared Deviations (75): A calculation based on the computation of all the deviations or distances from the mean of a set of scores, squaring these deviations and adding them all together.

Surveys (17): A research method that collects information from people about opinions or facts. Participants are asked to reconstruct experience, rather than behaviour being manipulated, in order to establish a causal relationship.

Symbolic Interactionism (239): The theoretical perspective that suggests that people act towards things and events on the basis of the meaning they have for them arising out of social interaction.

Syntax (284): The structure of a language.

Text (287): A body of writing drawn from verified sources.

The Wilcoxon Signed-rank Test: A non-parametric alternative to the paired *t* test for the case of two related samples or repeated measurements on a single sample.

Theory (9): A body of knowledge and interpretation in a particular area, supported by testable observation, plus a particular interpretation. A theoretical discipline is concerned with developing, exploring or testing the theories or ideas that researchers have about how the world operates.

Thematic Analysis (274): An approach to dealing with data (such as interview transcripts, field notes, video footage, diaries) in which 'codes' can be applied. Codes refer to the categories within data that allow it to form groups or themes.

***t* test (107):** A test of the null hypothesis that the means of two normally distributed populations are equal. Given two data sets, each characterised by its mean, standard deviation and number of data points, the *t* test determines whether the means are significantly different, provided that the underlying distributions can be assumed to be normal. All such tests are usually called Student's *t* tests.

Trend (144): The general drift or tendency in a set of data; the direction demonstrated through observation of data and/or indicators over time or change of circumstances.

Two-Tailed Test (97): The type of test applied when the hypothesis is non-directional. The statistical procedure chosen must consider the separation of the two distributions down both tails of the probability distribution.

Type I Error (86): Rejecting the null hypothesis when it is true; one way of reducing the probability of Type I error is to use a smaller significance level.

Type II Error (86): Accepting the null hypothesis when it is false.

Variables (43): A set of scores that can vary.

Variance (76): A measure of the statistical dispersion of a data set or distribution, indicating how its possible values are spread around the mean.

Verbal Protocols (6): Systematic descriptions of procedures that an individual carries out.

Wilcoxon Test (113): A test of difference between two sets of ordinal data derived from the same group of participants.

Withdrawal (35): The participants' right to withhold permission to use the data they have contributed, or to remove themselves from the study at any time.

Within-Subjects (Related Measures) Design (107): A research design in which the same participants are allocated to each condition.

x and *y* (176): Co-ordinates on a graph.

z-score: *See* standard score.

REFERENCES

Alder, F. (1975). *Sisters in crime*. New York: McGraw-Hill.

Ahlum-Health, M., & Di Vesta, F. (1986). The effect of conscious controlled verbalization of a cognitive strategy on transfer in problem solving. *Memory and Cognition, 14*, 281–285.

Allport, G.W. (1935). Attitudes. In C.M. Murchison (Ed.), *Handbook of Social Psychology*. Winchester, MA: Clark University Press.

Andrich, D. (2005). The Rasch model explained. In Sivakumar Alagumalai, David D. Durtis and Njora Hungi (Eds.), *Applied Rasch Measurement: A book of exemplars*. Berlin: Springer–Kluwer, Chapter 3, 308–328.

Arnold, M.J., Reynolds, K.E., Ponder, N., & Lueg, J.E. (2005). Customer delight in a retail context: Investigating delightful and terrible shopping experiences. *Journal of Business Research, 58*(8), 1132–1145.

Artz, S. (1998). *Sex, Power, & the violent school girl*. Toronto: Trifolium Books.

Bakken, D. (2006). Renewing the original bonds – let's put psychology back into market research (and marketing!). ESOMAR, Annual Congress, London, September.

Baker, E., & Beech, A.R. (2004). Dissociation and variability of adult attachment dimensions and early maladaptive schemes in sexual and violent offenders. *Journal of Interpersonal Violence, 19*(10): 1119–1136.

Baron, R.S. (1986). Distraction-conflict theory: progress and problems. In L. Berkowitz, *Advances in experimental social psychology, Vol. 19*. Bocta Raton, FL: Academic Press.

Baron, R.A., & Richardson, D. (1994). Human Aggression. New York: Plenum.

Beech, A., Fisher, D., & Beckett, R. (1999). *STEP 3: An evaluation of the prison sex offender treatment programme*. London: HMSO.

Bellezza, F.S. (1984). The self as a mnemonic device: the role of internal cues. *Journal of Personality and Social Psychology, 47*(3), 506–516.

Ben-Zeev, T., Fein, S., & Inzlicht, M. (2005). Arousal and stereotyping threat. *Journal of Experimental Social Psychology, 41*, 174–181.

Billig, M. (1992). *Talking of the Royal Family*. London: Routledge.

Black, D. (1976). *The behavior of law*. New York: Academic Press.

Bleecker, M.L., Bolla-Wilson, K., Agnew, J., & Meyers, D.A. (1988). Age-related sex differences in verbal memory. *Journal of Clinical Psychology, 44*, 403–411.

Blumer, H. (1969). *Symbolic Interactionism, Perspective and Method*. Englewood Cliffs, NJ: Prentice Hall.

Boyatzis, R.E. (1998). *Transforming qualitative information: thematic analysis and code development*. Thousand Oaks, CA: Sage.

Bradford, J.M.W. (1990). The antiandrogen and hormonal treatment of sexual offenders. In W.L. Marshall, D.R. Laws, & H.E. Barbaree (Eds.), Handbook of sexual assault: Issues, theories, and treatment of the offender (pp. 297–310). New York: Plenum Press.

Bradford, J.M.W. (1995). Pharmacological treatment of the paraphilias. In J.M. Odham and M.B. Riba (Eds.), *Review of Psychiatry*, Vol. 14, Chapter 29, 755–777.

Brewer, N., & Burke, A. (2002). Effects of testimonial inconsistencies and eyewitness confidence on mock-juror judgments. *Law and Human Behavior, 26*, 353–364.

Brewer, N., & Well, G. (2006). The confidence–accuracy relationship in eyewitness identification: effects of lineup instructions, foil similarity, and target-absent base rates. *Journal of Experimental Psychology: Applied, 12*(1), 11–30.

Brown, G., & Yule, G. (1983). *Discourse analysis*. Cambridge: Cambridge University Press.

Brown, J.R. (1996). The I in science: Training to utilize subjectivity in research. Oslo, Norway: Scandinavian University Press.

Bruner, G.C., II (1990, October). Music, mood and marketing. *Journal of Marketing*, 94–104.

Bumby, K.M. (1996). Assessing the cognitive distortions of child molesters and rapists: Developments and validation of the MOLEST and RAPE scales. *Sexual Abuse: A Journal of Research and Treatment, 8*, 37–54.

Bureau of Justice Statistics (2002). Homicide trends in the US: Clearance www.ojp.usdoj.gov

Burgess, A.W., Hartman, C.R., Ressler, R.K., Douglas, J.E., & McCormack, A. (1986). Sexual homicide: A motivational model. *Journal of Interpersonal Violence 1*, pp. 251–272.

Burns, A., & Bush, R. (2000) Marketing Research: Prentice-Hall.

Campbell, A. (1984, 1991). *The girls in the gang*. Cambridge, MA: Blackwell.

Chesney-Lind, M., & Brown, M. (1999). Girls and violence: an overview. In D.J. Flannery and C.R. Huff (Eds.), *Youth violence: Prevention, intervention, and social policy*. Washington, DC: American Psychiatric Press.

Chesney-Lind, M., & Pasko, L. (2003). *The female offender: girls, women and crime*. Thousand Oaks, CA: Sage.

Coleman, E., Cesnik, J., Moore, A., & Dwyer, S. (1992). An exploratory study of the role of psychotropic medications in the treatment of sex offenders. *Journal of Offender Rehabilitation. Special Issue: Sex offender treatment: Psychological and medical approaches. 18*(3–4), pp. 75–88.

Cottrell, N.B. (1972). Social facilitation. In C. McClintock (Ed.) *Experimental Social Psychology*. New York: Holt, Rinehart & Winston, 185–236.

Denzin, N.K., & Lincoln, Y.S. (1994). *Handbook of qualitative research*. Thousand Oaks, CA: Sage.

Department of Health (2005). *Research Governance Framework for Health and Social Care*. London: DoH.

Dilworth-Anderson, P., Burton, L.M., & Boulin-Johnson, L. (1993). Reframing theories for understanding race, ethnicity, and family. In P. Boss, W. Doherty, R. Larossa, W. Schumm, & S. Steinmetz (Eds.), Sourcebook of family theories and methods: A contextual approach (pp. 627–646). New York: Plenum Press.

Eagly, A.H., & Steffen, V.J. (1986). Gender and aggressive behaviour: a meta-analytic review of the social psychological literature. *Psychological Bulletin, 100*, 303–330.

Eggleston, E.J. (2000). New Zealand youth gangs: key findings and recommendations from an urban ethnography. *Social Policy Journal of New Zealand*, July 1.

Emmerson, P.G. (1986). Effects of environmental context on recognition memory in an unusual environment. *Perceptual and Motor Skills, 63*(3), 1047–1050.

Emory, L.E., Cole, C.M., & Meyer, W.J. (1992). The Texas experience with DepoProvera 1980–1990. *Journal of Offender Rehabilitation, 18*, 125–137.

Ericsson, K.A., & Simon, H.A. (1984). *Protocol analysis: Verbal reports as data.* Cambridge, MA: Bradford Books/MIT Press.

Eysenck, H.J. (1995). Can we study intelligence using the experimental method? *Intelligence, 20*(3) May–June, 217–228.

Eysenck, H.J. (1983). Psychophysiology and intelligence: New methods of measuring the I.Q. *Indian Journal of Psychophysiology, 1,* 33–39.

Fletcher, J. & Morgan, B. (2000). New directions in qualitative brand research, *Market Research Society Conference Papers.*

Flood-Page, C., & Taylor, J. (2003). (Volume Editors) Crime in England and Wales 2001/2002: *Supplementary HMSO publications.*

Francis, B., Barry, J. Bowater, R., Miller, N., Soothill, K., & Ackerley, E. (2004). Using homicide data to assist murder investigations. *Home Office Online Report 26/04.*

French, J.P.R. Jr, & Raven, B. (1960). The bases of social power. In D. Cartwright and A. Zander (Eds.), *Group Dynamics.* New York: Harper & Row, 607–623.

Furnham, A., & Thomas, C. (2004). Parents' gender and personality and estimates of their own and their children's intelligence. *Personality and Individual Differences, 37,* 887–903.

Gannon, T., & Polaschek, D. (2005). Do child molesters deliberately fake good on cognitive distortion questionnaires? An information processing-based investigation. *Sexual Abuse: A Journal of Research and Treatment, 17*(2), 183–200.

Gardner, M.P. (1985). Mood states and consumer behavior: A critical review. *Journal of Consumer Research,* 12 (December), 281–300.

Gavin, H. (2006). Intrusive music: the perception of everyday music explored by diaries. *Qualitative Report, 11*(3), 550–565.

Gavin, H., & Hockey, D. (2007). Criminal versatility and internalised justification explored by cognitive script theory. *3rd International Congress of Psychology and Law,* Adelaide Australia.

Giorgi, A. (1970). *Psychology as a Human Science: A phenomenologicallly based approach.* New York: Harper & Row.

Glaser, B., & Strauss, A. (1967). The discovery of grounded theory. Chicago: Aldine.

Glesne, C., & Peshkin, A. (1992). *Becoming qualitative researchers: An introduction.* New York: Longman.

Greenberg, D.M., & Bradford, J.M.W. (1997). Treatment of the paraphilic disorders: A review of the role of the selective serotonin reuptake inhibitors. *Sexual Abuse, 9,* 349–361.

Guba, E.G., & Lincoln, Y.S. (1981). *Effective evaluation: Improving the usefulness of evaluation results through responsive and naturalistic approaches.* San Francisco: Jossey-Bass.

Hanson, R.K., & Scott, H. (1995). Assessing perspective taking among sexual offenders, nonsexual criminals and nonoffenders. *Sexual Abuse: A Journal of Research and Treatment, 7,* 259–277.

Hanson, R.K. (2000). What is so special about relapse prevention? In D.R. Laws, S.M. Hudson, & T. Ward (Eds.), Remaking relapse prevention with sex offenders: A sourcebook (pp. 27–38). London: Sage.

Hanson, R.K., & Bussiere, M.T. (1998). Predicting relapse: A meta-analysis of sexual offender recidivism studies. *Journal of Consulting and Clinical Psychology, 66,* 348–362.

Haraway, D. (1988). Situated knowledges: the science question in feminism and the Home Office (2006). Crime in England and Wales. In S. Nicholla, C. Kershaw & A. Walker (Ed.) Home Office: London.

Harvey, A.S. (1990). Time use studies for leisure analysis. *Social Indicators Research, 23*(4), 309–363.

Haworth, K. (2006). The dynamics of power and resistance in police interview discourse. *Discourse Society, 17*, 739–759.

Heydon, G. (2005). *The language of police interviewing.* Basingstoke: Palgrave-Macmillan.

Hicky, E. (1991). *Serial murderers and their victims.* Belmont, CA: Wadsworth.

Hollin, C.R., & Palmer, E.J. (Eds.) (2006). *Offending behaviour programmes: Development, application and controversies.* Chichester: Wiley.

Horowitz, R. (1986). Review of Anne Campbell 'Girls in the Gang: a Report from New York City'. *Contemporary Sociology, 15*(1), 66–67.

Husserl, E. (1910). *Philosophie als Strenge Wissenschaft (Philosophy as Rigorous Science)*, trans. in Q. Lauer (Ed.) (1965) *Phenomenology and the crisis of philosophy.* New York: Harper.

Hyde, T. S., & Jenkins, J.J. (1973). Recall for words as a function of semantic, graphic, and syntactic orienting tasks. *Journal of Verbal Learning and Verbal Behaviour, 12*, 471–480.

Jones, J. (1981). *Bad blood: The Tuskegee syphilis experiment: A tragedy of race and medicine.* New York: Free Press.

Kette, G. (1990). Person-environment correspondence and adjustment to conviction. Using a diary method. *Arch Psychol (Frankf), 142*(2), 123–148. (translated from German).

Klein, M.W. (2005). The value of comparisons in street gang research, *Journal of Contemporary Criminal Justice, 21*(2), 135–152.

Knight, R.A., & Prentky, R.A. (1990). Classifying sex offenders: The development and corroboration of taxonomic models. In: W.L. Marshall, & H.E. Barbaree, (Eds.), Handbook of sexual assault: Issues, theories, and treatment of the offenders. New York: Plenum Press.

Kornhauser, R., & Hirschi, T. (1986). Review of Anne Campbell 'Girls in the Gang: a Report from New York City'. *American Journal of Sociology, 92*(2), 514–516.

Kress, G. (2001). 'From Saussure to critical sociolinguistics: the turn towards a social view of language'. In M. Wetherell, S. Taylor and S.J. Yates (Eds.), *Discourse Theory and Practice: A Reader.* London: Sage.

Kreuger, R.A. (1988). *Focus groups: A practical guide for applied research.* London: Sage.

Kvale, S. (1996). *Interviews: An introduction to qualitative research interviewing.* London: Sage.

Lachman, M., & Andreolotti, C. (2006). Strategy use mediates the relationship between control beliefs and memory performance for middle-aged and older adults. *Journal of Gerontology Series B: Psychological Sciences and Social Sciences, 61*, 88–94.

Lagerspetz, K.M.J., Bjorkqvist, K., & Peltonen, T. (1988). Is indirect aggression typical of females? Gender differences in aggressiveness in 11- to 12-year old children. *Aggressive Behaviour, 14*, 403–414.

Lee, C. (2005). The value of life in death: multiple regression and event history analyses of homicide clearance in Los Angeles County. *Journal of Criminal Justice, 33*(6), 527–534.

Lincoln, Y.S., & Guba, E.G. (1985). *Naturalistic Inquiry.* Beverly Hills, CA: Sage.

Lindlof, T.R. (1995). *Qualitative Communication Research Methods.* Thousand Oaks, CA: Sage.

Lockhart, R., & Craik, F. (1990). Levels of processing: a retrospective commentary on a framework for memory research. *Canadian Journal of Psychology, 44*(1) 97–112.

Lofland, J., & Lofland, L. (1984). *Analyzing Social Settings.* Belmont, CA: Wadsworth.

Malamuth, N.M. (1981). Rape proclivity among males. *Journal of Social Issues. 37*(4), pp. 138–157.

Marshall, W.L. (1988). The use of sexually explicit stimuli by rapists, child molesters, and nonoffenders. *The Journal of Sex Research, 25*, 267–288.

Marshall, W. L., Anderson, D., & Fernandez, Y. (Eds.) (1999). Cognitive behavioural treatment of sexual offenders. New York: John Wiley & Sons.

Marshall, W.L., Barbaree, H.E., & Fernandez, Y.M. (1995). Some aspects of social competence in sexual offenders. *Sexual Abuse: A Journal of Research and Treatment 7*(2).

Marshall, W.L., & Anderson, D. (1996). An evaluation of the benefits of relapse prevention programs with sexual offenders. *Sexual Abuse: A Journal of Research and Treatment.* (*8*) 3/July, 209–221.

Marshall, W.L., & Pithers, W.D. (1994). A reconsideration of treatment outcome with sex offenders. *Criminal Justice and Behavior, 21*(1), 10–27.

Mehra, B. (2001). Research or personal quest: Dilemmas in studying my own kind. In B.M. Merchant, & A.I. Willis (Eds.), *Multiple and Intersecting Identities in Qualitative Research* (pp. 69–82). Mahwah, NH: Lawrence Erlbaum.

Memon, A., Hope, L., & Bull, R. (2003). Exposure duration: effects on eyewitness accuracy and confidence. *British Journal of Psychology, 94*, 339–354.

Merton, R.K. (1941) described in Merton, R.K. and Kendall, P.L. (1946) 'The focused interview', American Journal of Sociology, *5*(6), 541–57.

Merton, R.K., Fiske, M., & Kendall, P.L. (1990). *The focused interview: A manual of problems and procedures.* (2nd ed.). London: Collier Macmillan.

Milgram, S. (1963). Behavioral study of obedience. *Journal of Abnormal and Social Psychology, 67*(4), 371–378.

Mitchell, V., Walsh, G. (2006). Consumer vulnerability to perceived product similarity problems; scale development and identification. *Journal of Macromarketing, 25*(2), 140–152.

MORI (2003). *Crime and Prisons Omnibus Survey*, London: MORI.

Morris, C.D., Bransford, J. D., & Franks, J.J. (1977). Levels of processing versus transfer appropriate processing. *Journal of Verbal Learning and Verbal Behaviour, 16*, 519–533.

National Centre for Social Research (1999). *1999 British Social Attitudes Survey.* London: National Centre for Social Research.

Newell, A., & Simon, H.A. (1972). *Human Problem Solving.* Englewood Cliffs, NJ: Prentice Hall.

Nisbett, R., & Wilson, T. (1977). Telling more than we can know: verbal reports on mental processes. *Psychological Review, 84*, 231–259.

Olweus, D., Mattsson, A., Schalling, D., & Low, H. (1988). Circulating testosterone levels and aggression in adolescent males: a causal analysis. *Psychosomatic Med.* 50: 261–269.

Panksepp, J. (1995). The emotional sources of "chills" induced by music. *Music Perception, 13*, 171–207.

Paivio, A., Yuille, J.C., & Madigan, S.A. (1968). Concreteness, imagery, and meaningfulness values for 925 nouns. *Journal of Experimental Psychology Monograph Supplement, 76*, 1–25.

Parker, H.J. (1974). A view from the boys: a sociology of downtown adolescents. *British Journal of Law and Society, 1*(2), 207–210.

Parker, I. (1999). Critical psychology: critical links. *Radical Psychology: A Journal of Psychology, Politics and Radicalism, 1*, pp. 3–18.

Patton, M.Q. (1990). *Qualitative evaluation and research methods* (2nd ed.). Newbury Park, CA: Sage.

Perfetti, C.A. (1976). Level of comprehension of phrases. *Bulletin de Psychologie*, Special Annual, 346–355.

Perkins, P., Hammond S., Coles D., & Bishopp, D. (1998). *Review of Sex Offender Treatment Programmes.* High Security Psychiatric Services Commissioning Board (HSPSCB).

Platania, J., & Moran, G. (2001). Social facilitation as a function of the mere presence of others. *Journal of Social Psychology, 14*(2), 190–197.

Popper, K.R. (1959). *The Logic of Scientific Discovery.* London: Hutchinson.

Potter, J., & Wetherell, M. (1987). *Discourse and Social Psychology: Beyond attitudes and behaviour.* London: Sage.

Potter, R., & Brewer, N. (1999). Perceptions of witness behaviour-accuracy relationships held by police, lawyers and jurors. *Psychiatry, Psychology and Law, 6,* 97–103.

Ramos, L.V. (1993). The effects of on-hold telephone music on the number of premature disconnections to a state-wide protective services abuse hot-line. *Journal of Music Therapy, 30*(3), 119–129.

Rethinking Crime and Punishment (2002). *Briefing 3: What Do the Public Really Feel About Non-Custodial Penalties?* London: RCP, November.

Ring, K., Wallston, K., & Corey, M. (1970). Mode of debriefing as a factor affecting subjective reaction to a Milgram-type obedience experiment: an ethical inquiry. *Representative Research in Social Psychology, 1*(1), 67–88.

Robinson, J.P., & Nicosia, F.M. (1991). Of time activity and consumer behaviour: an essay on findings, interpretations and needed research. *Journal of Business Research, 22*(2), 171–186.

Roediger, H.L., & Payne, D.G. (1983). Superiority of free recall to cued recall with 'strong' cues. *Psychological Research, 45*(3), 275–286.

Roulston, K. (2001). Data analysis and 'theorizing as ideology' *Qualitative Research, 1*(3), 279–302.

Russel, G.W., & Baenninger, R. (1996). Murder most foul: Predictors of an affirmative response to an ounrageous question. *Aggressive Behaviour, 22*(3), 175–181.

Russell, G., Arms, W., & Robert, L. (1995). False consensus effect, physical aggression, anger, and a willingness to escalate a disturbance. *Aggressive Behavior, 21*(5), 1995, pp. 381–386.

Sanna, L.J., & Shotland, R.L. (1990). Valence of anticipated evaluation and social facilitation. *Journal of Experimental Social Psychology, 26,* 82–92.

Schegloff, E.A. (1992). Repair after next turn: the last structurally provided defence of intersubjectivity in conversation. *American Journal of Sociology, 97,* 1295–1345.

Shapiro, L. (2004). Store atmospherics: A retail study. Los Angeles: DMX Music.

Sherlock, J. (2005). Part 2: International marketing-principles and practice: methods of market research. In J. Sherlock and J. Reuvid (Eds.), *The Handbook of International Trade: A Guide to the Principles and Practice of Export.* London: Kogan Page.

Silberstein, A. R., & Scott, S. (1991). Expenditure diary surveys and their associated errors. In P. Biemer, R.M. Groves, L.E. Lyberg, N.A. Mathiowetz & S. Sudman (Eds.), Measurement errors in surveys (pp. 303–327). New York: Wiley.

Smith, G.H. (1954). *Motivation Research in Advertising and Marketing*, Greenwood Press, Westport, CT.

Smith, J.K. (1990). Alternative research paradigms and the problem of criteria. In E.G. Guba (Ed.), *The paradigm dialog* (pp. 167–187). Newbury Park, CA: Sage.

Solman, R., & Rosen, G. (1986). Bloom's six cognitive levels represent two levels of performance. *Educational Psychology, 6,* 243–263.

Spencer, S.J., & Steele, C.M. (1999). Stereotype threat and women's math performance. *Journal of Experimental Social Psychology, 35,* 4–28.

Sproles, G.B., & Kendall, E. (1986). A methodology for profiling consumers' decision-making styles. *The Journal of Consumer Affairs, 20* (Winter): 267–279.

Steele, C.M. (1998). Stereotyping and its threat are real. *American Psychologist, 53,* 680–681.

Stewart, D.W., & Shamdasani, P.N. (1990). *Focus groups: Theory and practice.* London: Sage.

Stollak, G.E. (1967). Obedience and deception research. *American Psychologist, 22*(8), 678.

Strauss, A., & Corbin, J. (1990). Basics of qualitative research: Grounded theory procedures and techniques. Thousand Oaks, CA: Sage.

Symons, C.S., & Johnson, B.T. (1997). The self-reference effect in memory: a meta-analysis. *Psychological Bulletin, 121,* 371–394.

Tabachnick, B.G., & Fidell, L.S. (2001). *Using multivariate statistics* (3rd ed.). New York: Harper Collins.

Tang-Martinez, Z., & Mechanic, M.B. (2000). Response to Thornhill and Palmer on Rape. *The Sciences:* NY Academy of Sciences.

Thornhill, R., & Palmer, C. 2000: A natural history of rape: Biological bases of sexual coercion. MIT Press, Cambridge, MA.

Trickett, P.K., & Putnam, F.W. (1993). Impact of child sexual abuse on females: toward a developmental, psychobiological integration. *Psychological Science, 4*(2), 81–87.

Tulving, E., & Osler, S. (1968). Effectiveness of retrieval cues in memory for words. *Journal of Experimental Psychology, 77*(4), 593.

Tulving, E., & Thomson, D.M. (1971). Retrieval processes in recognition memory: effects of associative context. *Journal of Experimental Psychology, 87*(1), 116–124.

Van Dijk, T.A. (2001). Principles of critical discourse analysis: In M. Wetherell, S. Taylor and S.J. Yates (Eds.), *Discourse Theory and Practice: A Reader.* London: Sage.

Ward, T., Hudson, S.M., Johnston, L., & Marshall, W.L. (1997). Cognitive distortions in sexual offenders: An integrative review. *Clinical Psychology Review, 17,* 1–29.

Ward, T., Hudson, S.M., Marshall, W.L., & Siegert, R.J. (1995). Attachment style and intimacy deficits in sexual offenders. *Sexual Abuse: A Journal of Research and Treatment, 7,* 317–335.

Wells, G.L., Small, M., Penrod, S., Malpass, R.S., Fulero, S.M., & Brimacombe, C.A.E. (1998). Eyewitness identification procedures: Recommendations for line-ups and photospreads. *Law and Human Behavior, 22*(6), 603–645.

Willig, C. (2001). *Qualitative Research in Psychology: A Practical Guide to Theory and Method.* Buckingham: OU Press.

Wixted, J.T., & Stretch, V. (2004). In defense of the signal-detection interpretation of Remember/Know judgments. *Psychonomic Bulletin & Review, 11,* 616–641.

WSIS Civil Society Consultations (2005). *WSIS Tunis, November 2005 Report.* Geneva: World Summit on the Information Society.

Zajonc, R.B. (1965). Social facilitation. *Science, 149,* 269–274.

INDEX

ABC model, attitudes 152–3
abstract, research papers 319
  example 320
advice, giving 31, 36–7
aggressive behaviour 266, 267
  see also sexual aggression
Ahlum-Heath, M. 7
Allport, Gordon 38, 152
alpha level 94, 95, 383
alternative explanation 47
American Psychological Association 24, 27, 31
analysis of covariance (ANCOVA) 209, 210–14, 211, 369
analysis of variance (ANOVA)
  between-subjects 140, 141, 142
  correlational analysis 182
  defined 369
  four-way 195
  mixed designs 205
  multi-factorial 199, 379
  one-way 126, 135, 136, 146, 163, 194, 204
  as parametric test 127
  post-hoc tests 133–5
  regression analysis 221
  repeated measures 140
  single factor designs 127
  source table *132*
  sum of squares between groups 129–30
  sum of squares within groups 130–3
  total sum of squares 129
  two-factor 195, 206
  two-way 163
  univariate analysis 198, 212, 215
anaphoric reference 285–6
ANCOVA (analysis of covariance) 209, 210–14, 211, 369
Andreolotti, C. 214
anonymity, preservation 35
ANOVA *see* analysis of variance (ANOVA)
anthropology 56
antidepressants 303
APA (American Psychological Association) 24, 27, 31
Asch, Solomon 38

Ashley, G.O. 41
Atkins, Daryl 78, 79
attachment difficulties, sexual dysfunction 304
attenuation 182, 369
attitudes
  ABC model 152–3
  to crime, measuring 154
  definition of 'attitude' 152
  functions 153
  measurement 153–4
  personality distinguished 153
authority, researchers representing 34
aversion therapy 305

backward selection, correlation design 227
Baenninger, R. 224–5
Bakken, D. 256–7
balanced designs 369
bar charts 68, 69
Baron, R.A. 106
Beech, A. 308
behaviour modification techniques 306
'Behavioural Study of Obedience' (Milgram) 23–4
beta level 369
beta regression coefficient 222
Between Mean Square 378
between-subjects designs
  analysis of variance 141, 142
  data analysis 115–18
  defined 107, 369
  experiments using 113–18
  non-parametric tests 117–18
  parametric assumptions *see* parametric assumptions
  post-hoc tests 133–5, 205
between-subjects variance 369
Billig, M. 295
bipolar scaling methods 159
Bjorkqvist, K. 267
Blumer, H. 239, 240
Bonferroni's correction 135, 369
box-and-whisker plots 370

BPsS (British Psychological Society)
   see British Psychological Society (BPsS)
Bradford, J.M.W. 303
Bragg, W.L. 169
Brandeis, Louis D. 66
branding 255
briefing 26, 370
British Crime Survey 154, 161
British Psychological Society (BPsS) 27–31, 163
British Sexual Offender Treatment Programme (SOTP)
   302, 306, 308, 309, 310
Bush, George 254

Campbell, A. 268, 271
case studies 60, 370
causal modelling, and partial correlation 182
causality 13, 370
CBT (cognitive behavioural therapy) 306, 310
cells 370
central tendency 70–4
   choice of measure 73–4
   defined 370
   mean 71
   median 71–3
   mode 73–4, 378
centroid 214, 370
Chesney-Lind, M. 267
Chicago School 237
chi-square test 83, 100, 178, 180, 370–1
Chomsky, Noam 241
clarification probes 259
classical test theory, and item response theory 16
clinical trials 24
Clinton, President Bill 25
closed questions 155, 156, 160
coding, grounded theory 58
coefficient of determination 174, 222, 371
coercion 33–4, 371
cognitive behavioural therapy (CBT) 306, 310
Coke, Sir Edward 230
colleagues 31, 37
communicating research 315–27
   books 317
   conference proceedings 317
   government/corporate reports 318
   Internet 318–19
   journal articles 317
   newspapers 318
   papers, requirements for 317
   research paper sections 319–27
   theses and dissertations 318
conceptually rich theory 58
concurrent validity 16, 371
conditioning, diary use 275, 276
confederate 23, 371

conference proceedings 317
confidence level 371
confidentiality 26, 29–30, 35–6
confirmability 249
confounding variables 44, 371
consciousness 238–9
consent 27–8, 33
construct validity 16
consumer psychology 254–5
Consumer Styles Inventory 256
context evaluation 18
contingency tables 68, 82, *179*, 371
continuous variables 229, 371
control 106, 173, 371
control groups 133, 371
Control of Substances Hazardous to Health
   (CPSHH) 36
convenience sampling 260, 382
conversation analysis 287
Corbin, J. 247
core theoretical concepts 58
correlation coefficient 170, 172, 174, 372
correlational designs and analysis 171–82
   adding further variables *184*
   assumptions made in analysis 182
   control, lacking 173
   and experimental approach 171
   extrapolation 55, 177, 178, 375
   frequency/nominal data 178–80
   interval-level data 173–6
   IQ and verbal ability *172, 177*
   line of best fit *177*
   matrix *185*
   measures *175*
   negative correlation, representing *173*
   non-continuous data, correlation with 178–80
   ordinal data 180–2
   partial correlation 182–3
   pitfalls in use 173
   'pure' correlation 171
   purposes 170
   ranked data *181*
   regression coefficients 176
   simple linear regression 176–8
   surveys 167
correlations 46, 372
COSHH (Control of Substances Hazardous to Health) 36
counterbalancing 139–40, 372
covariance 47, 372
covert observation 35, 36, 264, 265
Craik, F.I.M. 123, 124, 146, 147, 190
credibility 55, 238, 249
crime
   by adolescent boys 265
   criminal justice system 156, 157, 163, *164–5*

crime *cont.*
    measuring attitudes to 153–66
    sexual *see* sexual aggression
    violent *see* violent crime
    worry, demographic factors 163, *165–6*
criteria-related validity 372
criterion measures 16
criterion validity 372
critical psychology 242, 372
critical region 92
cut-off point 92

data analysis 248–9
    between-subjects designs 115–18
    focus groups 262
    interviews 262
    participant observation 270–1
    transcribing 262
    two conditions, experiments with 107, *108*
    within-subjects design 110–13
data audits 56, 372
data collection techniques 248, 261, 295
Data Protection Act 1998 36
data-based decision making 17
debriefing 12, 29, 35, 372
deception 28–9, 34–5, 372
decision making, data-based 17
deconstruction 241
deep processing 123
degrees of freedom 74, 101, 130, 372–3
delinquency 265, 266
demand characteristics 11–12, 373
Denzin, N.K. 240
dependability 55–6
dependent variables 44, 373
depth of processing hypothesis 126, 191
Derrida, Jacques 241
descriptive statistics 66–7, 373
design
    correlational *see* correlational design
    defined 373
    ethical research 32–4
    experimental approach 9
    factorial *see* factorial design
    mixed 202, 205, 378
    qualitative research 245–50
    quantitative research 46–9
    simple experimental 104–20
    two conditions, data analysis from
        experiments with 107, *108*
detail-oriented probes 259
deviance, sexual 301–2, 303, 305, 307
deviation 74, 373
df numerator 132
Di Vesta, F. 7

diaries
    defined 373
    effect of recording experience 275–81
    qualitative data collection 60–1
    research, thematic analysis 274–5
    research papers 323
dimensionality, in scales 156–7
direct observation 16–17, 59
directional hypothesis 118, 373
discourse 286, 373
discourse analysis 283–97
    assumptions 287–8
    data collection 295
    definitions 287
    dynamics of 289
    interpersonal communication 289, 290
    interviews, as institutional discourse 291
    language structure 284–7
    method 295–6
    natural discourse 295, 379
    performing 289–94
    perlocution 291
    reliability 288–9
    semantics 383
    validity 288–9
discursive psychology 242, 373
dispersion
    defined 74, 373
    interval-level data 81
    sample variance and standard deviation 74–7
    standard error of mean 77–9
    tabular presentation 82–3
    z-score 79–80
distribution
    areas of *80*
    building 68–9
    defined 67, 373
    frequency 68
    Gaussian 70, 376
    leptokurtic 81
    normal 70, 379
    platykurtic 81
    probability sampling 92, 381
Doyle, Arthur Conan 234
drive theory 105, 373
dummy variables 226
D-values 110

Eagly, A.H. 267
Ebbinghaus, Hermann 8
ecological validity 11, 14, 373
EER (experiment-wise error rate) 133, 134
Eggleston, E.J. 268
Einstein, Albert 10, 122
e-journals 319

elaboration probes 259
electric shock experiments 23–4
emic perspective 57, 373
Emmerson, P.G. 193
Emory, L.E. 304
empirical research 5, 270, 374
encoding specificity principle 192–3, 374
Enlightenment 241
enumeration statistic 178
epistemology 52, 374
equality of variances *see* homogeneity
    of variances
Ericsson, K.A. 7–8
errors in research decisions 87, 374
ethical dilemmas, observation technique 264–5
ethical research 32–4
    advice, giving 31, 36–7
    clinical trials 24
    codes of conduct 27–31
    colleagues 31, 37
    confidentiality 26, 29–30, 35–6
    consent 27–8, 33
    debriefing 29, 35
    deception 28–9, 34–5, 372
    defined 374
    designing 32–3, 32–8
    discomfort, unusual 34
    ethics of research 24
    issues 26–32
    longitudinal studies 34
    protection 30, 36
    service, right to 26
    surveys, ethical considerations 163, 167
    Tuskegee Syphilis study 25–34
    withdrawal from research 29, 35, 385
Ethnograph data package 61
ethnography 17, 56–7, 57, 374
ethnomethodology 239
etic perspective 57, 374
evaluation
    defined 299, 374
    formative 300–1
    in psychology 299
    range of research 17–18
    research *see* evaluation research
    sexual offending 302–3
    summative 301
    treatment programmes, sexual offenders 302
evaluation research
    see also evaluation
    effectiveness of therapy 309–11
    forms of 300
    purposes 299–300
    questions 300
    scientific-experimental model 300

evaluation research *cont.*
    sexual aggression *see* sexual aggression
    study design 309
evoked potential 185, 374
experimental approach 8–15
    and correlational analysis 171
    demand characteristics 11–12
    evaluation research 300
    falsifiability 9–11
    limitations of laboratory experiments 14
    'pure' experimentation 171
    quasi-experimental design 170
    when unsuitable 170
experimental group 374–5
experimental methods 15, 375
experimentation 12–15, 375
    research without 15–18
experimenter effects 375
experiment-wise error rate (EER) 133, 134
external validity 48–9
extrapolation 55, 177, 178, 375
Eyesenck, H.J. 169, 171, 185, 186

factor, factorial 375
factorial designs
    depth of processing, factor of 126, 191
    designs with more than two groups 125–6
    encoding specificity principles 192–3
    Friedman's test 206
    memory models 123–5
    mixed 202, 205, 378
    as more common experimental design 126
    multiple factors, analysis with 190–206
    non-parametric tests 205–6
    post-hoc analysis 202–5
    reporting of results 194–202
    single 122–47
    transformations 205–6
falsifiability 9–11, 86, 375
fatigue effect 139, 375
female violence 266–8, 271
feminist psychology 243
Fisher, R.A. 95, 102
fixed variables 43
Fletcher, J. 255
focus groups
    see also interviews
    data analysis 262
    data collection, common technique 254
    description 260, 375
    market research 260
    origins 259
    questions for 261–2
    recording techniques 261, 262
    size 261

focus groups *cont.*
   thematic analysis 280
   use of 260–1
forced-choice scaling methods 159, *160*
formative evaluation 300–1
forward selection, correlational design 227
Foucault, Michel 241
French, J.P.R. Jr 289
frequency, defined 375
frequency data 82, 178–80, 376
frequency distribution 68
Friedman's test 143, 206, 376
fully informed consent, ethical research 33
F-values
   analysis of covariance 210
   analysis of variance 131, 135–6, 142, 143, 194, 199
   degrees of freedom 132
   equality of variances test 117
   factorial designs 201
   post-hoc tests 203

Gallup Organisation 151
gang activity 265–6, 268
Gaussian distribution 70, 376
Gavin, H. 60
gender differences 114, 266–8, 271
General Problem Solver (GPS) project 7–8
generalisation 11, 376
generative questions 58
genocide 22–3
Giorgi, A. 57
Glaser, B. 236
Glesne, C. 262
Goclenius 4
goodness-of-fit 99, 178, 376
government and corporate reports 318
GPS (General Problem Solver) project 7–8
gravity theory 10
Greenberg, D.M. 303
grounded theory 58, 236–7, 376
Grundy, Kathleen 290, 292, 293
Guba, E.G., on qualitative research
   confirmability 249
   naturalistic observations 247
   qualitative vs. quantitative paradigms 235, 238
   validity 55
Guttman ('cumulative') scaling 157

Harvey, A.S. 275
Haworth, K. 290–4
Heller, John 25
hermeneutics 57, 240–1, 376
heteroscedasticity 205, 376
Heydon, G. 291
hidden observation 35, 36, 264, 265

histograms 91, 92
homogeneity of variance 100, 112, 128, 201, 376
homoscedasticity 182, 376
Horowitz, R. 271
HSD ('Honestly Significantly Different') test 133, 134, 144, 203, 204
Husserl, Edmund 238
Hyde, T.S. 124
HyperQual data package 61
hypotheses
   definition of 'hypothesis' 87, 93, 376
   directional hypothesis 118, 373
   non-directional 9
   null hypothesis *see* null hypothesis
   stating of 93–4
hypothesis testing
   computing test statistic 96
   decision making 96–7
   defined 86, 376
   errors in 94
   levels of significance 94–5
   region of rejection 95–6, 382
   setting criterion for rejecting 94–6
   stating of hypotheses 93–4
hypothetico-deductive models 50

identification codes 35
illocution 286, 376
independent measures *t*-test 377
independent variables 43, 377
in-depth interviews 58–9
induction 236
inferential statistics 85–102
   degrees of freedom 101
   description 377
   hypothesis testing 93–7
   parametric tests and assumptions 99–100
   power of tests 97–8
   probability 88–92
information society 150–1
integrative diagrams, grounded theory 58
interaction effect 194, 377
internal validity 47–8
Internet, communication of research 318–19
interpersonal communication, discourse analysis 289, 290
interpolation 177–8
interval variables 45
interval-level data 81, 173–6, 377
interviews
   see also focus groups
   attributes of good interview 259
   conducting 258–9
   conversational 258
   data analysis 262
   data collection, common technique 254
   description 377

interviews *cont.*
　discourse analysis 293
　ending 259
　form of 256–7
　group interviewing, focus groups distinguished 260
　guided 258
　in-depth 58–9
　as institutional discourse 291
　observation contrasted 264
　qualitative 257–9
　sensitive topics 37
　standardised open-ended 258
　thematic analysis 280
　transcribing 259
　unstructured 59, 257–8
introductions, research paper sections 320–3
introspection 6–8, 377
invisible phenomena, studying 5
Ipsos UK, MORI merging with 151
IQ scores *79*
　and verbal ability 172, *177*, 183
item response theory, and classical test theory 16

Jenkins, J.J. 124
Jonckheere's trend test 145, 146
Jones, William 78
journal articles 317

Kelvin temperature scale 45
Kette, G. 275
Kierkegaard, Soren 241
Klein, M.W. 265–6
Kolmogorov-Smirnov Test (K-S test) 99, 113, 128, 377
Kreuger, R.A. 260
Kruskal-Wallis test 136, 137, 138, 377
kurtosis 80, 81, *82*, 377
Kvale, S. 259

Lachman, M. 214
Lagerspetz, K.M.J. 267
Lang, Andrew 104
language
　comprehension 123–4, 286
　illocution 286, 376
　perlocution 286
　semantics 285–7
　structure 284–7
Lee, C. 227–8
leisure behaviour, diary methods 60
leptokurtic kurtosis 81
levels of measurement *see* measurement levels
levels of processing framework 123–5
　alternatives to 191–4
　conditions *141*
　depth of processing, factor of 126, 191

levels of processing framework *cont.*
　description 190
　experimental results *127*, 191
　mean differences *134*
　memory traces 132
　orienting tasks 125
　ranked levels *136*
　repeated measures experiment *142*
　testing 193–4
Levene's homogeneity of variances test 100, 112, 128, 376
Likert scales
　description 157–9, 377
　level of measurement 159–60
　market research 257
　scoring and analysis 159
　as summative scales 157, 159
Limits of Behaviour Scale (LOBS) 224, 225
Lincoln, Y.S., on qualitative research
　confirmability 249
　naturalistic observations 247
　qualitative vs. quantitative paradigms 235, 238
　semiotics 240
　validity 55
line graphs 69
line of best fit, correlation design *177*
linear regression 176–8, 225–7
literature review, research papers 321, 322
LOBS (Limits of Behaviour Scale) 224, 225
Locke, John 4
Lockhart, R.S. 123, 124, 146, 147–8, 190
Lofland, J. and L. 270
logistic regression 228–9, 378
logits 229, 378
longitudinal studies 34
long-term memory (LTM) 123

Madigan, S.A. 124
main effect 194, 378
maintenance rehearsal 123
Malamuth, N.M. 223
MANCOVA (multivariate analysis of covariance) 209, 369
manipulation 12
Mann-Whitney *U* test 117–18, 136, 378
MANOVA (multivariate analysis of variance) 209, 214–16, 379
market research 254–7
　description 255
　focus groups 260
　and psychology 256
Marshall, W.L. 305
mathematics, probability principles 88
Mattson, A. 267
McCarthy, Mary 264
mean
　defined 378
　and normal distribution 77

mean *cont.*
  population 42, 71
  standard error of 77–9
  sum of squares (SS) *130*
Mean Square 378
Mean Square error (MS$_E$) 131, 378
mean square (MS) 131
meaning
  in experiences, discovering 283
  morphemes 284
  semantics 285
  as socially constructed reality 239–40
  syntax 284
  in text 288
measurement error 56, 378
measurement levels 44–6, 100, 159, 377
median 71–3, 72, 378
memoing, grounded theory 58
memory
  analysis of variance 127–8
  between-subjects designs, experiments using 113
  change in context harmful to 193
  complexity of 190
  models of memory 123–5
mental health 301
mental lexicon 285, 378
Merton, R.K. 259
Milgram, Stanley
  'Behavioural Study of Obedience' 23–4
  and crime statistics 223
  on deception 34
  and ethical research 22
  life of 38
  Tuskegee Syphilis study 25–32
Minitab statistical package 50
'missing variable' problem 47
Mitchel, V. 256
mixed designs 202, 205, 378
mode 73–4, 378
moderators 260, 261–2
modernism 241
Moran, G. 109
Morgan, B. 255
MORI (Market & Opinion Research International) 151, 153
morphemes 284
MS$_E$ (Mean Square error) 131, 378
multicollinearity 226, 378
multi-factorial ANOVA 199, 379
Multiphasic Sex Inventory 306–7
multiple linear regression 225–7, 378
multivariate analysis of covariance (MANCOVA) 209, 369
multivariate analysis of variance (MANOVA) 209, 214–16, 379
multivariate statistics 209–18
murder statistics 223–5
music psychology 321

National Health Service, Research Governance Policy 26
natural discourse 295, 379
naturalistic observations 236, 379
naturalistic paradigm 379
naturalistic setting 235–6
need assessment 18
Nesbitt, Eric 78
neurotransmitter dysfunction 303
Newell, A. 7
newspapers, communication of research 318
Newton, Isaac 10
Nicosia, F.M. 60, 275
Nietzsche, Friedrich 241
Nisbett, R. 7
nominal data 82, 178–80
nominal variables 45
non-directional hypotheses 9
non-equivalent groups design 170
non-parametric tests
    see also parametric assumptions; parametric tests
    between-subjects designs 117–18
    defined 379
    Friedman's test 206
    Likert scales 159
    single factor designs 135–43
    transformations 205–6
    within-subjects designs 111–13
nonsense words 8
normal distribution 70, 379
  disruptions to 80–2
  illustrated *71*
  parametric tests 99–100
  and standard deviation 77
NUD*ist (Non-numerical Unstructured Data Indexing, Searching and Theorizing) 61, 62
null hypothesis
  correlational design 174
  decision making 96
  defined 49–50, 379
  hypothesis testing, errors in 94
  meaning of 'null' 87
  Page's test 144
  power of tests 98
  sum of squares (SS) 132
Nuremberg War Criminal trials 23, 24

Obedience to Authority (Milgram) 38
observation
  being watched 105–7
  challenges of 264
  covert 35, 36, 264, 265
  direct 16–17, 59
  interviews contrasted 264
  as method 268–9
  observational research 30–1, 36

observation *cont.*
   participant *see* participant observation
   thematic analysis 280
   theory, combined with in psychology 6
Olweus, D. 267
one-tailed significance test 97, 379
ontology 52–3, 379
open questions 155, 261
operationalised statements 49, 379
opportunity sampling 161, 379, 382
'orders', following 23, 34
ordinal data 159, 180–2
ordinal variables 45
orienting tasks, memory models 124, *125*
Osler, S. 192
outcome evaluation 18
outliers 75, 100, 379

Page's test 144, 145
Paivio, A. 124
Palmer, C. 303
paradigms 15, 380
parameters, population 42
parametric assumptions
   data conforming to 110–11, 115–17
   defined 380
   moderate violations of 99
   non-parametric tests 111–13, 117–18
   and *t*-test 112
parametric tests 99–100, 127, 380
   see also non-parametric tests
Parker, H.J. 265
Parker, I. 242
partial correlation 182–3, 380
participant observation 264–72
   access to group 269
   challenges of 271
   data analysis 270–1
   observation as method 268–9
   qualitative data collection 59–60
   recording techniques 270
   time taken 269–70
   violence, observing 265–6
   violent women 266–8
partitioning *140, 196, 197, 200*, 380
Pasko, L. 267
Patton, M.Q. 248
Pearson's *r* 173, 182, 183, 212, 380
Peltonen, T. 267
Perfetti, C.A. 123, 126
Perkins, P. 305–6
perlocution 286, 291, 380
personality, attitudes distinguished 153
Peshkin, A. 262

phenomenology 57, 238–9, 270, 380
phonemes 284
plastic interval scale 159, 380
Platania, J. 109
platykurtic kurtosis 81
point-biserial correlation 181–2
police, power of 290–1
Popper, K.R. 9, 20, 54, 86, 236, 238
population mean 71
populations 42, 380
positive correlation 380
positive skew 80
positivism 236, 237, 380
post-hoc tests 133–5
   between-subjects and within-subjects factors 205
   defined 132, 380
   factorial designs 202–5
   simple effects 203–5
post-modernism 241
Potter, J. 287, 288, 294, 295, 296
power
   expert 292
   interpersonal communication 289, 290
   police 290–1
   of tests 97–8, 381
pragmatics 285, 381
predictive validity 16, 381
predictor variable 15, 381
probability 86, 88–92
   relative frequency concept of 89–90
probability sampling/property sampling distributions 92, 381, 382
probes 257, 259, 381
Problematum logicorum 4
process evaluation 18
product moment correlation coefficient (Pearson's *r*)
   see Pearson's *r*
proof, quantitative research 236
protection of participants 30, 36
psyche 4
psychoanalysis 10
psycholinguistics 283, 285, 294, 381
psychological data, analysis 18–19
psychology
   biological theories 242
   consumer 254–5
   critical 242, 372
   discursive 242, 373
   empirical, requirement for 5
   evaluation in 299
   Eyesenck on interrelated divisions of 171
   feminist 243
   market research 256
   meaning in experiences, discovering 283
   music 321

psychology *cont.*
  non-experimental approach 170, 235
  observation, combined with theory in 6
  systematic approach to research requirement 46
  terminology 4–5
  theoretical basis of 5
  unconscious processing 123, 124
psychometrics 15–16, 77, 153, 309–10
p-value 97, 381

qualitative data collection
  direct observation 59
  handling qualitative data 61–2
  in-depth interviews 58–9
  participant observation 59–60
  and quantitative data 51–3
qualitative research
  aim 18
  alternative paradigm 234–8
  credibility 249
  data analysis 248–9
  data collection techniques 248
  designing 245–50
  ethnography 56–7
  ethnomethodology 239
  exploratory 52
  features 246
  focus groups 259–62
  grounded theory 58, 376
  hermeneutics 57, 240–1, 376
  inductive 52
  interviews 257–9
  modernism 241
  phenomenology 57, 238–9, 380
  post-modernism 241
  psychological approaches 242–3
  psychological enquiry 238–42
  and quantitative research 51–3, 235–8, 325
  reasons for using qualitative methods 53–5
  reports 324–5
  role of researcher 246–7
  sampling strategies 248
  semiotics 240, 383
  symbolic interactionism 239–40
  validity 55–6
quantitative research
  aim 18
  confirmatory 52
  criticism 235
  deductive 52
  design 46–9
  exploratory 52
  objectives 66
  populations 42

quantitative research *cont.*
  positivistic nature 236
  and qualitative research 51–3, 235–8, 325
quasi-experimental design 170
questionnaires
  defined 381
  market research 257
  question format 155–6
  scaling 156
  surveys distinguished 17
  writing 154–5
questions
  to be avoided 155
  closed-format 155, 156
  discourse analysis 295–6
  evaluation research 300
  for focus groups 261–2
  non-threatening 154–5
  open-format 155, 261
  police 291, 292

random sampling 162, 382
random selection 12–13, 44
randomness 88
range 74, 381
range of research 4–20
ranked data, correlation design *181*
rape 303, 305
rapport, interviews 258
Rasch Model 159
Rating Scale Model 159
ratio variables 45
Raven, B. 289
reconstructive techniques 15, 381
recording techniques 261, 262, 270
reference, semantics 285–6
reflexivity 54–5, 382
region of rejection 95–6, 382
regression analysis 178, 220, 382
regression coefficients 176, 221, 382
relativity theory 10
reliability 16, 48, 55, 288–9, 382
repeated measures, single factor designs with 139–43
  counterbalancing 139–40
  levels of processing experiment *142*
  sum of squares in *140*
  trend tests 144
replicability 11, 48, 382
research
  communicating *see* communicating research
  direct observation 16–17
  ethical, design of 32–4
  evaluation *see* evaluation
  observational 30–1, 36

research *cont.*
  psychometrics 15–16
  range of 4–20
  self-reports 6, 7, 17, 383
  surveys 17, 384
  taking part in 42–3
  without experimentation 15–18
research diaries 274–5
Research Governance Policy, NHS 26
research paper sections
  abstract 319, 320
  discussion sections 325–7
  introduction 320–3
  method and research design 323
  qualitative results 324–5
  results 323–4
  statistical results 324
researcher, role 246–7
residual value 222
response scale, questionnaires 156, 158–9
Robinson, J.P. 60, 275
Rosen, G. 141
Rossetti, Christina 274
Rothamsted Agricultural Experiment Station 102
R-square 222
R-square 381
Russell, G.W. 224–5

sample variance 74–7
samples and sampling
  convenience sampling 260, 382
  definitions 382
  judgement sampling 161
  non-random non-probability sampling 161
  opportunity sampling 161, 382
  populations 42, 43
  quota sampling 161
  sample mean 71
  snowball sampling 161
  strategies 248
  surveys 160–3
  systematic sampling 162
sampling bias 162, 382
sampling frame 161
Sanna, L.J. 105–6
Sartre, Jean-Paul 241
SAS (statistical package) 50
scaling
  Likert scales *see* Likert scales
  in questionnaires 156
  unidimensional types 157
Schalling, D. 267
science 9, 170
  quantitative approaches *see* quantitative research

Second World War 22–3, 259
Selective Serotonin Reuptake Inhibitors (SSRIs) 303
self-esteem problems, sexual aggression 304
self-reports 6, 7, 17, 383
SEM (standard error of mean) 77, 79
semantics 285–7, 383
semiotics 240, 383
sentences and phrases 284, 285
sexual abuse 267
sexual aggression
  see also violent crime
  biological and evolutionary explanations 303–4
  biological-medical model 304
  primary and secondary targets 307
  reoffending 305
  social and psychological explanations 304–5
  theory and research 302–3
  treatment of sex offenders 305–9
  types of sexual offending 302
sexually transmitted diseases, withholding of treatment 25–6
shallow processing 123
Shamdasani, P.N. 261
Shapiro-Wilk's W test 99
Shipman, Harold 290–4
shopping behaviour 255
short-term memory (STM) 123
Shotland, R.L. 105–6
significance 85, 97
significance level 94, 95, 383
signs 240, 284, 285–7
Simon, H.A. 7–8
simulations, computer 7
single factorial designs
  analysis of variance *see* analysis of variance (ANOVA)
  between-subjects design 133–5
  comparison of two conditions 123
  with more than two groups 125–6
  non-parametric tests 135–43
  post-hoc tests 133–5
  with repeated measures 139–43
  repeated measures 144
  single factor designs 127
skew
  central tendency 73
  defined 80–1, 383
  positive 80
social facilitation 105, 106, 383
social skills deficits, sexual aggression 304
Solman, R. 141
SOTP (British Sexual Offender Treatment Programme) 302, 306, 308, 309, 310
soul 4, 5
Spearman's Rho 180–1
sphericity 201, 383

SPSS (Statistical Package for the Social Sciences)
  correlational design 227
  examples of output *330–68*
  handling statistical data 50
  logistic regression 229
  logit coefficients 229
  surveys 162
  and trend 146
SS *see* sum of squares (SS)
SS_B (sum of squares between groups) 129–30, 137
SSRIs (Selective Serotonin Reuptake Inhibitors) 303
SST (total sum of squares) 129
SS_w (sum of squares within groups) 130–3
standard deviation 74–7
  calculating 75, 76
  correlational design 174
  defined 383
  and normal distribution 77
  populations 42
standard error of mean 77–9
standard score 384
statistical data, handling 50–1
Statistical Package for the Social Sciences (SPSS) *see* SPSS
    (Statistical Package for the Social Sciences)
statistical results, research papers 324
statistical tests, choosing 328–9
Steele, C.M. 114
Steffen, V.J. 267
stereotype threat theory 114
Stewart, D.W. 261
STM (short-term memory) 123
store atmosperics, concept 321
Strauss, A. 236, 247
street gangs 265–6
structured interview 384
student's *t* test *see* *t*-test
subjective adequacy 270
subjective experience 7
sum of squares between groups (SS_B) 129–30, 137
sum of squares (SS) 75, 128, 129, *140*, 384
sum of squares within groups (SS_w) 130–3
summative scaling 157, 159
summative evaluation 301
Sun, gravity of 10
surveys
  attitudes, measuring 152–60
  characteristics 151
  comparative 161
  correlational design 167
  crime 162–3
  cross-cultural 161
  defined 384
  objectives 154
  polls 151

surveys *cont.*
  purposes 151–2
  questionnaires distinguished 17
symbolic interactionism 239–40, 384
symbols 56
syntax 284
syphilis 25
systematic sampling 382
syntax 384

tabular presentation 82–3
TBR (to-be-remembered) 192
temporal precedence 46
testosterone, male violence 267, 303
text
  defined 384
  discourse analysis, basic unit of 287
  meaning 288
  as social practice 294
  structured nature of 287
  thematic analysis 277, 280
  written 284
textbooks, communication of research 317
thematic analysis 274–81
  defined 384
  description 277
  development of themes and sub-themes *279*
  outcomes 280–1
  recording of experience, effect 275–81
  research diaries 274–5
  stages *278*
  uses of 274
theory
  core theoretical concepts 58
  defined 384
  experimental approach 9
  observation, combined with in psychology 6
  qualitative research *see* qualitative research
  scientific 10
  sensitivity to 247
  theoretical basis of psychology 5
  verifying 11
theses and dissertations, communication of research 318
Thomson, D.M. 193
Thornhill, R. 303
Thurstone ('equal-appearing interval') scaling 157
time diaries 60
total sum of squares (SST) 129
transferability 55
treatment programmes, evaluation 302
trend 144–6, 385
Treponema pallidum, and syphilis 25
Triplett, Norman 105
trustworthiness 238

t-test
    attitude measurement 158
    description 107, 385
    experiments with two conditions 108–9
    formula 108–9
    one- and two-tailed 118–19
    and parametric assumptions 112
Tukey HSD test 133, 134, 144, 203, 204
Tulving, E. 192, 193
Tuskegee Syphilis study 25–32, 34
two-tailed significance test 97, 385
Type I error
    analysis of variance 126
    correlational design 181
    defined 86, 385
    inferential statistics 86, 87, 94, 95, 98
    post-hoc tests 133
    power of tests 98
    significance level 94, 95, 383
Type II error
    analysis of variance, multiple univariate 215
    correlational design 181
    defined 86, 385
    inferential statistics 86, 87, 97, 98
    power of tests 98
    significance level 94

uncertainty 88
unconscious processing 123, 124
univariate analysis 67
utterance acts 286

validity
    concurrent 16, 371
    construct 16
    criterion 372
    discourse analysis 288–9
    ecological 11, 14, 373
    external 48–9
    internal 47–8
    predictive 16, 381
    psychometrics 16
    in qualitative research 55–6
    qualitative research 238
    in quantitative research 55
variables
    adding, to correlational design *184*
    confounding 44
    defined 43, 385
    dependent 44, 373
    distribution 67

variables *cont.*
    dummy 226
    fixed 43
    independent 43, 377
    interval 45
    measurement levels 44–6
    'missing variable' problem 47
    nominal 45
    ordinal 45
    random selection 44
    ratio 45
    relationship between 15
variance 76, 385
verbal ability, and IQ scores 172, *177*, 183
verbal protocols 6, 7, 385
violent crime
    see also sexual aggression
    gender differences 266–8, 271
    observation 265–6
    rape 303, 305
    statistics 223–5
    weapons 266
voluntary participation principle 26

Walsh, G. 256
Watson, J.B. 7
Wetherell, M. 287, 288, 294, 295
Wikipedia 319
Wilcoxon signed-rank test 111–12, *115*, 384
Wilcoxon test 113, 385
Willig, C. 54
Wilson, T. 7
withdrawal 29, 35, 385
Within Mean Square 378
within-subjects design
    data analysis 110–13
    defined 107, 385
    experiments 110–13
    non-parametric tests 111–13
    parametric assumptions *see* parametric assumptions
    post-hoc tests 205
words 285
Wundt, Wilhelm 6, 8, 19

x and *y* coordinates 176, 385

Yuille, J.C. 124

Zajonc, R.B. 105, 106, 120
z-score 79–80, 384
Zukav, Gary 85